Cultural Differences in Human-Computer Interaction

Towards Culturally Adaptive Human-Machine Interaction

von
Rüdiger Heimgärtner

Oldenbourg Verlag München

Bibliografische Information der Deutschen Nationalbibliothek

Die Deutsche Nationalbibliothek verzeichnet diese Publikation in der Deutschen
Nationalbibliografie; detaillierte bibliografische Daten sind im Internet über
http://dnb.d-nb.de abrufbar.

© 2012 Oldenbourg Wissenschaftsverlag GmbH
Rosenheimer Straße 145, D-81671 München
Telefon: (089) 45051-0
www.oldenbourg-verlag.de

Lektorat: Kathrin Mönch, Dr. Gerhard Pappert
Herstellung: Constanze Müller
Titelbild: Rüdiger Heimgärtner
Einbandgestaltung: hauser lacour
Gesamtherstellung: Books on Demand GmbH, Norderstedt

Dieses Papier ist alterungsbeständig nach DIN/ISO 9706.

ISBN   978-3-486-70584-3

"The real voyage of discovery

is not in seeking new landscapes

but in having new eyes."

(Marcel Proust)

Dedicated to my brother Sandro

and all the people who believe in me

"You cannot control what you cannot measure."

(De Marco, 1983: 3)

Acknowledgements

It is a great honor to spotlight some individuals who supported the completion of this work in a special way.

At first, sincere thanks go to the academic supervisors of this project, Prof. Dr. Rainer Hammwöhner and Prof. Dr. Christian Wolff, for inspiring discussions regarding this topic. In addition, I am very thankful to Prof. Dr. Kerstin Röse to whom I owe the foundation of this work as well as innumerable notes and suggestions with regard to intercultural HMI design. Furthermore, I thank Prof. Dr. Alexander Thomas, Prof. Dr. Daniel Draszek, PD Dr. Jürgen Reischer, Dr. Andreas Ratzka, John Loutzenhiser and Helmut Windl very much for proofreading this dissertation and for their valuable hints thereby.

Additionally, thanks are given to my supervisors at Siemens VDO, Dr. Volker Sasse and Lutz-Wolfgang Tiede and additionally to Steffen Zehner, Markus Schupfner and Dr. Nhu Nguyen-Thien. They supported this undertaking not only with ideas and with useful stimuli in the area of driver navigation systems, but also facilitated all development regarding resources within Siemens VDO that was necessary to do this dissertation project.

This venture received support by Genoveva Brunner and Erhan Ercan providing ideas from their master's theses as well as by the trainees Katharina Sieber, Matei Sescu, Franz Kreissl, and Danny Schneider. The trainees contributed to this dissertation project by supporting the implementation of the IIA tool and the CAHMI demonstrator. Moreover, many thanks go to Jia Zhang, Peter Niebergall and Craig Mabrey for Chinese and English proofreading as well as the translation of the test material. Heartfelt thanks are due to Kathrin Mönch from Oldenbourg Verlag as well as Sigrun Wieand and Monika Kleinert for their support to bring this work into the format for publication.

Finally, yet importantly, I thank Maria Heimgärtner very heartily for her support, dependability, and motivation from the start of my scientific career, as well as my parents Christa and Karl Heimgärtner for patiently bearing and supporting this enterprise, as well as my ideas and the course of my life.

In conclusion, I thank all who supported me and believed in me regarding this dissertation project, but whom I did not mention here explicitly.

Undorf, September 2011   *Rüdiger Heimgärtner*

Abstract

The work in hand makes a contribution to the investigation of cultural factors in Human-Machine Interaction (HMI). Cultural influences can be described by intercultural variables which are imprinted differently depending on the respective specific culture and provide concrete design tasks for the design of HMI. Different cultural models are presented. Assumptions are derived from them regarding the influence of culture on HMI. These assumptions encompass differences about information processing and interaction style between Chinese and German users. Cultural differences in Human-Computer Interaction (HCI) and culturally adaptive systems are not separable from each other because of safety issues. On the one hand, the regulation of cultural differences in HCI represents the first step towards developing culturally adaptive systems. On the other hand, the results of the cultural differences only become applicable in HCI by culturally adaptive systems in areas relevant to safety. E.g. a cultural customization is only automatically possible for driver navigation systems during the journey. Technical products like the driver navigations systems treated as examples in this dissertation are becoming more complex in functionality and interaction possibilities. Additionally, due to the expansion of global markets, products and systems need development for possible worldwide usage. One possible method of coping with intercultural complexity is to apply adaptive systems. The concept of cross-cultural adaptive HMI is discussed and the influence of culture on driver navigation systems and cases of cross-cultural adaptability in driver navigation systems are presented. Thereby, the reasons, advantages and problems of using adaptability will be addressed. An important prerequisite for cultural adaptability is to classify the user quantitatively by the system according to culturally influenced interaction patterns. This work concentrates on describing a method to obtain quantitatively discriminating cultural interaction indicators and their values for cross-cultural Human-Computer Interaction design as preparatory work for culturally adaptive navigation and multi-media systems. The method has been implemented in a tool for intercultural HCI analysis. Two empirical studies have been carried out providing HCI analysis during several test sessions. Test persons of different cultures did several tasks using this test tool. A first offline pre-study indicated interesting results and provided new insights that have subsequently been verified by two online studies. These studies revealed differences in human-computer interaction that depend on the cultural background of the users (e.g., attitude, preference, skill, etc.) and proved that the test tool was working properly. Furthermore, doing those empirical studies, the cultural differences in HCI have been found quantitatively, which fulfills a prerequisite for automatic cultural adaptability. Cultural dimensions are related to culturally different conceptions held by human beings about space, time and communication, which have implications for their expectations (e.g., number and order of information units). Several cultural interaction indicators exhibiting informational characteristics are presented which taken together describe an interaction pattern of the user with the system. Additional qualitative studies confirmed the necessity of the quantitative studies as well as confirming the truth of the results in this study. The results are presented and discussed to demonstrate the difficulties, but also the importance of understanding cultural differences in HCI to clear the way for cultural adaptability. Moreover, theoretically postulated correlations between cultural dimensions and variables for HMI design have been analyzed using statistical methods. Based on the results, a model with cultural variables for intercultural HMI design has been developed from which a usability metric trace model containing quantitative cultural interaction indicators was derived and empirically verified. This model served to adapt rules that have been implemented in a demonstrator to prove that cultural adaptability works in reality and not only statistically. The basic postulated principle of culturally adaptive human-machine interaction (CAHMI) can be improved upon empirically as found in the results of this work. The user interface can be adapted automatically according to the culturally influenced interaction patterns of the user. From this, also with regard to driver navigation systems, several recommendations for the design of 'intercultural user interfaces' are derived and culturally adaptive interface agent architecture as well as a generic adaptability framework is suggested.

Zusammenfassung

Diese Arbeit leistet einen Beitrag zur Untersuchung kultureller Faktoren in der Mensch-Maschine-Interaktion (MMI). Kultureller Einfluss kann mit interkulturellen Variablen beschrieben werden, die je nach Kultur konkrete Anforderungen für das interkulturelle MMI-Design liefern. Aus verschiedenen kulturellen Modellen werden Annahmen bezüglich des Einflusses von Kultur auf die MMI bezüglich der Art der Informationsverarbeitung und des Interaktionsstils zwischen chinesischen und deutschen Benutzern abgeleitet. Kulturelle Unterschiede in der Mensch-Computer-Interaktion (MCI) und kulturell-adaptive Systeme sind für sicherheitsrelevante Bereiche nicht voneinander trennbar. Zum einen stellt die Bestimmung kultureller Unterschiede in der MCI den ersten Schritt für kulturell-adaptive Systeme dar. Andererseits werden die Ergebnisse der kulturellen Unterschiede in MCI erst durch kulturell-adaptive Systeme für sicherheitsrelevante Bereiche nutzbar. Z.B. ist bei Fahrernavigationssystemen kulturelle Anpassung während der Fahrt nur automatisch möglich. Technische Systeme, in dieser Arbeit beispielhaft gezeigt an Fahrernavigationssystemen, werden immer komplexer hinsichtlich Funktionalität und Interaktionsmöglichkeiten. Zusätzlich muss ihr Nutzungspotential aufgrund globaler Märkte auf die ganze Welt ausgedehnt werden. Das Konzept der kulturellen Adaptivität bietet Methoden, um interkultureller Komplexität zu entgegnen. Daher wird das Konzept kultureller Adaptivität diskutiert und der kulturelle Einfluss auf Fahrernavigationssysteme und die Anwendungsfälle kultureller Adaptivität in Fahrernavigationssystemen präsentiert. Voraussetzung für kulturelle adaptive Systeme ist deren Fähigkeit, kulturell beeinflusste Interaktionsmuster des Benutzers quantitativ zu klassifizieren. Deshalb liegt der Schwerpunkt der Arbeit in der Beschreibung einer Methode zur quantitativen Bestimmung von klassifizierenden kulturellen Interaktionsindikatoren und ihrer Werte für das interkulturelle Mensch-Maschine-Interaktionsdesign als vorbereitende Arbeit für kulturell adaptive Navigations- und Multimediasysteme. Diese Methode wurde in ein Werkzeug für interkulturelle Interaktionsanalyse im MCI-Bereich implementiert. Zwei empirische Studien wurden mit diesem Tool durchgeführt, um die MCI innerhalb von Testsitzungen zu analysieren. Die Testpersonen bearbeiteten verschiedene Testaufgaben. Eine erste Vorstudie zeigte interessante Ergebnisse und neue Einsichten in das interkulturelle Interaktionsverhalten, welche in zwei Online-Studien verifiziert wurden. Diese Studien zeigten Unterschiede im Interaktionsverhalten, welche vom kulturellen Hintergrund der Benutzer (z.B.

Einstellungen, Vorlieben, Erfahrungen etc.) abhängen, als auch die Reliabilität des Test-Tools auf. Außerdem wurden durch diese Studien die kulturellen Unterschiede in der MCI quantitativ ermittelt. Dabei wurde gezeigt, dass eine grundlegende Voraussetzung für kulturell-adaptive Systeme, nämlich die automatische Anpassung an kulturelle Anforderungen ohne Verwendung expliziter menschlicher Interpretationsleistung zur Laufzeit, erfüllt ist. Kulturdimensionen beziehen sich auf kulturell unterschiedliche Vorstellungen von Menschen hinsichtlich Raum, Zeit und Kommunikation, was Auswirkungen auf deren Erwartungen während der Informationswahrnehmung und Informationsverarbeitung hat (z.B. Anzahl oder Anordnung von Informationseinheiten). Es wurden kulturelle Interaktionsindikatoren gefunden, welche Variablen für das MMI Design repräsentieren und zusammen im Verbund Interaktionsmuster des Benutzers mit dem System beschreiben. Zusätzlich bestätigten qualitative Studien die Notwendigkeit der quantitativen Studien in dieser Arbeit sowie die Richtigkeit deren Ergebnisse. Die Ergebnisse werden präsentiert und diskutiert, die Schwierigkeiten, aber auch die Wichtigkeit der Bestimmung kultureller Unterschiede in MCI demonstriert, um den Weg für kulturelle Adaptivität zu ebnen. Darüber hinaus wurden theoretisch angenommene Korrelationen zwischen Kulturdimensionen und Variablen für das MMI Design mittels statistischer Methoden untersucht. Basierend auf den Ergebnissen wurde ein Modell mit kulturellen Variablen für das interkulturelle MMI Design entwickelt und ein Usability Metric Trace Model bestehend aus quantitativen kulturellen Interaktionsindikatoren abgeleitet und empirisch verifiziert. Dieses Modell dient zur Ableitung von Adaptionsregeln. Einige davon wurden in einem Demonstrator implementiert, um zu belegen, dass die kulturelle Klassifikation nicht nur statistisch, sondern auch im realen Anwendungsfeld funktioniert. Das in dieser Arbeit postulierte Prinzip kulturell-adaptiver Mensch-Maschine-Interaktion konnte so optimiert werden, dass es die Anpassung an kulturell geprägte individuelle Unterschiede erlaubt. Die Benutzungsschnittstelle kann anhand der kulturell geprägten Interaktionsmuster des Benutzers automatisch an dessen kulturellen Hintergrund angepasst werden. Bezüglich interkultureller adaptiver Systeme generell und Fahrernavigationssysteme im Besonderen wurden einige Empfehlungen für das Design interkultureller Benutzungsschnittstellen abgeleitet und eine kulturell-adaptive Interface-Agenten-Architektur sowie ein generisches Adaptivität-Framework vorgeschlagen.

概要： 本文旨在研究人机交互中的文化因素。文化的影响可以通过多元文化的变量来描述，此变量因不同的文化而不同，为多元文化的人机交互设计提供了具体的要求。通过许多有着不同文化背景的模型，我们可以得出关于文化对于人机交互（HMI）影响的假想，这些假想包括信息处理的种类以及中国，德国用户不同的互动方式。人机交互（HMI）和文化适应系统中的文化差异对于安全相关的领域是相辅相成，不可分割的。一方面，为规定HCI中的文化差异首先需要文化适应系统。另外一方面，HCI中文化差异的结果先通过文化适应系统才被用于跟安全相关的领域。比如说，在车辆行驶中，车载导航系统的对于不同文化的适应，只能是自动的。本文中所举例的汽车导航系统的功能性正在变得越来越复杂，其互动的可能也越来越多。此外，由于市场全球化的扩张，导航系统潜在的运用将会延伸至全世界。应对多元文化所带来的复杂情况的一个可行办法就是使其适应。因此，需要讨论多元文化适应性这个概念，尤其是针对汽车导航系统。展示多元文化对汽车导航系统的影响以及导航系统适应多元文化的案例。此外，考虑到驾驶安全性和用户的偏好，不能遗漏使用文化适应性的原因，优势和存在的问题。适应多元文化的先决条件是通过系统对用户进行定量的分类，这个分类要考虑到受多元文化影响的人机交互的样本。因此本文的一个重点就是描述一个方法，这个方法用来定量确定已分类的人机交互的指数以及这些指数的值，它们被用来为人机交互作为导航和多媒体系统文化适应的筹备工作。这个方法被编写成在人机交互领域研究多元文化人机交互的工具软件(IIA-Tool)。运用这个软件进行了两个实证研究，用于分析在特定测试情况下的人机交互(Human-Computer Interaction, HCI)。

不同文化背景的测试者使用这个软件来完成各种测试任务。第一个在线测试取得了令人感兴趣的结果，让人对人机交互行为有了新的了解。这些结论在那两个长达一年的研究中得到了验证。这两个研究证实了不同的人机交互行为在很大程度上依赖于用户的文化背景（比如说，观点，偏好，经验等等），并证明了该工具软件(IIA-Tool)正常工作。此外通过这两个研究，在人机交互范围内定量找出文化的差异，这样就满足生成了人机交互系统自动适应文化能力最重要的先决条件。此外，过统计的方法分析了由理论生成的文化层面和跟信息有关层面的相互关联。文化层面指的是不同文化背景的人关于空间，时间和交流不同的观点，这些都影响到他们的期望值(比如说信息单位的数量和整理)。已经找到了一些人机交互的指标，可以代表某些跟信息有关的层面。这些指标和系统一起可以描绘出用户的人机交互样本。额外的数量研究证明了本论文进行定量研究的必要性以及其结果的正确性。这些结果将被展示和讨论，用于演示某些文化差异对于人机交互的重要性，以便为适应文化铺平道路。基于研究结果，开发并试验验证了定量文化交互指标的可用性度量追踪模型 (usability metric trace model)。这个模型为推导适应性的算法服务，他被编译在一个模拟器里面，用来证明文化的适应性不仅是数据统计，在现实当中也能运用。这个模拟器证明了多元文化人机交互(culturally adaptive human-machine interaction, CAHMI)
的原则是正确的：用户界面会自动按照用户的文化背景进行修改。此外，有迹象表明，文化适用性可以提高可用性，并改善所有系统的入口。
由此可以为设计汽车导航系统的用户界面和通用的适应性框架（generic adaptability framework）做出借鉴。

Foreword

Cultural differences will – paradoxically – gain in effect in a globalized world, where products and services are offered and sold without respect to the borderlines of traditional culture. Even the handling of modern technologicial devices is influenced by culturally dependent assumptions and habits. Modern products – especially in the sector of information and communication – that can adapt to the resulting user-behaviour should have a significant advantage on the market.

As a prerequisite of such design efforts empirical studies about cultural aspects of human information behaviour have to be undertaken.

The dissertation thesis of Rüdiger Heimgärtner drives the necessary research in this relevant field ahead significantly. He provides a thorough discussion of the state of the art of cultural studies over and beyond the tradition of Hofstede. A collection of large emprical studies is designed, implemented and evaluated. The immediate application context is that of car navigation systems. The discussion of relevant approaches, critique of methods and the empirical findings, however, will be valuable for other application fields as well.

I wish that this thesis will find the interested readers and the research impact it deserves. It has been a pleasure to be involved in this demanding research project.

Regensburg 2011   *Dr. Rainer Hammwöhner*

Content

1 Motivation, Objektive and Approach

"Wer sich selbst nicht misst, wird gemessen."
(German saying)[1]

This dissertation project started in 2003 with the cooperation of SiemensVDO (now Continental Automotive GmbH)[2] whose objective was to export European driver navigation systems to the Asian market (first of all to China).[3] However, there was little information about the market and the users of driver navigation systems in China. Furthermore, there were no concrete intercultural HMI design guidelines for the intercultural development of driver navigation systems.[4] Hence, it has been necessary to consider culture in HMI design. In academic literature, this requirement has been propagated since about 1990. However, cultural differences in the interaction of users with computers as

Industrial cooperation

Lack of intercultural HMI design guidelines

---

[1] "He who does not measure himself will be measured." This proverb has been downloaded from the WWW (cf. URL = http://www.folklore.ee/rl/date/saksa/teil01.htm, last access 4/26/11). Most of the proverbs used in this work are from URL = http://www.zeno.org/Wander-1867/A/Messen, last access 4/26/11, which are saved in file "Sprichwörter mit messen.txt" in the online appendix. Proverbs contain deep human experiences (cf. section 3.3.3, footnote 121 on page 71). They are used in this work to briefly express the summary and meaning of the content of the corresponding chapter (or a very important section). The cited proverb above should indicate that "if this work is not done by the author, another person will do it...". The meanings of the remaining proverbs used in this work are left to the interpretation of the readers. The corresponding interpretations of the author are stored in file "proverb meanings.xlsx" in the online appendix attached to the work report, which is an additional document to this dissertation published online at the publication server of Oldenbourg Verlag. The structure of the work report is identical to the structure of this dissertation and contains additional information or details focusing on the topic of the corresponding section.

[2] Siemens VDO was acquired by Continental AG on 12/5/07 and is no longer part of Siemens AG.

[3] These activities have been taken place within the so called "Fortuna" project for developing a mobile driver navigation system at Siemens VDO in Regensburg. The name "Waytona" replaced "Fortuna" in the course of the project.

[4] Cf. state-of-research in section 2.3.7 in this work.

well as with driver navigation systems have not been investigated exhaustively so far. This work is a contribution to reduce this gap regarding the area of culturally influenced human-computer interaction.

Complexity of systems increases density of information presentation and interaction effort

Ongoing technical progress leads to computer systems that provide more and more knowledge and have greater artificial intelligence. Similarly, in the area of automotive products, this phenomenon can also be observed (cf. Michon 1993 or Salvucci et al. 2001). Knowledge based systems, such as driver information and assistance systems, support humans in getting information and making decisions. These systems are becoming more complex in terms of functionality, and hence, need higher interaction efforts by the user (cf. Kolrep & Jürgensohn 2003). Thus, the complexity and the density of information presentations and interactions have increased.

Driver navigation systems require high interaction efforts

Automatic adaptation of HMI at runtime

Within driver information and assistance systems, driver navigation systems require the highest interaction efforts of the user with the system. Interacting with the system should be easy (cf. Shneiderman 2009 and enjoyable (cf. Hassenzahl 2001, Norman 2004) and should support concentrating on the driving tasks (cf. Kolrep & Jürgensohn 2003). In addition, using automotive navigation systems must not lead to the driver being distracted from driving (cf. Zimmer 2001). One problem in attaining driving safety is the fact that driver navigation systems are highly complex having up to 1,000 functions and demanding many interactive actions from the driver. A possible method to consider all of these aspects is to adapt the human-machine interaction according to the needs of the user. Adaptability can be a means to reduce the complexity of interaction according to the situation and user needs (cf. Piechulla et al. 2003). During driving, these systems have to adapt correctly to the expectations of the user in the current driving situation to avoid mental distress and hence, avoid accidents. Furthermore, adaptation of HMI (e.g., color, object and widget position or shape, speed or density of information presentation as well as type and way of interaction) has to take into account that the user's workload related to the user's interaction with the system and vice versa has to be as adequate as possible (cf. Piechulla et al. 2003).[5]

Globalization requires culturally adapted software

All these aspects must be considered according to the requirements and desires of the user (if compatible with driving safety) and his[6] respective culture. Moreover, globalization and new emerging markets require special software that is adaptable to the cultural demands of the users. The Asian market is

---

[5] The driver workload has to be as appropriate as possible and not as low as possible (because too low mental workload can lead to drowsiness of the driver). An adequate mental workload can be ensured by adapting the HMI (e.g., frequency or arrangement of information presentation) to the current driving situation depending on driver preferences (cf. Piechulla et al. 2003; Röse & Heimgärtner 2008).

growing enormously (especially in China), which requires software that is adapted to the cultural needs of Asian people.[7]

Figure 1: Multimedia shop in Japan presenting many driver navigation systems[8]

Globalization and growing automotive markets require driver navigation systems to be developed so that they can be used without expensive changes in the program code for all desired countries all over the world ("internationalization"). To use the systems in a special country, only adequate parameters should be switched to the required values ("localization").[9]

Internationalization and Localization

---

[6] For reasons of the readability the mention of both sexes is avoided. With the masculine form, of course the feminine form is always meant, too.

[7] Especially in 2000-2006, the sales numbers of cars in China have increased steadily and long term (cf. Berger & Grassl 2008). In January 2009, cars sales in China overtook those in USA (cf. URL = http://www.crossculturalreviews.blogspot.com/2009/02/chinas-january-car-sales-overtake.html, last access 2/28/11).

[8] I thank Lutz-Wolfgang Tiede, supervisor of this dissertation project at SiemensVDO for providing this picture.

[9] Internationalization and localization of software will be explained in detail in section 2.3.5 in the work in hand.

Information density

For example, Figure 1 shows a range of driver navigation systems in a multimedia shop in Japan. This picture demonstrates the large number of different systems and the fact that navigation systems are a common everyday product in Japan, as well as demonstrating the high information density expressed by the high number of pieces of information per space unit (e.g., the products are arranged side by side) which is also the case in other Asian countries as in China.[10]

Culturally adaptive HMI

The most important reason for employing cross-culturally adaptive HMI lies in the possibility of adapting HMI automatically at runtime to a special cultural group by using standard parameters to respond to more fine-grained differences in the interactive behavior of the user with the system. Therefore, this work is in the focal point of internationalization, localization and personalization of user interfaces (UI) using adaptive HMI.[11] The product will be more comprehensive and thereby easier and readily to use (cf. Honold 2000; Jürgensohn et al. 2001; Röse 2002 and Sun 2001), which leads to greater driving safety (cf. Jürgensohn et al. 2001). Moreover, the possibility that the user will buy a device from the same company again increases with usability, functionality and hedonic and communicative aspects of the device. However, these aspects can only get better, if the designers really take recommendations for cultural HMI design into account in the developmental phase of global products (as this work suggests, e.g., in section 8.3). Additionally, this work serves as a basic interaction analysis in intercultural HMI. Its results form the basis and the precondition for culturally adaptive systems.[12]

Aims of Culturally
adaptive HMI
⇨   Default parameter
⇨   User profiles

Culturally adaptive HMI (CAHMI) mainly should serve to:

- adapt the HMI during use of the system to the average expectations of culturally different users – this is known as default parameters from design phase, and to

---

[10] This high information density does not only exist spatially as presented in Figure 1, but also sequentially in time (very high information frequency in contrast to Germany) as shown in a short video file that has been recorded by the author in the train at the railway station in Hangzhou in March 2006 (cf. file "Sitting down in the train.mpg" in the online appendix).

[11] Furthermore, even if the cultures will grow together over time and the cultural distances will become smaller, e.g., because of the process of globalization, this work promotes personalization of HMI because individuals do have their own "culture" (cf. Heimgärtner et al. 2007 as well as sections 8.1 and 8.4 in the work in hand).

[12] Here "real" culturally adaptive systems are meant. "Real" means systems that do the complete adaptation process on their own and furthermore, partly explore the adaptation means as well as the adaptation information as explained in section 2.4.

- analyze the individual user preferences and expectations during interaction with the system at runtime and transfer them into user profiles over time to adapt a more fine-grained HMI and hence, more adequately adapt to the user needs.

Hence, this dissertation integrates two aspects: First, a method to obtain cultural differences in HCI purely quantitatively by empirical studies is provided. Second, the results found are applied to real systems exemplified by a mobile driver navigation system adapting its HMI (automatically) to the cultural needs of the user.

Aims of dissertation project:
⇨ Ascertaining cultural differences in HCI by empirical studies
⇨ Applying results in a real mobile driver navigation system

Therefore, the main focus of the work is the empirical acquisition and verification of cultural differences in human-computer interaction and to show how the results and the concepts can be made available for culturally adaptive systems.

In chapter 2, the state of research and the theoretical and empirical background regarding the most important concepts relevant to culturally adaptive HMI will be presented. Thereby, some important concepts regarding HMI, adaptability, intercultural HMI design, as well as driver navigation systems that are used in this work will be laid down to provide a common background for the reader.

Chapter 2:
Theoretical and empirical background of culturally adaptive HMI

In chapter 3, the concept of culturally adaptive HMI (CAHMI) will be explained and a short overview about the methods used in intercultural HMI research is given. Then, a methodological approach to CAHMI is developed and the methods used in this work are described, e.g., how to obtain cultural variables and their values for intercultural HMI design as well as the steps necessary to develop culturally adaptive systems.

Chapter 3:
Methods in intercultural HMI research and path to CAHMI

In chapter 4, the connection between culture and HMI design will be made explicit in detail by analytical means. Two decisive models have been developed reasonable for the interculturally adaptive HMI design. First, a potential model for the intercultural HMI design which contains variables concerning the relationship between culture and variables relevant for HMI design with different values depending on culture and second, a potential usability metric trace model, which contains concrete measurement parameters according to the variables in the potential model for intercultural HMI design, will be presented. Those parameters can be used to really measure, express and compare the cultural differences in HMI quantitatively. From this, the working hypotheses are generated.

Chapter 4:
Development of two models describing the relationship between culture and HMI

Chapters 5, 6 and 7 contain the main empirical research part of this work. The data collection concept and its application are explained in detail as well as test planning, test execution and analysis of collected data. An important part herein concentrates on the IIA tool, which the author designed and imple-

Chapter 5:
Creating test setting

mented for this purpose: it serves to analyze cross-cultural differences in HCI by data collection and data analysis.

Chapter 6:
Verifying empirical
hypothesis

The results of two empirical online studies regarding the data collection of the parameters of cultural variables for HCI are presented and discussed in chapter 6. Relevant empirical findings serve to verify the postulated hypotheses as well as to come to the verified model for intercultural HMI design.

Chapter 7:
Creating CAHMI
demonstrator to verify
methodological
hypotheses

The results found do have practical relevance along the long lasting benefits mentioned before by describing a working demonstrator exhibiting the principle of culturally adaptive HMI implemented in a real mobile driver navigation system in chapter 7. The most significant results form the parameters culturally classifying the users by adaptation rules, which will be presented and evaluated.

Chapter 8:
Discussion of the
methods, implications and
future research

In chapter 8, the methods, results and implications of this work will be interpreted and discussed in light of the theoretical background, and their meaning will be presented and made available for today's research. The implications of the results of this work concern intercultural usability engineering, internationalization of driver navigation systems (including recommendations for intercultural HMI design) and future intercultural HMI research. Furthermore, a culturally adaptive interface agent architecture is suggested that serves as a first basis for a generic adaptability framework representing the general principle of adaptive HMI.

Chapter 9:
Summary and future tasks

In chapter 9, this work is summarized, followed by the conclusions provided by this work and yielding perspectives into the future tasks emerging from this dissertation project. Finally, the used literature used is presented. Supporting material to this dissertation thesis can be found in the appendix as well as in electronic form in the work report and in the online appendix providing supporting information that is too complex or extensive to be printed in this document or that only can be presented electronically such as video or statistic files.[13]

---

[13] Documents in ownership of Siemens VDO (now Continental Automotive GmbH) (e.g., source code and its documentation) may not be published. SiemensVDO offered to use their facilities in Regensburg because of their support of this dissertation project and provided a stipend for three and a half years, from October 2003 to March 2007. For that, SiemensVDO obtained the usage rights for the executable program files, the demonstrator and the IIA tool developed within this dissertation project, including the source code as well as architectural models. Hence, in this work only screenshots of these programs can be depicted but not the detailed source code or architectural secrets (exceptions are, e.g., code extracts to exemplify some abstract aspects). The quality of this dissertation is not affected by this circumstance because the dissertation mainly focuses on the conceptual aspects for scientific progress and not so much on standard technical implementation details.

2   Basis for Culturally Adaptive Human-Machine Interaction

„Mit gleicher Elle messen.“
(German saying)[14]

In this chapter, the theoretical background regarding cross-culturally adaptive human-machine interaction is illuminated. The main topics are intercultural HMI design (section 2.3), containing cultural aspects (section 2.2) related to HMI (section 2.1) and adaptability and adaptivity (section 2.4), which together lead to the methodological approach to culturally adaptive HMI (CAHMI) presented in chapter 3.

Theoretical background of culturally adaptive HMI

"Intercultural research in Information Systems is a relatively new research area that has gained increasing importance over the last few years [..]" (Kralisch 2006: 17). According to Röse 2002, intercultural HMI design describes the user and culture oriented design of interactive systems and products taking into account the cultural context of the user in depending on the tasks and product usage (Röse 2002: 87). Intercultural HMI design means the process of HMI design in the cultural context (cf. Honold 2000: 42-43). Honold presented the steps of this process called "intercultural usability engineering" (cf. Honold 2000: 60 et seq.). This approach has grown academically in literature from 1990 to 2000 and emerged from the processes of globalization, internationalization, and localization of products (cf. section 2.3.5).

Intercultural HMI studies

Intercultural usability engineering

Cultural studies provide profound cultural aspects regarding the interaction of the user with the system. The focus will be on those cultural aspects that can be related to information science to enable the derivation of implications for intercultural HMI design. Even if there are many more disciplines that are

Intercultural HIM design related to cultural studies and information science

---

[14] "Measure with the same yardstick." (cf. footnote 1 on page 1 and file "Sprichwörter mit messen.txt" in the online appendix).

relevant to reach the objective to elucidate the connection between culture and HMI design, the theoretical basis of this work is "fed" mainly from information science and cultural studies.[15] Tackling this task needs a short presentation of the results and basic findings in cultural studies and information science. Hence, in the next sections, an overview of the parts, steps to and activities in intercultural HMI design as well as the influences of culture on HMI design is given.

2.1   Human-Machine Interaction Design in Information Sciences

Information science

Information science deals with all aspects concerning information (cf. Kuhlen 1991, Hammwöhner & Kuhlen 2004).[16] Whereas computer science is concerned with processing the computational and technical aspects of an information processing system, information science cares more about the user and the methods using such systems, including all techniques of processing and using information (collection, classification, manipulation, storage, retrieval, distribution and usage) (cf. Hammwöhner & Kuhlen 2004). Furthermore, all subject areas concerning the design of information processing systems and their user interfaces like usability, ergonomics and HMI, fall into the school of information science in combination with theories and methods from neighboring disciplines like psychology, social sciences, engineering sciences or the comparative study of civilization (cf. Eibl et al. 2005; Jacko 2007).

Intercultural HMI in information science

Cultural dimensions relevant for HMI design

The topic of intercultural HMI analysis is particularly interesting from the information scientific point of view since this can yield new knowledge, requirements and tasks for the design of information processing systems involving e.g., software engineering, software ergonomics and usability engineering. Intercultural topics in information science have not yet been discussed in breadth until now.[17] To reveal new insights and perspectives in this area, this work is concerned with the analysis of the suspected relations between culture and variables relevant for HMI design that can be classified

---

[15] Some other disciplines are mentioned in the work report in section 2.3.7.

[16] The "knowledge map" of information science by Zins 2007 in the work report in the corresponding section 2.1 in Table 1 gives a short and compressed overview of the relationships between the tasks, theories and applied fields of information science.

[17] Even though there are some information scientists who have already researched intercultural aspects in depth (cf. e.g., Mandl et al. 2003, or Smith & Yetim 2004).

into dimensions relevant for HMI design like information density or interaction frequency postulated by the author.[18] Cultural dimensions[19] serve for the description of cultures and refer to the culturally marked ideas and requirements of people, which have an effect on their expectations regarding information processing during the HMI with information processing systems (e.g., to the number of reported information units).

In the next sections the most important concepts from the information scientific point of view regarding HMI design will be presented and discussed.

2.1.1   Human-Machine Interaction

In human-machine systems both human and machine pursue a common objective (cf. Charwat 1992). According to Timpe 2000, the user acts together with a human-machine system to reach the objective of solving a user-selected or predefined task.

User acts together with human-machine system

The interaction, at which information is exchanged between user and system via a user interface (UI), is called "human-machine interaction" (HMI) or "human-computer interaction" (HCI) (cf. Jacko & Sears 2003).[20] The user initiates tasks with the system and the system responds with the results to the user and vice versa.

HMI – HCI

HMI takes place within a human-machine system which consists of three parts embedded in a working environment: the task, the user and the system (cf. Wandmacher 1993: 1). The user interface contains the components of a human-machine system which are relevant for interaction with the user (cf. Timpe & Baggen 2000). The tasks are split up gradually in hierarchically structured steps (cf. Herczeg 2009: 10-11). The environment and the tasks are taken into account and human abilities should be in the centre of the design considerations (cf. Röse 2002: 10). HMI is also called human-machine communication because information is exchanged and it can even be regarded as intercultural communication (cf. Fischer 2006). However, the question as to

Three parts: task, user, system

---

[18] These dimensions are called "HMI dimensions" (HMIDs) and will be presented in detail in section 4.2.

[19] Cf. section 2.2.3 for more information on cultural dimensions.

[20] The system can be e.g., a machine or a computer. In this work, the concept of HMI is used so that it subsumes human-computer interaction (HCI) because computers are special machines.

whether people do communicate or interact with computers is strongly discussed.[21]

Communication model of Shannon and Weaver

The communication model of Shannon and Weaver is often used as the basis for HMI models (cf. Shannon 1948). News, i.e. encoded information is exchanged between the communication partners over a channel. The transmission can be disturbed and the messages distorted thereby. The communication partners need codes for the coding and decoding of the information. Herczeg 2005 provided a six-level model for human-machine communication as well as for communicative systems (cf. section 5.2.2) that is not very different from the model of Shannon and Weaver: The user wants to solve a certain task with the help of the system. Hence, the user has to interact with the system to obtain information or relevant knowledge.[22]

HMI relevant concepts:
⇨ Interaction
⇨ Information
⇨ Dialogue

In particular, cultural influences affect especially interaction and dialog design (cf. Röse 2002). Therefore, the most important information scientific concepts regarding intercultural HMI design are "interaction", "information" and "dialog", which will be introduced in the next sections.

2.1.2   Interaction

Concept of interaction

Along a typology of human-machine interaction (cf. Schomaker et al. 1995), there is a reasonable working definition for interaction between human and technical systems that is based on Stary 1994: "Interaction" in HCI between user and system means the process of using interaction means and application functions. (Stary 1994: 35).[23] Interaction is therefore a specification of

---

[21] To ease things and not to fall into heavy discussions in this work, it is assumed that the user communicates with the system as he communicates with other people (applying the "computer talk hypothesis" (cf. Krause & Hitzenberger 1992, Kritzenberger 1998): The user acts as if he is communicating with the computer as with a human partner even if he knows that he is communicating with a computer. Using this view (cf. "register" according to Krause & Hitzenberger 1992) allows the description of the HMI principles in accordance with the principles in human-human communication (even if the "register" approach is improved by the "description" approach in the sense of Fischer 2006, cf. also Fischer 2007 and my discussion in the corresponding section 2.1.1 in the work report). Communication models that can be used, were developed e.g., by Shannon 1948 or Watzlawick 2011. The boundaries between communication and interaction concepts are presented, e.g., in Herczeg 2005: 79. The analysis of HMI relevant for this work follows in section 4.2.

[22] For more information and some personal thoughts on verbal and non-verbal interaction, please refer to section 2.1.2 in the work report.

[23] „Als Interaktion [zwischen Benutzer und System] wird dabei jener Vorgang im Rahmen der Mensch-Maschine-Kommunikation verstanden, welcher die Betätigung von Interaktionsmedien sowie Anwendungsaktionen zum Inhalt hat." (Stary 1994: 35).

communication and implies that a person acts in accordance with the interpretation of the received signs (Hohmann 2003: 29).

Interaction depends on and happens over time. It is possible to analyze the process of interaction over time (interaction process analysis) (cf. Bales 1950, Frey & Bente 1989). There are many aspects, which have to be considered and can be monitored during the interaction of the user with the system.

Interaction analysis

Long interaction breaks possibly indicate "problems" in the interaction ("communication") between user and system and vice versa. By logging the history of interactions and their analysis, solutions can be derived and suggested to the user.

Not only can the usage of the system's interactive facilities like soft keys (e.g. buttons or "links") be recorded and analyzed, but also interaction times, interaction paths as well as interaction frequency. For instance, analyzing interaction breaks can reveal important information about the user. Why are there breaks of interaction by the user? Is the user active or passive? Does he consume information of software messages, e.g., by reading or hearing? Does he try to input something (via mouse or keyboard)? Which input device is used and how often?[24]

Data recording

Many rather heterogeneous parameters can be analyzed during interaction: user, session time, mouse coordinates, number of mouse clicks and menu items/entries as well as button states, context state (position of mouse, menu etc.), explicit, implicit, and incremental prompts, messages, speed of speech, speech breaks, etc.

Analyzing heterogeneous parameters

Graphical design also influences the interaction behavior (e.g., colors, icons, font, line distance, etc.). Additionally, interactive behavior can be influenced by functional depth, which is different depending on the system and application types. For example, when driving a car the number of (simultaneously available) functions should be very low (every licensed user should be able to drive a car)[25] in contrast to applications in research and development in industry or science where it can be very high (only experts can cope with these user interfaces).

Interaction behavior influenced by:
⇨ *Graphical design*
⇨ *Functional depth*

By analysis of the interaction of the user with the system, relevant information can be obtained that describes or at least indicates the characterization of the user in interaction and in communication ("interaction/communication type").

Interaction type

---

[24] From the answers to these questions, the interface can be "designed by the user" manually (personalization) as well as by the system automatically (cf. adaptivity in section 2.4.1).

[25] This effect can change when cars will drive automatically by themselves.

The most relevant aspects of interaction for this work will be worked out in detail in section 4.2.

2.1.3   Information

Multifold concept

Reischer 2006: 8-11 describes very clearly the state of research regarding the concept of "information". There are many approaches but no uniform terminology. The meaning of the concept "information" is rather fixed respective to the context of the discipline, which uses it.

Information as knowledge in action

For example, Kuhlen 1991 defines the concept of information for the area of information science as "knowledge in action and context" (cf. Kuhlen 1991: 100, Hammwöhner & Kuhlen 2004 and Reischer 2006: 112).

Information by daily life

Reischer 2006 uses a semiotic concept of information integrating syntactical, semantic and pragmatic aspects motivated by everyday usage of the concept of information in life. In contrast, Fuchs & Hofkirchner 2002 argue that the concept of information can be specified very clearly and it cannot be derived from daily life (cf. Fuchs & Hofkirchner 2002).

Amount of syntax in information

Another definition of information stated by Shannon uses a syntactic-quantitative concept of information representing the amount of information expressed by the reciprocal value of the redundancy measured in [bit] (cf. Shannon 1948).

Amount of semantics in information

Floridi's semantic-quantitative concept of information measures the amount of semantic information in [sbit] (cf. Floridi 2004).

There are many more definitions (cf. Reischer 2006). However, neither is it the task of this thesis to define the concept of information nor to create a new terminology or to optimize the existing concept of information because new and deep profound considerations would be necessary that surely widen even the frame of an extra thesis. Furthermore, up to this day no one has yet done this (cf. Reischer 2006: 10).

To summarize the research about the concept of information in a nutshell:

1. There is no uniform information concept.
2. The information concept must be defined in the context of use.

Focus of this work:
⇨ Empirical analysis of interaction of HCI
⇨ Working definition of information

The focus of this work lies on the empirical analysis of the interaction of HCI. Therefore, the rather more pragmatic than syntactic concept of information of Kuhlen 1991 "information as knowledge in action" will be used as a working definition in this work especially from the point of view of information perception and information processing. Furthermore, in contrast to purely syntactic concepts of information like those of Shannon, the concept of Kuhlen comes closer and has more affiliations to cultural concepts, which can be extended to the relevant information related concepts necessary in this work (cf. sections 4.1 and 4.2).

2.1.4   Dialog: Combination of Interaction and Information

A reasonable means for exchanging information with the communication partner is the dialog. Dialogs embrace both information and interaction because they present information and need interaction. Therefore, the principles for interaction design and information processing rule over the principles for dialog design (cf. Dybkjær & Dybkjær 2004). In this work, the focus lies on the investigation of dialogs exhibiting "interaction with implicit information" between user and system (cf. Bernsen et al. 1998).[26]

Dialog = information + interaction

According to Wittig 1979, interaction of the user with the system is carrying on dialogs. He specified five criteria to identify a dialog between human and machine (Wittig 1979, p. 86):[27]

Dialog between user and machine

(i)   A "dialog" is a dialogue during which one of the two partners can be a machine.
(ii) Thematically certain remarks are judged and answered to the partner (intentionality is therefore dropped).[28]
(iii) Knowledge expansion appears for at least one of the partners.
(iv) The dialog must not be communicative but can be an instrumental action with a rational purpose.
(v)   The roles of the two partners regarding the items (i) to (iv) are exchangeable.

---

[26] For more information about "interaction with implicit information" or "informative interaction" for short, please refer to the corresponding section 2.1.4 in the work report.

[27] The five items have been translated analogous to the original text from Wittig 1979 into English by the author. The original text is "Definition DIALOG: 1. Ein Dialog ist ein Zwiegespräch, bei dem einer der beiden Partner eine Maschine sein kann. 2. Thematisch bestimmte Äußerungen werden an den Partner gerichtet und beantwortet (Die Intentionalität fällt damit heraus). 3. Bei mindestens einem Partner tritt eine Wissenserweiterung auf. 4. Der Dialog muß keine kommunikative, sondern kann eine zweckrationale Handlung sein. 5. Die Rollen der beiden Partner sind bzgl. der Punkte 1 bis 4 vertauschbar." (Wittig 1979: 96).

[28] "Intentionality" sometimes is referred to as "ghost in the machine" (cf. e.g. Searle 1992 or Hofstadter & Dennett 1981). There is a vehement philosophical discussion and much literature about the questions if computers can think or communicate or if they have intentions and so on. Please refer for detailed discussion, e.g., to Dennett 1998, Searle & Gavagai 1987 or Hofstadter & Dennett 1981 as well as Heimgärtner 2001 and Heimgärtner 2002. In this dissertation the discussion about intentionally loaded inter-human dialogs is excluded using the concept of "dialog" of Wittig 1979.

Reversible interaction

In my opinion, "interaction" with today's computer systems is having "dialogs" in the above meaning because the direction of interaction is reversible, the speech act types can be the same and knowledge expansion appears.[29]

Dialog windows

There are several kinds of dialogs in HMI (called "dialog windows") as described by Wittig.[30] Therefore, the dialog principles in HMI (e.g., turn-taking, dialog initiation, multimodal principles, etc., cf. McTear 2002 or Searle & Kiefer 1980) should be regarded to be similar to those in inter-human communication because human understanding is involved (cf. Reeves & Nass 1998).

HMI depends on many parameters

Furthermore, HMI depends on many parameters relating to situation, context, user preferences and real-world knowledge as well as aspects of space and time (cf. Del Galdo & Nielsen 1996). All these aspects are interwoven with culture. Therefore, it is important to consider fundamental intercultural differences when dealing with the interaction of members of different cultures with machines. In addition, knowledge about the cultural characteristics of the communication partners as well as their culturally imprinted communication behavior in intercultural communication situations is needed. The system should behave at best as if it were a human being in the same situation except making errors.

2.2   Basic Concepts from Cultural Studies Relevant for Intercultural HMI Design

Cultural studies

Cultural studies deal with all aspects concerning culture. All disciplines influenced strongly by culture contribute to cultural studies as a multi-disciplinary subject, e.g., art, literature, media, linguistics, philosophy, religion, psychology or sociology. Cultural studies are concerned with the investigation of human behavior creating culture in relation to social, histori-cal, political, literary, artistic, economical, judicial and spatial conditions according to cultural differences regarding, e.g., gender, age, education, nationality, etc. (cf. Straub 2007, Jäger 2004 and Hansen 2003).

Ethnocentrism

---

[29] A fortiori, this is the case among the dialog partners represented by agents within the agent paradigm (cf. section 8.5.1 in the work report).

[30] Dialogs can be represented in HMI using "dialog windows", i.e. places on the screen that the user can interact with (cf. e.g. according to Zeidler & Zellner 1992). Examples are mentioned in the work report in section 2.1.4.

One important phenomenon that has effects on intercultural interaction situations is ethnocentrism: people tend to regard their own culture as the centre of the world as well as the scale of all things (cf. Maletzke 1996: 23-24). Moreover, other people are looked at from their own point of view, the customs and one's own norms that are used as a standard for all judgment (cf. also Heimgärtner & Tiede 2008). Hence, often the habits and requirements of other cultures are not perceived or not taken into account by the developers for HMI design.

2.2.1   Concept of Culture

Culture is a very complex concept whose meaning differs according to its context of usage (topical, behavioral, functional, structural, historical, mental, symbolic and normative) (cf. Cf. Kralisch 2006: 12, table 2). "Culture" has its etymological roots in the Latin word *colere* which means "build on, order, care" and describes the way people model their life which includes, e.g., thinking and creating (cf. Maletzke 1996: 22-23).

Culture: Complex concept

In modern cultural anthropology, culture is understood as a system of convictions, attitudes and value orientations, which finds expression in the behavior of the people and in intellectual and material products. The cultural reference group conveys cultural standards to the individual (cf. Thomas & Eckensberger 1993: 112). According to Thomas 1996, culture expresses the attributes of orientation systems.[31]

Cultural standards

Culture is a generally valid system of orientation, which obtains a typical form within a certain group, organization or society. This system contains symbols and standards. According to Hansen 2003, culture embraces all of the habits of a collective and the standardizations that are true within this collective, i.e. culture consists of standardization, communication and collective. Collective is the main driving factor so that "intercultural" is also "inter-collective" which contains "interactions" (cf. Hansen 2003). Here, there is an important connection between cultural studies and information science through the connection of intercultural communication and interaction.

System of orientation

---

[31] "Kultur ist ein universelles, für eine Gesellschaft, Organisation und Gruppe [...] sehr typisches Orientierungssystem. Dieses Orientierungssystem wird aus spezifischen Symbolen gebildet und in der jeweiligen Gesellschaft usw. tradiert. Es beeinflusst das Wahrnehmen, Denken, Werten und Handeln aller ihrer Mitglieder und definiert somit deren Zugehörigkeit zur Gesellschaft. Kultur als Orientierungssystem strukturiert ein für die sich der Gesellschaft zugehörig fühlenden Individuen spezifisches Handlungsfeld und schafft damit die Voraussetzung zur Entwicklung eigenständiger Formen der Umweltbewältigung. " (Thomas 1996: 112).

Culture as
"programming"
of the mind

Furthermore, Hofstede's definition of the concept of "culture" contains (even) the concept of "programming" (which is a very commonly used concept in computer and information science): "It [culture] is *the collective programming of the mind that distinguishes the members of one group or category of people from others*." (Hofstede & Hofstede 2005: 4, emphases in original).

These definitions of "culture" so far have been pre-selected by the author to fit into this dissertation project. To avoid conceptual and philosophical discussions as far as possible as well as because of time and space restrictions of this work, other possible definitions of the concept of "culture" will not be investigated.[32]

Working definition of
culture for this work

Instead, the definition of Röse 2002: 7 (mainly based on the definitions presented so far) will be used as a working definition for "culture" in this work suitable also for analyzing the connections between culture and HMI design:

Common values influence
behavior patterns

Culture affects technology
handling

Culture represents the common values of a group that enables community and communication in contrast to other groups.[33] This is a rather pragmatic, systematic and structural notion of "culture" relevant for research in intercultural HMI design. The common values of a group (= culture) influence one's behavior patterns, learning and cognitive processing styles (cf. Röse 2002: 3-4). Therefore, culture also has an effect on dealing with technology in general (cf. also Hoft 1995 and Honold 2000).

2.2.2   Cultural Differences

Differences among
cultures

To obtain an impression of how culture possibly affects the user needs in HMI, it is reasonable to first have a closer look at the differences among cultures. Miscommunications are a main cause of conflicts between cultures and can be avoided by taking into account the signs and symbols of the other culture respectively. The form of communication can play a more important role than the content of the communication itself (cf. Maletzke 1996). Western culture is marked by the inheritance of a Greek intellect, Roman law, Germanic idea of society and Christian faith. This has led to the modern scientific character through the epochs of the Renaissance and Enlightenment. Characteristic for

---

[32] For more information about the analysis of some useful terms for this work like "communication", "symbol", or "system", please refer to Heimgärtner 2002.

[33] "[Kultur ist] das Abbild gemeinsamer Werte, Denk- und Handlungsweisen einer Gruppe von Individuen, die zur Bildung und Formung dieser Gemeinschaft beitragen und die Kommunikation darin ermöglichen. Sie dienen als Norm zur Orientierung der Gruppenmitglieder und als Abgrenzungskriterien zu andern Gruppen mit einer anderen Kultur." (Röse 2002: 7).

Western culture in comparison with Asian culture are particularly the following qualities: individuality, rationality, orientation to contracts and law as well as ethical performance. Of these qualities, Western individualism is the strangest one for Asians which is derived from the free will originating in the Christian faith. In contrast, the group is in the foreground in Asia (cf. Weggel 1997: 38). Harmony influences both, the thinking and the individual behavior, as well as the structure of society and conflicts with the Western distinction and splitting effort (cf. Nisbett 2003). The basis for inter-human dealings between Asian and Western people forms the striving for harmony and the avoidance of any kind of open conflict in Asia (face saving mentality, cf. Victor 1997).

This results in different communication behavior between Europeans and Asians. Europeans express things directly and clearly, without big introductions, in contrast to Asians, who often use indirect paraphrases, hints and symbols. The more important a message is, the more cautiously the arrangement and the content of the utterances is built. However, there are also cultural differences concerning cognition and perception (e.g., thinking styles or colors).[34] For example, visual information processing contains the processes of perception and classification (cf. Zimbardo 2008: 106). Physical energy in the form of light waves will be changed into nerve pulse-propagation velocities, which are organized and changed into recognizable samples in the brain. The qualities of the objects are put into known categories. These categories count on knowledge acquired in the past, expectations and conclusions (cf. Anderson 1996). Hence, culture has an influence on learning styles, anticipations and cognitive processing styles (cf. e.g., Brunner 2005, chapter 2.5.1). According to Röse 2002, there are cultural differences regarding information perception, information processing and information presentation as well as in problem solving strategies, language and behavior (cf. Röse 2002: 17 et seqq.).

There are also culture overlapping factors like the gestalt law of organization (cf. Röse 2002: 6) or universals in the content and structure of values (cf. Schwartz 1992) as well as common social factors (cf. Parsons 1964). However, Schwartz & Bardi 2001 as well as Inglehart et al. 1998 investigated these universals across cultures and found out that even they can vary or at least cause other differences to a certain degree.

Different communication behavior (Europeans – Asians)

Culture influences information
⇨ Perception
⇨ Processing
⇨ Presentation

Cultural differences in:
⇨ Problem solving
⇨ Learning style
⇨ Behavior patterns

---

[34] "Beliefs and consequently attitudes are formed through cultural values (e.g., Spence-Oatey, 2000)." (Kralisch 2006: 17). Cf. also Cole & Scribner 1974.

Many disciplines

There is much literature and there are many disciplines regarding cultural differences that are relevant for intercultural HMI design (cf. Röse 2002: 17-40). For example, Berry 2007 presents the research and applications of cross-cultural psychology (cf. also Altarriba 1993). D'Andrade 2001 described the development of cognitive anthropology and Tomasello 2006 explains human cognition. Lee et al. 1999 shows the differences of personality and person perception across cultures using the "Big Five" as a means of explanation (cf. Paunonen et al. 2000, Paunonen et al. 2001).[35] Wierzbicka 1991 explains the differences in English, Japanese and Chinese communication considering cross-cultural pragmatism and the semantics of human interaction (cf. also Chen 1993). Matiaske 1997 investigated the structure and meaning of orientation to virtues with managers from China and Germany. He found out that "new" Chinese businesspersons are individual materialists.[36]

E.g. cross-cultural psychology

Cultural differences in mentality and thought

Nisbett 2003 points to cultural differences in mentality and thought. Asian people concentrate their perceptions on context rather than on the relevant. Chinese people repeat important things very often especially at the end of the talk (cf. Fanchen & Yao 2007). There are also differences in complex decision making (cf. Strohschneider 2002).

All of these aspects influence the design of information systems (i.e., interaction and dialog design in intercultural user interface) and should be taken into account very carefully in the HMI development process.

2.2.3   Cultural Models

Cultural distance

As presented and explained in the previous section, the analysis of the cultural shaping of people from Western and Asian regions reveals a large cultural distance (cf. also Inglehart et al. 1998: 16 seq.). The distance felt between peoples and culture plays an important role in intercultural communication situations. It arises from the different expressions of the structural features of a specific culture. The probability of misunderstanding is proportional to the size of the cultural distance (cf. Maletzke 1996: 33-34).

Cultural models describe cultural distance

Cultural differences can be described and put in order with the help of cultural models. Cultural models describe the cultural distance, i.e. the differences

---

[35] "BigFive" denotes a model for describing the personality of a human being containing the following five dimensions of psychological categories: openness, conscientiousness, extraversion, agreeableness and neuroticism (cf. John & Srivastava 1999). These dimensions describe psychological differences in personality which also serve to compare national characteristics (cf. Peabody 1999).

[36] This supports the results in this work (cf. sections 6.2 and 6.4).

between cultures and allow the comparison of them with each other (cf. Hofstede 1984). The most important ones for this work are introduced in the following.

One of the best-known cultural models is the iceberg model of culture (cf. Hoft 1996). Only 10% of the attributes of a culture are visible and conscious, the rest is invisible and unconscious and hence, difficult to research. Cultural models help to overcome this methodological gap using cultural standards and dimensions to look beneath the water surface, i.e. to research the unconscious areas of culture.

Iceberg model of culture

10% visible attributes of culture

The organizational psychologist Alexander Thomas established the concept of "cultural standards", which expresses the normal, typical and valid attributes for the majority of the members of a certain culture regarding the kinds of perception, thoughts, judgments and actions (cf. Thomas 1996: 112).[37] Cultural standards serve as an orientation system for the members of a group and regulate action. The individual grows into its culture by taking over and internalizing these cultural standards. This process contains learning basic human abilities in the social arena, control of one's own behavior and emotions, the satisfaction of basic needs, worldview, verbal and nonverbal communication and expectations of others as well as the understanding one's role and scales for judging.

Cultural standards

Another key concept for describing a cultural system is that of "cultural dimension", which can serve as a basis for the identification of cultural standards (cf. Hodicová 2007: 38). According to the often cited organizational anthropologist Geert Hofstede, cultural dimensions are models to describe the behavior of the members of different cultures allowing the analysis and comparison of the characteristics of different groups *quantitatively* (cf. Hofstede & Hofstede 2005). They represent an aspect of a culture, which is measurable in relation to other cultures. Hence, cultural dimensions can be used to classify kinds of behavior within and between cultures. Cultural dimensions are indicators showing tendencies in the interaction and communication behavior of members of cultures. Overall, Hofstede postulated five cultural dimensions (cf. Hofstede 1984). The extent of the membership in a

Cultural dimensions

---

[37] „[...Kulturstandards sind] alle Arten des Wahrnehmens, Denkens, Wertens und Handelns [...], die von der Mehrzahl der Mitglieder einer bestimmten Kultur für sich persönlich und andere als normal, selbstverständlich, typisch und verbindlich angesehen werden. Eigenes und fremdes Handeln wird auf der Grundlage dieser Kulturstandards beurteilt und reguliert" (Thomas 1996: 112).

dimension is indicated numerically with an index (PDI, IDV, MAS, UAI and LTO):[38]

- Power distance (PDI): Power distance index represents the acceptance of social inequality and the relationship to authority, i.e. the extent up to which the less powerful members of institutions or organizations of a country expect that power is distributed dissimilarly (cf. Hofstede 1991: 42).
- Individualism vs. collectivism (IDV): This dimension describes the attitude of an individual towards living in groups. A high individualism index points to societies in which the relationships are loose between the individuals: One expects everybody to take care of himself and his immediate family. A low individualism index points to collectivistic societies, in which persons are integrated into collective groups from birth, which protects them for life and expects unconditional loyalty from them (cf. Hofstede 1991: 67).[39]
- Femininity vs. masculinity (MAS): This dimension represents the social implications from gender. A society indicates how clearly the roles of sexes are delimited from each other: masculinity means being forceful and strong as well as having a materialistic orientation. Femininity means being modest, more sensitive and attaching importance to quality of life. Femininity indicates a society in which the roles of the sexes overlap: Both women and men should be modest and sensitive and put value on quality of life (cf. Hofstede 1991: 101).
- Uncertainty avoidance (UAI): This index represents the degree to which members of a culture feel threatened by uncertain or unknown situations. It is also an indicator for expressing the way of dealing with uncertainty regarding controlling emotions and aggression (cf. Hofstede 1991: 133).
- Long-term vs. short-term orientation (LTO): Long-term oriented cultures stands for staying power, relation resistance and the retention of these relations to foster virtues toward future rewards, in particular perseverance and thrift (cf. Hofstede 1991: 401). Short-term oriented societies show a high personal stability, keeping dignity (preservation of face), respect for tradi-

---

[38] Hofstede 1991 determined values of the indices of his five cultural dimensions for 56 countries and regions. All of Hofstede's indices can be looked up in the appendix or at URL = http://www.geert-hofstede.com/hofstede_dimensions.php (last access 1/8/11). For a detailed description and discussion of the cultural dimensions of Hofstede, please refer to Reimer 2005.

[39] Hofstede 1997: "Individualismus beschreibt Gesellschaften, in denen die Bindungen zwischen den Individuen locker sind. Kollektivismus beschreibt Gesellschaften, in denen der Mensch von Geburt an in starke geschlossene Wir-Gruppen integriert ist, die ihn ein Leben lang schützen, dafür aber bedingungslos Loyalität verlangen. Ein hoher IDV steht für einen starken Individualismus." (Hofstede 1997: 66).

tion and fostering virtues related to past and present (cf. Hofstede 1991: 403).

Hofstede applied the cultural dimensions to nations. Their specific values represent the character of the nation. For example, in China, there is high 'power distance' in contrast to Germany. 'Power distance' represents a quantitative measurable aspect of a national culture, which quantifies the degree to which less powerful members of institutions and organizations in a country expect and accept disparate distribution of power (cf. Hofstede 1984). The power distance index (PDI) ranges from zero to about 100.[40] Hofstede found out that the power distance in China is high (PDI=80) compared to Germany (PDI=35). This may be relevant in cross-cultural HMI design, e.g., in accepting help or commands (given by the system) by the user according to his acceptance of external power.

Cultural dimensions applied to nations

Example: China – Germany

Figure 2 shows the values of Hofstede's cultural dimensions for China and Germany (cf. Hofstede 1991) indicating high cultural distance because the shapes for Germany and China in Figure 2 are not congruent.

High cultural distance between China and Germany

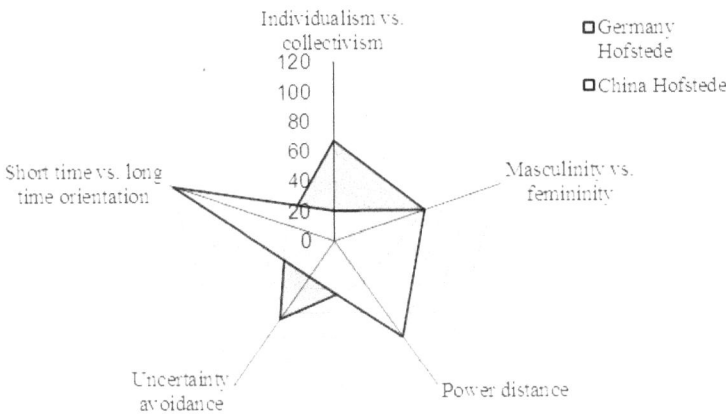

Figure 2: Different indices for China and Germany according to Hofstede

---

[40] Cf. VSM in Hofstede 1994. Originally, the values were on a scale of 0-100 in which 100 corresponded to the extreme value. Not all five dimensions of Hofstede have been empirically researched by Hofstede's first studies. Later on, additional research of Hofstede has shown values that exceed this value of 100 (e.g., 120 for LTO for China). Hence, Hofstede extended the range of values beyond 100.

Culture:
⇨   unconscious steering
⇨   "hidden dimension"
⇨   "silent language"

According to the anthropologist Edward T. Hall, culture is a "silent language" or "hidden dimension" which steers people unconsciously (cf. Hall 1959). Difficulties in communication with members of other cultures arise from that. If one is not conscious of one's own motives, which are culturally influenced, one cannot understand the motives and actions of others. Hall 1990 founded his findings regarding cultural dimensions like context information, message speed, mono-chronic or poly-chronic time orientation on interviews and field studies.[41]

However, there are many more founders of cultural dimensions like Trompenaars & Hampden-Turner 2007, Adler & Gundersen 2008, Condon 1984, Kluckhohn & Strodtbeck 1961, Victor 1997, etc. who postulated e.g., the following cultural dimensions:[42]

- Universalism vs. Particularity
- Role vs. Relationship Orientation
- Result vs. Ascription Orientation
- Neutral vs. Emotional Behavior
- Individualism vs. Community, or
- Achievement vs. Status Orientation.

In this work, the concept of cultural dimensions is more suitable than cultural standards because a system needs numbers provided by quantitative variables to culturally adapt HMI to the user. The idiosyncratic values of these dimensions have been determined for many nations by their authors (cf. Levine & Norenzayan 1999 or Inglehart et al. 1998). Baumgartner 2003 compiled a comprehensive list of 29 cultural dimensions extracted from literature in her master's thesis.[43] For this work, I analyzed the compiled cultural dimensions of Baumgartner 2003 and Marcus & Baumgartner 2004 to assign a value to the cultural dimensions for China and Germany through the study of the literature and my own considerations as well as using the indexes from Hofstede. The results are presented in Figure 3.

---

[41] The cultural model of Hall will be explained in detail in chapter 4 to derive relevant hypotheses for intercultural HMI design.

[42] Please refer e.g., to Cramer 2008 for a detailed description of those and some more cultural models (e.g., those of Pinto or Schwartz).

[43] For a detailed list with all the descriptions and explanations of these cultural dimensions, please refer to Baumgartner 2003.

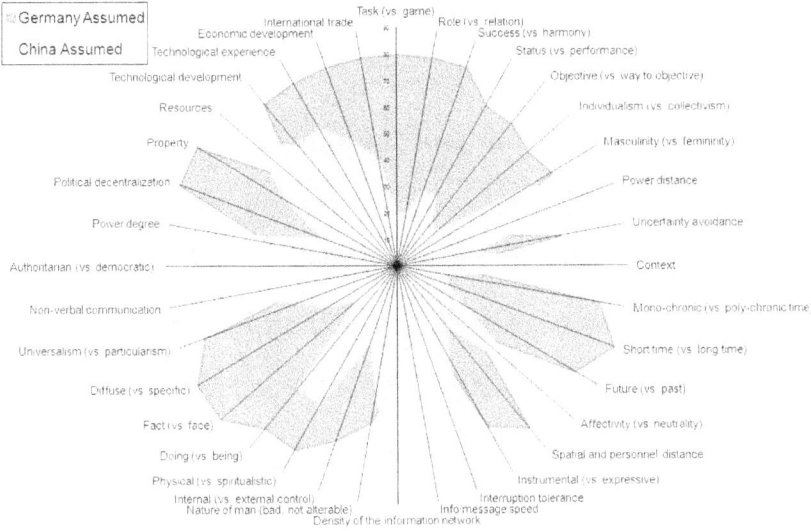

Figure 3: Postulated values for the analyzed cultural dimensions according to estimations of the author justified by literature study (Source: file "041213 Modell interkultureller Variable55 überarbeitet am 30-04-2009_pres.xls" in the online appendix)

Table 1 shows the attributes of the cultural dimensions that serve as working ground in this work suggested by Baumgartner 2003, Khaslavsky 1998, Marcus & Baumgartner 2004, Röse 2002 and the author.[44] The high cultural distance between China and Germany is obviously because they differ in most values of the cultural dimensions.

---

[44] Cf. also Table 10 in section 4.1 in the work report as well as the file "041213 Modell interkultu-reller Variable55 überarbeitet am 30-04-2009_pres.xls" in the online appendix. The values in Figure 3 have been estimated by the author similar to the estimations of Hofstedes indices using the basic range of 0 to 100.

Table 1: High cultural distance between China and Germany because most of the cultural dimensions have different values (Source: results from literature compilation by the author cf. file "041213 Modell interkultureller Variable55 überarbeitet am 08-01-2009_pres.xls" in the online appendix)[45]

Dimension of Culture	China	Germany
Context (Hall 1959)	High	Low
Message Speed (Hall 1959)	High	Low
Space (Hall 1959)	Close	Distant
Time orientation (Hofstede 1984)	Long-time oriented (LTO=118)	Short-time oriented (LTO=31)
Time orientation (Hall 1959)	Poly-chronic	Mono-chronic
Power Distance (Hofstede 1984)	High (PDI=80)	Low (PDI=35)
Collectivism vs. Individualism (Hofstede 1984)	Collective (IDV=20)	Individualistic (IDV=67)
Uncertainty Avoidance (Hofstede 1984)	Middle (UAI=30)	High (UAI=65)
Diffuse vs. Specific (Trompenaars & Hampden-Turner 1997)	Diffuse	Specific
Particularity vs. Universalism (Trompenaars & Hampden-Turner 1997)	Universalism	Particularity
Role of Gender (Hofstede Hofstede 1984)	Feminine (MAS=66)	Masculine (MAS=66)
Relationship vs. Task/Role orientation (Halpin & Winer 1957)	Relationship oriented	Task/Role oriented

Cultural dimensions describing tendencies

Cultural change is gradual

However, cultural dimensions merely describe behavioral tendencies because cultural change is gradual: Generalization is not tenable but (considering big groups) at least sustainable, i.e. acceptable as a first value of orientation (cf. Nagy 2003). Furthermore, knowledge of the values of cultural dimensions provides an impression of the culture to which a user might belong. Hence,

---

[45] Cf. e.g., Inglehart et al. 1998. In 2008, the Hofstede's indices for MAS were estimated for China as follows: MAS China = 66. The other values are MAS Hong Kong = 57 and MAS Germany = 66 (cf. Table 50 in the appendix). The value for China was estimated in contrast to the value for Hong Kong, which was determined by the empirical studies of Hofstede. In 2002, Röse used the value MAS Hong Kong = 57 instead of MAS China = 66 because the MAS value for China had not been estimated by Hofstede at this time. Hence, some of the conclusions of Röse 2002 regarding the expectations of Chinese users in contrast to German users are based on this fact and are therefore different than the expectations in this work presented in Table 1 (e.g. role of gender is feminine for China according to Röse 2002: 137, table 6-2). Therefore, the color expectations at the presentation layer in user interfaces are assumed to be feminine for China (cf. section 2.3.2, Table 2). How to apply this value depends on interpretation. The value of 66 is almost in the middle of Hofstede's scale of MAS representing femininity or masculinity. When taking the overall impression of the most important colors of China (red (royalty), yellow (richness), both for happiness) as well as the ascribed relationship orientation to China into account then it is reasonable to attribute "femininity" to MAS index.

cultural dimensions are indicators for differences between cultures that can give an impression of possible differences in cross-cultural HMI of users from different cultures.

Moreover, cultures do have many aspects in common: every culture has metrological relations[46] and basic metaphysical views, because they consist of human beings, society and knowledge of traditions and so on. Actually, most constituents of a culture are shared by all other cultures (cf. Moeschler 1989). Only some differences do exist. However, if these are significantly different, then it is very important to consider them by analyzing the interactions between members of cultures as well as by taking the culturally conditioned aspects into account in HMI design.[47]

Cultures have many aspects in common

Different aspects musts be considered in intercultural HMI design

2.2.4   Communication (and Culture)

According to the cultural anthropologist Edward T. Hall, culture comes along with communication. Even more, culture is mainly a communication system (cf. Hall 1959).[48] Therefore, Hall is regarded as the founder of intercultural communication (cf. Moosmüller 2007: 16). Communication is made by verbal or non-verbal interaction and information transfer is up to 80% non-verbal in human-human communication. Communication embraces language (understanding, cognition), material property (power and status) and behavior (emotion, conflict behavior). Perception of information depends on activity, situation, status, experience and culture (Hall 1983: 21).[49]

Culture as a communication system

Culture is learned and forms identity: by learning certain kinds of behavior, the human being matures according to his cultural environment. Basic patterns of behavior deal with time, the density of the communication network, the communication speed and the significance of time for action chains. Space and time as basic physical factors influence the communication behavior of the human being, which has an effect on the sociological processes of a group of

Basic patterns of behavior: space and time

Communication formed and influenced by culture

---

[46] „Metrology" is the science that deals with measurement (cf. e.g., Dotson 2006). It can also refer to a system of measurement. Hence, "metrological relations" are relations that can be measured and represented as metrological, i.e. by a metrics or at least expressed by a number (e.g., IDV of Hofstede).

[47] For example, it cannot be intended to create a culturally adaptive system, which makes hard and sharp decisions but fuzzy ones. This aspect is discussed in detail in section 8.4 and applied in section 8.5.

[48] „Kultur ist immer und vor allen Dingen ein System von Kommunikation." (Hall 1983: 19).

[49] "Kultur ist das wichtigste Bindeglied zwischen den Menschen und die Grundlage für jeden zwischenmenschlichen Kontakt." (Hall 1983: 21).

human beings and hence, on their culture. Inter-human communication has developed over the course of many millennia and has been characterized by social and cultural influences in the course of time (Röse 2002: 42).

Communication = special case of interaction

Originally, communication rules were used for the description of interpersonal communication. However, they can also be applied to decrease regional differences. Communication is a special case of interaction because interaction can also take place without transmission of messages.[50] Communication only happens if information is exchanged successfully; hence, interpretation processes are involved. Communication comprises, in contrast to pure interaction, the understanding of meanings by reciprocal processes and using language (i.e. a common code – whether verbal or non-verbal) (cf. Dennett 1998). Communication between human and computer requires interaction between the user and the system. As soon as information is to be transmitted, interaction turns into communication at the same time. HMI will not be initiated by the user without any purpose or intention, e.g., by forcing the system to do anything "communicating with it" by "sending a message to it".[51]

Cultural aspects to consider in HMI research

Hence, HMI often happens (in the authors view even mostly) to process information. For example, the driver uses a driver navigation system to obtain (e.g., maneuver guidance) or to provide (e.g., destination input) information or to initiate a process (e.g., calculating the shortest route). Thereby, the mental models of the communication partners should match as well as possible to grasp the dialogs. The less this is the case, the more errors and misunderstandings will take place in communication, and hence, in HMI. This has to be taken into account, especially in respect to designing human-machine dialogs in cross-cultural user interfaces (i.e. user interfaces that are used by users of different cultural needs across the cultures). However, up to now, cultural aspects have not been considered in depth in the design of the interaction process within HMI research (cf. section 2.3.7).

---

[50] Cf. also section 2.1.2.

[51] This view of the author is supported by the fact that communication presupposes interaction as well as intentional use of signs (cf. Reischer 2002: 297).

2.2.5 Mental Models (and Culture)

Mental models are a means to form common knowledge of the communication partners. In psychology and other scientific disciplines models serve as a means for the acquisition of knowledge (cf. Johnson-Laird 1983). In HMI research mental models or user models serve for the explanation of the user's expectations about the system (cf. Herczeg 2009: 9; Schlungbaum 1996; Schlungbaum 1997 as well as Blank 1996).[52] They are simplified models of complex events which a user forms about the operational and the functional possibilities of a system to work with it (cf. Herczeg 2009:17).[53] Therefore, there is the need for mental models in HMI design (cf. Jarz 1997). Mental models represent the subjective view of reality within the brain (cf. Zimmer 1985, Johnson-Laird 1983 and Hasebrook & Graesser 1995). The best HMI takes place, if user and system models agree. Then the system meets the expectations of the user. Furthermore, if the models agree, the system has self-description capability and therefore, its usage can be easily and "intuitively" learnt by the user.

Mental models in psychology and in HMI research

Cultural aspects have to be considered if one or more cultures are affected during HMI. This is the case, if the user of the system is not of the same culture than the developer, as well as if the user's culture changes (it changes permanently) (cf. Honold 2000, Röse 2002, cf. also section 8.1). Therefore, for intercultural HMI research, the conceptual models of the developers also have to be taken into account because systems reflect the same cultural imprint as their developers. Human-machine communication is intercultural communication at the same time if the user has another culture than the developer of the system (and hence, the "system itself") (cf. Honold 2000). Hence, the successful use of a computer system depends on the compatibility of the user's and system designer's mental models (cf. Herczeg 2009: 18-20; Honold 2000: 45). This means that the product developer must anticipate and develop suitable models of the possible user's mental models that can be used by the system after designing it at runtime. Therefore, *intercultural* usability engineering is necessary (cf. section 2.3.6).

Compatibility of mental models

Benefit of matching the user with the system model
⇨ Intuitive usage

---

[52] Blank 1996: 22 states that there are several dimensions of a user model for their administration: static, dynamic, individual, general, in the short and in the long run. Blank also explains the most important concepts for user modeling like human-computer communication, shell systems, generating stereotypes by observation, architecture components like inference, acquisition, in/output, interface, user model administration, as well as tools for building these components. Blank also presents applications of user modeling.

[53] Cf. also Brunner 2005 for a overview regarding definitions of mental models e.g., by Norman 1986, Dutke 1994, Zimmer 2001, Johnson-Laird 1983, 1988, Jacko & Sears 2003 and Van der Veer & Del Carmen Puerta Melguizo 2007.

Behavior patterns

Cultural schemes also influence the mental models that are restricted to the application domain. Rößger 2003: 130 describes culture as a phenomenon, which shows itself by persistent interaction samples with the environment. In addition, cultural differences influence the expectations about handling technical systems. The connection between culture and mental models lies in the permanent behavior patterns forming mental models. Hence, the focus in this work is to investigate the behavior patterns regarding the interaction of the (culturally different) users with the system.

Mental models formed and influenced by culture

2.3   Integrating Culture into HMI Design

2.3.1   Influence of Culture on User's Interaction with the User Interface

Influence of culture on HMI

The cultural distance between Western and Asian regions supports the assumption that it is reasonable to expect cultural differences in HMI (regarding interaction style, thinking and action models) of users from these regions (cf. section xxxx before). Therefore, the design, implementation and use of interactive systems should not only meet the general usability criteria but also take into account cultural issues which address relevant topics such as schedule, presence, privacy, authority, control, awareness, safety, error, trust, comfort, coordination, conflict, communication and collaboration (cf. Liang 2003).

Interculturally overlapping situations

Culture can influence HMI in different ways. The "interculturally overlapping situation" arranged by a technical system is the most interesting (cf. Honold 2000: 42 seq.).[54] These situations arise if a product is defined and formed within one culture and this product is then transferred and used in another culture. Broader forms of intercultural overlapping situations are interpersonal interculturally coincidental situations as well as culture comparative examinations arranged by technical systems directly from cultural influence factors on HMI (cf. Honold 2000: 42-43).

To be able for original equipment manufacturers (OEM) to compete on the world market, it is important that users accept the product. Therefore, one must consider this point of view during the development of products for other markets. The same data can have different meanings in different cultures due

---

[54] Honold 2000 made the approach of Thomas 1996 using "overlapping interaction situations" available for HMI design. Additional information and benefits from employing this method can be found in section 2.3.6 (in this work as well as in the work report).

to the experiences within one's own, since every culture has its own values, symbols and behavior patterns with meanings and interpretations connected to them.

These aspects have an effect on the coding or decoding of news during the communication (cf. Röse 2002: 21). The developer from culture A must make the operation of the product understandable to the user from culture B (cf. Röse 2002: 68 et seqq.). The messages and pieces of information must be formed so that the user of culture B can understand them without problems. It is important that there is an agreement between the developer and the users in different cultures about the meaning and interpretation of information; otherwise, misunderstandings or even not-understandings result (cf. section 2.2.5). Miscommunication has negative effects on the usability of the product (cf. section 2.3.6). Meanwhile, several experts point out that a change of cultural environment takes place at the transfer of a technology or a product from the manufacturer's country to another country (cf. e.g., Hoft 1995, Honold 2000, Hermeking 2001: 55, Röse 2002).

Agreement between developer and user from different cultures about meaning and interpretation of values, symbols and behavior patterns

Masao Ito and Kumiyo Nakakoji demonstrated already in 1996 the influence of culture on user interface design for the modes „hear" and „speak" between user and system (cf. Masao & Kumiyo 1996). In the „hear mode", the presentation of information from system to the user takes place within the phases perception, association and inference. From the first to the last phase, cultural dependency increases: colors and forms in the perception phase depend less strongly on culture than standards in language and metaphors within the phase of associating meaning. Finally, the inference mechanisms in the last phase that are based on logic and social norms depend strongly on culture. In the „speak mode", the instructions of the system by the user happens in four phases. First, the user recognizes the possibilities of system usage. For example, he grasps the meaning of the layout, selects alternatives, or initiates functions. Then he tests their applicability by checking semantic consistency using trial and error. In the third phase, he determines the expectation of the system regarding his actions and acknowledges the system instructions in the final phase.

Influence of culture on user interface design for the modes "hear" and "speak"

These process phases involve the perception of time, which is strongly dependent on culture (cf. Hall 1959). In addition, cultural dependence increases from phase to phase. For example, in Japan, on the one hand, short system response time is very important. On the other hand, Japanese users are obviously more patient doing long-winded tasks than users from European countries (cf. e.g., Lee 2002 or Rößger & Rosendahl 2002).

Strongly related to 'time' depending on culture

Culture influences HMI on all levels of interaction	Moreover, according to the cultural models of Hofstede, Hall and Thomas, culture influences HMI on all levels of the interaction model (cf. acting level model according to Herczeg 2005 and Heinecke 2011, as well as Norman 1986).[55]
Phases of cultural imprinting ("mental programming of the mind")	Following Hofstede & Hofstede 2005, during the intensive learning phase in childhood, primary culture imprints the human being with certain rules, norms and desired ways of behavior to which the members of the group adhere (cf. section 2.2.1). Secondary cultural imprint happens if the child (mainly from about 10 years onwards) adapts to other cultures that cover but not substitute the primary cultural imprint.[56]
Culture changes – Orientation may remain	Moreover, although culture changes permanently, i.e. even if the contents of the cultural standards can change, the possibility of orientation remains. Hence, in any case, there is something to orient oneself within a group of persons, region, or nation, which can be described as a cultural standard or by cultural dimensions.
	For HCI, those cultural standards and dimensions are most interesting that are directly connected to communication, information, interaction and dialog design, i.e. the cultural dimensions concerning the culturally different concepts of space, time and communication (cf. chapters 1, 5 and 10 in Hall 1959).[57]
Space and time: variables influencing communicative behavior	Space and time are physical variables influencing the communicative behavior of human beings, which form the social processes of a group of humans and their culture: by learning certain kinds of behavior, the human being matures according to his cultural environment. The influence of cultural imprinting of the user on his behavior in interactions with other communication partners is immense. This is also valid for HMI because communication in HMI is determined by the user and the system. For example, Vöhringer-Kuhnt 2002

---

[55] This is shown in this work in detail in section 5.2.2.

[56] In contrast, Inglehart 1990 describes a cultural shift in advanced industrial society: human behavior is not only influenced by primary but also even stronger by secondary, tertiary and even quaternary cultural aspects (cf. also the model of Sundermeier 1996 as well as Thissen 2008 about the statements of Inglehart). However, this view is discussed controversially and even not tenable (cf. Thomas 1996). I believe that primary culture imprints mostly, and hence, I suppose that if the user is exposed to mental distress, he shows a behavior which is directed by primary cultural imprint (which is partly supported by literature, cf. e.g., Aranda & Knight 1997 or Hobfoll 2004). However, this assumption must be verified by future empirical studies in several HMI contexts. Nevertheless, some confirmation has been found for the hypotheses presented in this work (cf. section 5.2.2): Even if the Chinese speaking users employed in the studies of this work exhibit high IDV contrary to the expected low IDV according to Hofstede, their interactive behavior is as expected (i.e. as Chinese users are assumed to do).

[57] These aspects will be presented in detail in section 4.3.3.

investigated the influence of culture on usability. The individualism index of Hofstede is significantly connected to the attitude towards satisfaction of the user and the attitude towards product usability. In his conclusion, Vöhringer-Kuhnt stated, "Individualism/Collectivism is connected to and has an effect on usability." (Vöhringer-Kuhnt 2002: 17).

Hence, cultural differences in interpersonal communication can and must be transferred to the interaction with technical devices (Röse 2002: 74 seq.).[58] Cultural dependencies in user system interactions (HMI) particularly concern interaction and dialog design (cf. Röse 2002). According to Röse, the effect can also be seen if the communication partner of the user is a computer system: culture influences the interaction of the user with a computer system or a machine because of the movement of the user in a cultural surrounding (cf. Röse 2002: 18). Therefore, cultural imprint has direct influence on the interaction of the user with the system.[59] This statement will be called the "fundamental abstract hypothesis" (FAH) henceforth. If the work in hand reveals cultural differences in HMI, then FAH is confirmed anew.

Cultural differences to be transferred to interaction

Culture influences HMI
⇨ fundamental abstract hypothesis (FAH)

2.3.2   User Interface Characteristics

To make cultural dimensions available for user interface design, Marcus 2001 developed characteristic factors for user interfaces and gives examples that can have an effect on user interface design. The user interface characteristics 'metaphor', 'mental model', 'navigation', 'interaction' and 'presentation' are connected to the five cultural dimensions of Hofstede. However, Marcus used a purely deductive approach to obtain these connections. Many possible recommendations for web design have been derived by Marcus & Gould 2000 mainly from Hofstede's knowledge without empirical foundation of all connections. Therefore, this formulated model still needs empirical validation (even if, meanwhile, there is some empirical work from Marcus itself, cf. e.g., Marcus 2006).

User interface characteristics

Connected to cultural dimensions

Need for empirical validation

Röse contrasted the user interface characteristics for China and Germany (cf. table 6-3 in Röse 2002: 138). A summary of the attributes of the user interface characteristics have been rearranged by the author by classifying the user

---

[58] For cultural background in the context of the design of intercultural information systems which is not directly in the center of this work, please also refer to Kralisch 2006, Röse 2002, or Honold 2000.

[59] This statement is based on the field theory according to Lewin 1993. From this, Eckensberger 2003 developed a rule and interpretation system as described in Röse 2002: 18.

interface characteristics into additional subcategories to make the cultural aspects relevant to HMI design more clear (cf. Table 2).

Table 2: Differences in user interfaces characteristics for China and Germany (rearranged by the author in accordance to table 6-3 in Röse 2002: 138)

User Interface Characteristics	Subcategory	China	Germany
Metaphor	Orientation	hierarchical	event, work, competition
		relationship	goal
		role	task
	Thinking	concrete	abstract
	Structure	fixed	changeable
		hierarchical	flat
Mental Model	Reference to prioritized data	yes	no
	Orientation	role	task
	Structure	social	work / business
	Mental model	simple	complex
	Articulation	clear	ambiguous
	Choice	limited	multiple
	Kind of logic	binary	fuzzy
Navigation	Choice	limited	multiple
		predetermined	arbitrary
	Paths	limited	open
		predetermined	individual
	Navigation	role dependent	role independent
		non-uniform / inconsistent	uniform / consistent
	Paths	long	short
		ambiguous	clear (referenced, taxonomy)
Interaction	Kind of error messages	direct	supportive
	Help	wizards	cards
	Search	limited	keyword
	Profile based on	role	user
	Orientation	function	game
		team	individual
	Preferred interaction	face-to-face	distance
	Messages	personalized	anonymous
Presentation	Speech	formal	informal
	Context	high	low
	Colors	feminine	masculine
	Orientation	relationship	task

According to Marcus 2001 and Röse et al. 2001, Chinese people (and hence users) are rather relationship and family oriented based on traditional powerful social hierarchical structures. In contrast, German users are described as event oriented regarding acts, tools, work, jobs and competition. Hence, they are more product and task as well as work and objective oriented using business type structures.

In contrast to Chinese users, the navigation and interaction behavior of German users does not depend on roles but on user profiles, i.e. user specific behavior, which is game, level, and individual oriented including distanced communication. Chinese users respect roles and appreciate practicability, function, team, and cooperation orientation preferring face-to-face communication. They like intermediation of intimacy and social group membership with high context relatedness (i.e. they need not say much to grasp the meaning because the communication partners know a lot already by frequent former communication) in contrast to German users, who concentrate on the task or product to present while having low context relatedness, i.e. using mainly explicit communication.

2.3.3   Potential Guidelines for Intercultural HMI Design

Some hints regarding cultural differences given in Table 2 can be used for the intercultural user interface design and further reflections and research. More detailed attributes and properties of the user interface characteristics can be derived that could also be regarded in intercultural HMI design. Table 3 shows a summary of implicated general recommendations for intercultural user interface design based on Röse 2002.

Table 3: Summary of recommendations for intercultural HMI design according to the user interface characteristics regarding China and Germany (summarized by the author in accordance to table 6-3 in Röse 2002: 138 as well as to Röse 2002: 305-317)

User Interface Characteristics	China	Germany
Metaphor	Use clear hierarchy and representation instead of abstraction	Use representation instead of abstraction
Mental model	Use many references without sequence of relevance, simple mental models, clear articulation, limited choice and binary logic	Use few references with sequence of relevance and fuzzy logic
Navigation	Use limited and predefined choice and navigation	Use open access and arbitrary choice and unique navigation
Interaction	Use personalized but team-oriented systems giving direct error messages, guided help and providing face-to-face interaction	Use distant but supportive (error) messages providing open and flexible interaction with the system (e.g., full text search)
Presentation	Use formal speech providing high contextual relationship-oriented information as well as feminine colors	Use informal speech providing low contextual task-oriented information as well as masculine colors

Need for empirical validation

However, not all recommendations have been proved yet empirically according to the five areas of user interface characteristics even if there is some research in this area. Röse validated some of the aspects pointed out by Marcus doing qualitative studies in China e.g., regarding different layout for Chinese and German users (cf. Röse 2001).[60] Moreover, regarding metaphors, taxonomies as hierarchical and classifying instruments are applied in China rather than in Germany because of the high power distance values. Most of the recommendations presented must be tested and confirmed empirically in detail by additional studies before being suggested as best practices or even useful guidelines, if not already done so. Furthermore, parallel to the research literature, empirical investigations regarding intercultural user interface characteristics are necessary, e.g., by comparing several systems of different cultures (benchmark tests) as well as usability evaluations (usability testing) to determine the usability of different systems.

2.3.4 Intercultural and Cultural Variables

According to Röse 2002: 93-96, intercultural variables describe the differences in HMI design regarding the preferences of the users of different cultures (cf. Table 4).

---

[60] Therefore, the arrangement of widget in layout has also been investigated by the author in accordance to Röse 2002 (cf. URD test task in Figure 16 in section 5.2.2).

Table 4: Intercultural variables according to Röse 2002: 97 et seqq. (estimated values regarding the difficulty to recognize the variables are added by the author)

Intercultural variable	Level of localization	Relation to HMI design	Perceivability of the variables	Estimated difficulty to recognize [0 (easy) – 10 (difficult)]
Dialog design	Interaction	Direct	Hidden / Over long time and deep analysis	10
Interaction design	Interaction	Direct	Hidden / Over long time and deep analysis	9
System functionality	Function	Indirect	Visible / Immediately	8
Service (Maintenance)	Function	Indirect	Visible / Immediately	7
Technical documentation	Function	Indirect	Visible / Immediately	6
Information presentation	Surface	Direct	Visible / Immediately	4
Language	Surface	Direct	Visible / Immediately	2
General system design	Surface	Indirect	Visible / Immediately	0

"Intercultural" variables represent knowledge that can be obtained only by observing at least two cultures and their differences, i.e. doing intercultural research (cf. Honold 1999) to obtain relevant knowledge for internationalization of software and system platforms. However, they can also be called simply "cultural" variables, because the values of those variables represent knowledge for a specific culture (relevant for system and software localization).

Intercultural research necessary to obtain cultural variables

Hence, in this work, I will use "intercultural variables" in cases where the intercultural research character for obtaining the values of the variables is meant and I will speak of "cultural variables", when mainly the usage of the values of the variables themselves (concerning a specific culture) is important.

Intercultural vs. cultural variables

There are "direct" and "indirect" variables affecting HMI parameters either directly (e.g., interaction, information presentation or language) or indirectly (e.g., via maintenance, documentation or technical surroundings).

Direct vs. indirect variables

Direct cultural variables are the most important, because they have direct and essential influence on the design of HMI. According to Röse 2002, direct variables can be divided into "visible" variables concerning surface levels and "hidden" variables affecting interaction levels, together mirroring the concept of the iceberg metaphor.[61] Both kinds of variables have strong influences on the design and determination of the usability and acceptance of the system. Visible intercultural variables concern presentation (e.g., colors, time and date

Visible vs. hidden variables

Visible variables

---

[61] Cf. also section 2.3.7. For more details about the iceberg metaphor in HMI design, please refer to Hoft 1996: 45 or e.g. to Brunner 2005: 22.

format, icons, font size, window size, form, layout, widget position like the position of navigation bar) and language (e.g., font, direction of writing, naming) level of a product (appearing above "water surface"). They can be recognized very easily because they are directly accessible and less determined by cultural context.

Non-visible (hidden) variables

Non-visible or "hidden" intercultural variables (below the "water surface") affect dialog design (e.g., menu structure and complexity, *changing* of dialog form, layout, widget positions, information presentation speed, frequency of changing dialogs, screen transitions) and interaction design (e.g., navigation concept, system structure, interaction path, interaction speed, usage of navigation bar, etc.) which have strong correlations to the cultural context. These variables concern interaction and dialog level of a product.

Visible / hidden intercultural variables

Additionally, the time aspect extends the definition of visible and hidden intercultural variables. "Visible" intercultural variables are immediately perceivable at a particular time (font, color, window size, navigation bar, etc.). It is very easy to grasp that intercultural dependencies of static aspects for the HMI design are easy to recognize because they exhibit contrast in direct comparison, i.e. if they do not normally change, they can be investigated more easily than those aspects that only can be determined by observing them over time. Therefore, it is relatively simple to obtain access to them and they are easy to analyze. In contrast, "non-visible" (or "hidden") intercultural variables are very elusive and only perceptible over a certain period of time (interaction speed, information presentation duration, dialog presentation frequency, usage of the navigation bar, etc.). Therefore, it is relatively difficult to analyze those variables and to obtain access to them.

Time dependent patterns

Dynamical aspects, firstly, need to be recognized by observing parts of the aspects over time, and secondly, they require a comparison of the patterns built up by the single parts. Hence, time dependent patterns play a decisive role here. The realization of localization in this area is very difficult because the contextual relation to the cultural background as well as to the product is very high for interaction and dialog design. However, it is exactly this high context, and hence culture dependency, that explains why those patterns and the non-visible intercultural variables are so important for the design of interaction and for the resulting dialogs (and dialog windows) thereof (Röse 2002: 98).

Direct hidden intercultural variables help to determine main "cultural effects"

They do have "inherent culture" which strongly helps to determine the main "cultural effects" in the contents of the intercultural variables. Table 5 shows some examples of visible and non-visible direct intercultural variables as well as the values postulated by the author, which are partly confirmed in literature (cf. footnotes in Table 5).

Table 5: Examples of visible and non-visible direct intercultural variables (partly from Röse 2002: 125 et seqq., extended by the author with postulated values)

	Characteristics / Value	
Variable / Parameter	Germany	China
Visible intercultural variables (VIV)		
Color of warning[62]	Red	Red / Orange
Color of normal operating state[63]	Green	Yellow
Degree of using colors[64]	Low	High
Disposition to touch on device[65]	Low	High
Number of words in messages	Low	High
Number of explanation dialogs	High (very important)	Low (less important)
Structure of explanations[66]	X, because Y	Because Y, X
Non-visible (« hidden ») intercultural variables (NVIV)		
Number of sequentially presented pieces of information[67]	Low	High
Number of system messages	Low	High
Number of mouse moves	Low	High

---

[62] Cf. the color study of Röse 2002: 125 et seq., as well as Vanka 1999.

[63] Cf. Röse 2002: 31 as well as Courtney 1986: 90. There is an inhomogeneity concept of colors in mainland China. Attention has to be paid to normal warning colors like red, yellow and green. Whereas in the USA or Germany the meanings of these colors (red = danger, yellow = attention, green = start/go/ok) are clear to nearly 100% of the people asked, in China these meanings are only clear to about 50% of the people tested (cf. Röse 2002: 32, figure 2-17).

[64] Cf. Röse 2002: 32 as well as the results of the qualitative study conducted by the author in China (cf. section 6.1).

[65] Cf. Rößger 2003.

[66] Cf. Scollon & Wong Scollon 2008.

[67] The author has estimated the values of the numbers of information pieces, system messages, mouse moves, word count and the importance of explanation dialogs from the reflections on Hall 1976 (cf. potential model for intercultural HMI design (PMICHMID) in section 4.4 as well as in file "041213 Modell interkultureller Variable55 überarbeitet am 30-04-2009_pres.xls" in the online appendix). Some of them will be confirmed by the studies presented in this work in section 6.2.

2.3.5   Internationalization, Localization and Globalization

In connection with the culture specific design of human-machine systems there are some other important concepts: internationalization (I18N) and localization (L10N) of software as well as globalization (G11N).[68]

Localization

Localization means the adaptation of the system to certain cultural circumstances at a certain local market e.g., the adaptation of the look and feel of the user interface or the internal data structures to the cultural needs of the user (cf. VDMA 2009). The localization of the product aims at special countries and culture specific requirements. Hence, in the localization process of the product will be adapted to the country and its culture specific needs. Localization of software is adapting and translating a software application in order to make it linguistically and culturally appropriate for a particular local market using internationalized software (Schmitz & Wahle 2000: 3-4).[69] The localization process comprises, e.g., adapting the following aspects to the desired culture:[70]

* Character set
* Differences in color meanings (concepts)
* Formats (e.g., date, address, currency)
* Documentation, online help
* Icons and metaphors.

Internationalization

Internationalization requires reflection about the general preparation of the system for localization. Internationalization of a product means that the product will be prepared for its usage in the desired (in the best case in all) countries (cf. International 2003). The internationalization of a software

---

[68] The localization industry standard association (LISA) provides a great deal of information on localization and internationalization of software as well as on globalization regarding the commercialization of products worldwide (cf. URL = http://www.lisa.org/Homepage.8.0.html, last access 6/8/11. However, "as of 2011 February 28, the Localization Industry Standards Association (LISA) was declared insolvent. The results of the Extraordinary General Assembly meeting and ballot of 2011 April 21 LISA has formalized the dissolution of the association and the transfer of the LISA Standards to the public domain. The company Société fiduciaire Zemp & Associés, SàrL in Geneva is designated as the liquidator of the association's assets." (cited from the URL).

[69] Sometimes, "localization" is used in the wrong sense embracing the concept of "internationalization". However, internationalization is the process of architectural preparation of a system for attractive localization at a later stage.

[70] More information about localization aspects can be found, e.g., in VDMA 2009, Esselink 2000, or in International 2003.

product delivers a basic structure on which a later cultural customization (localization) can be carried out. According to Esselink 1998, internationalization is designing software in a way that allows translation[71] into other languages without the need for re-design or re-compilation. However, internationalization is more than this. It is the process of preparing software so that it can be used in any country in the world (cf. VDMA 2009). Internationalization means the development of (software) products with regard to easy adaptation to other markets, i.e. to other (technical) conventions, cultural peculiarities *and* languages (Schmitz & Wahle 2000: 3). The internationalization process comprises, e.g.:[72]

- Support of Unicode strings
- Strings separated from source code
- Support for all date formats
- Support for all languages (e.g. providing correct writing systems, typography and input methods, e.g., by an input method editor (IME), cf. Lunde 1999).
- Generalizing online-help, documentation, project management, localization resources
- Generalizing HMI-forms and HMI-logic (cf. Stephanidis 2001 and Stephanidis 2007: "User Interfaces for All").

On the one hand, the process of internationalization does not start with delivering the product, but already with the product idea and affects product planning, product development, production and quality management (product test and evaluation). In this sense internationalization concerns the complete process of product management. On the other hand, the concepts of localization also have to be integrated into the development process from the beginning to reach optimal internationalization effect. Therefore, internationalization and localization can also be considered to be interwoven processes. It must be possible to adjust the parameters so that the product is usable with ease in the target country and in accordance with the respective culture.

Interwoven processes: Internationalization and localization

Hence, results of cultural and cognitive anthropology as well as psychology must be integrated into the internationalization concept to create in this stage

---

[71] Translation in this context means the conversion of written or displayed texts or spoken words into another language, i.e. all aspects concerning language within software.

[72] For more information please refer e.g., to VDMA 2009 or to International 2003. One of the first handbooks for developing international products was developed by Siemens-Nixdorf 1992 for the I18N and L10N of SINIX systems (cf. URL = http://serviceportal.fujitsu-siemens.com/i/de/support/technics/fgm/unix/fgc0385_gr.htm, last access 2/28/09).

the conditions necessary for successful subsequent localization.[73] Therefore, software internationalization research and design must also strongly consider the basic principles of software ergonomics for dialog design (i.e. general psychological norms valid for all human beings) along with intercultural differences.[74] Furthermore, the localization parameters have to be such that the product is appropriately usable in the respective country of destination. These processes primarily concern the functionality and the user interfaces of the product (e.g., graphic user interface, keyboard, buttons, controls, language, dialogs etc.).

Employing software
ergonomics and usability
engineering methods

Although this process implies greater efforts to analyze, plan, design and implement software, the long lasting benefits result in higher product acceptance by the user because the HMI has been optimized very carefully by employing software ergonomics and profound (intercultural) usability engineering methods. Furthermore, an improvement in the software ergonomics and human-machine interaction leads to better system acceptance by the user, if the system model matches with the culturally specific ways of thinking of the user (as explained in section 2.2.5).

Importance of considering
cultural background

Therefore, there is a great need to take into account the different cultural backgrounds of the users when applying the processes of internationalization and localization and to create user models in order to adapt the system to the cultural needs of the user.

Globalization

Finally, globalization encompasses all activities with regard to the marketing of a (software) product outside a national market (e.g., including I18N and L10N software). The objective is to run successful marketing in one or several regional markets by taking into account the technical, economic and legal conditions there (Schmitz & Wahle 2000: 2).[75]

---

[73] For example, within the process of localization of products for China it should be considered that Chinese people can be mentally overloaded (or can forget already known icons) during recognition of new icons because their language already embraces iconic characters (cf. Zimmer 1985 and Schmack & Wandke 1989).

[74] Relevant principles for HMI design are e.g., task adequacy, directness, self explanation ability, controllability, expectance conformity, error robustness, consistency, transparency, intuitiveness and user friendliness (cf. ISO DIN 9241 part 10, DIN 1996 as well as Schneider 2008). These principles can be used also in intercultural context because they mostly concern the basic human cognitive capabilities, which are the same in every human being. Following the mentioned principles for HMI design supports the user's understanding the system's functionality and thereby supporting satisfaction of the user as well as using the system efficiently and effectively, i.e. contributes to good usability (cf. section 2.3.6).

[75] Checklists for I18N and L10N are available e.g., by Esselink 2000, VDMA 2009, or the project "eCoLoRe" at URL = http://ecolore.leeds.ac.uk/ (last access 2/28/09), now URL =

2.3.6   Intercultural Usability Engineering in HMI Design

"Intercultural" usability engineering is a method for designing products of good usability for users from different cultures (Honold 2000). "Intercultural" in this context refers to the special methods that are necessary to do usability engineering for different cultures (cf. Honold 1999).[76]

Intercultural usability engineering

The work of Honold 2000 deals with the question of whether there is a reduction of the fit between user and product if products of one culture are used in another. At the collection of culture specific user requirements and culture specific assessment of the concepts used, it has to be examined how far approved methods of usability engineering are suitable. The existing cultural models should be taken into account in the process of product design in the context of intercultural usability engineering. First, the product developers must be sensitized to the difficulties of cultural influences on product development and product use. Then cultural factors influencing HMI must be provided to the developers and integrated into the product. The procedures, which serve to realize the knowledge acquired in concrete product design, must be institutionalized.

Culture specific user requirements

It must be distinguished between the desired functionality by the user concerning the system and the functionality of the system actually implemented. Analysis and implementation of the functionality desired by the user with regard to an optimally useable system with joy and ease are decisive for software with ergonomic and intercultural demands. This requires knowledge in software ergonomics and intercultural user interface design as well as the application of usability evaluation methods. In contrast, if the currently implemented functionality of a system of a certain culture is used as a basis for the analysis of user interface characteristics, it may lead to erroneous or simply wrong design guidelines because those requirements need not necessarily match the real needs of the user. Therefore, the user's needs must be collected for every user or at least for the desired user groups (e.g., Chinese and German users).

Creation of optimal useable system

---

http://corpus.leeds.ac.uk/mellange/ecolore_tmx_corpus.html (last access 2/8/11). Several aspects regarding I18N and L10N of driver navigation systems have been compiled by Ercan 2005. Sturm 2002 analyzed the usage of localization and internationalization chronologically and developed the TLCC model comprising the levels technical affairs; language, culture and cognition (cf. section 2.3.5 in the work report).

[76] The term "intercultural usability engineering" is commonly used by German usability engineers (cf. Zühlke 2004).

The usability of a system strongly depends on how the user can cope with the system. This knowledge can be obtained "simply" by observing and asking the user during his interactions with the system. In this case the user articulates his desires and hence his needs regarding the usability of the system. This is trivial and easy, but unfortunately, this method is applied too little in industrial HMI design even today.

Wrong design
⇨   No use

However, if there is a lack of that knowledge the final product will not be desired by the user: the customer (user) cannot use it because of the lack of important features or it takes too long to do a certain task using this system because of wrong design.

Precondition: knowledge about the cultural differences in HMI

The preconditions for intercultural usability engineering are knowledge about the cultural differences in HMI and its considerations in product design and product realization (Honold 2000; Röse 2002; Heimgärtner 2005). In addition to the common misunderstandings between developers and users, which lead to different product design, there are also misunderstandings because of cultural conditions. There is not only a different comprehension of the requirements of the product but also culturally dependent perspectives and views of them (cf. Heimgärtner & Tiede 2008). Hence, the developer needs much intercultural knowledge to understand the user of another culture. Furthermore, he needs competency regarding intercultural communication to enable the exchange of information with the user and to know exactly which product the user is likely to have (cf. Honold 1999).

Saving costs by doing intercultural usability engineering before starting the development process

Moreover, bad or lacking intercultural usability engineering within the development process of the product increases the development and maintenance costs through requests for a change. Detailed analysis of product requirements can save up to 80% of maintenance and implementation costs of such requests for a change (cf. Mutschler & Reichert 2004). Therefore, intercultural HMI design must already begin with the analysis of requirements before starting the design. This is also valid and especially necessary for driver navigation systems, because in the driver-oriented design of HMI for global markets, good usability increases driving security by preventing cognitive mental overload of the driver during driving. Furthermore, preferences of many people all over the world can be taken into account using intercultural usability engineering methods, which essentially enables the expansion into greater markets (Holzinger 2005) as well as broadening universal access (Heimgärtner et al. 2008).

Increased customer satisfaction and functional safety

The results for intercultural HMI design and software architecture from cultural studies in HMI are a necessary precondition for the usability and the sale of software for global markets. An international software product, which can be used effectively and efficiently by users of different cultures, increases customer satisfaction as well as functional security. A satisfied user will not change product brand because he appreciates the efforts of the manufacturer to develop usable products having optimized HMI.

2.3.7   State Of Research in Intercultural HMI Design

In the area of intercultural user interface design, the research of difficult to access methodological intercultural factors like different habits of interacting with the system, different expectations regarding the navigation within hyperspace or different mental models stands at the beginning of acquiring results.

Intercultural user interface design – research at the beginning

Two of the first important books regarding internationalization of HMI are *Designing User Interfaces for International Use* from Nielsen 1990 and *International User Interfaces* from Del Galdo & Nielsen 1996. *A Practical Guide to Software Localization* of Esselink 1998 is about how to write software for other countries. It provides a useful checklist for this purpose. Another very good introduction to the study of cross-cultural of HCI is Day 1991. A newer overview of culture and its effects on HCI is given by Cagiltay 1999.

However, to capture the newest aspects regarding methodology, technology transfer and the diffusion of innovation, one has to browse through the literature up to now to get an impression about what the most important tasks in intercultural HMI research can, should or must do in the future. The results of this browsing process by the author are presented in the following.

The number of studies supporting the importance of taking cultural aspects into account in user interface design is growing steadily (Evers 2003; Smith & Chang 2003). This is also the case for driver navigation systems (Rößger 2003). However, there is relatively little literature and few guidelines for intercultural dialog and design for interaction (e.g., Kamentz 2006, Kralisch 2006) and very few especially for driver navigation systems (e.g., Rößger 2003). Most studies concern the presentation of information on web pages (e.g., Hodemacher et al. 2005, Marcus 2003, Dormann & Chisalita 2002, Baumgartner 2003, Marcus & Gould 2000, Stengers et al. 2004, Sun 2001 and Callahan 2005). Even though there are already the first pragmatic guidelines e.g., for intercultural web design (cf. Marcus & Gould 2000) or intercultural HMI design (cf. Röse 2001), there are none for intercultural user interface design in driver navigation systems which could be used easily and effectively by HMI designers in this area. This is also supported by the overview of Sturm & Mueller 2003 as well as Fitzgerald 2004 presenting many activities and models for intercultural website design. There are no new insights regarding interactive design but those presented in this work until now as the most recent overview of Thiessen regarding intercultural information design also shows

Growing importance of cultural aspects in user interface

(cf. Thissen 2008) – even if, for a short time, there have also been studies examining stand-alone systems and applications other than web applications (e.g., Kralisch 2006, Kamentz 2006, Lewandowitz et al. 2006, Braun & Rößger 2007). Röse 2002 and Zühlke & Röse 2000 also explicitly mention intercultural HMI design as well as design of global products for the Chinese market. On the one hand, most of these studies concentrate on "visible" intercultural variables[77] such as:

Many studies concentrate on visible intercultural variables

- Colors (e.g., NASA standard for colors (Currie & Peacock 2002 or Ou et al. 2004))
- Icons (e.g., use of pictorial or abstract icons (Röse 2002: 135))
- Date and time, phone numbers and address formats, spelling, typography, reading and writing directions, sorting methods (Shneiderman 2009: 23-24)
- Extension of texts, text processing, amount of characters (Rätzmann 2004: 77)
- Multimedia (e.g., Krömker 2000).

Research on additional aspects in intercultural HCI

On the other hand, there is activity investigating the trends in intercultural HCI (cf. Jetter 2004). Lee 2002 did a cross-cultural study on how users and developers experience their use of information systems and found differences in mobile Internet usage between users from Japan (e.g., high email traffic) and Korea (e.g., many downloads) depending on different value structures in Japan and Korea imprinted by culture.

Need for personalization of internet services

Hence, personalization and adaptation to the different user needs is necessary: "[..] Internet strategies should be localized or adjusted to unique cultures, since people want different values even from the same services across different cultures. [..] Mobile Internet services need to be personalized to individual users because value structures and usage patterns are influenced by various factors across countries. To develop personalized services, mobile Internet service providers need to segment user groups by cultural, demographical, or socio-economic factors and monitor them, which may enable them to chase users' fast changing needs or values efficiently." (Lee 2002: 237).

Information seeking process

Komlodi 2005 investigated the cultural differences in the information seeking process. Guidelines are available on building IT architecture (cf. Koning et al. 2002).

Holistic vs. analytic thought patterns

Nisbett 2003 proposed that the thought patterns of East Asians and Westerners differ greatly (holistic vs. analytic). Holistically minded people have a tenden-

---

[77] Cf. section 2.3.4.

cy to perceive a scene globally; they are more field-dependent.[78] Analytically minded people are more field-independent because they have a tendency to perceive an object separately from the scene and tend to assign objects to categories.

Dong & Lee 2008 studied the relationship between cognitive styles and webpage perception and presented the culturally different behavior of eye movement. The different viewing patterns of Chinese, Korean and American people suggest that webpage designers should be aware of the cognitive differences existing among holistically minded people and analytically minded people and that web pages should be designed to match the users' cognitive styles in order to enhance usability. Holistically minded people (e.g., Chinese people) scan the entire page non-linearly. Hence, the design of content should show the whole context of the website and the harmony between the foreground and background as well as the relationship among all the content areas. In contrast, the webpage design should be as clear and simple as possible for analytically minded people (e.g, German people). They tend to employ a sequential reading pattern among areas and to read from the center to the periphery of the page. Hence, the arrangement of all content areas must be considered carefully. Category titles and navigation items should be named as clearly as possible since analytically minded people tend to pay more attention to these items and gain an overall picture of the website from them.

Study of cognitive styles and webpage perception

In future studies, Dong & Lee 2008 intended to define the relationship between cognitive styles and webpage layout design. This indicates once more that most intercultural studies concentrate on researching web pages.

Hence, in the area of intercultural HMI design there is much research regarding the design of cross-cultural web pages and research of international product design (cf. international workshops of internationalization of products and systems (IWIPS)) as well as many guidelines regarding the visible areas of graphic user interfaces for the internationalization and localization of software (cf. section 2.3.5).

Intercultural HMI design: research restricted to visible areas

In addition, the cultural influences on the values of direct visible cultural variables of HCI is proven empirically in the literature on internationalization and partly implemented in products (cf. Nielsen 1990, Evers & Day 1997)

---

[78] In psychology, often the two contrasting cognitive styles for teaching and studying, called field dependent vs. field independent (often also paraphrased as global vs. analytically) are used to describe the style of cognitive processing of learners (cf. Witkin et al. 1977) which exhibit similar attributes corresponding to the cultural dimension relationship vs. role orientation or to collectivism vs. individualism (cf. section 2.2.3), e.g., social vs. impersonal orientation, organizational need vs. self-structuring, helping vs. competition, data vs. theory-driven, global vs. analytical perception.

regarding surface level (presentation of information, speech and general design of machine) and functional level (machine functions, service and technical documentation) of localization.

Lack of research on direct hidden intercultural variables

However, the detailed survey of current research in cross-cultural user interface design also showed that some intercultural variables have not been thoroughly investigated so far. Study of the literature does not reveal much about research on direct hidden intercultural variables at the interactional level: cultural influence on HMI at the interactional level, e.g., regarding navigation, system structure and mental models or varying functionality has not yet been investigated in detail to develop optimal products for the specific culture.

There is little literature about the connection between cultural aspects and directly hidden intercultural variables for HMI design. For example, Evers et al. 1999 examined cultural differences in the understanding of metaphors applied in user interfaces.[79] Since the real world changes from culture to culture, the metaphors referring to the real world that are used in HMI must also be considered for the localization of user interfaces. Examination has shown that test subjects from different cultures understand metaphors differently and their expectations, which they combine with the metaphors, are also different. However, these variables are also mostly regarded as an open field for research in intercultural HMI design.

Hence, it is decisive in the area of intercultural user interface design to bridge the gap between cultural aspects and those specifically for user interface design, e.g., the current lack of research regarding culturally imprinted interaction and dialog design.

2.3.8   Methodological Problems in Intercultural HMI Design

Combination of culture and HMI design challenging

According to Hall 1976, the methodological problem in researching culture is the fact that the transmission of simple systems is easier than the integration of complex systems that can only be connected together by human creativity.[80] This applies primarily to cultural questions, which integrate the complete context of a member of a culture. This problem also confronts intercultural user interface design, which makes it compellingly necessary to deal with the combination or linkage of culture and HMI design. Many aspects have to be taken into account simultaneously to obtain possible cultural explanations for their effect on HMI. Alternatively, the effects of culture on HMI cannot be

How to acquire the relationship between cultural and HMI?

---

[79] Cf. also section 2.3.2 or e.g., research on desktop metaphor (cf. Herczeg 2005: 59 seq.).

explained by only one single aspect but by many different influences.[81] Another problem in cultural research is that one cannot predict how the single parts of the cultural puzzle will fit together (cf. Hall 1976: 130).

Furthermore, different approaches exist for determining intercultural variables and their values. For instance, cultural dimensions arise from cultural studies that can give insight into the diversity of cultures (cf. section 2.2.3). From cultural dimensions, intercultural factors for HMI design can be derived (cf. section 2.3.2). The results received are supported argumentatively and deductively, but not confirmed empirically (Marcus & Gould 2000: 5 et seq.). Also, Cyr & Trevor-Smith 2004 state that the connection between cultural dimensions and HMI design has not been researched as yet in depth. Either detailed empirical studies will follow or the results can only serve as exemplifications, but not as a scientific foundation for further research.

Determining intercultural variables

Deductive approaches lacking empirical confirmation

User interface characteristics

The complement to this deductive approach is the inductive approach: Cultural markers have been determined by empirical studies (e.g., Badre & Barber 1998, Dormann 2006, Sun 2001), which are specific for a certain culture and which are preferably used within this certain culture. Badre & Barber 1998 showed the direct influence of cultural markers on the performance of users interacting with the system and hence the connection between culture and usability (confirmed, e.g., by the studies from Sun 2001 or from Vöhringer-Kuhnt 2002, cf. section 2.3.1). However, these results cannot be generalized, e.g., to a complete country because of the small sample sizes and the limited representativeness of the test persons for obtaining statistical results of high quality. This is one reason why there are few evident qualitative empirical studies and even fewer purely quantitative studies (cf. Smith & Yetim 2004 as well as Maier et al. 2005) researching the interaction of culturally different imprinted users with the system.

Inductive approaches lacking generalization

Cultural markers

Hidden variables are difficult to make out because they are only recognizable over time (cf. section 2.3.4). Therefore, the reason for the lack of results regarding direct hidden intercultural variables at the interaction level is also grounded in the difficulty of accessing and measuring them.

Difficult accessibility of hidden intercultural variables

---

[80] „Die Übertragung einfacher, wenn auch hochentwickelter mechanischer Systeme, die wenige Hintergrundinformationen erfordern, ist weniger problematisch als die Integration hochkomplexer mehrstufiger Systeme, die nur mit menschlichem Einfallsreichtum erfolgreich miteinander verknüpft werden können." (Hall 1976: 54).

[81] „Kultur ist aber ein komplexes Phänomen und ihre Auswirkungen auf die MMI lassen sich nicht durch die Betrachtung einzelner isolierter Kulturdimensionen erklären. Es handelt sich vielmehr um ein Zusammenspiel vieler unterschiedlicher kultureller Einflüsse." (Brunner 2005: 106).

Investigation of interaction and dialog design

To work against these methodological difficulties in researching hidden variables, it is reasonable, to a certain degree, to regard interaction and dialog design separately. First, the cultural differences in the interaction between user and system must be investigated, and then, how the interaction affects information flow between user and system.[82] Finally, how dialog windows should be designed for culturally different users also needs investigation which should lead to preliminary design recommendations.[83]

2.4   Adaptability and Adaptive Systems

Adaptability: capability of system to adapt automatically to user's needs

Adaptability is the capability of the system to adapt itself automatically to the user needs and expectations in accordance to situation and context, which can be a means to compensate cultural differences adequately, i.e. automatically but smoothly. According to Neuss 2001: 17 system adaptivity is the situation dependent customization of a system which can contain triggering from the environment or from functional activity and interactive behavior by the user. In any case, system adaptivity presupposes identification of the triggers of adaptation, the adaptation objective (e.g., automatically adapt the system to the user needs) as well as what has to be adapted. Hence, for all adaptive systems, at least the following four questions must be answered (cf. Holzinger 2001):

- Adaptation objective: Why adaptive? According to Brusilovsky 1996, there are at least two good reasons to create adaptive systems. First, there are different user expectations and differently thinking users. Second, getting lost in hyperspace and information overload should be avoided by adapting navigation and flow of information (cf. Hammwöhner 1997). Furthermore, the objective is to avoid cognitive overload and to reach a level of high usability for the system.
- Adaptation means: What has to be adapted? Adaptive parts of the HCI can be, for example, the number of information units presented in parallel (e.g. Points of Interest (POI) per map page in a driver navigation system).
- Adaptation information: The adaption is according to what? The number of information units presented in parallel can be adapted according to the different cultural preferences of the users (e.g., Chinese vs. German user).
- Adaptation process: How is adaptation achieved? By recording and analyzing the dialogs as well as the user interaction with the system (e.g., getting the average number of selected pieces of information from the us-

---

[82] Cf. sections 4.2 and 4.3.

[83] Cf. section 8.3.

er), an interaction model[84], as well as a domain model[85] according to the user tasks must be created. Inference mechanisms can match current interaction patterns with stored (e.g. culturally dependent) ones, i.e. inferring components make decisions regarding the adaptation means based on decision models. Inference mechanisms trigger adaptation mechanisms, which are components that implement the adaptation means (e.g., presenting the adequate number of information units according to the user preferences recorded earlier). Evaluation mechanisms are research components that collect information about the user by observing the user's behavior. They are used to verify whether the performed adaptation corresponds to the user-model by checking whether the system model and the user model match. Hence, adaptivity can be achieved by adjusting the domain model as well as the system-model to the user model by generating decision models from the interaction model (Bra et al. 2004, Holzinger 2001).

Some of these components and mechanisms are also used for the principle for culturally adaptive HMI, which will be explained in section 3.2.1. The user likes to see the system as a tool (cf. Herczeg 2005). Hence, the system should recognize what tool it has to be for the certain task the user wants to do and it should adapt itself to become the required tool in the corresponding situation. The minimal constituents to achieve adaptivity are observing the interaction of the user with the system, generating a user model by the system to acquire adaptation rules as well as automatically adapting the system to the user (cf. Mandl et al. 2003 and Brusilovsky & Maybury 2002). Kühme et al. 1992 suggest a taxonomy of adaptive user interfaces. A very detailed presentation of the types of adaptive systems as well as a taxonomy of their components can be found in Malinowski et al. 1992, Malinowski & Obermaier 1993 as well as in Dieterich et al. 1993.

Minimal constituents to achieve adaptivity

2.4.1   Kinds of Adaptability

There are at least three ways of adapting a system to user-specific requirements to optimize HMI (cf. Heimgärtner 2005 on the basis of Malinowski et al. 1992 and Bra et al. 2004):

---

[84] Interaction models describe how the user interacts with a system (cf. e.g., Hubner 1990, Schlegel et al. 2003, or Herczeg 2003). The interaction model of Herczeg 2009 has been implemented in an intercultural interaction analysis tool (cf. section 5.2).

[85] A domain model describes the various entities involved in a system or of an application area and their relationships. It is commonly used in user modeling (cf. e.g. Dix et al. 2001) and in applying UML (cf. Balzert 2005).

Manual adaptation

(i) Manual adaptation means that the user adapts the system manually to set his preferences, i.e. the user adapts the parameters of the system in accordance with his wishes. This is known as "personalization". Personalization means an individual (quite specifically a single user) manually adapts the system driven by the preferences of this individual (often also storable in user profiles within the system) (cf. Van Kleek & Shrobe 2007). The user keeps control over the system on that occasion. Furthermore, the user workload is not taken into account. The likelihood that both the user model and system model match over a long time is relatively low.

Adaptivity
(automatic adaptation)

(ii) Adaptivity (automatic adaptation) is the ability of a computer system to adapt itself automatically to user-specific peculiarities (user preferences) using a formerly created user model to fulfill the user's expectations. Moreover, it is called "self-adaptivity" if the system takes over all possible tasks to fulfill adaptivity (cf. Malinowski et al. 1992). This embraces the initiation of adaptation, the proposition of changes, the decision upon action to be taken as well as the execution of the change. Furthermore, real time monitoring is an essential precondition for adaptivity (i.e. for the possibility of the system to adapt to the user automatically). The main advantage of this kind of adaptive HMI (especially in vehicles) is the reduction of the mental workload (for the driver) by taking into account user preferences and user workload in the actual (driving) situation to adapt the system correctly and automatically (cf. Piechulla et al. 2003). In addition, interaction adaptivity can suppress interaction offerings if they are misleading in a certain context (cf. Hollnagel 1995).[86] Furthermore, the interaction between user and system improves and becomes easier, which optimizes HMI in general (and increases driving safety). This effect is even stronger when additional cultural aspects are taken into consideration in the user model. The advantages of adaptivity are that the user does not have to know the system in detail. The user automatically determines the type and degree of adaptivity of the system by his interaction with the system. Thus, the HMI is continually being simplified and the likelihood increases that user model and system model will continue to match over a long time. However, the system can over-adjust or can adjust incorrectly.

Semi-Adaptivity –
Hybrid of (i) and (ii)

(iii) The third kind of adaptability is semi-adaptivity. The system recognizes the interactive behavior of the user and derives the necessary HMI adjustments using its collected knowledge about the user. The system then

---

[86] Unsuitable interaction offerings cause the most frequent misinterpretations by the user (cf. Hollnagel 1995).

automatically suggests possible adjustments to the user,[87] which can then be manually approved or rejected. Thus, the user is made aware of system changes. This hybrid solution tries to unite the advantages of approaches (i) and (ii) and to avoid their disadvantages as far as possible. The user retains full control over the system, but does not need to know the system in detail. The HMI is simplified and the likelihood is high that user model and system model will (even probably completely) match over a long time period. Therefore, unfulfilled expectations of the user are avoided and usability is optimized. Moreover, this approach takes into account also the user workload by causing the system to switch into a fully adaptive mode automatically in situations where the workload of the user is too high (e.g., blocking a system message or a phone call when approaching a crossing).

2.4.2   Adaptivity Methods – User Modeling

Adaptivity of HMI needs to support the identification and personalization of the user by storing the type of interaction of the user with the system in a database in order to recognize the user to adapt to him.[88] The system must recognize interactive patterns in order to adapt its own interaction patterns to those of the user and his situational needs. This can be done by adapting the HMI according to the user model (cf. section 2.2.5). However for this, the system has to know the different user models of the different users employing user identification mechanisms (like password locking or fingerprint recognition, etc.).[89] Hence, a user model has to be built and kept up to date by observing the user (e.g., the driver whilst he is driving).[90]

Interactive patterns

---

[87] Only in appropriate situations, i.e. when the user is not overloaded by the actual (driving) task.

[88] Please refer to sections 6.6.2 and 8.5 for detailed information on these aspects.

[89] Cf. also the overview of identification methods from Amberg et al. 2003. For instance, Bartmann 1997 developed a method to identify the user by analyzing the way of entering the user name and password at login prompt called "Psylock" (cf. also Bartmann et al. 2003, Bartmann & Wimmer 2007 and Bartmann et al. 2007). This identification method has been extended by the author employing analysis of mouse events (cf. section 6.6.2). It is possible to identify the user within several minutes because of mouse usage (cf. section 7.5). However, such systems are not fraud-resistant because the security key of keyboard and mouse event driven systems can be cracked by listening to the event streams using a mouse event or keystroke logger.

[90] For example, by recognizing and observing the facial expressions or the sitting position of the user, the character, workload and emotion of the user can be analyzed to identify the user (hectic, calm, affective, etc.). Cf. also sections 3.1.1 and 8.3 as well as Röse & Heimgärtner 2008.

Methods of generating
user models

According to Kobsa 1993, there are several methods for the system of acquiring necessary information about the user to generate a user model (= implanted knowledge in the system about the user). Primary acquaintance heuristics can be domain-specific (rules by direct interaction) or independent of a domain, e.g., correct and incorrect usage of objects, queries of explanations and details as well as feedback. Finding stereotypes in user behavior is another method and involves three steps: determination of user group, identification of the key features of the user and hierarchical representation of stereotypes. There are many other methods such as recognition of the intentions of the user using libraries of plans or plan composition as well as error libraries and inferences.

Several adaptation
algorithms

Several algorithms can be used to implement adaptability. Simple adaptation rules are implemented directly in program codes in the form of production rules (cf. Görz 2003).[91] More complex rules for adaptation can be realized using a knowledge base, either as adequate facts and rules within an expert system or as beliefs (B), desires (D) and intentions (I) using a BDI logic that can help to model and to hold consistent the beliefs, desires and intentions (as well as the factual and contra factual presumptions) of agents within a BDI system (cf. Georgeff et al. 1999).

In any case, the knowledge found about the user must be kept as consistent as possible by complex but adequate forms of representation such as predicate or modal logic as well as neural networks or hybrid representation systems.[92] For this purpose, and to simplify the realization of adaptive systems, shell systems (e.g., BGP-MS from Kobsa & Pohl 1995) as well as special functional programming languages (e.g., Prolog or Lisp, cf. Görz 2003) for user modeling components can be used (cf. Kobsa 1993).

For example, variable adaptation rules are implemented using neural networks that are able to learn the rules before runtime and to adapt the learned adaptation rules as well as to learn new adaptation rules during runtime (cf. Zaphiris & Kurniawan 2007). Hackos & Redish 1998 describe in detail how to obtain the user models by applying user and task analysis methods for interface design (cf. Hackos & Redish 1998: 12, figure 1-4).[93] Further methods to reach these objectives by the system are exhibiting cooperative behavior e.g., using

---

[91] This method is also used in the CAHMI demonstrator presented in section 7.3. For more details regarding the logical programming of artificial intelligent systems, please refer e.g., to Görz 2003.

[92] Please refer to Heimgärtner 2002 for elucidating representation handling within different representation systems.

[93] Cf. also "usage centered design" by Constantine & Lockwood 1999.

clarifying dialogs to reduce underspecified information as well as providing explanation dialogs to make decisions of the system clear to the user (cf. Shneiderman 2009). Similarly, structure and size of menus have to be adapted according to the capabilities and expectations of the user. Even if there is vague or missing data, the user assumes that the expertise of the system is correct. Hence, the system should inform the user about deviations or doubtful information (or it should be able to correct the wrong data by itself). Algorithms of artificial intelligence (e.g. data mining methods)[94] can handle this problem.

2.4.3 Overcoming Problematic Aspects of Adaptivity

Adaptivity is achieved by adjusting the correct user models (already available from the design phase) according to the current context of use at runtime. Automatic adaptation (= "adaptivity") depends on maximum data when observing new users: the system needs much data in order to capture information about the user as well as to infer the characteristics of the user regarding information presentation, user interaction and using dialogs. The system needs a certain time from the first start up to obtain enough data to be able to adapt itself to the user. Hence, there is the so-called "bootstrapping problem".[95] As long as no solution is available that can achieve meaningful adaptations from minimum data automatically, it remains necessary to investigate standard parameters and their values very early in the design-phase, and long before runtime, in order to integrate them into the system.[96] Before using the system for the first time, it must be adjusted e.g., to the nationality of the user (which indicates the main affiliation of the user to a cultural group e.g., a certain country) and the corresponding cultural parameters can be simultaneously postulated as standard parameters for the desired country. Thus, the adaptive system also obtains adequate characteristics of the user more quickly at runtime, because there is "more time" to collect the culture-specific data of the

Bootstrapping problem

---

[94] Data mining methods like classification, clustering, regression, summarization, dependency modeling, change and deviation detection derived from techniques of machine learning, pattern recognition and statistics are used for the investigation of unknown, but mostly structured amounts of data (cf. Fayyad et al. 1996). Text mining methods are used to analyze *unstructured* amounts of data (cf. Mehler & Wolff 2005).

[95] "[..] is the bootstrapping problem, that very little about the user is known when the application is first installed on the user's system." (Van Kleek & Shrobe 2007: 1).

[96] According to an additional study by the author, first indications are present to suggest that these times can be reduced for some domains to several minutes or even shorter (cf. section 7.5 for details).

user and a basic adaptation to the most important user preferences was already performed before runtime (by putting the standard parameters into the system at design phase). Therefore, it is necessary that the system already has corresponding user-knowledge (standard parameters) before the user's first contact with the system occurs. Designing an appropriate system in the design phase helps to avoid some of the problems arising from adaptivity at runtime.

Reliability of assumptions However, the knowledge gathered about the user can be misleading or simply false: the reliability of assumptions can be a problem (cf. Kobsa 1990). The system model has to be in common with the user model to prevent unexpected situations for the user, which may confuse him.

Legal restrictions Another problem is that legal restrictions also have to be taken into account: only the effects of user actions in a user model (e.g., interaction type) are allowed to be stored permanently, but not the log file of the personalized user sessions themselves (e.g., interaction data) (cf. Bra et al. 2004).

Design rules From the known problems with adaptivity mentioned above, some design rules can be derived to work around the problems (cf. Kobsa 1993). The user must be aware of the user-modeling component and of the fact that the system can make errors or even pursue non-cooperative interests.[97] Hence, the user should be allowed to switch off adaptivity. Modeling long-term user features should be avoided because they can change according to the situation and over time. Furthermore, it is necessary to make personal entry possible due to the analysis of user intentions. Adaptability should not surprise the user but must be in accordance with the mental model of the user. Hence, sudden changes must be prevented. Additionally, e.g., space limits for the automatic enlargement of buttons for handicapped users have to be taken into account during the design process to support the "universal design" or "user for all" paradigms (cf. Stephanidis 2007) that call for adaptive systems.

---

[97] E.g. an artificial agent, cf. section 8.5.1 in the work report.

3 Towards Culturally Adaptive Human-Machine Interaction

"Lepší míra nežli víra."[98]
(Czech saying)

To prepare a technical product for global markets, intercultural user interface design as well as intercultural usability engineering is necessary (cf. sections 2.3.6 and 2.3.7). In addition, to achieve culturally adaptive HMI (CAHMI), extended methodological research in intercultural HMI design regarding adaptability is required. In section 3.1, the current state-of-research in CAHMI is summarized. Subsequently, I define the concept of CAHMI, postulate the principles of CAHMI, sketch the architecture to implement CAHMI, as well as briefly describe the scope, the problems and benefits of CAHMI (cf. section 3.2) by integrating the basic reflections from chapter 2. Then, a methodological approach to CAHMI will be developed (cf. section 3.3) based on the quantitative recognition of cultural differences in HCI. Existing methods relevant for this approach are presented followed by finding appropriate methods to be used in this work. Finally, the objectives and main research questions of this dissertation project and the scope of this work are stated (section 3.4).

Path to Culturally Adaptive HMI – CAHMI

3.1 State Of Research in CAHMI Design

So far, culture has played a minor role in the design of adaptive (software) systems and this statement is supported by the study of research literature. In particular, purely quantitative differences in interaction behavior depending on

---

[98] "It is better once to measure self than to believe someone else twice." (cf. footnote 1 on page 1 and file "Sprichwörter mit messen.txt" in the online appendix).

culture have not been investigated very intensively until now (cf. section 2.3.7).

Minimal research in quantitatively analyzing cultural differences in HMI

The content of the fundamental abstract hypothesis (FAH, section 2.3.1) that is used in this work, has been stated by Röse 2002 mainly using literature study and analytical reasoning, as well as the results from qualitative studies (e.g., focus groups and usability testing) mostly without using log files containing recorded data regarding the interaction of the user with the system. There is relatively little empirical research and a lack of well-elaborated theoretical work based on empirical results in the area of intercultural interaction and dialog design. However, if an automatic cultural adaptation of HMI should be done by a machine then cultural differences have to be recognized purely quantitatively. In fact, nothing could be found on this topic in the literature.[99] Until now, no empirical studies have analyzed the cultural differences in the interaction of the user with the system purely quantitatively. Therefore, in this work, the interaction of the user with the system is measured empirically using a special test tool including several potential cultural interaction indicators to prove the precondition for CAHMI that cultural differences in HMI can be recognized purely quantitatively.

Idea of culturally adaptive software

Proved by CAHMI demonstrator

The first paper promoting the idea of culturally adaptive software as well as the first step to prove that culturally adaptive systems are possible was provided by Heimgärtner 2005[100] and the proof itself has been presented in Heimgärtner et al. 2007 with the CAHMI demonstrator that will be described in detail in chapter 7 of this work. Therein, the author introduced the principle of culturally adaptive HMI and presented the first results of quantitative empirical studies regarding cultural differences in HCI in Heimgärtner 2006 as well as the final results in Heimgärtner 2007b. This proved that culturally adaptive systems are possible in the first place because cultural interaction differences in HMI can be recognized and measured quantitatively by a computer system. This happens merely by monitoring and analyzing the interaction of the user with the system resulting in adequate quantitative culturally dependent values for the intercultural variables.

---

[99] This is especially valid for the beginning of the dissertation project in 2003. Cf. also the corresponding section 3.1 in the work report.

[100] In 2007, Reinecke & Bernstein 2007 proposed the idea that culturally-adaptive systems would go beyond internationalization.

3.1.1   CAHMI in Driver Navigation Systems

A driver navigation system is an electronic device, which consists of a display, a data carrier and operating equipment to support the driver in the navigational task. It serves to determine the current position of a vehicle and to support the driver by guidance to the desired destination.[101]

Description and task of driver navigation system

The driver consistently needs information about the next maneuvers provided by maneuver guidance and the map display to react to changes in the route tracking (e.g., traffic jam or construction sites). Therefore, besides his actual task, steering the vehicle in the traffic, the driver must also turn his attention towards communication with the driver navigation system (cf. Röse & Heimgärtner 2008). This demands additional attention of the driver (cf. Gstalter & Fastenmeier 1995). The user's expectations of the system must be met to allow efficient, effective and satisfactory use (i.e. the system must provide good usability).[102]

In this sense, the driver navigation system plays a prominent role of intersection within the sphere of driver information and assistance systems.

Research of interaction by use cases of driver navigation systems

Therefore, in this work, user system interaction will be researched and demonstrated by use cases of driver navigation systems to elucidate cultural adaptability.

The most interesting use cases possess tasks with a high degree of interactivity.[103] Moreover, the main interactive activities in driver navigation systems are connected to their main functions and most used 'use cases' (also called application cases):[104] destination input, map display, route guidance and setting of options (cf. Heimgärtner 2005).

Application (Use) Cases

By associating the aspects of the use cases with cultural models, implications can be made to adapt the HMI culturally. For example, "presentation of

---

[101] For more information on the kinds, architecture and use cases of driver navigation systems, please refer to section 3.1.1 in the work report.

[102] Cf. e.g., to Preece 1993, Dumas & Redish 1999, or Mayhew 2008 for more information on the usability concept.

[103] The tasks within these use cases will be explained in detail in section 5.2 where design and usage of the tool for intercultural interaction analysis (IIA tool) is presented.

[104] A use case defines all possible scenarios, which can happen if the user tries to accomplish a certain technical goal (business goal) with the help of the system examined. The main emphasis is on the question, 'what' happens and not 'as' it happens (cf. e.g., Kulak & Guiney 2000 or Bittner & Spence 2003).

information" covers visual cultural variables such as colors or arrangement of widgets. The dependence on driver situations can be regarded using e.g., several modes of information presentation (e.g., navigation, cruise or vigilance mode)[105] which can be selected manually or automatically according to driving situation. According to the active mode of information presentation, information is presented with adequate density, frequency and "speed" (presentation duration).[106]

Driver navigation
systems:
⇨   No cultural
    adaptivity up to now
⇨   Change of basic
    settings available

At present, driver navigation systems are manually adaptable only to a certain degree according to the user needs. They can be personalized but they do not provide extensive adaptivity of HMI. There is adaption of HMI to driving situations (e.g., vibrating the steering wheel when changing the lane without using the indicator or when crossing the medial strip or leaving the roadside). Regarding cultural preferences, currently only basic settings can be changed like language or color using styles or color schemes. However, further cultural aspects like layout or different frequency and speed of information presentation flow or interaction behavior as well as the adaptation of these aspects to the driver workload are not available.

Differences in the
interaction of drivers
according to cultural
background

For example, even if Rößger & Rosendahl 2002: 135-146 show some differences in the interaction of drivers with driver information systems, they focus on the user preferences concerning interaction means and interaction behavior from a general perspective, less than regarding the principle of culturally adaptive HMI and cultural adaptivity. They propose e.g. that Japanese (in general) do not mind "deeply structured" menus, like "Hi-tech" interfaces, want entertainment and games, accept parallel interfaces (like multiple maps on a display) in contrast to Europeans (in general) who want sequential, easy-to-use interfaces that are obvious and clear. Use of local language is important. Americans (in general) want to talk; they are lonely in their cars. Like Europeans, they tend to be sequential. Moreover, cultural adaptivity in vehicles does not only concern the look and feel of the user interface at the driver work place, but also the number and the kind of system functions that can dynami-

---

[105] Navigation mode is selected if navigation commands have to be taken or there are many maneuvers to execute. Cruise mode is set when driving on highways where the mental workload for the driver is relatively low and the driver can e.g., listen to music and set up the equalizer to change the attributes of the sound while driving. Vigilance mode will be activated if a dangerous situation emerges or mental workload increases dramatically, e.g., if the phone rings while approaching an intersection (cf. personal communication with Tertoolen, S., Groenland, F. and Rühl, H.W. within the project "Drive-IT Adaptive HMI" at SiemensVDO in 2004).

[106] Cf. HMI dimensions in section 4.2.

cally change according to driver preferences, driver state, driving situation and driving behavior.[107]

Hence, culturally adaptive driver navigation systems must adapt not only the human machine interaction but also vehicle specific functions, such as automatic gear change, braking, parking, etc. Some of these functions also need human machine interaction. Hence, culturally adaptive HMI of a driver navigation system needs or depends on driving dependent functionality and data (e.g., automatic gear change to display the actual gear, speed or acceleration) which have to be taken into account in HMI design. Generally, the design and development of user interfaces for vehicles includes manifold aspects e.g., information visualization, haptic technology, etc. which are challenges to software developers. The most common use cases that need massive interaction in navigation systems are destination input, map interpretation and maneuver guidance.

Adaptation of vehicle functionality along HMI in automotive context

To take into account these complex information structures simultaneously, and to optimize the driver's mental workload at the same time, it is necessary to employ adaptability in addition to pre-settings or profiles. Adaptivity is reasonable because the driver does not have the opportunity to adapt the setup of the information presentation manually according to special situational requirements. Hence, either the system suggests the adequate form of information presentation to the driver (computer supported adaptation) or it adapts it automatically (automatic adaptation) while the driver is actually concentrating on driving (cf. section 2.4.1). For example, difficult routes with high rate of accidents can be avoided most notably for beginners by analyzing the routes as well as the driving behavior and by adapting route calculation and information presentation according to the recognized facts.

Necessity of adaptability in automotive context

Hence, the importance of CAHMI in driver navigation system will be increasing steadily. However, according to literature studies, there is no driver navigation system that automatically adapts to the cultural needs of the driver. Furthermore, CAHMI in driver navigation systems has not yet been realized because CAHMI has not been used in general until now. This gap should be reduced by this work by developing an integrated concept of cultural adaptability including all the aspects mentioned. According to the principle of culturally adaptive HMI (cf. section 3.2.1), the culturally dependent behavior of the driver has to be measured and recorded over time in order to obtain information about the parameters necessary to culturally adapt the HMI as proposed in Heimgärtner 2005.

Increasing importance of CAHMI in driver navigation systems

Integrated concept of cultural adaptability in this work

---

[107] Cf. Timpe & Baggen 2000. In the future, probably also the interaction devices can change dynamically in form and functionality adequately to the current use case.

3.2   Concept of Culturally Adaptive HMI

Cultural vs. individual aspects

User-individual adaptation requires person-bound identification

Cultural aspects are not to be confused with individual aspects. Only a single user owns individual aspects as opposed to all users of a common culture who have cultural aspects at their disposal in common. For example, in an adaptive personalization mode, the system adapts to the individual features (personal characteristics) of the user.[108] This kind of user-individual adaptation requires a corresponding person-bound identification.[109]

Concept of cultural adaptivity

In contrast, the concept of cultural adaptivity does not mean adaptive personalization at an individual level but integrates internationalization and localization at a cultural level. Cultural adaptivity in this sense is equivalent to adaptivity of cultural elements, i.e. the automatic adaptation of HMI to cultural characteristics: all users who can be assigned to a certain culture are consequently tossed into the same pot. Hofstede proved that there are quantitative differences in human behavior between countries (Hofstede 1991). Hence, the HMI can be adapted according to the characteristics of cultural dimensions at country level first. One approach is to transfer these quantitative differences to differences at HMI where possible and to provide this knowledge to the system for adapting the HMI to the cultural needs of the user.[110]

Culturally adaptive HMI

Culturally adaptive HMI applies user models that are averaged across all users of a certain cultural group (similar to the concept of user stereotypes).[111] Culturally adaptive HMI does not perform person-identification but applies an identification of the user's culture by the recognition of culture-specific interaction patterns of the user and his preferences in the system. In this sense, culturally adaptive HMI is adaptation neither to a particular national culture

---

[108] Personal characteristics are e.g., Carl Gustav Jung's four categories that reappear in the Myers-Briggs-Type-Indicator (MBTI) (cf. Keirsey 1998): extroversion vs. introversion, sensing vs. intuition, perceptive vs. judging and feeling vs. thinking (cf. also Shneiderman 2009).

[109] User identification can be achieved, e.g., using static methods like personalized car keys, password or fingerprint or new dynamic methods like "Psylock" by analyzing the style of using the keyboard (cf. Bartmann 1997) or mouse (cf. section 7.5).

[110] This work also provides a method to evaluate whether Hofstede's indices can be used for this purpose (cf. section 3.3). The discussion of the results of this work indicate that Hofstede's dimensions only partly provide the knowledge necessary for culturally adaptive systems (cf. section 8.1).

[111] A stereotype is a phrase relating to all the members of a class or a set and often form the basis of prejudice as well as usually being employed to explain real or imaginary differences due to race, gender, religion, ethnicity, socio-economic class, disability, occupation, etc. (cf. Monfared & West 2002).

nor to a particular individual. Rather it comprises the recognition of culture-specific interaction-patterns of the user with the system (because of acting in a cultural surrounding (cf. the fundamental abstract hypothesis in section 2.3.1) as well as the corresponding culture-specific adaptation of the HMI (either as suggestions to the user or automatically, cf. section 2.4.1).

3.2.1   Principle of Culturally Adaptive HMI

All reflections from chapter 2 so far can be reasonably integrated into a principle of culturally adaptive HMI in accordance e.g. with Stephanidis 2001; Stephanidis & Savidis 2001, Maybury & Wahlster 1998, Baumgartner 2003 and Leuchter & Urbas 2004 regarding the basic principle of automatic adaptation of HMI. The principle of CAHMI (cf. Figure 4) represents a feedback control system which allows the derivation of the values of the cultural dimensions by analyzing the monitored user interaction behavior and by retrieving associated cultural parameters stored in a database format (both during design phase and at runtime).[112]

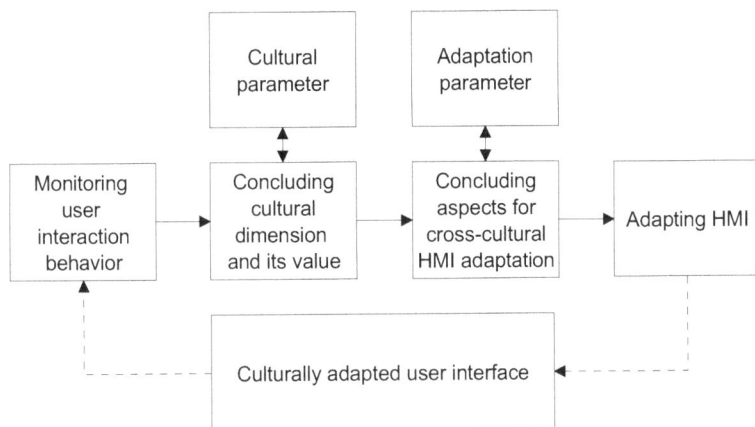

Figure 4: Principle of Culturally Adaptive HMI

The system monitors and records the user interaction with the system. Then, the system analyses this data using cultural interaction criteria to determine the

Parameters for cultural adaptation

---

[112] The relationship of the user interaction and the cultural parameters is postulated in detail in chapter 4 and empirically determined and partly verified in chapter 4. The final model for intercultural HMI design (MICHMID) can be found in section 8.2.

cultural characteristics of the user by comparison with predefined cultural patterns. From this suitable aspects for intercultural user interface design (parameters for cultural adaptation) can be derived that allow the adaptation of both "look" (appearance) and "feel" (behavior) of HMI according to the cultural needs of the user. Adaptation parameters are direct visible intercultural variables concerning "look" like color, font and menu position that are immediately visible. The "feel" of HMI is affected by direct hidden intercultural variables which are perceivable over time like menu structure, usage of scroll bars, information presentation speed or frequency of displaying messages (cf. section 2.3.4). Finally, the system adapts the HMI according to the cultural preferences of the user employing HMI design guidelines for intercultural interface design after asking the user or automatically if expectance conformity is not damaged or an emergency situation forces it to do so.

Implementation of CAHMI into architecture

The principle of CAHMI can be implemented in architecture for culturally adaptive systems. Users with different cultural needs use the device. The system monitors and records the interaction patterns and then classifies the interaction patterns into interaction classes using its knowledge about culturally dependent variables.[113] After recognition of the interaction pattern, the device adapts to the cultural interaction preferences of the user and, if defined at the design phase by the guidelines for intercultural HMI design, to the cultural imprinted preferences of the user regarding surface, interaction and functionality.[114]

3.2.2   Scope, Problems and Benefits of Culturally Adaptive HMI

Advantages of adaptivity

According to Jameson 2007, the advantages of adaptivity lead to better usability by adapted user and system models, shorter training times by fast adaptation to the user and less mental workload by automatically optimizing and adapting the HMI according to the current situation (and in less distraction from traffic in the case of driving a vehicle).

The acceptance of interculturally adaptive intelligent user interfaces is given when the user is aware of the changes in the user interface driven by the system or if the changes are very small. If many small changes occur distri-

---

[113] Cf. cultural interaction indicators (CIIs) in section 6.6.2 as well as HMI dimensions (HMIDs) in section 4.2.

[114] More information on the CAIAA can be found in the work report in section 8.5 as well as in section 8.5 in the work in hand.

buted over a long time period, the user does not recognize them because he is being slowly familiarized to them.

For adequate usability of culturally adaptive HMI, it is vital to connect cultural influences to the surface, function and interaction level of a system. Cultural adaptation of HMI requires knowledge about intercultural differences and commonalities as well as their implications for the HMI (cf. Röse 2002). Not only cultural aspects identified by comparative usability studies are necessary, but also an intercultural understanding of the context of usage, thereby deriving adequate test settings by employing focus groups and interviews (cf. Honold 2000 in section 2.3.6). This is the reason why intercultural usability testing does not only embrace the comparison of cultural aspects but also the understanding of intercultural aspects.[115] It is necessary for designers to have intercultural knowledge because the context of system usage changes the design requirements as well as the test settings and test scenarios (cf. Honold 1999, Honold 2000).

Intercultural knowledge

Intercultural understanding

Usability studies

The disadvantages of culturally adaptive HMI are the same as those for all adaptive systems, as stated in section 2.4.3. In addition, "culturally" adaptive systems need special attention regarding the cultural aspects and this requires effort at the development stage (design phase).

Standard cultural parameters have to be determined that can be changed by the system over time with analysis and evaluation of the ongoing user interaction behavior at runtime. The problem to initially determine these parameters can be solved at the design phase (cf. Holzinger & Weidmann 2005) by researching literature, doing usability testing and conducting empirical studies as well as employing logging and artificial learning mechanisms to draw relevant conclusions and compute adequate values for these parameters during runtime (cf. Bra et al. 2004). In the case of no scientifically sound values being available for a parameter, the adaptive system should be able to observe the user and to estimate adequate values over time during runtime.

Determination of standard cultural parameters at design phase

Furthermore, direct hidden intercultural variables cannot be easily accessed and it is difficult to measure their values as explained in section 2.3.4. One possible solution is to simulate use cases at the design phase to measure potential parameters (cf. chapter 3.3.3). Therefore, real-time-adaptive solutions (cf. chapter 7) need not necessarily rely on previous measurement data (cf. chapter 6), but can orient themselves to basic cultural standards and culture-related psychological research (default parameters) obtained by analytical

Simulating use cases

Obtaining default parameters

---

[115] Cf. section 2.3.4 for the difference of the notions "cultural", "cross-cultural" and "intercultural" as well as their usage in this work.

reflection in the design phase (cf. chapter 4). The advantages and disadvantages of both approaches are described and discussed in detail in this work (cf. chapter 8).

3.3   Methodological Approach to Culturally Adaptive HMI

> "Measure everything which can be measured,
> and make everything measurable which cannot be measured."
> Galileo Galilei, 1610

First, possible methods and tools usable in CAHMI research for eliciting cultural differences in HMI (sections 3.3.1 to 3.3.3) to achieve the given objectives in this work will be presented and reflected on. Before illustrating the methods applied in this work (section 3.3.5), the steps on the way to systems with culturally adaptive HMI (Path-To-CAHMI) is described (section 3.3.4).

3.3.1   Methods and Tools for Research and Evaluation of CAHMI

Determination of cultural parameters for intercultural user interface design

It is important to consider fundamental cultural differences when dealing with members of cultures interacting with machines. Hence, the most important step is to bridge the gap between cultural aspects (e.g., derived from cultural dimensions) and HMI design by determining relevant cultural parameters for intercultural user interface design using analytical research and empirical tests. These tests should show whether or not human-machine interaction comes along with cultural dimensions, and if so, in which way. Possible approaches to accomplish this are presented now.

"Grounded Theory"

The "Grounded Theory" is a method that can be used for research areas such as intercultural HMI design, which are not analyzed in detail. Hence, it is reasonable to apply the fundamental process, stated by the grounded theory in this work because of the lack of research or the gaps in CAHMI research today. According to the grounded theory, a multi stage process has to be used to generate new theories. Using analytical reflection of known theories, models and intuitive ideas, hypotheses for a new integrating theory should be generated. Then, empirical data have to establish a basic foundation (initial position) to test the hypotheses and to verify the theses to obtain a new theory. From this theory, new hypotheses and predictions can be derived to test them again empirically (cf. Vollhardt et al. 2008). Furthermore, it constitutes an iterative scientific process similar to iterative software development cycles (cf. Balzert

2005). Both, grounded theory and iterative software development are used in this dissertation project.

Hence, it is necessary to perform research in this area by using existing, or introducing new, methods such as analyzing critical interaction situations between humans and computers or machines.

Need for analyzing critical interaction situations

Good opportunities for the transmission of intercultural competence are "critical incidents" (cf. Brislin & Yoshida 1994). Analyzing critical interaction situations between humans is a well-known method to find differences among cultures (cf. Thomas 1996).[116]

This method can be also used for analyzing critical situations between a driver and driver navigation system. As an example, the driver gets the advice to turn left in 200 meters but there is no intersection. Does the driver expect new correct advice or an excuse? Is the driver patient and quiet or does he interrupt the system to obtain correct information? These questions need answers in the proper cultural context e.g., by observing Chinese drivers using a German driver navigation system and vice versa.[117]

One objective in intercultural HMI design is to show developers of international products a way to develop these products such that they can be offered successfully in the global market.

Hence, one of the most important tasks is to explore the intercultural differences (e.g., different color meanings or cognitive styles) and then to consider the implications of the identified differences in designing intercultural HMI (e.g., different operation state colors, browsing style). Relevant cultural variables for intercultural HMI design have to be determined and specified by literature review and requirements analysis. The values of cultural variables show culture-dependent variations that can be exploited for intercultural user interface design. They can be found on all levels of HMI localization (surface, functionality, interaction) (cf. Röse 2002). Then, the empirical qualitative and quantitative analyses of the values of the cultural variables need to integrate the results into cross-cultural HMI.

Determination of cultural variables for intercultural HMI design

---

[116] In my view, another reasonable method to identify cultural differences and probably to extend the explanation power of cultural dimensions could be to analyze the proverbs of a culture since they reflect the historical culturally developed cognitive structure of the members of the corresponding culture. However, this method has to be developed in detail and must be verified by empirical studies in future.

[117] Cf. also the results of the benchmark test in section 6.1 regarding the differences between the user preferences and the interaction behavior provided by the system.

Method of culture-oriented design (MCD)

Röse 2002: 108 developed an approach for the design of intercultural human-machine systems using the "method of culture-oriented design" (MCD). The MCD integrates factors from established concepts of culture-oriented design into existing concepts of HMI design. Thereby, knowledge about cultural differences is integrated into existing methods. To include intercultural aspects in human-machine interaction, a simplified version of this method will be applied in this work (Figure 5).

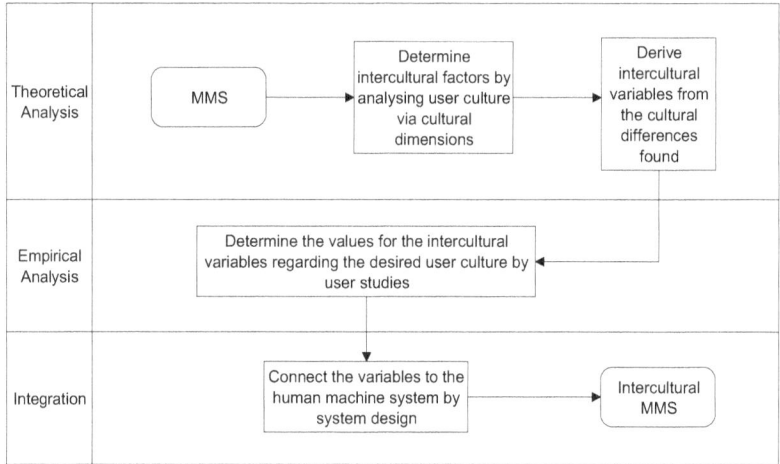

Theoretical Analysis

MMS → Determine intercultural factors by analysing user culture via cultural dimensions → Derive intercultural variables from the cultural differences found

Empirical Analysis

Determine the values for the intercultural variables regarding the desired user culture by user studies

Integration

Connect the variables to the human machine system by system design → Intercultural MMS

Figure 5: Simplified version of the Method of Culture-oriented Design (MCD) (Source: own illustration)

Steps necessary to design HMI

In sections 3.3.2 and 3.3.3, the steps necessary to design HMI are derived from MCD such that a system is able to adapt to users from different cultures automatically. Finally, a path to CAHMI including the required methods to obtain usable values for cultural variables in intercultural HMI design is presented (cf. section 3.3.4).

3.3.2 From Cultural Dimensions to Cultural User Interface Design

Cultural dimensions for intercultural HMI design

A cultural dimension represents an aspect of a culture, which is measurable in relation to other cultures (cf. section 2.2.3). Cultural dimensions are good indicators of possible differences between cultures (cf. Hofstede 1991). Furthermore, recommendations are available regarding which cultural dimensions are most interesting for intercultural HMI design (cf. section 2.3.2). However, most of the cultural dimensions known are still not made usable for intercultural HMI design.[118]

Knowledge about the values of cultural dimensions provides an impression of the possible cultures to which a user might belong. For example, relationship-oriented cultures accept high information speeds in contrast to task-oriented cultures that like to concentrate on their tasks instead of wasting time chatting with other people when the communication information is not related to the task (cf. Halpin & Winer 1957; Hall 1959). Task-oriented users prefer fulfilling tasks to relationships (during working hours, e.g., professional drivers). The knowledge, whether the user is rather relationship-oriented or task-oriented, may be derived from the user interaction behavior. For example, pressing buttons very exactly and navigating very directly without permitting disturbances or interruptions by other people or the system increases the probability that the user is task-oriented because he takes the task very seriously.

Relationship-oriented vs. task-oriented users

These explanation tests also raise some questions, though. For example, Hofstede 1991 suggested that Chinese people are more relationship oriented and have lower uncertainty avoidance than German people. It is difficult to explain and decide which culture dimension predominates.[119]

In addition, culturally adaptive HMI depends on many parameters relating to situation, context, user preferences and world knowledge as well as aspects of space and time (Del Galdo & Nielsen 1996). All these aspects constitute culture. In turn, all these aspects are also influenced by culture.

3.3.3   Measuring the User Behavior

Areas strongly influenced by culture, e.g., ethical values, do not come to the surface directly (cf. Röse 2002). Only behavior is visible on the surface, which is imprinted by cultural aspects over time and, hence, only the user behavior itself yields insights about the cultural imprint of the user. The behavior on the surface can be measured very well, because it is visible. Therefore, regarding the interaction analysis, the character of a human being can be identified (cf. Bales 1950, Jordan & Henderson 1995, Smith & Bugni 2006). This is also valid for HMI design and can be applied in HCI (cf. Card et al. 1983, Nardi

User behavior culturally imprinted over time

Interaction analysis identifies the character of a person

---

[118] This task will be tackled in this work in section 4.1 (cf. the results in Table 8).

[119] During this dissertation project, doubts about the explanatory power of cultural dimensions have arisen and will be discussed as a result of this work in detail in sections 6.6.3 and 8.1.

2001). For instance, facial expressions or utterances reveal a certain ethical attitude if observed over certain time (cf. Koda et al. 2008, or Endrass et al. 2008).

Furthermore, by both qualitative and quantitative analysis of the visible behavior of the user with the system, the patterns of action and their causes as well as mental models are ascertainable (cf. Rehm et al. 2007). Hence, there is a good chance of getting relevant cultural information from the user interaction with the system (e.g., by recording the number of actions per minute, speech input speed, analyzing word meaning, etc.) which can then be used for cross-culturally adaptive HMI. If the culturally dependent user behavior can be analyzed and described functionally, the system can be provided with intercultural knowledge related to the interaction behavior of the user (cf. Seitz et al. 2000). This enables the system to determine the user's culture to a certain degree, which allows the system to adapt the user interface to culturally imprinted user preferences and needs. Hence, it is reasonable to measure user behavior.

Methods of measuring user behavior

Most methods for measuring the user behavior are located in the domain of psychological research (cf. Eysenck & Eysenck 1985, Krauth 1995 or Eysenck Eysenck & Keane 2004). They are designed with respect to intercultural phenomena concerning inter-human and inter-cultural communication (cf. Neuliep 2008, or Revel & Andry 2009). In contrast, measuring user behavior in cross-cultural HCI has not been investigated in detail (cf. section 3.1). Therefore, the objective of this work is to study the behavior of the users from outside their culture and to compare it with different cultures. Table 6 shows the two approaches for conducting cultural research according to Donsbach 2008.[120]

Table 6: Emic vs. etic approach (Source: own illustration)

	Emic approach	Etic approach
Perspective	Study behavior from within the system	Study behavior from a position outside the system
Culture	Examine only one culture	Examine many cultures, comparing them
Results	Structure discovered by the analyst	Structure created by the analyst
Relation	Criteria are relative to internal characteristics	Criteria are considered absolute or universal

Etic approach used in this dissertation project

The analyst (the author) a priori defined the structure of the culture (cf. chapter 4). Furthermore, the criteria for the differences of the cultures are regarded as universal (cf. Inglehart et al. 1998). Hence, in this work the etic approach is

---

[120] The terms have been introduced by Kenneth L. Pike (cf. Peterson et al. 2002).

used (cf. Table 6). However, in any case, i.e. irrespective of which approach is used, it is important to avoid cultural prejudices (cf. Thomas 1996) which is very difficult (cf. Heimgärtner & Tiede 2008).[121] Hence, this work will attempt to conform to strict and objective rules of academic inquiry.

3.3.4   Path-To-CAHMI

Derived from the general course of action as well as from the suggested method of cultural design (MCD) and the reflections before, the following adapted steps for intercultural HMI design towards CAHMI (Path-To-CAHMI) may help to reach the objectives of this dissertation project presented in section 3.4:

1. Find and use the most important use cases (and their context of usage), which are used in all cultures (e.g., following maneuver guidance announcements, observing the map display or entering a new destination) (section 3.1.1).
2. Postulate hypotheses derived from this analysis (e.g., number of POI correlates with information density acceptance of the user and this in turn correlates to the degree of relationship-orientation of the user (cf. Hall 1959)) (section 4.3).
3. Determine cultural variables for intercultural HMI design and usability metrics from the literature and empirical studies that can be correlated with cultural dimensions (e.g., correlation of information density and speed to relationship-oriented cultures (cf. Hall 1959)) (section 4.4).
4. Set up the test setting by implementing the hypotheses and the use cases in a test environment. Localize all cultural variables that have not been investigated (independent variables). Do not localize cultural variables to be investigated (dependent variables). Implement the logging possibility of quantitative and qualitative information processing into the test environment (sections 5.1 and 5.2) by using a cross-cultural usability metrics (cf. section 4.5).
5. Do quantitative and qualitative intercultural usability evaluations with users from different cultures by using the adequately localized test environment (sections 5.3 and 5.4 as well as chapter 6).

---

[121] This old wisdom is also experienced in cultures expressed by proverbs, for example by the following one from Holland: „Hij beoordeelt een ieder naar zich zelven.". This proverb is also used in the English language e.g., "every one measures other people's corn by his own bushel" or "men muse as they use; measure other folk's corn by their own bushel". It is also known in Germany: „Jeder misst andere gern mit seiner eigenen Elle." (cf. also footnote 1 on page 1 and file "Sprichwörter mit messen.txt" in the online appendix).

6. Design a culturally adaptive model including adaptation rules (Table 42, Table 44 and Table 47 in chapter 7) for the confirmed hypotheses (section 6.5) and the most important use cases (e.g., destination input, map display, voice guidance) and implement it in the test environment (chapter 7.1).

Steps 7 and 8 serve to enhance the outcome from the steps 1 to 6 of the Path-To-CAHMI. Therefore, they are not in the main focus of this work.

7. Do quantitative and qualitative intercultural usability evaluations with users from different cultures with the adaptive system version. (Set parameters to default and let the system work. The evaluations should measure the cross-cultural parameters according to the usability metrics established by the hypotheses and adjust the culturally dependent variables (e.g., interaction style, menu position) automatically according to the cultural context of the user) (chapter 7.3).
8. Finally step towards and build a theory of cultural HMI based on the verified model for intercultural HMI design (section 8.2) to allow and perform (in best case) automatically deducing recommendations for intercultural HMI design of arbitrary use cases and cultures (cf. section 8.3), which is still done mostly manually up to now.

3.3.5   Applied Methods and Tools in this Work

To identify cultural differences in HCI or HMI, the user interaction with the system has to be evaluated. Hampe-Neteler 1994 classified nineteen evaluation methods (whereas usability testing is seen as an abstract method containing a mix of others, such as observation or log file recordings and hence, it is listed in Table 7 as a dependent method in contrast to all other independent methods).

Table 7: Possible and used methods (indicated by √) to reach the objectives of this work

Oral questioning (√)	Evaluation through a standard task (√)
Written questioning (√)	Group comparisons (√)
Online questioning (√)	Log file recordings (√)
Observation (√)	Simultaneous loud thinking ( )
Experiment ( )	Video confrontation user diaries ( )
Usability testing (√)	Secondary analysis (√)
Formal analytical procedures (√)	Expert judgments (√)
Experimental walkthrough ( )	Heuristic method (√)
Cognitive walkthrough ( )	Group discussion / Focus group (√)

Most efficient and cost effective methods

All methods in Table 7 can be used to determine the specific values of the dimensions relevant for HMI design regarding information, interaction and dialog. However, only the most efficient and cost effective methods that simultaneously support intercultural usability engineering have been used (because of resource restrictions).

To find the most appropriate methods, the methods above have been divided into three classes:

(i)   Questioning (oral, written, online, group discussion/talk)
(ii) Questioning (usability testing, evaluation accompanying a standard task, log file recordings, user diaries, experimental and cognitive walkthrough)
(iii) Reflection (formal-analytical procedures, secondary analysis, judgments of experts)

Three classes of methods

Ad (i):   Questionnaires can be used to determine the intercultural preferences of the user. Distributed online they reach a high number of users from different cultures. This quantitative data collection should yield cultural preferences and tendencies (if there any). Furthermore, interviews or focus groups can be used to enrich the results by qualitative aspects.

Ad (ii): Observing the interaction of cultural-specific users with the system should give insight into the cultural differences in interaction. The interaction can be analyzed and evaluated partly automatically using an adequate tool for this purpose (cf. section 5.2). This tool has been used for a quantitative survey that can be done via Internet or Intranet to reach many culturally different users. This quantitative data collection with this tool should also reveal cultural preferences and tendencies in the interaction of users from different cultures with the system (if there are any). All qualitative data should be captured using open questions.

Ad (iii): Finally, the conclusions from the analysis of questions and observation of test persons have to be fed back iteratively by reflection into the evaluation process to optimize the test equipment as well as the set of hypotheses.

In sum, a mix of approaches derived from the method of culture-oriented design must be employed, to obtain a model for intercultural HMI design consisting of intercultural variables or even a theory of cultural HMI. Hence, the methods used for this project (indicated in Table 7 by √) have been taken from all three areas to allow for recording and analysis of subjective and objective as well as qualitative and quantitative aspects by an optimal mix of methods.

Mix of approaches leads to model for intercultural HMI design

The analysis of the relationship between culture and HMI design can be done analytically (chapter 4) as well as empirically (chapter 6) to obtain usable guidelines for intercultural interaction and dialog design. This also helps to tackle the research questions from different sides to identify the connection between culture and HMI design.

Analytical and empirical analysis

Using tools for obtaining cultural differences in HMI

Hence, the most promising method to obtain cultural differences in HMI a posteriori is to observe and analyze the user interaction with the system by appropriate automated analysis tools employing usability metrics because of their empirical value (cf. Nielsen 2001, Shneiderman 2002; Shneiderman 2009, Dix 2007). The values can be compared simply and used quantitatively in computer systems without external human interpretation.

Quantitative metrics to measure cross-cultural HMI

To put it briefly, there are no well-established metrics for measuring quantitative variables in cross-cultural HMI. Hence, the objective is to find quantitative metrics for HMI by relying on existing metrics in HMI that are adequate to measure cross-cultural HMI. This can be achieved by finding actual hypotheses (cf. section 4.3) concerning the correlation of the cultural variables and their values in different cultures (cf. potential model for intercultural HMI design in section 4.4) according to step three of Path-To-CAHMI (cf. section 3.3.4). Empirical work must show if the results are compatible with cultural models and if they correspond with cultural dimensions and HMI dimensions only conceptually or even quantitatively e.g., with the quantitative indexes of Hofstede's studies (according to the steps four to seven of Path-To-CAHMI).

Test tool

To test some of the most important interrelationships between culture and information processing, a test tool for conducting user studies has been developed and used by the author (cf. sections 5.2 and 5.3) that allows the measurement of numerical values of the dimensions relevant for HMI design such as information speed, information density, interaction speed and interaction frequency in relation to the user (according to step five and seven of the Path-To-CAHMI).

These dimensions are hypothetically correlated to cultural variables in the sense of Röse 2002 (cf. section 2.3.4) concerning the surface level, for example, number or position of pictures in the layout or affecting the interaction level or frequency of voice guidance. This tool can also be used to investigate the values of variables like widget positions, menu structure, layout structure, interaction speed, speed of information input and output, dialog structure, etc.

Cultural interaction indicators

The main empirical objective of this work is to obtain a set of cultural interaction indicators (cf. section 6.2), which builds the basis for a model (step six of Path-To-CAHMI) that describes cultural differences in interaction behavior of the user by representing the relationship (cf. section 8.2) between the values of cultural dimensions (cf. section 2.2.3) and information scientific categories (cf. section 4.2).

If there are any differences, they will be interpreted and discussed, followed by an analysis of implications for intercultural HMI design (cf. chapter 8). An objective of future research is to develop an overall theory that explains the mutual relationship between the cultural interaction indicators and their interrelationship with the cultural background of the user (according to step eight of Path-To-CAHMI). However, there is a long way to go to achieve this goal and this work can only make a start (cf. also section 8.6.7 in the work report).

The advantages in this work of the developed method mix of using the test tool lie primarily in the possibility to employ abstract use cases that can be used to achieve functional equivalence according to Honold 2000: 92 seq. through which intercultural usability research is made possible in the first place. This requires the creation of equal test conditions as far as possible, reached e.g., by the following means recruiting employees from SiemensVDO worldwide (cf. section 6.4) that use a tool (cf. chapter 5) especially developed for this purpose by the author:

- Translation of the test tasks into the mother tongue of the test persons   Equal test conditions
- Carrying out the test only once
- Recruiting test subjects with similar experience with respect to dealing with PCs
- Similar educational level of the test persons
- Local analysis of the cultural differences by measuring them in the desired cultural environment
- Identical and easily understandable tasks for all test subjects
- Use many test persons (large sample size)
- Ensure high reliability of the data collection method

Furthermore, quantitative data offers broader advantages (cf. Kralisch 2006).   Quantitative data collection
For example, the results are more easily comparable. Qualitative methods are unsuitable for measuring dynamic interaction patterns since the user cannot explain why he has proceeded in a particular way. The user's mind is deeply (unconsciously) culturally imprinted; therefore, he cannot explicitly explain his behavior ad hoc without previous deep reflection (if he can explain his behavior at all). The reasons behind his behavior are unconscious for him (cf. ice berg metaphor, Hoft 1996).[122]

---

[122] If only the interaction behavior of the users without regarding informational issues shall be measured, it would be rather beneficial if none of the subjects of a test would understand the formulation because then only the reaction of the user on the system without conscious considerations regarding the contents of the test tasks would be independently measured. In addition, this constellation would represent a stress situation for the user, which would primarily result in culturally marked behavior (cf. Aranda & Knight 1997). Cf. also Hobfoll 2004: stress comes also from collective stimuli and not only from deprivation of resources, which indicates that cultural imprint plays a decisive role in stress situations.

3.4   Objectives, Main Tasks and Research Questions

As shown until now, within the process of culturally adaptive HMI design, the most challenging step today is to bridge the gap between cultural aspects and HMI design by determining relevant cultural variables and their values to derive practical guidelines for intercultural user interface design (that lack totally for driver navigation systems). The major objective of this project is to show if culturally adaptive HMI is possible by determining which "direct hidden cultural variables" (cf. section 2.3.4) have a fundamental effect on localization and must be considered and applied quantitatively for culturally adaptive HMI. The outcome of this dissertation should be a concept to adapt HMI automatically to the preferences of culturally different users. Therefore, the empirical objective of this work is to identify cultural differences in HCI as well as to analyze if such differences can be determined quantitatively to lay down the foundation for CAHMI. Cultural differences in the interaction of users of different cultures with the system must be analyzed in detail. In addition, the theoretical objective of this work is to develop a concept for culturally adaptive HMI (CAHMI). Thereby, the main influences must be examined: intercultural HMI design, adaptivity, and the connection between culture and HMI dimensions (cf. section 4.3).

Identifying "cultural interaction indicators"

An analysis of research on the interaction of the user with the computer to identify "cultural interaction indicators" mainly regarding "direct hidden cultural variables" (cf. section 2.3.4) at the interactional level (dialog and interaction design) suggests the following general course of action:[123]

a. Determining all used concepts (definition of terminology) (chapter 2 and section 3.2)

b. Determining a methodology (definition of Path-To-CAHMI) (section 3.3)

c. Determining necessary preconditions (presenting assumptions) (section 4.3)

d. Defining a potential model of cultural criteria for the intercultural HMI design (generation of hypotheses) (section 4.4)

e. (i) Reflecting, (ii) creating and (iii) executing empirical tests (test of hypotheses) (chapter 5)

---

[123] This course of action determined the structure of this document in hand even if according to iterative design principles some actions have been done in a loop (cf. file "iterative_design.ppt" in the online appendix).

f. (i) Analyzing test data, results and (ii) optimizing the cultural model of HCI from the results by using a tool for intercultural interaction analysis for HMI (chapter 6): a considerable amount of data will be collected largely automatically for carefully selected countries (especially for China and Germany)

g. (i) Reflecting, (ii) creating, (iii) implementing and (iv) testing of architecture for culturally adaptive HMI within a demonstrator using knowledge about the cultural aspects in HMI (chapter 7)

h. (i) Discussing and (ii) deriving implications for research and (iii) HMI design (chapter 8)

j. Testing whether the usability of the device can be improved by culturally adaptive HMI using intercultural usability engineering methods. By means of usability tests with users from different cultures, the usability of a culturally adapted system in contrast to a system that is not culturally adapted can be compared.[124]

3.4.1   Scope of this Work and Project Overview

It is not possible for this work to analyze all mentioned aspects in detail because of time and space restrictions. Therefore, the objective of this work is rather to generate a concept, which gives direction to culturally adaptive HMI (exemplified by a mobile driver navigation system) in terms of a "foresighted" development by a new internationalization platform sui generis to yield lasting benefits for research and industry. For example, it is not the objective of this project to analyze or to fix the concepts of "culture" or "information", but to describe the relationship as far as possible between cultural differences and information scientific categories as well as the cultural influence on variables used within HMI design by analyzing the interaction between user and system.

Concept to CAHMI exemplified by driver navigation system

There are several limitations of the scope of this work:

Reasons for the limitation of the scope of this work

- Limitation to direct hidden cultural variables, because of their direct influence on HMI design and the determination of the usability and acceptance. According to Röse 2002, hidden intercultural variables (for interaction and dialog design) depend most strongly on the context and culture at

---

[124] Task j could not be done in this work because of resource restrictions. This task remains for future research. Nevertheless, some results from usability tests done in the pre-studies are presented in the work report in section 6.1 as well as in the online appendix in the folders "pictures", "pdf" and "videos".

the deeper level of the iceberg metaphor where all those cultural dimensions and information scientific categories play a prominent role that are affected by time. Direct hidden cultural variables have not yet been investigated very well. Generally, the time aspect has not been investigated in HMI research in great detail so far, even if there is some initial research (e.g., Gellner & Forbrig 2003, Röse 2001).[125] Hence, hidden variables are investigated because they are only recognizable over time.

- Limitation of the two countries, China and Germany, because this is the first project in this direction regarding driver navigation systems for China. The cultural distance between China and Germany is very high and hence, also the probability is higher that culturally dependent variables can be recognized, if there are any, than investigating cultures with low cultural distance (like Germany and Austria).[126]

- Limitation to use cases in the HMI of driver navigation systems in order to restrict the scope of research, representative and demonstrative use cases for cross-cultural human-machine interaction (cf. Heimgärtner 2005).

- Limitation to simulate the use cases on a personal computer (PC) instead of a real driver navigation system, because there is no driver navigation system, which is facilitated with interaction monitoring. There is no driver navigation system adequately localized for China. Possibilities of recording and controlling the interaction behavior of the user can be implemented very easily and fast using a PC in contrast to an embedded system with restricted resources. There are many instances of test programs to do quantitative remote studies all over the world with PCs in contrast to real driver navigation systems. Short manual changes or optimization of the test equipment on a PC are easier than on driver navigation systems in hardware targets. Initial results regarding the localization of the interaction behavior of the system can be implemented very fast on a PC. Hence, it is easier to simulate and implement use cases on a PC.

- Limitation of topic and implementation of the demonstrator to the area of adaptability (graphical user interface (GUI) and speech user interface

---

[125] By the way, the time aspect has not been investigated in much detail in scientific research generally so far because it is very difficult to do so (even if there are some exceptions like the theory of dynamical systems (cf. Van Gelder 1998), chaos theory (cf. Haken 1983) and even Einstein's relativity theory (cf. Einstein 1919).

[126] Cf. Hofstede's scores in Table 50 in the appendix.

(SUI)), because the effort to integrate external car data requires too many resources for this dissertation project.[127]

In spite of these limitations in the scope of this dissertation project, there are still enough items to investigate. Figure 6 gives a rough overview of the most important work packages and the sequential milestones of the CAHMI project according to the steps of Path-To-CAHMI.

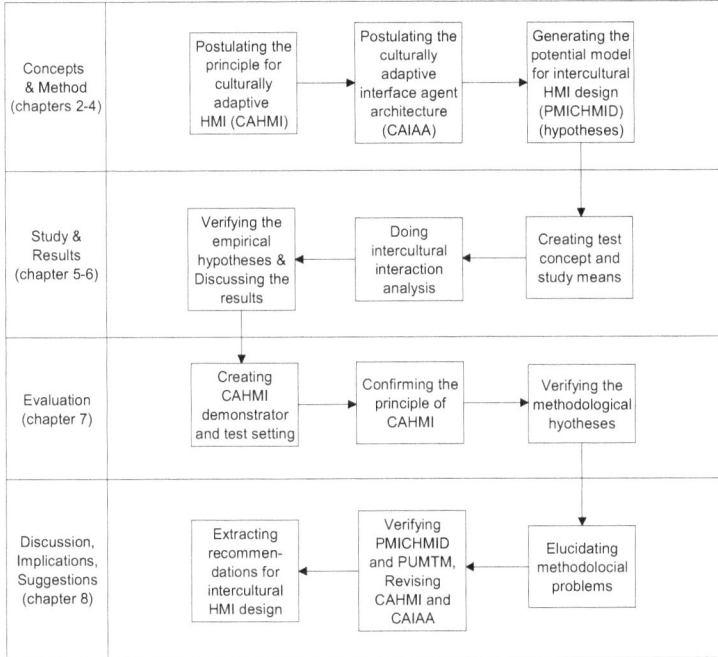

Concepts & Method (chapters 2-4)	Postulating the principle for culturally adaptive HMI (CAHMI)	Postulating the culturally adaptive interface agent architecture (CAIAA)	Generating the potential model for intercultural HMI design (PMICHMID) (hypotheses)
Study & Results (chapter 5-6)	Verifying the empirical hypotheses & Discussing the results	Doing intercultural interaction analysis	Creating test concept and study means
Evaluation (chapter 7)	Creating CAHMI demonstrator and test setting	Confirming the principle of CAHMI	Verifying the methodological hyotheses
Discussion, Implications, Suggestions (chapter 8)	Extracting recommendations for intercultural HMI design	Verifying PMICHMID and PUMTM, Revising CAHMI and CAIAA	Elucidating methodolocial problems

Figure 6: Milestones of this dissertation project

---

[127] Nevertheless, some work has been done by the author in this area by creating the generic adaptability framework (GAF) as indicated in section 8.5 and the corresponding section in the work report (cf. also Heimgärtner 2008b) as well as applying this GAF to driver navigation systems (cf. also Heimgärtner 2009a).

4   Towards a Model for Intercultural HMI Design

"When you can measure what you are speaking about, and express it in numbers, you know something about it, but when you cannon measure it, when you cannot express it in numbers, then your knowledge is of a meager and unsatisfactory kind."
Lord Kelvin, 1882

Theoretical research in this work embraces a top down strategy using an analytical approach to investigate the relationship between culture and HMI design. This approach involves the generation of a model for the connection of cultural background and interaction of the user with the system consisting of cultural variables in the potential model for intercultural HMI design (cf. section 4.4). This model includes concrete hypotheses (cf. section 4.3) to be tested in this dissertation project. In this chapter, first the complexity of cultural models will be reduced (cf. section 4.1) to facilitate identification of new clues in the field for intercultural HMI design (HMI dimensions (HMIDs), cf. section 4.2) allowing the derivation of the postulated results (cf. section 4.5) in the form of potential cultural interaction indicators (PCIIs) as well as a test concept for empirical research.[128]

---

[128] The test concept and the test setting are presented in detail in chapter 5.

4.1   Reduction of the Conceptual Complexity of Cultural Models

Cultural dimensions

Part of cultural models

Can be compared because of similar qualities

Culturally dependent dimensions (cultural dimensions) are part of cultural models that allow the comparison of the behavior of human beings from different cultures (cf. section 2.2.3). Thereby, according to Reimer 2005: 39, many of the cultural dimensions of the different authors have similar qualities, which allow them to be compared to each other (even if they can differ in their usage).

For example, the cultural dimension "individualism vs. collectivism" can be used dichotomously (as Hofstede does) or holistically (as Trompenaars does). Moreover, there is a close semantic relationship of some cultural dimensions (cf. Hodicová 2007: 38).[129] For example, the cultural dimension "role vs. relationship-orientation" correlates strongly with Hofstede's concept of "individualism vs. collectivism", which describes societies with loyal members. Furthermore, the cultural dimension "role vs. relationship-orientation" also correlates with Trompenaars cultural dimension "specificity vs. diffusion"[130], which means the separation of working and private areas (cf. Hodicová 2007: 38).

Connection of "Individualism" and "Power Distance"

Besides, obviously some cultural dimensions cannot be separated from each other because they are inherently connected: "In contrast to previous studies, we argued that both Individualism and Power Distance affect privacy attitudes and cannot be considered independently from each other. Empirical results provided evidence that the combination of both cultural dimensions has in fact the strongest impact." (Kralisch 2006: 209).

Cultural model in OSLS

In addition, the Ohio State Leadership Study (OSLS) (cf. Halpin & Winer 1957) revealed a similar cultural dimension, contrasting task and people orientation, even if the results OSLS must probably be relativized because of methodological deficiency (cf. Schriesheim et al. 1995). Nevertheless, the most important attributes of the postulated cultural model in the OSLS can be used for this work. In task-oriented cultures, people with a task focus put getting the job done as the highest priority before any people considerations,

---

[129] To explain intercultural communication and collaboration, many cultural dimensions have to be taken into account at the same time (cf. e.g., Rösch 2005).

[130] "In spezifisch orientierten Kulturen trennt [man] säuberlich die dienstliche Beziehung [...] von Beziehungen anderer [privater] Natur. [...] In manchen Ländern jedoch gibt es die Tendenz, dass jeder Lebensbereich und jeder Aspekt der Persönlichkeit alle anderen durchdringt." (Trompenaars 1993: 109).

which is in contrast to people-oriented cultures.[131] Hence, many cultural dimensions coincide with each other.

The reduction to some main cultural dimensions is also supported by the compilation of Cox 1993 who lists the dimension of individualism vs. collectivism which is immediately related to task/role vs. relationship orientation. Moreover, many authors of cultural dimensions use the individualism vs. collectivism dichotomy (cf. Cramer 2008: 37). This implication can also be based on the findings by Vöhringer-Kuhnt 2002 that only one of the five cultural dimensions of Hofstede, namely "individualism vs. collectivism", is correlated with the usability of a system (Vöhringer-Kuhnt 2002: 17), which indicates that it is most important for intercultural HMI design. In addition, Podsiadlowski 2002: 43 has used the one-dimensional construct "individualism vs. collectivism" as the basis for their extension to a multidimensional construct to obtain many cultural and individual sub-dimensions. Podsiadlowski 2002: 45 also highlights the time and space as well as the communication aspects brought forward by Hall 1959.

Reduction to main cultural dimensions

All these aspects in combination with the arguments of Hall and Kant (cf. section 4.2) support the fact that almost all compiled and analyzed cultural dimensions in this work can be reduced to one basic cultural dimension (BCD) combining the very similar dimensions "individualism vs. collectivism", "task vs. person orientation" and "role vs. relationship-orientation".[132]

Thereby, it is assumed that the differences in the behavior in relationship-oriented cultures to task-oriented cultures are larger than the difference in the behavior within relationship-oriented cultures or task-oriented cultures.[133] For example, Chinese and French people exhibit in relationship orientated aspects similar behavior because both cultures are strongly relationship oriented. German and US-American people exhibit in relationship orientated aspects similar behavior because both cultures are task-oriented. It is assumed that the differences in the interaction behavior between German and US-American people or between Chinese and French people are lower than between German/US-American and Chinese/French people.

---

[131] Cf. also section 4.1 in the work report.

[132] Cf. also section 4.1 in the work report for the relationship between the constituting cultural dimensions of the basic cultural dimension (BCD = combination of the first three cultural dimensions in Table 8) and others as well as section 4.2 in the work report for analyzing the dimensions using the analytical approach of Immanuel Kant.

[133] This equals assumption A4. All assumptions made in this work are listed in section 4.3.1.

The cultural dimensions "activity orientation" (doing – becoming – being), nature of the human being (good, bad / changeable, unchangeable), instrumental vs. expressive (depending on the nature of the human being), universalism vs. particularism and all cultural dimensions, which concern the development of a country, are difficult to subsume beyond the basic cultural dimensions. These dimensions contain rather common personally motivated objectives than group motivated ones. Therefore, they cannot be classified so easily into role/task/individualism or relation/person/collectivism-oriented categories at the society oriented level.

Influence of cultural dimensions on user interface design

All cultural dimensions and specific values are indirectly relevant and the ones directly relating to the condensed basic cultural dimension are directly and most relevant for intercultural HMI design because they indicate different user behavior depending on his role or relationship orientation. Baumgartner 2003 asked thirty international usability experts from twenty-one different countries about their opinion on the influence of these cultural dimensions on user interface design and asked them to judge the dimensions in accordance with their importance for HMI design. Her results include a summary of the following relevant cultural dimensions for HMI design in the order of their importance according to the asked experts (Baumgartner 2003: 46):

- context
- technological development (combination of environment/technology and technological development)
- avoidance of uncertainty
- perception of time
- conception of authority.

The dimension "context" is related to the required amount of information that is necessary in a culture in a certain situation (cf. Hall 1976). "Technological development" covers both the technological progress and the experience in dealing with technology, which is found in a culture. "Avoidance of uncertainty" describes the circumstances of how far the members of a culture feel threatened by unknown situations (cf. Hofstede 1991). "Perception of time" refers to mono-chronic, i.e. doing things rather scheduled and sequentially and poly-chronic time orientation, i.e. doing things rather seemingly arbitrarily and in parallel (cf. Hall 1976: 17 seq.). "Concept of authority" contains the attitudes of power distance, organizational power and leadership, as people are aware of members of an organization (cf. Hofstede 1991).

Postulated values for cultural dimensions

Until now, these results were based on the assessment by usability experts alone and still require empirical validation. Also, according to the analysis of the author, out of the 29 cultural dimensions (cf. Figure 3 in section 2.2.3) the following four super categories that are directly and immediately relevant for intercultural user interface design have been found by analytical reasoning (light grey background in Table 8):

- Individualism (task) vs. collectivism (relationship) (therein contained related cultural dimensions like face saving or power distance)
- Non-verbal communication
- Perception of space (e.g., distance between user and system, network density, context)
- Perception of time (therein all related cultural dimensions like contained uncertainty avoidance or communication speed).

Four super categories relevant for intercultural user interface design

These super categories mostly overlap with the results of Baumgartner 2003. However, the additional aspect "Technological development" according to Baumgartner 2003 is, in my opinion, a trivial factor because it represents a necessary precondition for comparing technical aspects like intercultural HMI design in different cultures. Nevertheless, this aspect is fulfilled in this work by recruiting test persons exhibiting similar characteristics from a company of a high technological standard (cf. section 5.1.3).

Moreover, Khaslavsky 1998 supports the relevance of the four super categories providing "a package of nine descriptive variables useful for assessing culture and design" (Khaslavsky 1998: 365 seq.). This package contains the well known cultural dimensions from Hall (communication speed, density of information nets, personal space and time orientation), Hofstede (power distance, collectivism vs. individualism and uncertainty avoidance) as well as Trompenaars (diffuse vs. specific and particularism vs. universalism) to derive relevant variables for intercultural HMI design expressed by message speed, i.e. the speed at which people decode and act on messages and the amount of information depending on context in which it occurs.

Supported by related work

Table 8 presents a summary of the most important cultural dimensions considered as relevant for intercultural interaction analysis (IIA) within intercultural HMI design in this work. It is clear that by reducing the number of cultural models an information loss happens. However, for the sake of argument to proof concepts and to get first tendencies in cultural differences in HCI while not exceeding the boundaries of this work, the reduction is justified and reasonable. The same argumentation takes effect for the HMI dimensions presented in the next session.

Most important cultural dimensions for intercultural HMI design

Table 8: Cultural dimensions most relevant for intercultural interaction analysis (IIA) in intercultural HMI design (Source: own illustration)

Author(s) of cultural dimension	Cultural dimension most relevant for intercultural interaction analysis (IIA) in intercultural HMI design	China	Germany
Hofstede	Individualism vs. Collectivism	Collectivism	Individualism
Trompenaars	Role vs. Relationship Orientation	Relationship	Role
Halpin & Winer	Task vs. Person Orientation	Person	Task
Hall	Context	High	Low
Hall	Communication Speed	High	Low
Hall	Time Orientation	Poly-chronic	Mono-chronic
Hall	Action Chain Orientation	Parallel	Sequential
Hall	Information Network Density	High	Low
Hall	Personal Space	Low	High
Hall	Nonverbal communication	High	Low

4.2   HMI Dimensions Relevant for HMI Design

HMI dimensions (HMID)

Derived from physical dimensions space and time

The relevant variables for HMI design can be derived from dimensions for HMI design (called "HMI dimensions" (HMIDs) in the following). In this work, the term "HMID" will be used to denote classes containing variables useful for HMI design (cf. section 2.1). By analogy with the terminology in cultural studies, the concepts of "informational dimension" and "interactional dimension" are compared to the concept of "cultural dimension". The mentioned peculiarities of informational and interactional dimensions are referred to in this work as "HMI dimensions" relevant for HMI design regarding the "style of information processing" and the "interactional characteristics" of the user with the system.

Information related dimensions

Using statistical methods

According to Schlögl 2005, who uses dimensions of information management, information related dimensions can be determined using factorial analysis and multidimensional scaling.[134] The mentioned methods allow identifying factors or dimensions by grouping the variance in the data (cf. section 5.4) and are applied to verify the HMI dimensions (cf. section 6.6.1) concerning the

---

[134] Graham et al. 2000 similarly provide dimensional spaces for the design of interactive systems exposing familiar attributes of the HMI dimensions applied in this work. Further aspects that contribute to clarify the term 'information dimensions' are provided by Lange et al. 2005 as well as in the work report in section 4.2.

information processing style or interaction characteristics as postulated in this section, which contain the properties of the style of the user to use the system (exposing his "HMI style").[135]

Dialogs, interaction, information presentation and with that HCI and HMI generally are strongly linked with time (interaction, communication) and space (layout, structure) as well as the mental aspects (relations, thoughts). Since the view of space, time and mental aspects is strongly culture dependent (cf. section 2.3), also HMI is culture dependent (which supports FAH in section 2.3.1). HMIDs can be derived from the basic physical dimensions of space and time as well as from their sub-dimensions (e.g., speed, frequency or density).

Everything in our world underlies space and time and thus, one can assign the dimensions "space" and "time" to all cultural dimensions. Concrete, as well as physical and material things can be perceived only in space and involving time. Ideal as well as non-physical and immaterial things are part of the mental aspects involving only time but not needing space.[136]

The basic physical sub-dimensions relevant for HMI design can be derived from the basic physical dimensions (space and time) and by classification of the attributes of "culture" described by cultural models of cultural standards and cultural dimensions.[137] Table 9 shows these basic physical dimensions as well as from which cultural model and cultural dimension they come from.

---

[135] Probably, the information processing style or interaction characteristics of the user can be subsumed to the concept of "style of use" or "HMI style". Moreover, in parallel to the term "user interface characteristics" describing the properties of a user interface (cf. Marcus 2001), the term "user interacting characteristics" can be used – meaning the interaction style as well as the information processing behavior of the user with the system. However, it must be noticed that the terminology used in this work can only be an outline for this new topic and must be developed still further by future work.

[136] All derived categories from space and time (like density, speed or frequency) as well as the category of space itself are based on time (cf. Kant 2006).

[137] For further details about the derivation, please refer also to section 4.2 in the work report.

Table 9: Physical sub-dimensions derived from the basic physical dimensions and cultural models relevant for HMI design

Derived Physical Sub-dimensions [Basic Physical Dimension]	Cultural model(s) / concept(s)	Cultural Dimension(s)
Frequency [Time]	Hall: Usage of Time	Mono/poly-chronic time orientation
		Density of information network
Speed [Time]	Hall: Communication tempo	Density of information network
Sequentiality / Priority / Order [Time and Space]	Hall: Action chains	Mono/poly-chronic time orientation
Context [Time and Space]	Hall: Context density	Density of information network
		low vs. high context orientation
Density / Quantity [Time and Space]	Hall: Context density	Density of information network
		low vs. high context orientation
Structure [Time and Space]	All cultural models	All cultural dimensions
Complexity [all categories]	All cultural models	All cultural dimensions
Quality [all categories and user characteristics]	All cultural models	All cultural dimensions

Frequency and speed are derived from the usage of time and they depend on the kind of time orientation and communication tempo. Action chains can explain order and sequential interactions. Density of communication networks and context orientation determine the context used in HMI.

Postulated empirical hypotheses are mainly based on Hall's work

Hall's approach is the cultural and information scientific fundament of this work as well as that of intercultural user interface design, because his cultural model relates especially to the culturally different concepts of time, space and communication. This is the reason, why the postulated empirical hypotheses in section 4.3.3 are mainly based on the works of Edward T. Hall.[138]

HMI dimensions for dialog design

To limit the scope of research and because dialogs are basically composed of information and interaction (cf. section 2.1.4), this work concentrates on the dimensions of "information" and "interaction" by putting all the parameters found above into one nutshell of the following HMI dimensions (HMIDs) for dialog (information and interaction) design:

Information related sub-dimensions

- Information: At least the following aspects form the information processing type / style / "culture" of the user:
  - Frequency (sequential density)

---

[138] Similar to Kant's categorization system (quantity, quality, relation and modality) (cf. Kant 2006), which is totally interspersed with the Kantian base category of "time", time permanently saturates any communication. This is also supported by the fact that the Gricean cooperation principle, whose application is a precondition for successful communication, can be also traced back to Kant's categorization system (cf. Grice 1993).

- o   Density (static: spatial distance, dynamic: temporal distance)
- o   Order / Sequentiality
- o   Structure / Arrangement

- • Interaction: At least the following aspects form the interaction characteristics / type / style / "culture" of the user:
  - o   Frequency
  - o   Speed
  - o   Order / Sequentiality
  - o   Kind of interaction means

Interaction related sub-dimensions

Quality of information and interaction processing is represented respectively by their efficiency and effectiveness. To measure the parameters, the specific values of those HMI dimensions (HMIDs) must be very concise and concrete.

Hence, in the following sections, the HMIDs will be operationalized to several quantitative variables to build the basic measurement instrument and to subsequently generate the empirical hypotheses of this work by relating them to cultural dimensions. The quantitative and statistical variables for the final test setting will be generated in chapter 5.

4.3   Relationship between Cultural Dimensions and HMI Dimensions

Cultural influence can be connected with HMI design via the relationship between the specific values of cultural dimensions and the values of the variables relevant for HMI design. Using cultural dimensions, it is possible to derive hypotheses relevant for intercultural HMI design. Hence, from the work of Hall and the findings until now, several fundamental statements regarding the connection between cultural dimensions and HMI dimensions will be drawn. This section gives a summary of the analytical results so far by generating the hypotheses that have to be tested empirically in this dissertation project. However, before generating the hypotheses, the assumptions presupposed in this work will be presented.

Cultural and HMI dimensions:
basis for finding hypotheses relevant for intercultural HMI design

4.3.1   Presuppositions

In this work, the computer-talk-hypothesis is applied (cf. section 2.1.1). It is presumed that human-machine communication can be regarded as if it works similarly to human-human communication to apply reasonable and known methods to solve communication problems between user and the system.

Furthermore, the following already verified hypotheses in research are used as presuppositions for this work:

- Presupposition #1 (P1): Adaptive systems need a *quantitative* "apparatus of recognition" (Homann 2002).[139]
- Presupposition #2 (P2): Cultural distance (which results in differences in behavior and communication) is the case between humans (e.g., users and the designer of the systems) as well as between the user and system (Honold 2000). A logical consequence of this is that cultural distance takes effect also between systems.
- Presupposition #3 (P3): The differences in behavior and communication are the greater; the greater the cultural distance is (Thomas 1996).
- Presupposition #4 (P4): The cultural distance between China and Germany is high (Hofstede & Hofstede 2005) (cf. Table 1 in section 2.2.3).
- Presupposition #5 (P5): Relationship oriented countries like China exhibit higher communication speeds, more dense communication networks and hence higher context, poly-chronic time orientation and lower uncertainty avoidance in human-human communication than task-oriented countries like Germany according e.g., to Hofstede & Hofstede 2005, Hall 1959, or Halpin & Winer 1957 (cf. also Table 1 in section 2.2.3). This presumption will be strongly supported by analyzing Hall's work and deriving empirical hypothesis in section 4.3.3.
- Presupposition #6 (P6): HMI is influenced by culture (Röse 2002). The kind of user interaction with a system (computer, machine, driver navigation system, etc.) is culturally different (Röse 2002). This is because there are intercultural influences on hidden variables of HMI (design of interaction and design of dialogs) (Röse 2002: 98 et seq.) which are strongly context dependent due to the cultural background (Röse 2002: 97). This equals the fundamental abstract hypothesis (cf. section 2.3.1) underlying and motivating this dissertation project (i.e. P6 = FAH).
- Presupposition #7 (P7): Mainly the user's behavior gives insight to his cultural characteristics (Röse 2002: 72).
- Presupposition #8 (P8): The hypotheses concerning information processing in this work are posited under the assumption of equal information transmission between cultures, which is reasonable for high test samples (cf. sections 4.3.3 and 6.2).

Furthermore, the following assumptions have been postulated in this work (derived from literature research):

- Assumption #1 (A1): Interruption tolerance of Chinese users is higher than those of German users (cf. section 4.2).

---

[139] The necessity of adaptive systems (at least in automotive context) has been substantiated in chapter 1 as well as in sections 2.4 and 3.1.1.

- Assumption #2 (A2): For the automatic identification of the user culture and the automatic adaptation of the system to this user culture at runtime, a few discriminative intercultural variables should suffice, which can quantitatively include and describe the user and his interaction with the system (cf. section 4.4).
- Assumption #3 (A3): The preferred language used in the IIA test indicates the culture of the user with which he is most familiar (cf. section 6.2).
- Assumption #4 (A4): The differences in the behavior in relationship-oriented cultures to task-oriented cultures are larger than the difference in the behavior *within* relationship-oriented cultures or task-oriented cultures (cf. section 4.1).

In the course of this dissertation project, it has been attempted to find empirical proof to confirm these assumptions as well as the hypotheses stated in the next sections.

4.3.2   Methodological Hypotheses

From literature study and reflection, methodological hypotheses can be generated that cannot be quantitatively operationalized by variables, but must be verified very carefully by qualitative interpretation. Some of those methodological hypotheses form the most abstract and hence, main hypotheses of this work (indicated by MMH), because if they are true, it will turn out that culturally adaptive HMI is possible in the first place:

Main methodological hypotheses (MMH)

- Main methodological hypothesis #1 (MMH1): There are significant different patterns of interaction in HMI according to culture (composed of combinations of cultural interaction indicators) depending on the cultural imprint of the user, i.e. the interaction of the user with the system depends on the cultural background.
- Main methodological hypothesis #2 (MMH2): Cultural interaction differences in HMI can be recognized and measured quantitatively by a computer system. This happens merely by monitoring and analyzing the interaction of the user with the system quantitatively, resulting in adequate culturally dependent values for the intercultural variables.
- Main methodological hypothesis #3 (MMH3): The HMI can be automatically adapted by the system to the culturally dependent interaction characteristics of the user. Hence, systems with culturally adaptive HMI are possible and the principle of culturally adaptive HMI is correct (cf. section 3.2.1).

Moreover, based on the presumptions in section 4.3.1, the following methodological hypotheses (indicated by MH) can be postulated regarding culture (additionally indicated by C):

Methodological hypothesis concerning culture (MHC)

- Methodological hypothesis concerning culture #1 (MHC1): The difference in the kind of interaction of humans with a system (computer, machine, navigation system, etc.) is greater the greater the cultural distance is. For this hypothesis, at least three different cultural groups are needed (to compare the results according to their mutual (different) cultural distances). In this dissertation project, users from several countries were recruited for this purpose (cf. sections 5.1.3 and 6.2).
- Methodological hypothesis concerning culture #2 (MHC2): It is possible to determine the culturally imprinted characteristics of the user by analysis of the interaction of the user with the system.

Methodological hypotheses concerning determination of cultural variables (MHCV)

Further methodological hypotheses concern the determination of cultural variables (additionally indicated by V):

- Methodological hypothesis concerning cultural variables #1 (MHCV1): Intercultural variables can be determined purely by analysis of the interaction of the user with the system (considering only interaction tracing log files).
- Methodological hypothesis concerning cultural variables #2 (MHCV2): The idiosyncratic values of the intercultural variables can be determined purely by analysis of the interaction of the user with the system (considering only interaction tracing log files).

4.3.3   Empirical Hypotheses

Hall's cultural model most relevant for intercultural HMI design

In the following, the assumed influences of the values for the cultural dimensions on user interface design will be explained in detail. For instance, according to Hall 1983, relationship-oriented cultures have a higher communication speed in contrast to task-oriented cultures. They communicate more frequently with each other than task-oriented cultures. Hence, they interact more frequently with each other. Both, interaction frequency and interaction speed are higher. Hence, it is reasonable to assume that both information density and information speed are higher as well. From this, it can be assumed that Hall's cultural dimensions (mono vs. poly-chronic (sequential vs. simultaneous) and high vs. low context (for information density and information speed) are the most relevant for intercultural HMI design besides Hofstede's individualism vs. collectivism and Halpin & Winer's task/role vs. relation or neutral vs. emotional orientation provided by Trompenaars and Hampden-Turner (cf. Table 1 in section 2.2.3).

Generating hypotheses according to the work of Hall

Therefore, the empirical hypotheses will be generated in the following by investigating the relationship between cultural dimensions and HMI dimensions according for the most part to the work of Hall 1983 concerning the basic behavior patterns: contact with time, density of informational nets and communication speed as well as the time behavior of action chains (cf. Table 8 in section 4.1).[140] It may be possible to assign them to their corresponding categories regarding the HMI dimensions as shown in Table 10.

Table 10: Contrasting cultural dimensions and HMI dimensions

Basic pattern of kinds of behavior (cultural dimensions) according to Hall	Derived HMI dimensions from the dimensions "information" and "interaction" regarding information processing style and interaction characteristics
Dealing with the time	Information sequentiality (sequence, parallelism, type of information network etc.) - message complexity - information density / interaction speed and sequentiality
Density of the information network	Information context - information density - message complexity / interaction frequency and speed
Communication speed	Exhaustiveness of the contents, size of some information units, information speed, message speed, information complexity - amount of information / size / interaction frequency and speed
Significance of time for action chains	Information sequentiality (sequence, parallelism, type of information network) / interaction sequentiality

In this respect, it is reasonable to assume that variables connected to HMI design like information speed (distribution speed and emergency frequency of information), information density (number and distance of information units) or information order (appearing sequence and arrangement of information units) correlate with these culturally different basic patterns of behavior. If this is the case, the differences that Hall 1959 found between cultures imply differences, for example, in information speed ("duration of information presentation"), information density ("number of parallel pieces of information during information presentation") and information frequency ("number of information presentations per time unit") as well as in interaction frequency and style.

The assumed relationships presented in Table 10 can be turned into empirical hypotheses to be tested empirically in this work. For example, relation oriented cultures can exploit the higher communication speed at their disposal unlike task oriented cultures (cf. Hall 1959). Furthermore, it can be assumed that German users abhor redundancy in the presentation of information in contrast to Chinese users because they mainly prefer to obtain the essential information

Assumption: Variables connected to HMI design correlate with basic patterns of behavior

Empirical hypotheses

---

[140] Cf. also especially chapters 4, 6, 7 and 10 in Hall 1976. 7 out of 10 dimensions relevant for HMI design are related to Hall.

necessary to fulfill the required task. Thereby the following hypotheses can be postulated:[141]

Empirical hypothesis #0
(EH0)
Information processing concerning hypothesis #0 (IH0):

- Low context culture (e.g., Germany) corresponds to $(\sim)$[142] low number of redundant pieces of information
- High context culture (e.g., China) $\sim$ high number of redundant pieces of information

Additionally, the following hypothesis regarding interaction characteristics can be generated:

Interaction characteristics concerning hypothesis #0 (INH0):

- Low context culture (e.g., Germany) $\sim$ low number of redundant interaction activities
- High context culture (e.g., China) $\sim$ high number of redundant interaction activities

Basic patterns of behavior
To support these assumptions, the four basic aspects according to Hall 1983 (time, density of communication network, communication speed and time behavior of action chains, cf. Table 10) that underlie human behavior will be explained now in detail. Additionally, emotional, conversational and paralinguistic aspects will be elucidated.

---

[141] The empirical hypotheses generated in this work are correlations. For example: "There is a significant correlation between cultures that have low context orientation and the assumption that these cultures expect a low number of redundant pieces of information" (nominal metrics). The hypotheses can also be seen comparatively in the form "THE X, THE Y." (ordinal metrics). For example: "The lower the context orientation of a culture is, the lower the expected number of redundant pieces of information". If the results of this study yield very high selectivity then it is possible to also verify ordinal metrics in addition to nominal metrics. In addition, to simplify things, the antecedent of the hypothesis (the primary culture) is fixed to Chinese or German, adopting the findings in the literature of cultural studies (represented by the assignment of nationalities to cultural dimensions by the authors of the cultural dimensions) (cf. Table 1, section 2.2.3). Furthermore, the hypotheses regarding aspects of information processing are designated by 'I'. Every transmission of information needs communication and hence, interaction. Therefore, almost all hypotheses regarding information can be also transferred to hypotheses addressing interactional aspects (designated by 'IN'). The hypotheses can also be referenced according to their first or second part (e.g. INH1c1 and INH1c2). INH1c1 denotes the empirical hypothesis EH #1 of type IN (interaction context) *part 1* of the hypothesis (regarding high context oriented cultures) – INH2c2 denotes *part 2* of the hypothesis (concerning low context oriented cultures). Finally, to better memorize the hypotheses, they will be presented in a much-abbreviated form.

[142] "Corresponds to" will be abbreviated by "$\sim$" in the following.

Unlike time itself, language provides communication, which is based on, and can be manipulated, by time (cf. Hall 1983). Hence, every culture possesses a kind of "time language".[143] Time language arises from the basic rhythm (of life) of the human being from a culture which leads to organization, time schedules and appointments as well as to priorities which together also form spatial order (regularity, organization, arrangement). Order can be expressed also by aspects related to time like punctuality, handling time, timing, waiting time and daytime, as well as the perspective on time (past, future and present).

Language based on time

"Time language"

The time system serves as an order system for the organization of human life, which can be divided into two basic categories: linear/mono-chronic time division, which is objectively oriented placing sequentiality (e.g., regarding work and tasks) in the foreground, and nonlinear/poly-chronic time fragmentation, which is related to parallel planning and working often preferring family and friendship. The time system is neither learned naturally nor is it genetic, but it is a convention made by humans and is different in different cultures (cf. Hall 1990, Inglehart et al. 1998 and Levine 2007). Table 11 shows the differences in response behavior when mono-chronic or poly-chronic time oriented.

Time system

---

[143] „Jede Kultur hat ihre eigene Zeitsprache." (Hall 1983: 23).

Table 11: Differences between mono-chronic and poly-chronic time behavior according to Hall 1983 (adapted by the author)

Mono-chronic time response	Poly-chronic time response
Sequentiality (rigid action chains)	Parallelism (flexible action chains)
Work	Relation
Concentration	Diversion
Punctuality	Unpunctuality / temporal commitment unimportant
Weakly context oriented ➔ needs much additional information (few informal communication networks) [because life divided up very much, much individual information]	Backgrounds (many informal information networks) ➔ context oriented ➔ strong communication networks
Planning, Organization	Loosely organized
Short-lived relations	Long-lasting relations
Methodology	Capable but impatient
Individual possession intellect	Collective possession intellect
Strong inclination towards timing / low orientation at connections	Little inclination towards timing / strong orientation at connections
More stored than transmitted information	More transmitted than stored information
Germany, USA	China, France

Mono-chronic / Poly-chronic cultures

In dealing with time, Hall differentiates between cultures with mono-chronic and poly-chronic time orientation. "Mono-chronic time means paying attention to and doing only one thing at a time. Poly-chronic time means being involved with many things at once." (Hall 1990: 13). Mono-chronic people mostly finish one task after another and concentrate mainly on one thing. Poly-chronic time orientation is exactly the opposite. It stands out by the fact that many things are taken care of at the same time. Interpersonal relationships are very important. Poly-chronic people "live in a sea of information" (Hall 1990: 16). They must be permanently and exactly informed about everything that is going on around them to feel well. According to Hall 1983, Germany should be classified as a culture with mono-chronic time behavior in contrast to e.g., France, which has a poly-chronic culture, as does China as well e.g., due to the assumption (A1) that interruption tolerance of Chinese users is higher than that of German users (cf. section 4.3.1).[144]

---

[144] Hall & Hall 1990 investigated, in particular, the German and French cultures. Germany and the USA are task-oriented cultures whilst France and China are relationship-oriented cultures. All task-oriented cultures exhibit similar behavior in contrast to relationship-oriented cultures and vice versa (cf. Table 3 in section 4.1 in the work report). Therefore, Chinese and French people exhibit in some respect similar behavior because both cultures are strongly relationship oriented. Hence, Hall's findings for the French culture can be applied mostly also to the Chi-

China should be regarded as a poly-chronic rather than a mono-chronic culture, because the properties of poly-chronic cultures cover the properties of China like relationships and context orientation as well as acting collectively (cf. Table 11). This statement poses no hypothesis to be tested in this work but presents a fact that can be found to be widespread in literature. It will, however, be used as an ascertainment for further reflections in this work derived from presumption P5 in section 4.3.1 (cf. also Table 1 in section 2.2.3):

- Chinese users ~ poly-chronic, relationship and high context (team) oriented
- German users ~ mono-chronic, task and low context (individual) oriented.

Relation oriented cultures communicate, and hence, interact with each other more frequently than task oriented cultures because of more dense communication networks (cf. Hall 1959). "Communication network" in this case represents the structure of communication channels within a culture. The density of such a communication network depends on relationship orientation and context of information usage (cf. Hall 1989:61).[145]

Communication network represents structure of communication channels

The more dialogs are carried on in a particular time; the higher is the communication speed. The amount of data and data transfer speed is higher the more dialog steps are done within a certain time period as it is the case in relationship oriented cultures. This indicates to more dense communication networks.

More dialogs in same time period
⇨ higher communication speed

However, this assumption does not necessarily also imply that the transferred and understood content (e.g. information) is greater. Hence, high communication speed does not necessarily implicate high information exchange speed because there can be e.g., missing communication success factors or irrelevant data (cf. Austin & Savigny 1962 and Grice 1993). However, it is taken as given in this work for the sake of argument that in average the members of every culture exhibit the same quality of communication dismantling and recycling, i.e. the hypotheses concerning information processing are posited under the assumption of equal information transmission, which is reasonable to

---

nese culture because of their common propositional attitude towards relationship orientation. This is supported by the fact that the attributes of several cultural dimensions for China and France have almost the same values (cf. e.g. Table 12 and Table 13 below in comparison with Table 1 in section 2.2.3 or chapters 6.6 and 8 in Hall 1983), because of the similar relationship to the common cultural dimension "relationship vs. role orientation" (cf. Table 3 in section 4.1 in the work report, cf. also assumption A4 in section 4.3.1). This tendency is supported by the empirically obtained results in this work, which are discussed in section 6.6.

[145] "The matter of contexting requires a decision concerning how much information the other person can be expected to possess on a given subject." (Hall 1989:61)

assume for a high number of test samples.[146] Therefore, it can be supposed that interaction frequency and interaction speed as well as information density and information transfer speed is higher for relationship oriented cultures which exhibit rather parallel information processing in contrast to task oriented cultures.

In addition, different time orientation can also have implications concerning information density, information context and information speed. For example, parallel or sequential information processing can be explained by action chain orientation or poly-chronic vs. mono-chronic time orientation.

The above findings are reformulated in the following hypotheses:

Empirical hypothesis #1 (EH1)

Information processing concerning hypothesis #1a (IH1a):

- Poly-chronic time (e.g., China) ~ high information frequency
- Mono-chronic time (e.g., Germany) ~ low information frequency

Interaction characteristics concerning hypothesis #1a (INH1a):

- Poly-chronic time (e.g., China) ~ high interaction frequency
- Mono-chronic time (e.g., Germany) ~ low interaction frequency

Information processing concerning hypothesis #1b (IH1b):

- High density of communication networks (e.g., China) ~ high information density (sequentially and spatially) (e.g., high number of dialogs counted within a certain time)
- Low density of communication networks (e.g., Germany) ~ low information density (sequentially and spatially) (e.g., low number of dialogs counted within a certain time)[147]

Interaction characteristics concerning hypothesis #1b (INH1b):

- High density of communication networks (e.g., China) ~ high interaction frequency / high task interruption tolerance
- Low density of (loosely) communication networks (e.g., Germany) ~ low interaction frequency / low task interruption tolerance

Information processing concerning hypothesis #1c (IH1c):

---

[146] Equals presupposition (P8), cf. section 4.3.1.

[147] In this work, sequential or temporal information density is regarded to be the same as information frequency.

- High communication (data transfer) speed / high context (e.g., China) ~ high information (data) speed / frequency
- Low communication (data transfer) speed / low context (e.g., Germany) ~ low information (data) speed / frequency

Interaction concerning hypothesis #1c (INH1c):

- High communication (data transfer) speed / high context (e.g., China) ~ high interaction speed / frequency
- Low communication (data transfer) speed / low context (e.g., Germany) ~ low interaction speed / frequency

Information processing concerning hypothesis #1d (IH1d):

- Mono-chronic time behavior of action chains (e.g., Germany) ~ high information sequentiality
- Poly-chronic time behavior of action chains (e.g., China) ~ low information sequentiality

Interaction characteristics concerning hypothesis #1d (INH1d):

- Mono-chronic time behavior of action chains (e.g., Germany) ~ high interaction sequentiality
- Poly-chronic time behavior of action chains (e.g., China) ~ low interaction sequentiality

High vs. low context
communication

Furthermore, the density of the communication network has implications for information frequency (how fast sequential information comes in), the amount of information and the information context (low or high) according to the cultural dimension "high vs. low context".[148] The communication partners refer strongly to common contexts and knowledge in countries with high context communication (like China) in comparison to countries with low context communication (like Germany). In high context cultures, information is conveyed rather indirectly and implicitly. Background information for most events in daily life is not expected or even needed. This is because the members of such cultures permanently keep themselves informed about everything with the people who are important in their lives. Spacial communication networks exist in the family, within the circle of friends and between teammates. Explicit and direct communication is characteristic for low context cultures. In the interaction with other people, detailed background information is needed since the individual areas of life are separated from each other. Low context oriented human beings need more formal information to have the same knowledge as high context oriented people, who have acquired this knowledge already because of informal small talk. High context people would be rendered uncertain if suddenly, only a few pieces of information could be exchanged informally because of their habit to obtain and to hand over many pieces of information.

High context cultures

Low context cultures

Cultural dimension of
uncertainty avoidance

The cultural dimension of uncertainty avoidance comes into play here, too. The less the sensitivity for interference, the more the people feel safe and the less the people avoid uncertainty or unexpected situations because of feeling safe.[149] Kralisch 2006 writes: "It appears that the cultural dimension of Uncertainty Avoidance is the most important determinant of a user's perception of information need." (Kralisch 2006: 208).[150]

---

[148] „Menschen mit einer stark ausgeprägten Orientierung an Zusammenhängen, mit dichten Informationsnetzen, reagieren häufig ungeduldig, gereizt, wenn Mitmenschen mit weniger dichten Informationsnetzen ihnen Dinge erzählen, die sie bereits wissen. Umgekehrt sind solche Menschen völlig hilflos, wenn sie von den anderen nicht ausreichend informiert werden. Eine der wichtigsten Kommunikationsstrategien besteht somit darin, den Informationsumfang den jeweiligen Informationsbedürfnissen anzupassen. Gibt man überflüssige Informationen, wirkt dies belehrend. Bietet man nicht genügend Informationen an, stiftet dies Verwirrung." (Hall 1983: 40).

[149] „Allgemein lässt sich sagen: je größer, fester und dichter das Informationsnetz, desto stabiler ist das System und desto geringer ist seine Anfälligkeit gegenüber Störungen." (Hall 1983: 44). Cf. also Honold 2000: 35 et seqq.

[150] This is also supported in the HMI field by Trillo 1999 who investigated intelligent agents (shortly explained in the work report in section 8.5.1). He states that e.g., an intelligent agent provides information that is more explicit for low context oriented users and high context oriented users require less explicit information from intelligent agents.

In dense communication networks, there is higher information exchange because there are many senders per receiver. The probability of the arrival of another piece of information during an already ongoing process of information reception or processing is high.

Higher information exchange in dense communication networks

Hence, e.g., the mental stress of a recipient of a culture with a low density communication network exposed to a culture with high communication networks density is high, if many pieces of information have to be processed, because a low information frequency is expected. [151] For example, the high information flow in traffic crossing a junction in China is overwhelming and provokes a high mental workload for a German driver or passenger (cf. Figure 7).[152] The Chinese pedestrians (cf. black circle in Figure 7) deal successfully with the vehicles by bypassing them as usual without causing accidents.

High mental stress for people of low context culture being exposed to high context culture

---

[151] „Es gibt für jedes Land ein *Kommunikationstempo*, bei dem sich die Leute wohl fühlen. *Schnelle* Botschaften werden von Menschen, die an *langsame* Botschaften gewöhnt sind, normalerweise schlecht verstanden." (Hall 1983: 41, emphasized in original).

[152] Watching the video „Hangzhou.mpeg" stored in the online appendix, provides a multimodal "atmosphere" to feel the cultural differences regarding information perception speed, information density and interaction frequency in contrast to Figure 7 alone because along the dynamically changing visual also auditory impressions can be cognitively integrated over two minutes.

Figure 7: Typical traffic situation in a shopping road in China (Yanan Road, Hangzhou, 3/20/06, 2 pm) (Source: video file "hangzhou.mpg" in the online appendix taped by the author)

It seems that the denser the information network, the higher the information frequency and speed as well as the interaction frequency and speed reformulated in the following hypotheses:[153]

Empirical hypothesis #5
(EH5)

Information processing concerning hypothesis #5 (IH5):[154]

---

[153] Hypotheses 2 to 4 have been rejected. They were part of the two of the three originally developed test systems that have subsequently been abandoned, which can be found in file "050815 IIA-Erhebungskonzept.doc" in the online appendix (cf. also section 5.1.1, footnote 176). The finally used test system does not contain the hypotheses 2 to 4.

[154] The irregular numbering of the hypotheses came from the fact that some of the originally postulated hypotheses based on Hofstede's cultural dimension "individualism vs. collectivism" could not have been investigated (because the IDV of the test participants were identically, cf. sections 5.1.1, 6.2, 6.4 and 8.1) and, hence, do not appear here anymore.

- Communication network of high-density (e.g., China) ~ high information frequency
- Loose communication networks (e.g., Germany) ~ low information frequency

Interaction characteristics concerning hypothesis #5 (INH5):

- Communication network of high-density (e.g., China) ~ high interaction frequency
- Loose communication networks (e.g., Germany) ~ low interaction frequency

Action chains are represented by steps to reach an objective.[155] Examples of action chains are greetings, education and contracts of cooperation, joint ventures, stock emission, making a career, judgment processes or playing golf. Germans avoid interrupting or disturbing their sequential course of actions because they like to finish the work they started. They can only finish their work if not too many parallel actions destroy the action chain.[156] Here again, the cultural dimension of "uncertainty avoidance" is affected (as supposed in assumption A1 in section 4.3.1). German people feel uncertain if they cannot do the tasks sequentially one by one because they are more sensitive, in this regard, than people using very dense information networks (for instance, Chinese people who are relationship oriented). Obviously, people of high orientation to information sequentiality (like Germans) dislike being disturbed whilst working to avoid becoming cognitively distracted from the main task even by a short distraction and hence, exhibit high uncertainty avoidance. Thereby, they prefer sequential information processing. Hence, the following empirical hypotheses can be generated:

Cultures with high or low uncertainty avoidance

Information processing concerning hypothesis #6a (IH6a):

Empirical hypothesis #6 (EH6)

- High uncertainty avoidance (e.g., Germany) ~ high orientation to information sequentiality / low parallel processing / few simultaneous tasks
- Low uncertainty avoidance (e.g., China) ~ low orientation to information sequentiality / high parallel processing / many simultaneous tasks

---

[155] „Eine Aktionskette besteht aus Vorgängen, die nach einem bestimmten Schema aufeinanderfolgen und bei denen eine oder mehrere Personen auf ein bestimmtes Ziel hinarbeiten." (Hall 1983: 43, emphasis in the original).

[156] „Zu viele gleichzeitige Vorgänge führen zum Bruch einer Aktionskette." (Hall 1983: 44).

Interaction characteristics concerning hypothesis #6a (INH6a):

- High uncertainty avoidance (e.g., Germany) ~ high orientation to interaction sequentiality / low parallel interaction / few simultaneous interaction
- Low uncertainty avoidance (e.g., China) ~ low orientation to interaction sequentiality / high parallel interaction / many simultaneous interaction

Information processing concerning hypothesis #6b (IH6b):

- High uncertainty avoidance (e.g., Germany) ~ low task distraction tolerance / low disturbance tolerance during working / low tolerance for irrelevant information
- Low uncertainty avoidance (e.g., China) ~ high task distraction tolerance / high disturbance tolerance during working / high tolerance for irrelevant information

Interaction characteristics concerning hypothesis #6b (INH6b):

- High uncertainty avoidance (e.g., Germany) ~ low interaction distraction tolerance / low interaction disturbance tolerance during working
- Low uncertainty avoidance (e.g., China) ~ high interaction distraction tolerance / high interaction disturbance tolerance during working

Different personal space | A culturally different perception of space is expressed by the distance to the communication partner which can be measured e.g., by distance sensors as well as by the behavior regarding order (room layout, clearance, etc., cf. Hall 1983). Hereby, the territory, i.e. the personal space, is distinctive. For example, German people claim and defend a certain area and only a few people are allowed to penetrate this area. Otherwise indisposition or even aggressiveness arises, which is caused by uncertainty avoidance.[157] Furthermore, German people who are generally considered to be task oriented are very sensitive about noise if their work requires high concentration. Hence, an implication for cultural HMI design regarding German culture could be that e.g., no disturbing acoustic error messages should be given when their work requires concentration. In contrast, even in such situations, relationship oriented people need activity and like to know what is happening around them. In a test setting, the noise level during test tasks can be measured and even injected into the test

---

[157] „*Räumliche Bewegungsabläufe* verleihen unseren Äußerungen im Gespräch mit anderen Farbe und Betonung. Manchmal geben sie dem, was wir sagen, sogar einen anderen Sinn. *Bewegungsdynamik und körperliche Distanz* im Gespräch sind Teil des Kommunikationsprozesses. Der erträgliche Gesprächsabstand zwischen einander fremden Menschen zeigt, welche Dynamik in der Kommunikation durch Bewegung steckt." (Hall 1983: 47, emphasis in the original).

setting to check the confusion level of the user. Hence, the "distance" from user to system can be measured to ascertain the cultural imprint of the user. Moreover, cultural shock is a reaction to a lack of familiar signals and unfamiliar behavior.[158] Thereby, again, the cultural dimension of "uncertainty avoidance" is involved.[159]

Furthermore, space indicates power.[160] In Germany, the boss sits in a corner office, in France in the middle (center) of the building, which expresses the difference between the task oriented and the flat hierarchically organized Germans and the relationship oriented high hierarchically organized French with lower power distance orientation (cf. also Hofstede & Hofstede 2005).

Space indicates power

Hence, it seems that relationship oriented cultures (e.g., France or China) allow less distance to information sources and using rather hierarchical information structures than task oriented cultures (e.g., Germany or USA) (cf. Table 2 in section 2.3.2). This phenomenon will be captured by the following hypotheses:

Information processing concerning hypothesis #7 (IH7):

Empirical hypothesis #7 (EH7)

- Relationship oriented cultures (e.g., China) ~ low distance to information sources (e.g., spatial distance to communication partner like distance between user and system) / much context / no "fear of contact"
- Task oriented cultures (e.g., Germany) ~ high distance to information sources (e.g., spatial distance to communication partner like distance between user and system) / little context / "fear of contact"

Interaction characteristics concerning Hypothesis #7 (INH7):

- Relationship oriented cultures (e.g., China) ~ low distance to interaction sources (e.g., using touch screens) / much interaction context / no "fear of contact"
- Task oriented cultures (e.g., Germany) ~ high distance to interaction sources (e.g., using menu button controls (e.g., iDrive[161])) / little interaction context / "fear of contact"

---

[158] „Der oft zitierte *Kulturschock* ist nichts weiter als eine Reaktion auf das Fehlen uns vertrauter Signale und eine Bestürzung über die Konfrontation mit andersartigen, uns unbekannten Verhaltensweisen." (Hall 1983: 47, emphasis in the original).

[159] This aspect will be considered empirically in this work e.g., in the test setting using the "Virtual agent test task" presented in Figure 14 in section 5.2.2. See also the screenshot for the "UV test task" in section 10.3.4 in the work report.

[160] "Raum signalisiert Macht." (Hall 1983: 48).

[161] "iDrive" is the name of a special menu control button for interacting with interior equipment in cars invented and introduced by BMW (cf. Bengler et al. 2002).

Information speed
depends on
communication speed

The speed of information dissemination (depending on the bandwidth of the information channel as well as the number of modalities and media used in parallel) as well as the information flow appears in the speaking speed, interaction speed and dialog frequency. All these components are part of communication. Hence, information speed depends on communication speed (taking presupposition (P8) for granted). According to (Hall 1983: 49), information flow is not abstract, but it is very concretely identifiable (distinctly and clearly) and it is even measurable.

Hence, it seems that in role/task-oriented cultures the information speed is lower in contrast to relationship-oriented cultures, where information speed and frequency is higher which is formulated in the following hypotheses:

Empirical hypothesis #8
(EH8)

Information processing concerning hypothesis #8 (IH8):

- Relationship oriented cultures (e.g., China) ~ high information speed / frequency
- Task oriented cultures (e.g., Germany) ~ low information speed / frequency

Interaction characteristics concerning hypothesis #8 (INH8):

- Relationship oriented cultures (e.g., China) ~ high interaction speed / frequency
- Task oriented cultures (e.g., Germany) ~ low interaction speed / frequency

Non-verbal
communication

Non-verbal communication is expressed in emotional and affective behavior. Non-verbal language is a very important part of communication (more than 80% of the human-human-communication is non-verbal, cf. section 2.1.2). In particular, relationship-oriented cultures with high context orientation and high communication speed use non-verbal communication. For example, French people develop a complex play of facial expressions and gesticulation if they are affected by something. These aspects are covered by the cultural dimension "affectivity vs. neutrality".[162] However, logical argumentation is also very important for French people, because they are "reasonable logicians", pragmatists and realists, who are looking for practical solutions and strategies, which provide results very rapidly (cf. Hall & Hall 2004). Here, different cognitive

---

[162] Cf. Trompenaars & Hampden-Turner 2007: 69 seq.

styles are addressed (mono-causal and multi-causal reasoning).[163] Furthermore, non-verbal communication and context orientation are strongly involved. Hence, low context oriented cultures (like Germany) should use less non-verbal communication, are more neutral and less affected than high context oriented cultures (like China). From this the hypotheses IH9 and INH9 will be generated:

Information processing concerning hypothesis #9 (IH9):

- Low context oriented culture (e.g., Germany) ~ little non-verbal communication
- High context oriented culture (e.g., China) ~ much non-verbal communication

Empirical hypothesis #9 (EH9)

Interaction characteristics concerning hypothesis #9 (INH9):

- Low context oriented culture (e.g., Germany) ~ little non-verbal and affective or hectic interaction / few error clicks / few gestures and mimic signals / low acceptance of virtual agents
- High context oriented culture (e.g., China) ~ much non-verbal and affective or hectic interaction / many error clicks / many gestures and mimic signals / high acceptance of virtual agents

Furthermore, the density of the communication network and context orientation influences also the speed of information flow within the communication network. "Another important and closely related feature of both context and communication is the fast and slow message continuum." (Hall 1989:63). Hence, communication means to transport information quickly or slowly. For example, compared to Germany, in China there are many headlines, flashing advertisements or TV ads (even on city buses) which represent fast communication means, supporting a high communication speed. The message speed refers to the speed with which people decode news and react to these types of communication. Some cultures prefer slow news transport, other like fast news transport (cf. Table 12).

Influence of density of communication network and context orientation on speed of information flow

---

[163] Mono-causal reasoning means that syllogism is generated sequentially (e.g. if A then B then C then D). Multi-causal reasoning allows many causes in parallel, i.e. syllogism can be generated from a mix of sequential and parallel steps (cf. Röse 2002: 37).

Table 12: Fast and slow means of communication (according to Hall 1983)

Fast means of communication / media	Slow means of communication / media
Prose	Poetry
Headings	Books
Propaganda	Art, literature, research (slow messages with much content.)
Caricature drawings	Etchings
Watching TV commercials	Documentary films
Television	Print media
Fast acquaintances	Depth of relations

Information flow

People have a certain attitude concerning information flow and the speed of information dissemination all over the country according to their cultural imprinting (cf. Table 13). For example, it can be measured, how much time is needed for a message to travel from point A to point B, how long it takes for an action to be executed because of the triggering by a message and how information flows (kind and types).[164]

---

[164] Hall's findings for the French culture can mostly also be applied to the Chinese culture because of their common 'propositional attitude' concerning relationship orientation as explained before. Cf. also section 4.1 and the results in section 6.4 as well as their discussion in sections 6.6 and 8.1.

Table 13: Information flow in task-oriented countries and in relationship-oriented countries exemplified by Germany and France (according to Hall 1976)

Germany	France
Slow	Fast
Purposeful	Full-coverage
Focused (can't spread unhindered)	Network like ("everybody knows something about everybody – everybody knows everybody")
Low informal information transmission	High informal information transmission
Weak flow of information due to protection against environment ➔ the individual room to move is low, everything must have its order, everything is regulated	Strong flow of information and unhindered flow of information due to little protection against disturbing environmental influences because they do not disturb but are welcome according to the sociability
Less contact with each other ➔ not knowing the news permanently ➔ often information overload since much information is exchanged at one time ➔ appointments help to fix sociability	Much contact with each other ➔ permanently knowing the news ➔ seldom information overload since not much information exchanged at a time but at many times a little information is exchanged ➔ appointments only disturb sociability

These aspects can be demonstrated using an example from Hall. According to (Hall 1983: 49), German people use some rules to master high information flow:

Example from Hall: how Germans cope with high information flow

- Organize information (classification)
- Plan carefully to avoid disturbances and information loss
- Protect themselves spatially and temporally against others to increase concentration
- Prevent interruptions or diversions to avoid stopping the action chains and therefore provoke faults and manipulation of information

This has the following consequences:

Consequences

- Strongly prepared and formal information
- Soundproof doors, overloaded appointment books and dividing up of everything
- Entry to other people (relations) is aggravated
- Flow of information is restricted (and people seem to be stubborn and unapproachable).

The conversation dialogs are also affected by the directness or indirectness of the communication style determined by culture (cf. Table 14). Furthermore, the method of communicating is determined by face-saving considerations (cf. Victor 1998).

Conversation style

Table 14: Differences in conversation style between Germany and France (according to Hall 1983)

Germany	France
Blunt and direct	Restrained and tactful
Plain text (formal)	Hints (informal)
Straight, direct, facts, relevant	Wordily enriched, intellectually, vague, unclear
Detailed information, numbers, facts	Style is important

Face saving

For example, in China it is very important not to lose face. Hence, e.g., using help or user manuals to fulfill a task is avoided by Chinese users in contrast to German users (cf. Honold 2000), which can be measured e.g., by the number of online help initiations. In this sense, Chinese people exhibit similar behavior to French people presented in Table 14. They are tactful, informal and polite to save face.

Furthermore, there are differences in the complexity and in the importance of explanation dialogs as well as in the structure of the explanations themselves (cf. Table 15).

Table 15: Differences in dialog design for Germany and China (Source: own illustration)

Aspect	Germany	China
Complexity of dialogs	Low	High
Explanation dialogs	Very important	Less important
Structure of explanations[165]	X, because Y	Because Y, X

It can be assumed that task oriented cultures (e.g., Germany and the USA) use a direct conversation style, less complex dialogs as well as more and linearly structured explanation dialogs because of low context orientation in contrast to relationship oriented cultures (e.g., China and France). The latter use an indirect conversation style (e.g., low number of help initiations by the user) and implicit communication structures with inverted and less explanation but more complex dialogs because of dense communication networks and face saving mentality.

From this, the following hypotheses can be created:

Empirical hypothesis #10 (EH10)

Information processing concerning hypothesis #10 (IH10):

---

[165] Cf. Scollon & Wong Scollon 2008.

- Task oriented culture (e.g., Germany) ~ direct conversation style / exact interpretation style / high meaning precision
- Relationship oriented culture (e.g., China) ~ indirect conversation style / tolerant interpretation style / low meaning precision

Interaction characteristics concerning hypothesis #10 (INH10):[166]

- Task oriented culture (e.g., Germany) ~ direct interaction style / high interaction exactness / few functional initiations / few dialog steps
- Relationship oriented culture (e.g., China) ~ indirect interaction style / low interaction exactness / many functional initiations / many dialog steps

Interaction characteristics concerning hypothesis #11 (INH11):[167]

Empirical hypothesis #11 (EH11)

- Task oriented culture / low face saving mentality (e.g., Germany) ~ direct interaction style / many help initiations
- Relationship oriented culture / high face saving mentality (e.g., China) ~ indirect interaction style / few help initiations

Information processing concerning hypothesis #12 (IH12):

Empirical hypothesis #12 (EH12)

- Task oriented cultures (e.g., Germany) ~ low information speed / long duration of information presentation
- Relationship oriented cultures (e.g., China) ~ high information speed / short duration of information presentation

4.4 Potential Model for Intercultural HMI Design

To attain reasonable values for the hypotheses of this work, the informational and interactional aspects were analyzed as far as possible according to the HMI dimensions.

First, a collection of hypothetical cultural variables for the user interface design was generated and categorized. These variables should represent the relationship between culture and HMI design. Reflections regarding reasonable

---

[166] According to Rößger 2003, there is a different usage of interaction devices between Chinese and German users (near vs. far, touch vs. control button). Cf. also footnote 161.

[167] Cf. sections 2.2.2 and 4.1 (cf. also Victor 1997).

combinations of such variables finally led to a potential model for intercultural HMI design (PICHMID), in which potential cultural variables are assigned to the HMI dimensions. The combination of variables is the key to getting reasonable results for cultural classification (cf. section 6.6.2). Furthermore, the probability of getting correct results is the higher when more operationalized variables are applied.

Potential model for intercultural HMI design (PMICHMID) containing intercultural variables (extract)

It is not possible to present the total model with all included relationships in this book because of space restrictions.[168] To demonstrate the complexity of this first hypothetical model containing intercultural variables, a short extract is presented in Table 16.

---

[168] It would require several DIN A0 plots to read the whole content of the model at once as the model contains more than 300 potential intercultural variables. The complete potential model can be found in file "041213 Modell interkultureller Variable55 überarbeitet am 08-01-2009_pres.xls" in the online appendix.

Table 16: Extract of the potential model for intercultural HMI design (Source: own illustration from file "041213 Modell interkultureller Variable55 überarbeitet am 08-01-2009.xls" in the online appendix)

	What? (HMI dimension)	Information density	Information density	Information frequency	Information sequentiality	Information quality	Information priority
Inter-cultural variable (with direct relation to HMI)	Variable / parameter	Number of icons / pictures / side / propositions	Dialog number / min.	Note dialogs of the system/min.	System dialog order	keep pro-position	Sequence of information processing
Usability Metric	How to measure?	Count pictures, icons, propositions	Count dialogs per min	Count dialogs of the system per min	(Message dialogs, logical structure) record dialog	Find out share of real propositions	Use usability scenario
Value estimated by the author	China	0.5	0.8	0.8	0.3	0.4	0.9
	Germany	0.1	0.5	0.1	0.8	0.9	0.3
	Czech Republic	0.2	0.4	0.2	0.7	0.7	0.4
	France	0.1	0.2	0.3	0.6	0.7	0.5
	USA	0.3	0.6	0.4	0.6	0.8	0.6
	Japan	0.7	0.8	0.9	0.3	0.5	0.8
Cultural aspects	Why intercultural variable?	Picture / syllable language vs. alphabet	Openness for the communication / relation ability	Information perception	Way of thinking differently: Mono-causal vs. multi-causal (network like)	Loss of face	Loss of face
	Culture dimension	Game vs. task / mask. vs. Fem. index vs. Koll.	Individualism vs. /collectivism	News / information speed / uncertainty avoidance / time orientation and perception	Index vs. coll. / time orientation / task vs. person orientated	Face vs. Fact / task vs. person oriented	Face vs. Fact / task vs. person oriented
Use cases	General	Number of pictures, icons, propositions	Dialog number	Dialog number	Help / information / note dialog	Information	(Work-) instruction / task
	Driver navigation system	Card representation POIs	Note, clarification and confirmation dialogs	Voice guidance	Help steps	Aim leadership	Route planning / route representation
Classification and selectivity power	Methodical accessibility	easy	middle	easy	heavy	heavy	heavy
	Cultural dependence	middle	middle	middle	strong	strong	strong
	Information scientific / technical feasibility	simple (increase number POIs and representation density)	simple (change number of announcements per way unit)	simple (measure number of announcements per way unit)	difficult because analysis of semantically connection necessary	heavy	heavy
	Recognizability of the variable	easy	easy	easy	heavy	medium to easy	medium to easy
	Localization level	Surface	Interaction	Function / surface	Interaction	Function / surface / (interaction	Function / surface / (interaction

					consequences)	consequences)
Kind of intercultural variable	direct	direct	direct	direct	direct	direct
Context reference to system and situation	middle	middle	middle	high	high	high
Usability measurability	easy	medium	medium	heavy	heavy	heavy
Benefit of use for the Localization for the user	high	high	high	high	high	high
Methodical accessibility / variable detect ability / context / Def. acc. to Röse 2002	visible	hidden	hidden	hidden	hidden	hidden

Potential intercultural variables

Important classes of potential intercultural variables postulated in the model are e.g.:

- Interaction (e.g., frequency, path, speed, effectiveness)
- Information (e.g., density, complexity, quality, quantity, frequency, sequentiality / order, priority)
- Dialog (e.g., length, degree of detail, turn taking, complexity, structure, explanation capability, etc.)
- Language and paralanguage (e.g., speed, pitch, intonation, number of words, frequency and length of pauses).

The reflections on this model are concentrated within the hypotheses represented in postulated HMI dimensions. Figure 8 is showing the author's assumed relationships of the values for Chinese and German users for basic categories useful for HMI design.

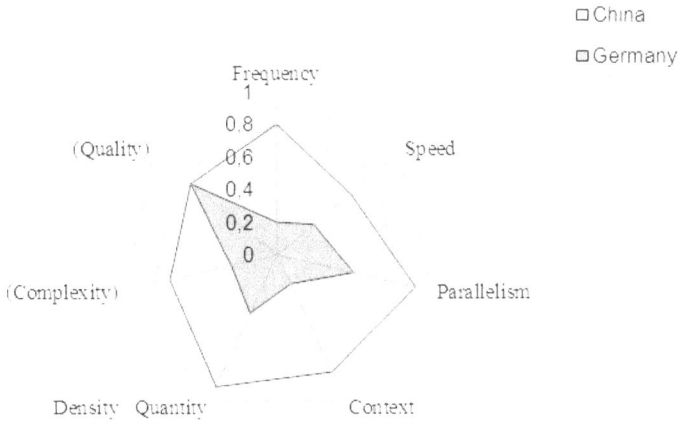

Figure 8: Postulated specific values of the basic categories relevant for HMI design based on the potential model for intercultural HMI design (Source: own illustration from file "041213 Modell interkultureller Variable55 überarbeitet am 08-01-2009_pres.xls")

The diagram indicates that the basic categories relevant for HMI design like frequency, speed, density, context, non-linearity and complexity are expected to be higher for China than for Germany regarding the HMI dimensions derived from the dimensions "information" and "interaction" and assuming the same level of quality. The values are estimated values, corresponding to the personal impressions of the author regarding the relationship of cultural dimensions and the HMI dimensions according to the basic cultural dimensions "role/task vs. relationship-orientation" and "individualism vs. collectivism" obtained by literature study, cultural experience in China and Germany, intuition and common sense.[169]

In the area of usability engineering (software ergonomics, Human Factors), several metrics have been developed to describe the quality of the interaction of the user with the system from some interaction attributes and characteristics. The following measurement possibilities emerge during task execution by the user using the system (according to Shneiderman 2009 and Dix 2007):

Metrics for describing user interaction

---

[169] The worksheet "Ausgewählte Kulturdimensionen" within the file "041213 Modell interkultureller Variable55 überarbeitet am 30-04-2009_pres.xls" in the online appendix shows a summary of the assumed influences of cultural dimensions on user interface design from the basic analytical reflections regarding the connection between culture and user interface design.

- time to complete a task ($\sqrt{}$)
- percent of task completed ($\sqrt{}$)
- percent of task completed per unit time ($\sqrt{}$)
- ratio of successes to failure ($\sqrt{}$)[170]
- time spent on errors ($\sqrt{}$)
- percent or number of errors ($\sqrt{}$)
- number of commands used ($\sqrt{}$)
- frequency of help and documentation use ($\sqrt{}$)
- number of repetitions of failed commands ($\sqrt{}$)
- number of runs of successes and of failures ($\sqrt{}$)
- number of available commands not invoked ($\sqrt{}$)

Metrics which requires
questionnaire / video
analysis

The following metrics require questionnaire or video analysis by a human being after executing the tests:

- number of good and bad features recalled by users
- number of users preferring your system (this can be asked in a query after the task)
- number of times user expresses frustration or satisfaction ($\sqrt{}$)
- percent of favorable/unfavorable user comments
- number of times the interface misleads the user
- number of times users need to work around a problem
- number of times the user is disrupted from a working task ($\sqrt{}$)
- number of times user loses control of the system

Final comparisons

The following can be determined by final comparisons:

- percent or number of competitors better than a reference user ($\sqrt{}$)

The problem with some of these parameters is that they are subjective, i.e. humans must interpret them. In machines, only quantitative parameters can be processed very easily without using complex architectures and methods of artificial intelligence for "subjective" interpretation. Hence, only those parameters from usability literature that can be counted simply by a machine have been used in this work (indicated by ($\sqrt{}$) above).

Creating PUMTM out of
PMICHMID

From the potential model for intercultural HMI design (PMICHMID) and the quantitative usable parameters from the metrics in software ergonomics, a model of measurements (metrics) to express the HMI dimensions can be

---

[170] Prümper 1994 gives an overview of erroneous judgments by users in HCI using action theoretical fault taxonomy. He also provides many variables and coefficients for measuring the errors made by the users in HCI.

derived: the potential usability metric trace model (PUMTM). It can be used to develop metrics to trace the user interaction for evaluating the usability of the system.

In contrast to PMICHMID, which also contains the relationship of the measurement variables to culture, PUMTM contains only measurement variables. The hope was that at least 10-30 of the about 300 postulated potential variables within the PMICHMID can be determined as significant, exposing a relatively high classification rate that supports the employed cultural dimensions and assumptions. The variables of this model can be implemented in a demonstrator and serve to check their cultural validity. In addition, it is reasonable to assume that for the automatic identification of the user culture and the automatic adaptation of the system to this user culture at runtime, a few discriminative intercultural variables should suffice, which can quantitatively include and describe the user and his interaction with the system (= assumption 2 (A2), cf. section 4.3.1). These must already be identified by tests before runtime, though. PUMTM allows conclusions to be drawn regarding the usability of the system for the particular user. During the interaction of the user with the system, the values of this model are determined and documented (traced).[171]

PUMTM contains only measurement variables

Table 17 and Table 18 present some of the parameters from PUMTM that will be applied in the empirical research in this work (cf. Table 20 in section 5.2.2). Table 17 represents the static measurement parameters and their values according to the HMI elements as well as their relationship to the characterization of the user and their relationship to culture. Many criteria for characterizing the user and his culture reduce the probability of classification errors by the system.

---

[171] Hence, this model is called „potential usability metric *trace* model".

Table 17: Static parameters of the Potential Usability Metric Trace Model (PUMTM) (Source: own illustration derived from potential model for intercultural HMI design, cf. file "041213 Modell interkultureller Variable55 überarbeitet am 30-04-2009_pres.xlsx" in the online appendix)

Static parameter	Value of parameter	HMI element possibly concerned	Possible user characteristics	Most relevant cultural dimension
Number	high vs. low	e.g., color, widgets, dialogs, interaction means	communicative, expressive, relationship oriented	relationship vs. task orientated
Color	warm vs. cold, colored vs. mono-chrome / half tone	e.g., background, font	task orientated, lively	relationship vs. task orientated, affective vs. neutral
Position	left vs. right, top vs. bottom	e.g., button, list box	task / objective orientated, game oriented, orientation, thinking style	relationship vs. task orientated, internal vs. external
Arrangement / order	dense vs. loose, grouped / structured vs. chaotic	e.g., widgets, layout	hierarchical orientated, collectivistic, discriminating	relationship vs. task orientated, power distance, individualism vs. collectivism, communication speed, network density

Dynamic measurement parameters

In contrast, Table 18 presents the dynamic measurement parameters and their values according to the HMI elements as well as their relationship to the characterization of the user and their relationship to culture. Also here, it is assumed that the more criteria are used for characterizing the user and his culture, the more the probability of classification errors by the system is reduced.

Table 18: Dynamic parameters of the Potential Usability Metric Trace Model (PUMTM) (Source: own illustration derived from potential model for intercultural HMI design, cf. file "041213 Modell interkultureller Variable55 überarbeitet am 30-04-2009_pres.xlsx" in the online appendix)

Dynamic parameter	Values of parameter	HMI element possibly concerned	Possible user characteristics	Most relevant cultural dimension
Number	high vs. low	e.g., mouse clicks, mouse moves, confirmations	expressive, motivated, task/objective oriented, reflective	uncertainty avoidance
Duration	short vs. long	e.g., confirmation, task	unreflective, motivated, experienced	activity orientation
Speed	high vs. low	e.g., mouse moves, double click, speech	unreflective, motivated, experienced	communication speed
Order	sequential vs. chaotic, linear vs. non-linear/network	e.g., clicking points, break points, steps	task/objective orientated, arbitrarily, mono vs. multi-causal thinking	action chains, cognitive style
Direction	straight vs. curvy, linear vs. non-linear	e.g., mouse movement, navigation	task/objective orientated, indecisive, expressive, mono vs. multi-causal thinking	time orientation, action chains
Breaks	short vs. long, many vs. few	e.g., mouse, keyboard, information reception, interruptions, keyboard input	task/objective orientated, indecisive, expressive	time orientation, action chains, activity orientation, uncertainty avoidance, communication speed

With the HMI dimensions (cf. section 4.2), it is possible to refine and operationalize the hypotheses to make them testable by connecting them to measurable variables, i.e. the postulated statements and assumptions will be reformulated adequately to obtain testable hypotheses for statistical processing. From the potential model for intercultural HMI design (cf. Table 16), "potential cultural interaction indicators" (PCIIs), which represent the measurable variables of the potential usability metric trace model, have been identified as hypothetically depending on culture by literature, study and reflection.

Measurable variables of the PUMTM

4.5   Potential Cultural Interaction Indicators

The factor "number of interactions with the system per time unit" (IN) is represented by the following measurement variables per time unit: number of mouse clicks (MC), number of key strokes (KS), number of mouse moves (MM), number of dialog/function initiations (FI), number of help initiations (HI) and number of nonverbal interaction (NVIN). Interaction break (¬IN) is the opposite of IN, i.e. the time in which no interaction happens. Mouse

Interactions per time unit represented by several variables

movement speed (MMS) is thereby represented by "($\neg IN_{Mouse}<1ms$) per time unit".[172]

Self-contained variables

The remaining variables are number of parallel tasks in task bar (PT), number of error clicks (EC), number of acknowledged (irrelevant) messages (RM), time to disable virtual agents (TDA), length of mouse tracks (LMT) and number of POI presented on map display (POI). The "number of presented pieces of information per time unit" (NIT) is e.g. represented by the number how often maneuver guidance (MG) announcements are desired by the user within a certain time period (cf. MG test task in section 5.2.2). Also the information presenting time, i.e. the duration of information presentation (DIP), can be measured (e.g., a visually presented MG announcement). Table 19 shows the expected values for the potential cultural interaction indicators. The hypotheses and variables are integrated into the test setting in the next chapter.

---

[172] Cf. section 4.5 in the work report for details of operationalization of variables.

Table 19: Expected tendency of the values for the measuring variables (PCIIs) from the Potential Usability Metric Trace Model (PUMTM) according to the hypotheses in this work (Source: own illustration)

Measuring Variable (operationalized hypotheses)	Germany	China	Short name of measuring variable
Information speed (time between two sequentially presented information units) (IH1a)	low	high	TPI
Number of interaction breaks (¬INH1a)	high	low	¬IN
Number of POI at the map display (IH1b1)	low	high	POI
Number of interactions with the system per time unit (IH1b2)	low	high	IN
Number of interactions with the system per time unit (IH1c)	low	high	IN
Number of mouse clicks per time unit (INH1c1)	low	high	MC
Mouse movement speed (INH1c2)	low	high	MMS
Number of mouse moves per time unit (INH1c3)	low	high	MM
Number of parallel tasks in task bar (IH1d)	low	high	PT
Number of pieces of information presented per time unit (IH5)	low	high	NIT
Number of interactions with the system per time unit (INH5)	low	high	IN
Number of parallel tasks in task bar (IH6a)	low	high	PT
Number of error clicks (IH5)	low	high	EC
Number of acknowledged (irrelevant) system messages (IH6b)	low	high	RM
Time to disable virtual agents (INH6b)	low	high	TDA
Number of non verbal interactions with the system per time unit (IH7)	low	high	NVIN
Length of mouse track (INH7)	long	short	LMT
Number of interactions with the system per time unit (IH8)	low	high	IN
Number of interactions with the system per time unit (INH8)	low	high	IN
Number of non verbal interactions with the system per time unit (IH9 + IH10)	low	high	NVIN
Number of function initiations per time unit (INH10)	low	high	FI
Number of help initiations per time unit (INH11)	high	low	HI
Duration of information presentation (IH12)	long	short	DIP

5 Intercultural Interaction Analysis Tool

> "Meten is weten, gissen is missen."
> (Old Dutch saying)[173]

Chapter 5 contains the preparatory part for the empirical research in this work concerning the investigation of the relationship between culture and HCI by the determination of the differences in interactions as well as the different interaction patterns of users with different cultural backgrounds. For this purpose, the most important use cases (application cases) in the area of driver navigation systems have been implemented in a tool developed by the author ("IIA tool", cf. section 5.2.1). Thereby, the interaction of culturally different users with the computer system can be recorded, analyzed and compared using a test setting that permits capturing values for some of the criteria of the HMI dimensions (HMIDs) for different cultures (e.g., the values of some hidden cultural variables). The test concept (section 5.1), test setting (section 5.2), test execution (section and 5.3) and data analysis (section 5.4) using this tool will be presented in this chapter.

5.1 Test Planning: Data Collection Concept

The data collection concept encompasses the following descriptions: Test planning

- the problem which needs statistical information (cf. the empirical hypotheses in section 4.3.3)
- the part of reality, which has to be modeled statistically (section 5.1.1)
- the statistical features and their values (section 5.1.2)
- participants and sample plan (section 5.1.3)

---

[173] "Measuring is knowledge, guessing is missing." (cf. footnote 1 and file "Sprichwörter mit messen.txt" in the online appendix).

- data collection material (such as interviewer handbook, coding instructions or information for participants) (cf. section 5.2 as well as section 10.3 in the appendix of the work report)
- the method of acquiring data using data collection tools (section 5.3)
- data preparation methods (e.g., plausibility check) (section 5.4)
- data analysis methods and tools (section 5.4)
- legal basics[174]
- organizational information (time schedule, costs, resources, planning).[175]

5.1.1   Description of the Statistically Represented Part of Reality

The hypotheses postulated in chapter 4 will be operationalized for statistical processing in this section. To test the hypotheses, three test systems have been developed according to the relationship between independent and dependent variables. However, only one test system could have been applied in this work because it is *not* based on Hofstede's IDV.[176] The following test system used for the first and second online survey regarding the relationship between cultural and HMI variables has been realized using the potential cultural interaction indicators (PCII) (cf. section 4.5) derived from PMICHMID and PUMTM (cf. section 4.4):

Independent / Dependent Variables

Independent Variables:

- Primary cultural imprint (defined by mother tongue and first nationality: both have to be of the same value)

Dependent Variables:

---

[174] Cf. e.g., Friedersen & Lindemann 2000 regarding the law of freedom of information. In the guide to the law of freedom of information of the country of North Rhine-Westphalia, it is e.g., explained which legal basics must be taken into account at the preparation of questionnaires. Detailed information is also given e.g. by GESIS (URL = http://www.gesis.org/das-institut/, last access 5/31/11).

[175] Cf. files "050815 IIA-Erhebungskonzept.doc" as well as "timetable.doc" in online appendix.

[176] The three test systems can be found in the online appendix in detail in file "050815 IIA-Erhebungskonzept.doc". In this work, only the finally used "test system 2" will be presented. The hypotheses postulated in the test systems 1 and 3 are connected to Hofstedes "individualism index". They cannot be tested because the obtained individualism index for the Chinese persons recruited for the online studies in this work is almost the same as for German test persons and the hypotheses presuppose different IDV values. Please refer to section 5.1.1 and to the same section in the work report as well as to file "050815 IIA-Erhebungskonzept.doc" the online appendix for a detailed discussion of this aspect.

- Number of POI at the map display (POI)
- Number of mouse clicks per time unit (MC)
- Number of mouse movements per time unit (MM)
- Mouse movement speed (MMS)
- Number of parallel tasks in task bar (PT)
- Number of error clicks (EC)
- Number of acknowledged (irrelevant) system messages (RM)
- Time to disable virtual agents (TDA)
- Number of non-verbal interactions with the system per time unit (NVIN)
- Length of mouse track (LMT)
- Number of function initiations (FI)
- Number of key strokes (KS)
- Number of help initiations (HI)
- Number of pieces of information presented per time unit (NIT)
- Duration of information presentation (DIP)
- Number of interactions with the system per time unit (IN): the sum of the number of all recorded user interactions with the system per time unit (MC, EC, FI, HI, KS, PT, NVIN) (cf. section 4.5)
- Number of interaction breaks ($\neg$IN)

Furthermore, to gain control over the most disturbing variables assumed to be exerting influence the following control variables are used:[177]   *Control variables*

- PC experience
- Gender
- Age.

The group of persons is restricted to the sample size used within this work comprising only of employees of SV (cf. section 5.1.3).

The empirical hypotheses (EH) have been created and described in detail in section 4.3.3. From them, statistical hypotheses (SH) can be generated. In contrast to empirical hypotheses, statistical hypotheses have the advantage that they can be verified with statistical methods in any case because they are transformed accordingly to be processed in statistics.   *Statistical hypotheses*

SH$_1$: $\mu IN_C > \mu IN_G$ $\leftrightarrow$ $\mu IN_C - \mu IN_G > 0$

The average value of "number of interactions with the system per time unit" (IN) is significantly higher for the group of persons assigned to be of Chinese culture than of German culture.

---

[177] Cf. section 6.3 for a detailed discussion of the "controlled disturbing variables".

SH$_2$: $\mu POI_C > \mu POI_G$ $\leftrightarrow$ $\mu POI_C - \mu POI_G > 0$

The average value of "number of points of interest at the map display" (POI) is significantly higher for the group of persons assigned to be of Chinese culture than of German culture.

SH$_3$: $\mu MC_C > \mu MC_G$ $\leftrightarrow$ $\mu MC_C - \mu MC_G > 0$

The average value of "number of mouse clicks per time unit" (MC) is significantly higher for the group of persons assigned to be of Chinese culture than of German culture.

SH$_4$: $\mu MMS_C > \mu MMS_G$ $\leftrightarrow$ $\mu MMS_C - \mu MMS_G > 0$

The average value of "mouse movement speed" (MMS) is significantly higher for the group of persons assigned to be of Chinese culture than of German culture.

SH$_5$: $\mu PT_C > \mu PT_G$ $\leftrightarrow$ $\mu PT_C - \mu PT_G > 0$

The average value of "number of parallel tasks in task bar" (PT) is significantly higher for the group of persons assigned to be of Chinese culture than of German culture.

SH$_6$: $\mu EC_C > \mu EC_G$ $\leftrightarrow$ $\mu EC_C - \mu EC_G > 0$

The average value of "number of error clicks" (EC) is significantly higher for the group of persons assigned to be of Chinese culture than of German culture.

SH$_7$: $\mu RM_C < \mu RM_G$ $\leftrightarrow$ $\mu RM_C - \mu RM_G < 0$

The average value of "number of refused system messages" (RM) is significantly lower for the group of persons assigned to be of Chinese culture than of German culture.

SH$_8$: $\mu TDA_C > \mu TDA_G$ $\leftrightarrow$ $\mu TDA_C - \mu TDA_G > 0$

The average value of "time to disable virtual agents" (TDA) is significantly higher for the group of persons assigned to be of Chinese culture than of German culture.

SH$_9$: $\mu NVIN_C > \mu NVIN_G$ $\leftrightarrow$ $\mu NVIN_C - \mu NVIN_G > 0$

The average value of "number of non verbal interactions with the system per time unit" (NIN) is significantly higher for the group of persons assigned to be of Chinese culture than of German culture.

SH$_{10}$: $\mu LMT_C > \mu LMT_G$ $\leftrightarrow$ $\mu LMT_C - \mu LMT_G > 0$

The average value of "length of mouse tracks" (LMT) is significantly higher for the group of persons assigned to be of Chinese culture than of German culture.

SH$_{11}$: $\mu HI_C < \mu HI_G$ $\leftrightarrow$ $\mu HI_C - \mu HI_G < 0$

The average value of "help initiations" (HI) is significantly lower for the group of persons assigned to be of Chinese culture than of German culture.[178]

SH$_{12}$: $\mu KS_C > \mu KS_G$ $\leftrightarrow$ $\mu KS_C - \mu KS_G > 0$

The average value of "keyboard strokes" (KS) is significantly higher for the group of persons assigned to be of Chinese culture than of German culture.

SH$_{13}$: $\mu FI_C > \mu FI_G$ $\leftrightarrow$ $\mu FI_C - \mu FI_G > 0$

The average value of "functional initiations" (FI) is significantly higher for the group of persons assigned to be of Chinese culture than of German culture.

SH$_{14}$: $\mu NIT_C > \mu NIT_G$ $\leftrightarrow$ $\mu NIT_C - \mu NIT_G > 0$

The average value of "number of presented pieces of information per time unit" (NIT) is significantly higher for the group of persons assigned to be of Chinese culture than of German culture.

SH$_{15}$: $\mu DIP_C < \mu DIP_G$ $\leftrightarrow$ $\mu DIP_C - \mu DIP_G < 0$

The average value of "duration of information presentation" (DIP) is significantly shorter for the group of persons assigned to be of Chinese culture than of German culture.

Finally, the statistical hypotheses (SH) can be reformulated by test hypotheses (TH) to apply the statistical mechanism of rejecting or accepting the test hypothesis (H$_0$) or the alternative hypotheses (H$_1$):

TH$_1$:   H$_0$: $\mu IN_C \leq \mu IN_G$ H$_1$: $\mu IN_C > \mu IN_G$

TH$_2$:   H$_0$: $\mu POI_C \leq \mu POI_G$ H$_1$: $\mu POI_C > \mu POI_G$

TH$_3$:   H$_0$: $\mu MC_C \leq \mu MC_G$ H$_1$: $\mu MC_C > \mu MC_G$

TH$_4$:   H$_0$: $\mu MMS_C \leq \mu MMS_G$ H$_1$: $\mu MMS_C > \mu MMS_G$

TH$_5$:   H$_0$: $\mu PT_C \leq \mu PT_G$ H$_1$: $\mu PT_C > \mu PT_G$

TH$_6$:   H$_0$: $\mu EC_C \leq \mu EC_G$ H$_1$: $\mu EC_C > \mu EC_G$

---

[178] Cf. table V333 in Inglehart et al. 1998.

TH_7: H_0: $\mu RM_C \geq \mu RM_G$ H_1: $\mu RM_C < \mu RM_G$

TH_8: H_0: $\mu TDA_C \leq \mu TDA_G$ H_1: $\mu TDA_C > \mu TDA_G$

TH_9: H_0: $\mu NIN_C \leq \mu NIN_G$ H_1: $\mu NIN_C > \mu NIN_G$

TH_{10}: H_0: $\mu LMT_C \leq \mu LMT_G$ H_1: $\mu LMT_C > \mu LMT_G$

TH_{11}: H_0: $\mu HI_C \geq \mu HI_G$ H_1: $\mu HI_C < \mu HI_G$

TH_{12}: H_0: $\mu KS_C \leq \mu KS_G$ H_1: $\mu KS_C > \mu KS_G$

TH_{13}: H_0: $\mu FI_C \leq \mu FI_G$ H_1: $\mu FI_C > \mu FI_G$

TH_{14}: H_0: $\mu NIT_C \leq \mu NIT_G$ H_1: $\mu NIT_C > \mu NIT_G$

TH_{15}: H_0: $\mu DIP_C \geq \mu DIP_G$ H_1: $\mu DIP_C < \mu DIP_G$

5.1.2   Statistical Features and Parameter Values (Measurement Variables)

The most important and operationalized parameters that will be used in this work to measure the interaction of the user with the computer have been shown in Table 19 in section 4.5. They represent the potential cultural interaction indicators (PCIIs) whose values will be determined in the empirical studies presented in the following sections.

5.1.3   Reflecting Subjects, Sample Selection and Participation

Influences on user interaction behavior

The basic idea of identifying cultural differences in HMI is to observe and analyze the user interaction with the system as explained in sections 3.3 and 4.2 taking into account e.g., interaction frequency, interaction breaks, interaction style, interaction efficiency, information speed, information frequency, information order and information complexity. These HMI dimensions (HMIDs) for user interface usage represent the effects of the cause-effect-diagram on the right hand side of Figure 9.

Cause-effect-diagram

However, besides culture, there are other influences on user interaction behavior such as aspects regarding the machine (system), method, means, environment, as well as the user himself as indicated on the left hand side of Figure 9.[179]

---

[179] These other influences in turn are influenced by culture.

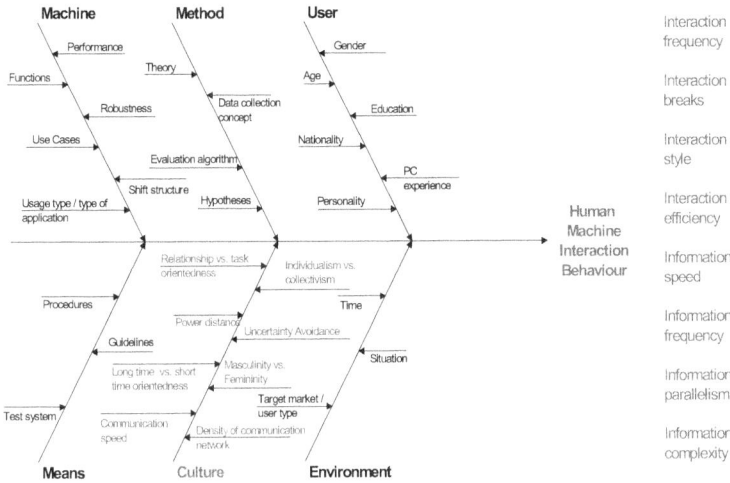

Figure 9: Possible influencing factors on the interaction of the user with the system

The arrangement of interaction cycles depends on the user, system and tasks (cf. e.g., Herczeg 2005, Dix 2007, or Shneiderman 2009). Hence, to measure the differences in the interaction behavior of different users, tasks and system must remain the same. Furthermore, to measure cultural interaction differences, at least two culturally different groups (e.g., Chinese and German users) must be examined. Furthermore, to identify only the cultural differences in HMI, all aspects other than culture (i.e. user, machine, environment, method and means) must be kept the same for all test participants. Hence, one should assume that only subjects that have a comparable experience background with regard e.g., to education, social environment and real-world knowledge may be employed to secure only the cultural differences. However, this assumption is problematic because all these parameters are already subject to the cultural stamp and contribute to user culture anyway.

Same test setting

Test persons with comparable background

Nevertheless, the minimal requirement for the test persons is that the values of the potentially disturbing parameters must be similar. This means e.g., that the test persons must exhibit similar computer experience to do the tests in the same way (e.g., using a PC) as well as belonging to a different culture e.g., different mother tongue and pure native speaker (i.e. the user never should have left the country). Hence, the main objectives of the sample selection can be stated as follows:

Similar target group

Employees of Siemens VDO

High rate of valid test results

- Similar character of the desired target group exhibiting equal distribution of all experience levels (high education level, high technical experience, low cultural experience abroad, car driver knowing about "driver navigation systems")
- High participation rate of all selected employees of Siemens VDO in the online tests in the desired countries (China and Germany)
- High amount of valid quantitative and qualitative test results.

All these requirements are fulfilled by doing online studies with similarly educated employees from Siemens VDO in China and Germany who have similar job equipment (systems) and using a special tool for this purpose, which provides the same tasks and systems (a PC). The following methods of data collection have been planned:

- Quantitative data collection with real random samples of at least 800 participants per country (China and Germany via intranet at SV)
- Qualitative data collection with 10–20 participants per country (in China and Germany).

Before information about the recruiting and the preparation of the participants in the studies will be given in detail in section 5.3, the hypotheses will be turned into reasonable test settings.

5.2   Test Design: Turning Hypotheses into Test Settings

To test the postulated hypotheses, a test setting using an automated tool has been developed which is described in this section.

5.2.1   Designing a Tool for the Analysis of Cultural Differences in HCI

Existing methods for determining cultural differences in HCI

The literature study showed that there are no adequate methods for determining cross-cultural differences regarding interactional aspects of HMI and none for driver navigation systems even if there is some work about the recording of interaction on PCs (cf. Spannagel 2003). For example, there are tools for user interaction logging. Some of the best known are e.g.:

- ObSys (recording and visualization of windows messages) (cf. Gellner & Forbrig 2003)
- Interact (coding and visualization of user behavior) (cf. Mangold 2005)

- Reviser (automatic criteria oriented usability evaluation of interactive systems, cf. Hamacher 2006)
- Tool set for log file analysis (cf. Köppen & Wandke 2002)
- UserZoom (recording, analyzing and visualization of online studies) and other instrumental tools for instance Noldus, SnagIt, Morae, A-Prompt or LeoTrace.[180]

All the existing tools provide some functionality for (partly remote) usability tests and interaction behavior measurement. However, none of the existing tools provide explicitly cultural usability metrics (cf. PUMTM in section 4.4) or measuring interaction behavior according to special use cases (e.g., use cases for driver navigation systems).

Furthermore, the required knowledge about variables, which depend on culture, could not be implemented in the existing tools mentioned above because the cultural parameters of the PUMTM had not been determined before. Not until the theoretical reflections on the literature by the author led to the potential model for intercultural HMI design (cf. PMICHMID (and PUMTM) in section 4.4) consisting of cultural variables representing the connection between culture and the HMI dimensions relevant for user interface usage (HMI characteristics). Moreover, even if the architecture of the new tool follows the already existing tools in some respect, the architecture of the existing tools could not have been changed in time for this dissertation project such that the potential parameters could be determined.[181]

Hence, a new special tool for measuring the interaction behavior of the user has been developed from scratch by the author for this purpose. With this new tool, the interaction of culturally different users doing the same test task can be observed (using the same test conditions i.e. the same hard- and software, environment conditions, language and the test tasks) as well as requiring the same experience in the use of the system.

Creation of new tool

A benchmark test of driver navigation systems from different countries with similar functions helped to determine the requirements for this tool and offered some differences in HMI (cf. section 6.1). Logging data of dialogs, debugging

Benchmark test

---

[180] Please refer to the web sites of these companies for further information (e.g., http://www.noldus.com, http://www.techsmith.de/, http://www.leotrace.de/, http://www.userzoom.com/, last access 5/31/09).

[181] Furthermore, it is not clear if the owners of these tools would have permitted the author to change the architecture of their products – beyond the fact that they would need to reveal their source code.

and HMI event triggering while using the system are highly valuable.[182] The requirements for recording these data can be found in the PUMTM (cf. section 4.4). This data can be logged during usability tests according to certain user tasks.

Creation of task scenarios

To motivate the user to interact with the computer and to verify the postulated hypotheses, adequate task scenarios have been created and implemented in this new test tool. The resulting tool for intercultural interaction analysis (IIA tool) provides a data collection, data analysis and data evaluation module for data collection, analysis and evaluation:[183]

- recording, analysis and visualization of user interaction behavior and preferences
- intercultural usability testing using use cases that are localized for different cultures
- usability evaluation for all interaction levels
- qualitative judgments from quantitative data to enhance test validity and reliability.

The collection and preparation of the data will be done mostly automatically by the IIA data collection module. This saves much time, costs and effort. The collected data can be quantitative (related to all test persons, e.g., the mean of a Likert scale, cf. Lienert et al. 1998) as well as qualitative (related to one single test person, e.g., answering open questions, cf. La Cruz et al. 2005).

Data stored in standard format

Using statistical software

Moreover, the collected data sets can be stored in standard format (e.g., CSV)[184] so that anyone can perform their own statistical analyses. This also means that the studies with this tool are completely reproducible using the IIA tool. The data will be stored in databases in a format that is immediately usable by the IIA data analysis module, which does subsequent data conversion or

---

[182] Kralisch 2006 explicitly encourages using log file analysis in online surveys: "The combination of log file analysis and online surveys appears to be an appropriate methodological combination for cross-cultural and cross-linguistic investigations, whose application for future research is hereby encouraged." (Kralisch 2006: 211). To obtain deeper insights, local offline studies can be used: "[..] think-aloud methods for gaining more detailed insight. [..]" (Kralisch 2006: 211).

[183] In this work, the IIA tool is described only as detailed as necessary to grasp its usage and functionality to verify the hypotheses of this dissertation project. For a more detailed description of the architecture and functionality of the IIA tool, please refer to section 10.2 in the work report as well as to the online appendix. However, the source code may not be published because of copyright restrictions.

[184] CSV means comma-separated values or character separated values and is described in the specification RFC 4180 (Cf. URL = http://tools.ietf.org/html/rfc4180, last access at 2/4/11).

preparation. Hence, common statistic programs like SPSS[185] can be deployed to apply statistical methods (cf. section 5.4). The IIA data evaluation module enables classification using neural networks to cross-validate the results from data analysis.

The programming language "Delphi"[186] was used to create one single software tool, which can be installed online via the Internet as well as offline via a CD. To avoid downloading and interaction delays, the IIA tool has been implemented as an executable program file on a server to be downloaded onto the local hard disk of users worldwide. The reason for this is that the tool has to measure the interaction behavior of the user during the online tests correctly and comparably in real time. This is only possible if the program runs on the target system to avoid delays in program flow because of high network traffic. The Delphi-IDE allows transformation of new HMI concepts very quickly into good-looking prototypes that can be tested very soon within the development process. For example, some of the hypotheses of this work have been confirmed quantitatively addressing many test users online using the IIA tool in one month (implementing the use cases as well as doing data collection and data analysis).[187] Hence, using the IIA tool means rapid use case design, i.e. real-time prototyping of user interfaces for different cultures as well as a huge amount of valid data collected rapidly and easily worldwide, i.e. online via internet or intranet.

Programming language „Delphi"

---

[185] SPSS is a statistical software package for the social sciences from SPSS incorporation and stands for "superior performing software system". It is almost free of charge for scientific usage at universities. For using SPSS, please refer to Kockläuner 2000, Fromm 2007, or Ho 2006. The statistical program SPSS has been renamed to PASW Statistics (Predictive Analytics Software) with software version 17.0.2.

[186] Delphi Version 7 from Borland (cf. Cantù 2003). Cf. Doberenz & Gewinnus 2007 for further information on the integrated development environment (IDE) for Delphi.

[187] The development process of the IIA tool took about two man-years to be usable at first time in 2005.

5.2.2   Implementation of Test Tasks and the PCIIs into the IIA Tool

Intercultural Interaction
Analysis Tool (IIA tool):
⇨ Analyses cultural
differences in HCI

⇨ Provides basis for
general guidelines in
intercultural HMI
design

The IIA tool has been developed to determine and analyze cultural differences in HCI. Therefore, it can be used to illuminate the basic user behavior with computers as well as with use cases related to special products (e.g., driver navigation systems as for the case of this dissertation project). This suggests that the results could be general guidelines for every kind of intercultural HMI development as well as context specific recommendations for the design of special products tested using special use cases. Furthermore, some results are expected to be valid for HMI design in general because the context of usage is eliminated by abstract test settings, which are independent from application dependent use cases. Hence, the test setting within the IIA tool contains two scenarios:

Abstract scenario for
general use

Concrete scenario for
driver navigation systems

- an abstract scenario with test tasks (abstract use cases) for general usage of widgets
- a concrete scenario with test tasks (special use cases) for the usage of driver navigation systems.

In the first scenario, the user uses certain widgets. Those tasks can only be done by persons that have used a PC before. The second scenario takes into account concrete use cases from driver navigation systems. This additionally requires that the test participant has some knowledge and interaction experience regarding driver navigation systems.

Technical and linguistical
localization of test tasks
enables worldwide
extension

The simulation of special use cases within the IIA tool can highlight any usability problems and differences in user interaction behavior (similar to "paper mock-ups").[188] Every one of the test tasks serves to investigate other cultural aspects of HCI. The test tasks (use cases) are localized at the technical and linguistic level, but are largely semantically identical for all users[189], so that participants of many different cultures can do the test tasks (according to step four of Path-To-CAHMI, cf. section 3.3.4).[190] Hence, the study can be

---

[188] Paper mock-ups are prototypes of user interfaces drawn on paper to manually „simulate" the user interface behavior and its outfit to test its usability very cheaply (cf. Holzinger 2005).

[189] For details on levels of localization, please refer to sections 2.3.5 and 2.3.7 in this work as well in the work report.

[190] In this work, the test tasks are described to illustrate their working principle. For descriptions of the test tasks in detail as well as for tests not presented here, please refer to section 10.3 in the appendix of the work report as well as to file "050815 IIA-Erhebungskonzept.doc" in the online appendix.

extended from the Chinese and German cultures to other cultures by using the same (adequately localized) test tool.

The IIA tool provides an implementation of the PUMTM and therefore the ability to determine the values of the specified cultural variables. Thereby, the values of the following HMI dimensions can be determined quantitatively:

Values of HMI dimensions to be determined quantitatively

- Information density (spatial distance between informational units)
- Information speed (time distance between informational units to be presented)
- Information frequency (number of presented informational units per time unit)
- Interaction frequency (user) (number of initialized interaction steps by the user per time unit)
- Interaction frequency (system) (number of initialized interaction steps by the system per time unit) (this equates to time distance between interaction steps)
- Interaction style (e.g., kind of mouse moving)

During the whole test session, the IIA tool records the interaction between users and the system (cf. Gerken et al. 2008), e.g., mouse moves, clicks, interaction breaks or the values and changes of the slide bars set up by the users in order to analyze the interactional patterns of users from different cultures.[191] Thereby, all levels of the interaction model (physical, lexical, syntactical, semantic, pragmatic and intentional, cf. Herczeg 2009) necessary for dialog and interaction design can be analyzed using the IIA tool (cf. Heimgärtner 2007a and Heimgärtner 2008).

IIA tool: Recording and analyzing interaction permanently

In accordance with the methods of "interaction course analysis" in Hohmann 2003, Figure 10 shows a part of a course of interaction of a user with the system during a test session represented by some parameters like mouse moves or mouse clicks as well as keyboard presses (at y-axis) displayed over time (at x-axis).

Extract of a test session

---

[191] The test procedure within a test session will be explained in detail in section 5.3.

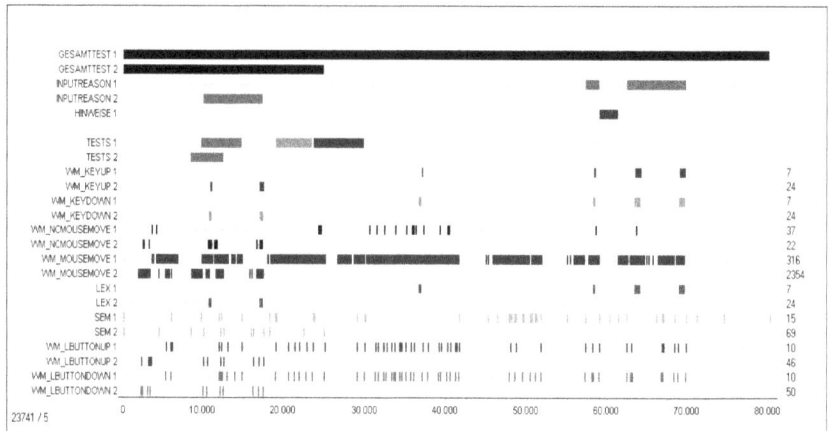

Figure 10: Part of a course of interaction of a user with the system during a test session done with the IIA tool

High number of potentially culturally sensitive variables

The IIA tool allows the measurement of numeric values for information speed, information density and interaction speed in relation to the user. These are hypothetically correlated to cultural variables concerning the surface level like number or position of pictures in the layout or affecting the interaction level like frequency of voice guidance. More than one hundred potentially culturally sensitive variables for HMI from the potential model for intercultural HMI design (PMICHMID, cf. section 4.4) have been implemented into the IIA tool and applied by measuring the interaction of the test persons with a personal computer system in relation to the culture (cf. Table 20).

Most relevant variables

The most relevant variables for interaction analysis will be explained in the following sections. Furthermore, which data has been collected, and why and how will also be presented.[192]

---

[192] The variables are described in detail in the source code of the IIA tool as well as in the statistical data processing files of SPSS in the online appendix (e.g. in "060124 Most Discriminating Use case Independent Cultural Interaction Indicators.spo"). Their detailed description is given in this work where necessary. Not all PCIIs from the PMICHMID and PUMTM could have been implemented in the IIA data collection module because of time and budget restrictions. Only the most promising PCIIs requiring the least integration effort have been implemented. Furthermore, only the most relevant variables for the presentation of the results in this work are listed in Table 20.

Table 20: Implemented variables from the PUMTM in the IIA tool

Kind of measurement variable	Concerned test task(s)	Measurement variables (parameters)
Measurement variables measured at each test task	all	test task duration, total dialog time, number of error clicks[193], number of mouse clicks, entered characters (where possible)
Measurement variables measured over the whole test session	all	test duration, total dialog time, maximal open tasks, number of scrolls, all mouse clicks, number of error clicks, number of mouse clicks, mouse left ups, mouse left downs, click distance, click duration, number of mouse moves, mouse move distance, number of agent moves, number of agent hides, number of shown messages, number of refused messages, number of acknowledges messages, number of acknowledged decision questions, number of refused decision questions, number of help calls, number of syntactical interaction ("Lex"), number of semantically interaction ("Sem"), (Interaction-) breaks less than 1 ms, interaction breaks of 1ms, interaction breaks of 10ms, interaction breaks of 100ms, interaction breaks of 1s, interaction breaks of 10s, interaction breaks of 100s, interaction breaks of 1000s, interaction breaks of 10000s
Measurement variables measured before starting the test session	all	number of open tasks before test
Measurement variables measured within a single test task	User Requirement Design (URD) test task	position X begin (URD), position Y begin (URD), position X end (URD), position X Back (URD), position Y back (URD), position X next (URD), position Y next (URD), position X end (URD), position Y end (URD), position X ready (URD), position Y ready (URD), position X display (URD), position Y display (URD), position X list box (URD), position Y list box (URD), position X status (URD), position Y status (URD)
"	Map Display (MD) test task	number of textures (MD), number of POI (MD), number of street names (MD), number of streets (MD), number of maneuvers (MD), number of restaurants (MD)
"	Maneuver Guidance (MG) test task	message distance (MG), display duration (MG), car animation speed (MG)
"	Information Order (IO) test task	information order index (IO), factor of disorder (IO), number of pixels in disorder (IO), number of overlapping pixels (IO), coverage factor (IO), image size (IO), distance between image margins (IO), image distance (IO)
"	INteraction Exactness (INE) test task	interaction speed (INE), interaction exactness (INE)
"	INteraction Speed (INS) test task	interaction exactness (INS), interaction speed (INS)
"	QUEStionnaire (QUES) test task	time to change value in questionnaires (QUES)
"	Information Hierarchy (IH) test task	information hierarchy index (IH)
"	Uncertainty aVoidance (UV) test task	uncertainty avoidance value (UV)

---

[193] Error clicks are mouse clicks that do not have any functional effect. This is a very simplified and limited view of error possibilities in HCI. For a detailed overview of errors in HCI, please refer e.g., to Prümper 1994.

Aim of test tasks: reveal decisive cultural variables

The test tasks with the IIA tool were designed to help to reveal the empirical truth regarding the different values in cultural variables. Some of those aspects and use cases will be explained in more detail on the following pages.

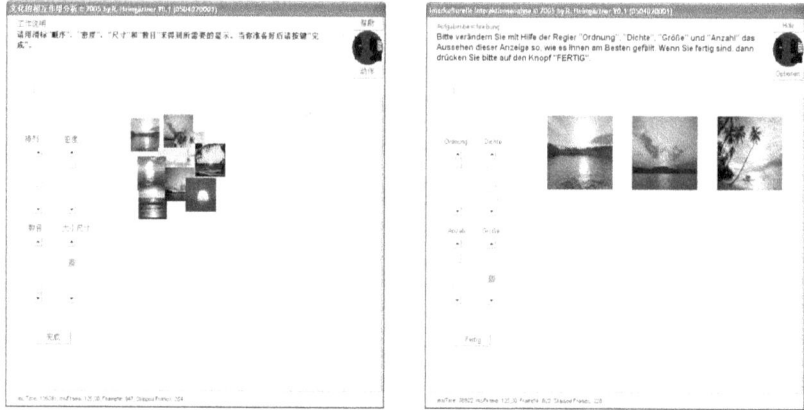

Figure 11: Expected results from Chinese and German users

Confirming the hypothesis by test cases

Abstract use cases

Both abstract and special use cases have been implemented in this way as test scenarios in the IIA data collection module in order to obtain results for the design of navigation systems (cf. Heimgärtner 2005). For example, a hypothesis such as "there is high correlation of high information density to relationship-oriented cultures like the Chinese" (cf. hypothesis IH1b in chapter 4) should be confirmable by setting low distances between a set of many small pictures by Chinese users compared to German users. Figure 11 shows the expected results regarding this hypothesis in the study. Chinese users are assumed to adjust the arrangement of the pictures in the left image of Figure 11 whereas German users should rather arrange the pictures during the test as shown in the right image of Figure 11. This expected result would support the hypothesis that "there is high correlation of low information density and high information order to task-oriented cultures like Germany" because of less but well ordered pictures.

Special use cases

"Map display test task"

To transfer the results of these general use cases within the abstract test settings to use cases of driver navigation systems, special use cases have to be implemented as test scenarios in the test tool. For example, the number of pictures can be correlated to the number of POI displayed on the map display by replacing the abstract context of sunset-pictures by a navigation map with POI on it. This use case "number of POI displayed" has to be tested by studies with Chinese and German users to investigate the context of usage and to verify the general validity of the results by comparing them with the results of tests with other use cases. The results will probably show that there are differences in information density expressed by the number of POI in map display. Hence, the hypothesis "there is a high correlation of high information density to relationship-oriented cultures such as the Chinese" (equates to SH_2, cf. section 5.1.1 and IH1b, cf. section 4.3.3) should also be confirmable by adjusting more POI by Chinese users compared to German users.[194] Therefore, the use case "map display" has been implemented by the "map display test task" to measure the number of pieces of information on the map display regarding information density (e.g., restaurants, streets, POI, etc.) (cf. Figure 12).

The user can define the amount of information in the map display by adjusting the scroll bars (number of POI, number of maneuvers, etc.). The test tool records the values of the slide bars set up by the users. Based on this principle, the test tool can also be used to investigate the values of other cultural variables like widget positions, menu, layout and dialog structure, speed of information input, etc.

---

[194] Surely, to evaluate whether information density is different more measurement variables than solely number of POI should be used (cf. also section 8.1 regarding the methodological challenges). This is solved in this project by also measuring other variables like number of restaurants, number of streets, number of textures and number of maneuvers that contribute to represent information density.

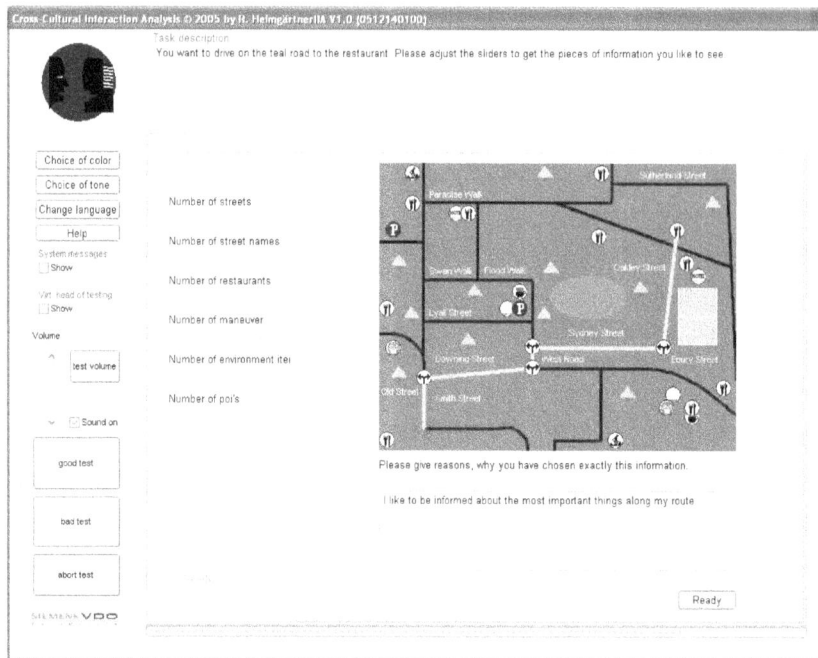

Figure 12: Screenshot of the "map display test task" during the test session with the IIA data collection module

"Maneuver guidance test task"

Along with the implemented use case "map display" in the map display test task shown in Figure 12, another important use case of driver navigation systems "maneuver guidance" has been implemented as a "maneuver guidance test task" in the IIA data collection module. The test user has to adjust the number and the time distance of the maneuver advice messages on the screen concerning the frequency and speed of information (cf. Figure 13). The effect of this test task can best be grasped by watching the maneuver guidance test task video[195] because there is animation of the car and the messages, which is only recognizable and evaluable over time.

---

[195] Cf. the clip 3:35s to 4:53s in the file "screencam_test.mpeg" in the online appendix. However, the best solution is to do the IIA test by executing the IIA data collection module by oneself (please contact the author for this purpose if you are interested).

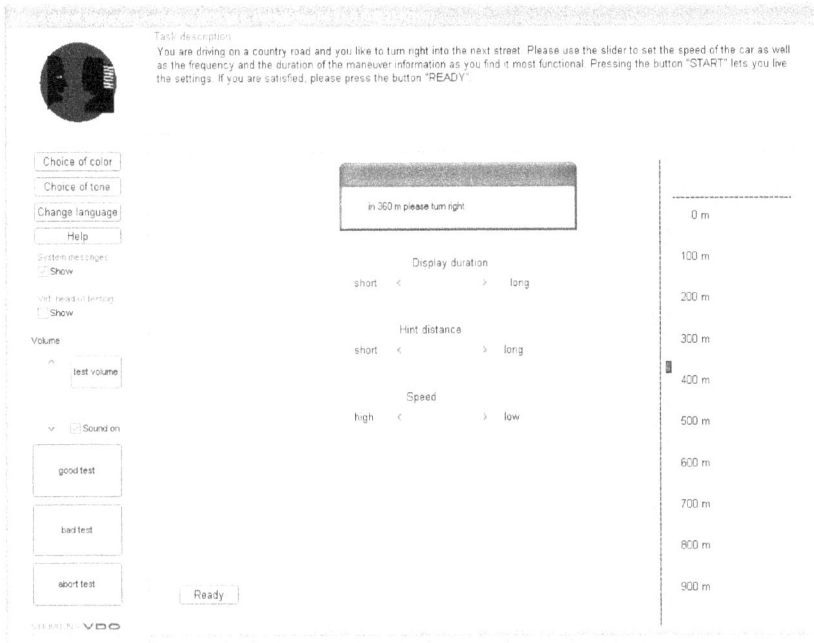

Figure 13: Maneuver guidance test task

According to Prendinger & Ishizuka 2004, avatars can reduce stress during interaction with the user. However, in this work the test has another objective. The main aim is to determine the difference in switching off the agent by the user because the agent is disturbing the user. Hence, another variable is measuring the acceptance of the "life-like" character "Merlin".[196] The agent

"Interruption sensitiveness test task"

---

[196] The virtual assistant "Merlin" is part of the interactive help system of Microsoft Office™. Cf. programming Microsoft agents in MSDN online (URL = http://msdn.microsoft.com/en-us/library/ms695875(VS.85).aspx and URL = http://msdn.microsoft.com/de-de/magazine/cc163649(en-us).aspx, last access 2/28/11). However, this test case can be improperly constructed because both, the successful interaction of German and Chinese users are disturbed by the agent. To capture this difference, it is important to frequently present the virtual agent to the user in such a way that both user groups, Chinese and German users, will switch off the agent because of his nerviness. After a certain time, both groups switch off the agent which does not disturb the test session any longer. Furthermore, with increasing time the test gets more reliable since the test participant thinks less about the test reasons and takes the test more and more unconcerned and naturally. This means that the user interacts close to his real cultural stamp which is exactly what should be measured within the IIA test. Hence, the system can be formed differently here. For example, the avatar can be much more defensive and in the background. Cf. also section 8.1.

"Merlin" was implemented into the IIA tool to offer his help every 30 seconds (cf. Figure 14).

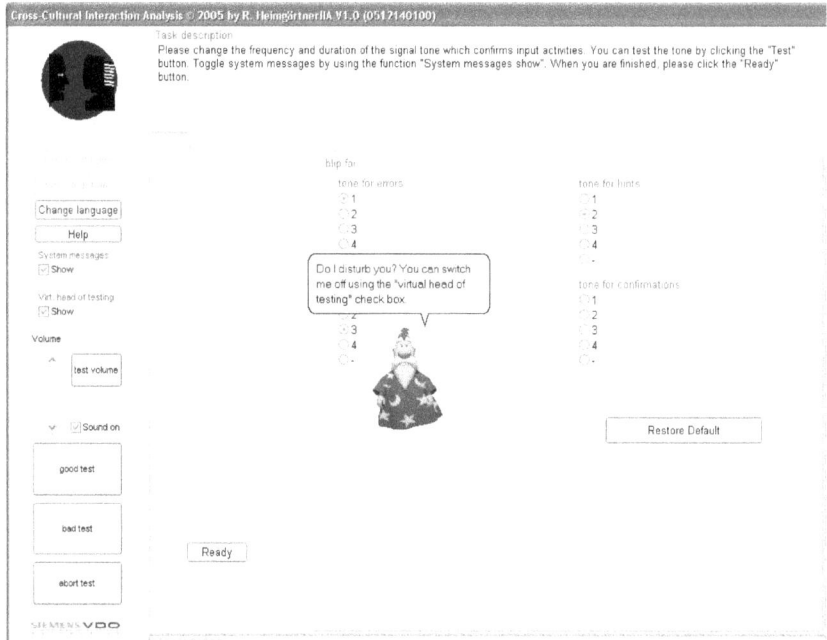

Figure 14: Interruption of the user's workflow by the system to test the uncertainty avoidance of the user

"Uncertainty avoidance test"

On the one hand, according to the cultural dimensions of "uncertainty avoidance" and "task orientation", it was expected that German users switch off the avatar much sooner than Chinese users. It is assumed that Chinese users bear the agent longer than the German users because of face saving and collectivistic orientation being used to use communication networks of high density. Moreover, German users fear uncertain situations (cf. Hofstede & Hofstede 2005) as well being mono-chronic oriented doing the tasks one by one and not in parallel like poly-chronic oriented cultures (cf. Hall 1959). Furthermore, they do not like to be distracted from achieving the current task (cf. Halpin & Winer 1957). On the other hand, if applying the cultural dimension of face saving, it should be the other way around. If Chinese users made use of help very often, they would lose face (cf. Victor 1997, Honold 2000).

It becomes clear here, that the situation can be explained in this or that way depending on which cultural dimension is used for the explanation. This shows that in this case only empirical studies have an actual explanatory value.

The "interaction speed test task" is very abstract and is not related to driver navigation systems. Figure 15 shows the screen shot of this test task.

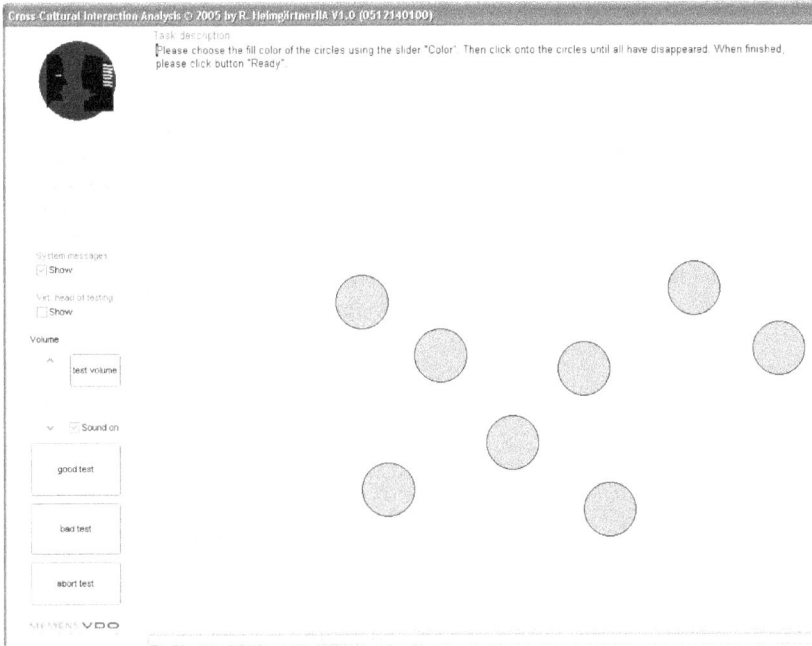

Figure 15: Abstract "interaction speed test task"

"Interaction speed test task"

The user has to click away at 16 randomly arranged points on the screen to measure interaction speed and sequentiality (clicking order). Similar to this test task is the "interaction exactness test task", which measures the same parameters, but displays the points sequentially one by one (to measure the clicking exactness, i.e. a deviation factor from the middle of the button). Thereby, the following PCIIs can be measured (according to the generated hypothesis in section 4.3.3 and to PMICHMID in section 4.4):

Relevance of test tasks for PCIIs

- Average time from clicking on one point to another. It is expected that this time is shorter for Chinese than for German users because of hypotheses INH1c, INH5/8/10 and IH10 (cf. section 4.3.3).
- Sequence of clicking on the points (linear for German, non-linear for Chinese because of hypotheses INH6b, IH1d and INH1d).

- Exactness of clicking the point in the middle. It is supposed that German users are clicking more exactly than Chinese users because of hypotheses INH1c, INH10 and IH5.
- Number of interaction breaks during doing the test task is expected to be lower for German users than for Chinese users because of hypotheses IH1a and IH7.
- Time between information presentation and next user interaction with the system (user response time). This period should be shorter for Chinese than for German users because of hypotheses INH8, INH6, INH1c1 and INH1c as well as IH10.
- Test task duration. Should be shorter for Chinese users than for German users because of hypotheses IH1c, IH6 and IH10 as well as INH6 and INH1c.

The user also has the possibility to specify his requirements for widget position directly and visually by designing the layout of the GUI by changing the widget position in the "user requirement design (URD) test task" (cf. Figure 16).

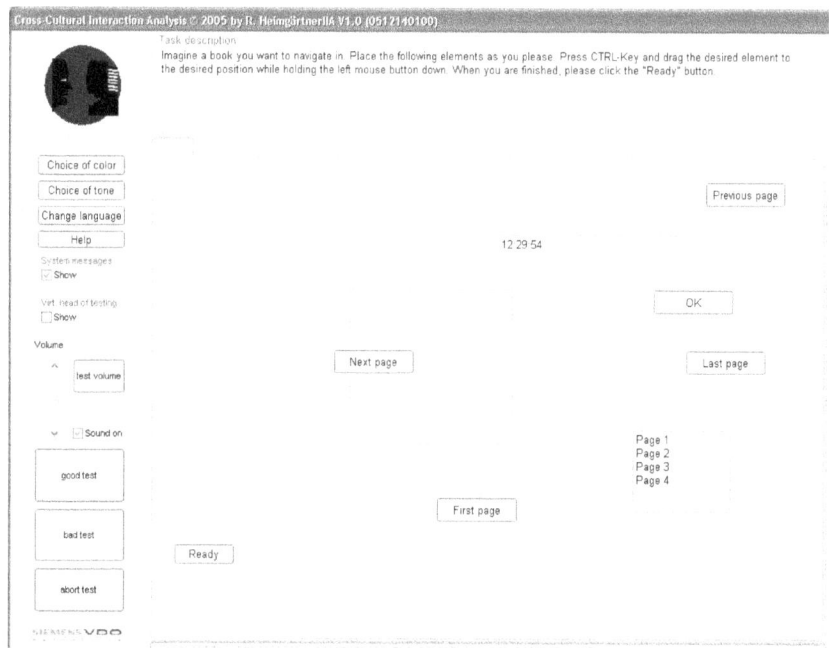

Figure 16: Changeable GUI integrated into the URD test task

Here, the following PCIIs can be determined:

- Position of widgets. According to hypotheses IH1a, IH1b1, IH1d and INH1d, it is assumed that German users arrange widgets rather mono-causally and with greater spatial distance to each other than Chinese users do.
- Duration of the drag and drop process. German users should need more time than Chinese users for the drag and drop process because of hypotheses INH1c2 and INH6b.
- Moving speed. Hypothesis INH1c2 implies that Chinese users move the dragged widget faster than German users.
- Sequence of handling the widget. Supposed to be linear for German users in contrast to Chinese users because of hypotheses IH1d and INH1d.
- Number of function initiations (e.g., during testing the widget functions after finishing their arrangement). Supposed to be lower for German users than for Chinese users because of hypotheses IN6b and INH6b.
- Sequence of function initiations (e.g., during testing the widget functions after finishing its arrangement). Supposed to be linear for German users in contrast to be non-linear for Chinese users because of hypotheses IH1d and INH1d.

Determination of PCIIs

The presented test tasks exemplified the functionality of the IIA tool.[197] In the next section, the procedure of collecting data with the IIA tool is explained.

---

[197] The screenshots of the remaining test tasks can be found in section 10.3.4 in the work report.

[198] The course of data collection flow is presented in section 5.3 in the work report.

5.3   Data Collection with the IIA Tool: Setup, Test Setting and Usage

Test setting, test procedure

In this section, the setup of the IIA tool, the test setting as well as the test procedure is presented in detail.[198] The test participant (SV employees) downloaded the IIA data collection module via the corporate intranet of SV locally on his computer, started the tool and completed all the test tasks. Before closing the tool, the collected data was transferred automatically onto a non-public and secure network drive on a SV server by the IIA tool.

Principle of usage of IIA tool

Figure 17 shows the principle of the usage of the IIA tool.[199]

---

[199] The aspects of the operative process can be found in detail in the online appendix in file "050919 Datenerhebung.igx". To view *.igx-files, please use the IGX-Viewer or e.g., the software "IGrafx Process" (URL = http://www.igrafx.de/products/viewerplus/index.html, last access 7/9/11).

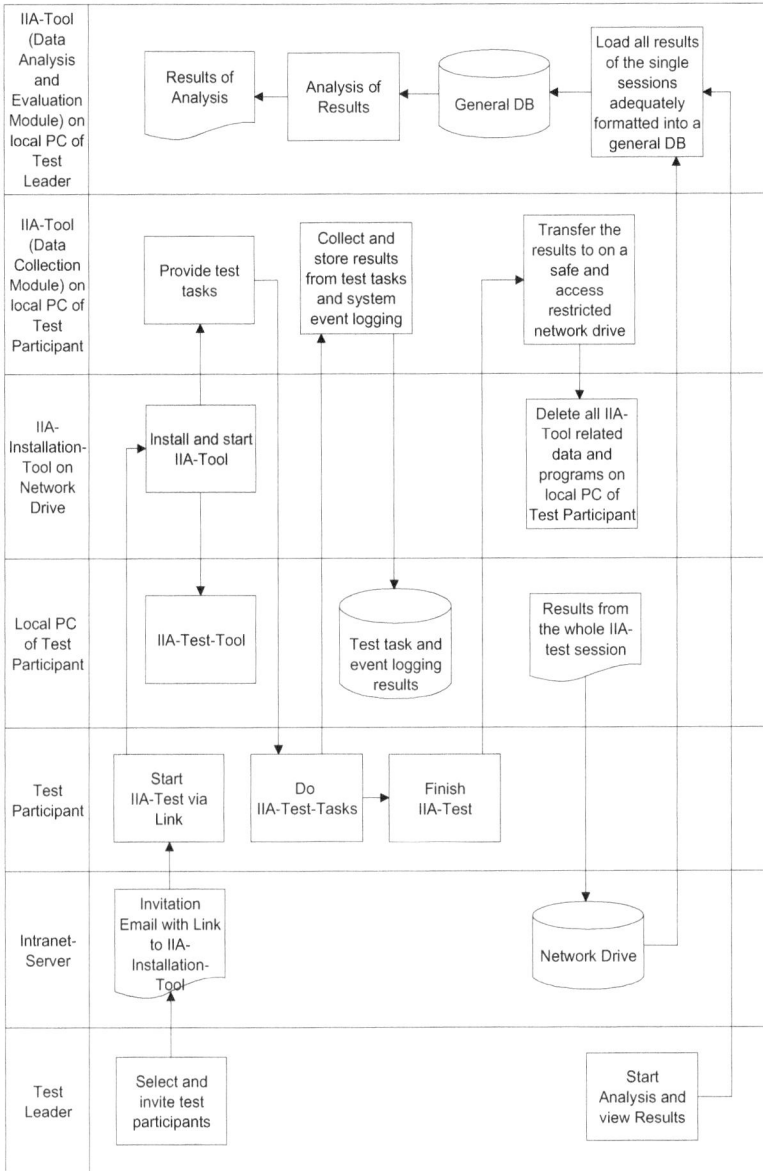

Figure 17: Principle of the usage of the IIA tool

The method of asking many users online by letting them do test tasks (use cases) and then collecting the qualitative data (user preferences) which emerged quantitatively through this process has mainly been used for Chinese

Use cases for quantitative data collection

(C), English (E) and German (G) speaking employees of Siemens VDO worldwide.

Test setting

The tests were carried out on the computer belonging to test persons, in which the test system had been installed automatically after confirmation of the participation of the test persons in the test. Therefore, the user could use his own PC and was not under time pressure to do the test because there was no need to use a foreign test device within predefined time slots. In the case of difficulties in understanding, the test participants could use the online help. The individual test meetings lasted for approximately 45-90 minutes and always took place using the same scheme.[200] Every meeting recorded all system events regarding usage of the keyboard and mouse as well as taking a screenshot after finishing every test task. Furthermore, the collected data is prepared for subsequently statistical analysis in SPSS using CSV format. The IIA analysis module instructs the data loader module to extract, load and prepare the data from the general database for analysis. The outputs of the IIA analysis module are network diagrams presenting the average parameters of the data collection, comparing different nationalities, countries or cultures.[201] Using the IIA data analysis module, the data could be analyzed anonymously, i.e. without using the personal data of the participants.[202]

Test session

A test session with the IIA data collection module comprised five main parts: collecting the demographic data, executing the test tasks, surveying the cultural values of the user, cross-checking the test results of the user and debriefing. Figure 18 reveals the IIA test procedure containing the sequence of test tasks presented to the test participant.[203]

---

[200] The average duration to complete the IIA test is 48 minutes for (C) and 55 minutes for (G) (cf. variable "Duration of Test" (mean in seconds) in Table 49 in the appendix).

[201] Cf. "cultural HCI fingerprints" in Table 30 in section 6.6.3.

[202] The data collection was agreed and approved by the working council of SiemensVDO for the duration of the dissertation project. After the dissertation grant at SiemensVDO, data was made anonymous, i.e. data that contained personal information of the employees were deleted. This allowed for post-project analysis of the anonymous backup data as well as the publication of results that do not allow the reader to obtain knowledge of or reference to the test participants.

[203] The brackets enclose the file names containing the source code of the modules written in Delphi7.

IIA Test Procedure	Select test language (choicelangform2.pas) → Agreement declaration (identdata.pas) → Identification page (identdata.pas) → Test description (testdescr.pas) ↓

Figure showing flowchart of test procedure with boxes:

- Select test language (choicelangform2.pas) → Agreement declaration (identdata.pas) → Identification page (identdata.pas) → Test description (testdescr.pas)
- Information order (infoorder.pas) ← Demographic Data Collection (userdata.pas) ← Selection of widget colors (options2.pas) ← Selection of tone types (options.pas)
- Information speed (infospeed.pas) → Interruption tolerance (irtol.pas) → Interaction exactness (interexact.pas) → Interaction speed (interspeed.pas)
- Map Display Test Task (poi.pas) ← User Requirement Design (Arranging widgets) (urd.pas) ← Information hierarchy (infohier.pas) ← Interaction sequentiality (interseq.pas)
- Information Tolerance (sensedisturb.pas) → Information sequentiality (comic.pas) → Debriefing questionnaire (endques.pas) → Result evaluation (testrep.pas)

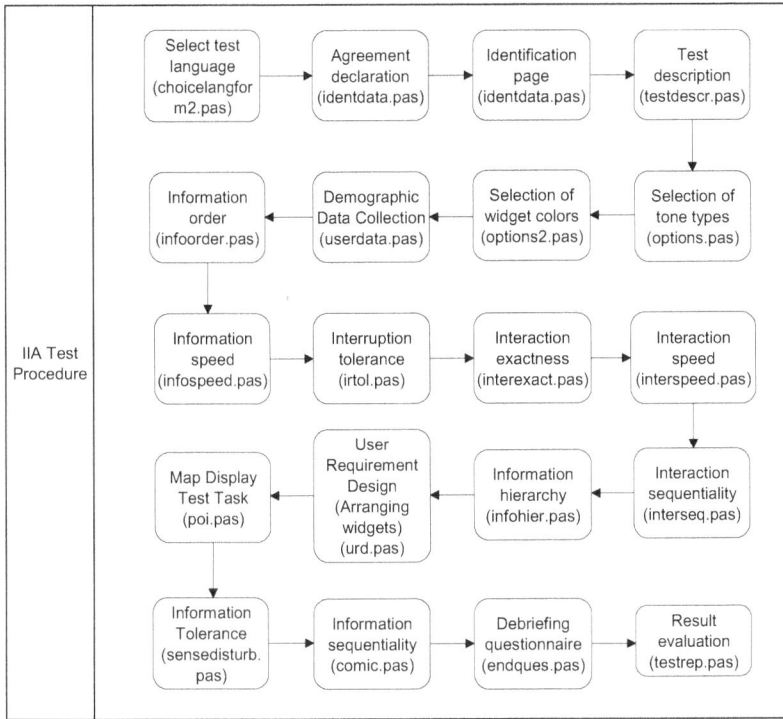

Figure 18: Test procedure of an IIA test session

After the start of the IIA data collection module, the user firstly had to select his preferred test language, i.e. the language in which the test takes place.[204]

Afterwards, acknowledgements and a legend will be presented followed by a declaration of consent from the users that the data collected from them may be used in this dissertation project. If a user disagreed, no personal data was collected: the data collection was then anonymous.

To analyze the cultural characteristics of the users, the value survey module (VSM94) has to be filled in by the user (cf. Hofstede 1994). The VSM94 contains 26 questions to determine the values of the cultural dimensions using the indices of Hofstede that characterize the cultural behavior of the users.[205]

Test proceeding:

Choice of test language

Declaration of consent

Answer questions of VSM94 (indices of Hofstede)

---

[204] Cf. also Figure 16 in section 5.3 in the work report.

[205] The VSM94 (Value Survey Model) has been established by Hofstede 1994. At least 20 participants per country are necessary to obtain reliable results from the VSM test. The ques-

The questions are implemented within the IIA data collection module using a questionnaire module with a flexible layout (cf. Figure 19).[206]

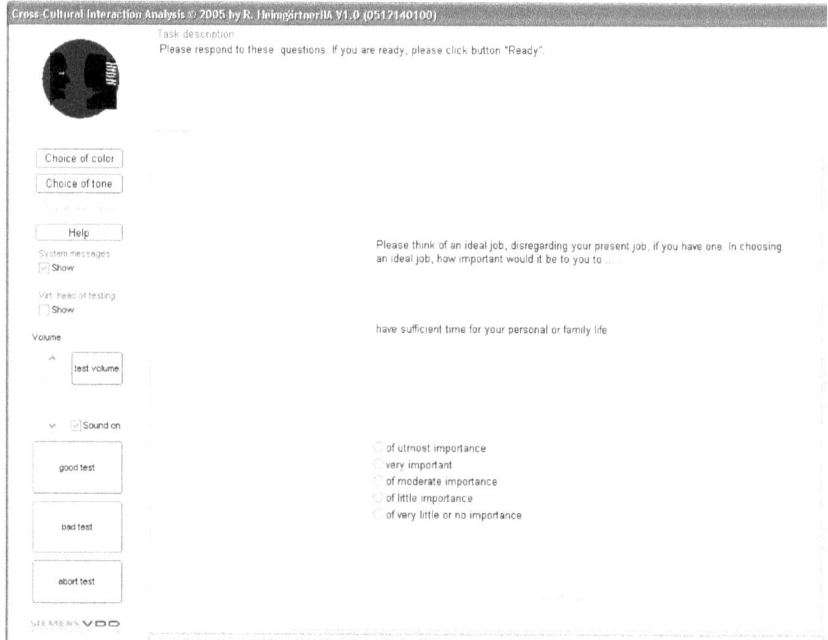

Figure 19: VSM94 questions in the IIA data collection module

Not only the contents of the questions but also the kind of the questions can be defined (nominal, ordinal, interval, with or without qualitative reason or text box, with or without numerical display, checkboxes or radio buttons) controlled by an excel sheet.

Results of VSM94 re-checked by test participant

After this, the results of the VSM94 and those of the test tasks are presented to the user who has to estimate whether or not the cultural, informational and interactional values found correlate or match with him.

tions in the VSM questionnaire can be seen in section 10.2.7 "IIA Questionnaire (Final questions in the IIA data collection tool)" in the work report (questions 1-23). The remaining demographical questions have been raised via the "special" demographic questionnaire (cf. Figure 18 in section 5.3 in the work report).

[206] Cf. also file "050815 IIA-Erhebungskonzept.doc" in the online appendix.

A part of the IIA data analysis module (integrated in the IIA data collection module) computes the most important coefficients regarding information speed, information density, information order, information sequentiality, interaction speed and interaction exactness as well as relationship-orientation, uncertainty avoidance and power distance using formulae derived from the hypotheses generated in chapter 4.[207] The preliminary results of the values of the cultural dimensions and of the HMI dimensions (HMIDs) are presented to the test user via progress bars. The test user can judge these values and decide if they are correct or not. He can enter the expected values estimated on his own using scroll bars to the right of the presented results.[208]

This method allows verification of the results as well as the formulae used to compute the results, and hence, allows verification of the hypotheses postulated in this work, cross validating along the statistical analysis of the collected data.

Verification of hypotheses

Cross validation along statistical analysis

The debriefing part reveals the purpose of the test to the test participant in detail. It collects data regarding the usability of the test system, the perceived difficulty of the test in general and whether the test person has recognized the implemented hypotheses in the test tasks during the test session, as well as e.g., recording the physical conditions of the test environment.

Debriefing part

5.4 Data Analysis Concept and Data Analysis

The data analysis concept gives an overview of the methods and means that are used to analyze the collected data obtained by applying the contents of the data collection concept. It provides methods to transform the content of an operative database filled solely with numbers into an informative database containing usable results by automatically predefined interpretation rules of the numbers. Only one person (the author) has access to the data and to the

Automatic data collection via IIA tool

---

[207] These formulae have not been verified because of time restrictions. Therefore, they cannot be shifted into the focus of this work. Furthermore, much research needs to be done on them in the future to obtain mature and reliable formulae containing adequate rules regarding the connection between cultural aspects and HMI dimensions as shown in section 8.6.7 in the work report. Nevertheless, first trials of preliminary formulae representing possible parts of adaptation rules for CAHMI that have been used within the IIA tool to compute the values for the "self-evaluation test task" in section 10.3.4 in the work report can be found in the work report in section 10.6.3.

[208] Cf. the screenshot „self-evaluation test task" in section 10.3.4 in the work report.

resulting information.[209] Descriptive and explanatory statistics, correlations and explorative or confirmatory factor analysis have been used to explore cultural differences in the user interaction as well as to find a cultural interaction model using structural equation modeling, data mining methods and statistics. Processing of the gathered data was carried out largely automatically via the IIA data collection module itself due to the well elaborated data structure concept.[210] The data was checked for plausibility and filed in a reasonably predefined format into a result database.[211]

Statistic software SPSS

The statistic software SPSS from V12.0 onwards was used for the analysis of the data. Several statistical methods had been applied to analyze the collected data: ANOVA, Kruskal-Wallis test, explorative factor analysis, discriminance analysis as well as multidimensional scaling and structural equation models.[212]

One-way ANOVA

One-way ANOVA as a statistical method for comparing the means of more than two independent samples was used to identify significant cultural differences in variables, which are distributed normally. The results of the test of homogeneity of variances indicate whether ($p>.05$) or not ($p\leq.05$) the variables are distributed normally. The potential variables that are distributed normally can be analyzed by ANOVA.

Tukey-HSD-Hoc test

The interactional differences between the user groups separated by the primary cultural imprint (e.g., using test language or nationality, cf. independent variable in section 5.1.1) can be identified using the Tukey-HSD-Post-Hoc test after one-way ANOVA.

---

[209] This was the requirement of the working council of Siemens VDO because of information security reasons to allow the conduction of this study at SV. Only the software developer responsible for the IIA tool (the author) knew the user name and password. This helped to increase assurance that no other person than the author had access to the gathered data as required by the working council of SV.

[210] Cf. sections 10.2.6 and 10.2.7 in the work report.

[211] Cf. work report in section 10.2.6 for the database format. More information about the data loader and the IIA data evaluation module as well as the software itself can be found in the online appendix in the files "dataloader.bmp", "IIA_SQL-Anfragen.txt", "ergebnisdaten.txt" and "IIA data evaluation module.bmp". The features of the IIA data collection and analysis modules together have been described in section 5.2. Cf. also section 5.2 in the work report.

[212] Cf. Bortz & Weber 2005, Arbuckle 2005, Backhaus et al. 2006, Lienert et al. 1998, Burzan 2005, Bühner 2004. It has to be considered whether one should reduce the alpha value adequately at the variety of the planned tests (multiple test problems, Bonferroni correction). At this point, I like to thank Ferenc Acs as well as Michael Wiedenbeck for their valuable hints regarding the application of statistical methods including structural equation models within this dissertation project.

For the remaining variables, which are not distributed normally, the Kruskal-Wallis test has to be applied to identify the differences in the mean values. The analysis of the empirically collected data comparing the average values using the IIA data analysis module, SPSS and neural networks within the IIA data evaluation module indicated whether the parameters really do depend on culture or not.

Kruskal-Wallis test

In addition, factor analysis served to structure and to select the derivation of the cultural interaction indicators of the HMI dimensions relevant for HMI design. According to Langer 2002, explorative factor analysis allows checking of the measuring relations of a hypothetic model of variables like the one used in this work (cf. PMICHMID in section 4.4). Therefore, explorative factor analysis can be used to determine the correctness of the conducted classification of the parameters into factors (i.e. into HMI dimensions derived from the dimensions "information" and "interation", cf. section 4.2).[213]

Explorative factor analysis

The objective of factor analysis is the grouping and reduction of the information quantity (judgments, questions and variables), simultaneously ensuring and protecting information content. The main tasks of factor analysis in this work are:

- Grouping variables to "factors" according to their correlation strength,
- Identifying variables / factors that correlate highly with HMI dimensions (HMIDs) or strongly predict them,
- Filtering of variables with a low explanation value in regard to the factor or the HMIDs they represent,
- Declaring variables to indicators on the basis of factor and item analysis as well as reflections regarding content,
- Deducing indicators representing (parts of) the HMIDs.

The methods used for these purposes (explorative factor analysis, regression analysis and item analysis) are all feasible in SPSS. Cluster analysis for classification or linear regression for correlations can be exploited to find

Mix of statistical methods

---

[213] Cf. Day 1991; Backhaus et al. 2006 for detailed explanations of the methods and usage of factor analysis. For the structure of "work values" as well as creating them for factor analysis, please refer to Holoch 1999. Cf. also Backhaus et al. 2006 as well as Hox & Bechger 1998. Good examples of using explorative factor analysis can be found in Wentura 2005. Further information can be also found in section 6.6.1 in the work report. In section 6.6.1 in the work in hand, the validity of the HMIDs found is discussed using explorative factor analysis.

correlations between the recorded cross-cultural user interaction data and the specific values of the cultural variables (cf. Kamentz & Mandl 2003).[214]

Structural equation models in AMOS

Structural equation models (SEM) belong to the statistical methods of confirmative factor analysis, which can be performed using e.g., AMOS.[215] It should be possible to optimize the model of culturally dependent variables for the HMI design using structural equation modeling. According to Kenny 1979, a structural equation model consists of a set of equations. The effect or endogenous variable is on the left side and on the right side is the sum of the causes with each causal variable multiplied by a causal parameter.

Neural networks to enhance plausibility of quantitative results

Furthermore, neural networks are used within the IIA evaluation module to verify and establish trends of cultural differences in the user interaction.[216] The IIA data evaluation module provides neural networks that can help to enhance the plausibility of quantitative results. For example, it might not be important which subjects take part in a test, if adequate neural networks are used, which can independently learn existing trends.[217] Therefore, such networks do not care about which test persons take part in the test. By connecting the categorized grouped test data according to the HMI dimensions to the input neurons and the cultural characteristics (represented e.g. by variables like nationality,

---

[214] The statistical methods commonly used in most scientific disciplines are explained in depth in Bortz & Weber 2005. Hence, they will not be explained in detail in this work. The more elaborated methods like factor analysis, structural equation models and neural networks will be explained to the degree that is necessary to apply them within this work. A very good overview with basic explanations of all statistical methods is given in the white paper of StatSoft for their statistic software (cf. Hill & Lewicki 2006). Grotjahn 2001 explains the basics of test theory regarding the measuring of the reliability, parallel test reliability as well as the retest reliability. Inner consistency of a test can be checked by analyzing the test splitting reliability or performing consistency analysis using Cronbach's alpha. Naumann et al. 2000 described how to design questionnaires and Nissen 2003 explained neural networks and their usage employing the fast artificial neural network library (FANN), which has been accessed by IIA data analysis and IIA data evaluation module. For more information about the statistical methods for multivariate analysis, please refer to Backhaus et al. 2006.

[215] AMOS is short for "analysis of moment structures". It is a statistical tool for data analysis providing structural equation modeling (SEM). For further details about AMOS and how to use it, please refer to Arbuckle 2005 as well as to Byrne 2001.

[216] The procedure described here, has been implemented in the newly generated FTE tool by the author to analyze the relationship between cultural imprint and interaction behavior of the user via neural networks. More information about the FTE tool can be found in the files "060529 FTE Processes.igx" and "060612 Fortuna Evaluation Flow.igx" in the online appendix.

[217] E.g., back propagation networks (cf. Rumelhart 1986) or self-organizing maps (cf. Kohonen 2001). Please refer e.g., to Haykin 2008 for a comprehensive foundation of neural networks. Cf. also Heimgärtner 2002 for a simplified exemplification of some aspects of neural networks.

mother tongue, etc.) of the users to the output neurons of the neural network, training of the network will reveal if there is a correlation of the HMI dimensions at the inputs and the culture at the output of the neural network. In other words, if cultural differences do exist, i.e. if there is a correlation between the corresponding test data of the test persons and the culture at the output of the neural network, the neural network will learn and reveal it. By means of connecting test data which is categorized or grouped according to hypotheses and the cultural variables to the output of the neural network, it will identify whether cultural differences exist or not. Thereby, on the one hand, it can be seen whether a correlation exists between the test data from the subject of a test at the inputs of the neural network and his cultural imprint at the outputs of the neural network. On the other hand, it should be possible to capture the correlation of the HMI dimensions at the input of the neural network and the culture indicated at the output of the neural network. Furthermore, neural networks can be used for the generation of hypotheses by applying the method of monitored learning.[218]

Finally, the data analyzed for the qualitative and quantitative studies that revealed a trend for the investigated cultures (cf. sections 6.1 and 6.2) will be described in detail at the relevant places in this work where required.

Further explanation of data analysis where required

---

[218] Please refer to section 5.4 in the work report for further reflections.

6   Cultural Differences in Human Computer Interaction

"Bättre twå gånger mätet, än en gång förgätet."
(Swedish saying)[219]

In this chapter, the qualitative offline studies (cf. section 6.1) and the quantitative online studies (cf. section 6.2) conducted using the IIA tool within this dissertation project and their results will be presented. Furthermore, the influence of disturbing variables (section 6.3) and the cultural imprint of the test participants (section 6.4) are shown. The most important empirical hypotheses (cf. section 4.3.3) will be verified as well (section 6.5). Finally, the reliability and validity of the results are discussed (cf. section 6.6). Thereby, the values of the intercultural variables and the selectivity (discriminatory power) of the information HMI dimensions (HMIDs) and their plausibility will also be investigated.

6.1   Pre-Studies: Capturing Impressions by Qualitative Studies

Pre-studies

Qualitative studies were planned to verify and support the results of the two main quantitative online studies (cf. section 6.2). However, in fact they served as pre-studies before doing the two quantitative online studies in this work. In spite of their small sample sizes as well as the limited resources to do them locally in several countries (e.g. lacking time to find and train test leaders

---

[219] "It is better to measure twice than to forget it once." (cf. file "Sprichwörter mit messen.txt" in the online appendix).

speaking the mother tongue), they provided some interesting results helping to verify the two main online studies that will be presented in section 6.2. A benchmark test, questionnaires, a focus group and usability tests (pilot studies with the IIA tool) have been carried out. To evaluate the usability of HMI, an additional tool was developed by the author.[220] Moreover, at Siemens VDO in Huizhou (China) a focus group was held with Chinese employees of Siemens VDO regarding questions about HMI design. In Regensburg (Germany), the requirements for driver navigation systems were discussed with German users in three focus group sessions.[221]

Several usability tests with students were conducted with the IIA tool as well as with the CAHMI demonstrator with both Chinese and German test participants in Hangzhou (China) as well as in Regensburg, Augsburg and Aachen (Germany).[222]

Usability tests

In addition, before doing the main online tests, a pilot test was carried out with German test subjects to reveal faults in the test settings of the IIA tool, such as problems with the formulation and the operation of the test. Some mistakes were eliminated, such as the incorrect formulation of the wording or the translation. No great difficulties were found regarding the understanding of the test tasks and the operation of the test. However, the results from the pilot tests could only serve as preliminary indications for further studies. The usability pretests with the IIA tool took place at the workplaces of the test subjects.

Pilot test

The test setting in the offline pilot studies was similar to those for the online tests described in section 5.3. In contrast to the online studies, the pre-studies were carried out using a single and specially prepared notebook. In addition, to recording all system events regarding the usage of the keyboard and mouse within a session also a video of the screen as well as the user in front of the computer has been captured. A task was set up at a table on which the notebook computer was placed with the test software installed (the IIA tool, cf. section 5.2). Two chairs were ready for the test person and the test leader so that the test leader could watch the events on the screen and perhaps step in if any problems arose. Before each meeting, the necessary material (test log,

Test setting in offline pilot studies

---

[220] Cf. screenshots of the ISO9421-Usability-Testing-Tool in the online appendix in the files "Usability-Testing-Tool_s1.bmp" and "Usability-Testing-Tool_s2.bmp".

[221] However, these results are the property of Siemens VDO and may not be published in this work. Nevertheless, the results inspired and influenced the work of the author.

[222] For further information on the qualitative studies as well as the tools programmed for this purpose, please refer to the work report (cf. sections 10.2, 10.3 and 10.5 in the work report as well as the file "Used Tools.doc" in the online appendix). Additional information about the pre-studies can be found in section 6.1 in the work report.

legend and posttest questionnaire) was prepared and the subject of the test was instructed. First, the test person was welcomed and some words were exchanged to create a more familiar atmosphere. After that, the purpose and the goal of the test were explained. The necessity for the video and screen recording was pointed out to the test person. Before processing of the tasks, consent was secured from the test person for the video and screen recording and general details about the person were collected. It was checked if the video was on and the test system was started. The participant was asked to read an additional introductory text himself. The test person himself started the test. Then, the processing of the test tasks was carried out. The test subjects had to be reminded by the test leader to express their thoughts aloud.[223] In the case of comprehension difficulties the test leader answered questions.[224] All participants were asked after finishing the test tasks how he had found the test and whether processing problems had appeared. Furthermore, they were asked to complete the questionnaire with general questions about the test. Test persons were given the opportunity to make general remarks about the test. To thank the test participants, each received a Siemens VDO gift from the test leader.[225]

Pre-study in China and Germany

The first efforts were made to identify cultural differences in HCI scanning interaction behavior in April 2005 by doing a very small local offline heuristic pre-study in Huizhou (China) and in Regensburg (Germany) with 9 Chinese (C) and 13 German (G) students and employees of Siemens VDO. The purpose of this study was to check the intercultural usability of the IIA tool for Chinese and German users. This qualitative offline pre-study, done by means of participative observation and personal interviews after the test sessions (as described above), showed very interesting preliminary results regarding culturally dependent differences in using the IIA tool running on single computer systems. Some of the results (e.g., number of error clicks and interaction speed) were confirmed later by the two online studies that have been conducted subsequently to verify the functionality and reliability of the IIA tool and to identify cultural differences in HCI in detail (cf. section 6.2).

Results

Differences were found (cf. Figure 20) in the interaction with the computer between C and G regarding the order of pictures (more ordered by G than by C, test duration (longer for C), error clicks (C more than G) and telling the

---

[223] In the online studies, a virtual test leader ("Merlin") was used instead of a real test leader locally on the spot (cf. screenshot "Greeting Screen" in section 10.3.4 in the work report).

[224] In the online studies, the test participants could press the online help button instead of asking a real test leader locally on the spot.

[225] In the online study, the gift was sent to the participant when the test provided valid test data that could be used for data analysis. They had been selected by random (cf. section 6.2).

truth regarding computer experience (C understated their experience significantly). Furthermore, the speed of doing the same tasks (clicking away dots with the mouse as explained in section 5.2.2., cf. also Figure 15) was done faster by C, hence exhibiting higher "interaction speed" than G. G clicked the dots more centered than C which indicates higher interaction exactness. However, C needed longer for the tests than G. This could have been due to the poor comprehensibility of the Chinese translation at this time. However, the quality of the Chinese translation was improved by experienced Chinese software developers of SV for the online studies. Therefore, the test duration in the second online data collection was considerably shorter for the Chinese employees from SV. This is mainly be the consequence of improvement in the usability of the IIA data collection tool by the results from the usability tests done in the previous quantitative pre-study (e.g., improvement of wording and comprehensibility of test tasks).[226]

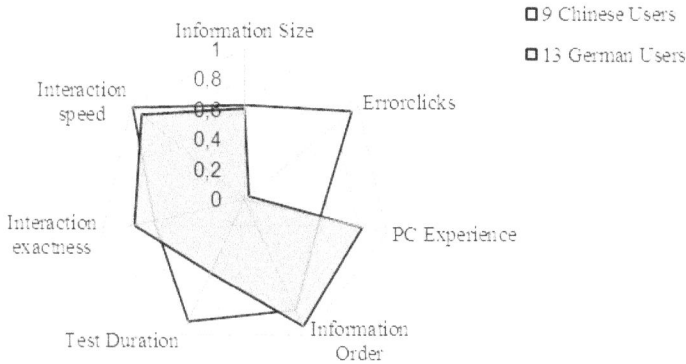

Figure 20: Results of the pilot study using the IIA tool (Source: files "mittelwerttest.spo" and "050726 Ergebnisse Pilotstudie.xlsx" in the online appendix)[227]

---

[226] I thank Mrs. Jia Zhang very much for supporting this task by translating all texts into Chinese as well as giving valuable hints for the comprehensibility of the test tasks for Chinese users.

[227] To view the SPSS output files (*.spv or *.spo) in the online appendix, please use the 'IBM SPSS Smartreader' or the 'SPSS legacy viewer' by downloading the file available from

Findings by usability tests

The most important findings of these offline studies regarding the intercultural usability of the IIA tool concerned language (English and especially Chinese) because of suboptimal information processing like wrong translations, missing/weak or insufficient visual attractiveness of the task descriptions or of the questions in the questionnaires, inconsistent entries for selection, and unclear wording or denotation of function names. Furthermore, technical problems, which occurred, have been fixed e.g., on recording the results of the questionnaire in the database or the lack of logging important events or values; excessive test session length; sound was turned down; different screen resolutions depending on the system; missing explanations, answering boxes or widgets and interaction means (e.g., the report evaluation test task needed progress indication and slide bars).[228] The findings led to modification requests in the test design and to the optimization of the implementation of test tasks within the IIA tool.[229]

Rectification of test tasks and IIA tool

Benchmark test with Japanese driver navigation system

A benchmark test (qualitative research by device tests) with a Japanese driver navigation system (J_{DNS}) sold in China (because at the time of doing this benchmark test in 2005 no driver navigation systems made in China were available) and a German driver navigation system (G_{DNS})[230] was conducted by the author in August 2005 using main parts of the questionnaire developed by Kamentz & Mandl 2003 for qualitatively evaluating a GUI according to cultural differences.[231] A Chinese employee[232] at Siemens VDO in Regensburg

---

SPSS web page at URL = http://www-01.ibm.com/support/docview.wss?uid=swg21479879, (last access 5/09/11).

[228] Please refer for details to the scanned hand written usability protocols from March to October 2005 in files "IIA-Usability-Tests.pdf" and "IIA-Usability-Tests2.pdf" in the online appendix.

[229] For the settings of the usability tests with the IIA tool as well as the findings and modification requests, please refer to the modification request list among other things for optimizing usability in the file "050425 IIA-Reqirements.xls" in the online appendix (cf. also section 8.6.1 in the work report).

[230] The Japanese system was "RNS-CN1 VW AN1" from Aisin AW Co Ltd. for VW. The German system was "E60 CCC D1 Sample B4502 (with pre-rendered images for China)" from Siemens VDO for BMW.

[231] The questionnaire is available online at URL = http://www.uni-hildesheim.de/~womser/ Lehre/WS01HSBewertung.pdf and URL = http://www.uni-hildesheim.de/media/ifas/ WS01HSBewertung.pdf, last access 2/28/09. For a very detailed and theoretically founded catalogue of criteria for the evaluation of learning software, please refer to Gottfried et al. 2002.

[232] I thank the test leader Mrs. Cia Luo Xin very much for her support.

evaluated the differences in HMI between the systems answering 229 questions using a special tool for this purpose developed by the author.[233]

Minimal differences in quantitative interpretation by the test leader were found. Even if, according to the subjective impression of the test leader[234], there are qualitative differences regarding degree of personalization ($J_{DNS} > G_{DNS}$), system feedback ($J_{DNS} > G_{DNS}$), help information ($J_{DNS} > G_{DNS}$) and system messages to be acknowledged ($J_{DNS} > G_{DNS}$) (which are also in line with the results of the two online studies presented in section 6.2), there are only minimal deviations between the two devices over all questions (<10%, cf. Figure 21) that can be recognized quantitatively regarding e.g., the following aspects:

Minimal quantitative differences

- Fewer vs. many maps (J_{DNS} : 42, G_{DNS} : 50) [235]
- Less vs. much usage of color (J_{DNS}: 75, G_{DNS}: 80)
- Continuous text vs. enumeration (J_{DNS} : 53, G_{DNS} : 49)
- Fewer vs. many objects of direct manipulation (Japanese: 80, G_{DNS} : 77)
- Fewer vs. many pictures (J_{DNS}: 81, G_{DNS}: 86)
- Low vs. high uniqueness (J_{DNS}: 31, G_{DNS}: 34)
- Textual links vs. iconic links (J_{DNS}: 90, G_{DNS}: 91)
- Fewer vs. many help texts (J_{DNS}: 19, G_{DNS}: 20)
- Short vs. long dialog cycles (J_{DNS}: 434, G_{DNS}: 475).

Hence, the data obtained by this benchmark test needs a great deal of interpretation effort, which results in different implications.[236] This indicates that the differences found cannot be considered as highly significant. Furthermore, obviously the results are also not very meaningful because the judgments of the systems did not differentiate enough (cf. Figure 21).

Results by benchmark test questionable

---

[233] A screenshot of this tool is shown in Figure 21 in section 6.1 in the work report.

[234] Cf. the handwritten and scanned notes in the file "Benchmark_JDNS_GDNS.pdf" in the online appendix made from the interview by the author with the test leader.

[235] The range of the slide bar to set an answer value was from 0 to 100 except for the duration of dialog cycles (cf. files "Questions.mdb", "Fragen Deutsch Transponiert Optimiert2.xls", as well as "fragebogen_ergebnisse.txt" in the online appendix).

[236] Moreover, interpreting similar things (like the small differences in the benchmark test) is very questionable for resching reasonable conclusions because the test results were interpreted employing much mental effort influenced by different cognitive styles, cultural backgrounds and real-world knowledge of the individual interpreter.

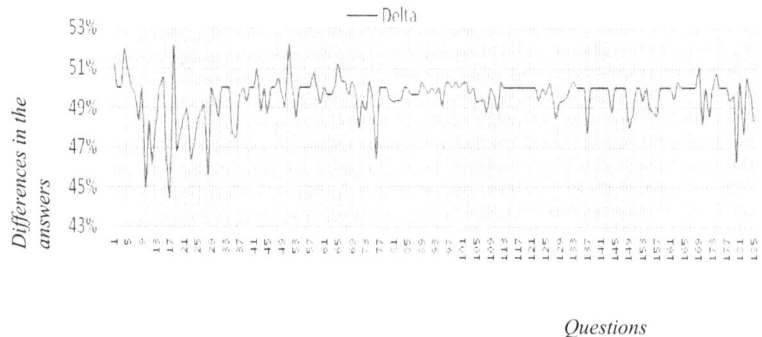

Figure 21: Delta of the HMI benchmark test between a Japanese and a German driver navigation system using an adapted version of the questionnaire developed by Kamentz & Mandl 2003 (Source: file "Questions.mdb" in the online appendix)

Hence, it is not recommended to use the results from this benchmark test, to support a well founded tendency of differences in the values of the HMI dimensions or any other variable relevant for intercultural HMI design at the interactional level of localization, i.e. apart from the superficial and functional level of localization (cf. section 2.3.7).

Qualitative studies amplified impressions about cultural differences in HMI

Another qualitative study with 20 Chinese students at Zhejiang University in Hangzhou in China from 3/6/06 to 3/20/06 confirmed the impression that there are cultural differences in HMI as well as in the perspectives of topics in intercultural HMI design. Finally, however, only eight test data sets were completely recorded and analyzed.[237] Hence, this qualitative study also has only a preliminary character like the other qualitative studies conducted in this work because they must be interpreted as strongly subjective, are not easy to reproduce and exhibit less reliable results.

In general, it seems that it is very difficult to obtain comparable results regarding user interaction by doing qualitative studies of this kind. It is much easier to interpret the results from observation and counting simply by comparing numbers in purely quantitative studies. Hence, using quantitative methods in this work (permanent and attentive observation by automatic test tools) is more adequate to identify cultural differences in HMI: to analyze the interaction of the user with the system, which is highly dynamical and there-fore only recognizable over time (cf. section 2.3.4), it is more reliable to monitor the user behavior (e.g., interaction style, information processing

---

[237] The summarized results are presented in section 6.1 in the work report.

characteristics) than to ask the user (cf. methodological discussion in section 8.1).[238]

Nevertheless, the qualitative studies yield valuable indications about the possible results from the main quantitative online studies presented in the next section.

6.2   Main Studies: Two Temporally Separated Online Surveys

Two online studies separated in date by one year (the first in 2006 and the second in 2007) served to identify the preferences of users according to their cultural background (especially regarding their interaction behavior) and to verify the functionality and reliability of the IIA tool. Randomly selected employees from Siemens VDO all over the world were invited by email to do the test session using the IIA data collection module.[239] Table 21 characterizes the two online studies done in 2006 and 2007 with 15100 employees of Siemens VDO in total regarding sample size, tests downloaded, tests aborted, valid test data sets and return rate.[240]

Table 21: Characterization of the two online studies conducted with the IIA tool

Stud y	Sample size	Survey period	Number of downloaded tests	Tests aborted [%]	Number of valid test data sets	Overall return rate [%]	Return rate of valid data sets [%]
1	600	12/14/05 - 01/14/06	166	41.5	102	27	16.6
2	14500	11/14/06 - 01/19/07	2803	66.8	916	16	6.3

---

[238] The methodological problems of qualitative and quantitative studies as well as the reliability of their results will be discussed in detail in this work in the sections 6.6 and 8.1.

[239] To motivate the employees to participate in the test, firstly, the author appealed to their cooperativeness as Siemens VDO employees. Secondly, a raffle with small but nice prizes was organized. All participants who delivered valid test data automatically took part in the raffle. The prizes were distributed at the end of the dissertation project. Furthermore, the test results were sent to all interested participants.

[240] For possible explanations about the behavior of respondents, non-respondents and refusers across mail surveys, please refer e.g., to Brennan & Hoek 1992 or to Rogelberg et al. 2001.

Return rates

Out of the 14500 test persons invited to participate in the larger second main study, 2803 downloaded and started the test. This return rate of 19.3% is sufficient for reasonable statistical analysis. 66.8% of the tests were aborted. The remaining 33.2% of the tests were completed by the test persons and analyzed by the author (916 valid data sets).[241] The return quota of 27% in the first survey is relatively high because the employees of Siemens VDO interact globally. In the second survey, the return rate was only 16% because many employees had been informed by their bosses, colleagues and working council, so that it was no longer new and as interesting as in the first study.[242] Therefore, the return rate of valid data sets was 16.6% for the first and only 6.3% for the second survey.[243]

Some tests were aborted due to the following reasons: download time too long[244], no time to do the test now or test is not interesting or appealing.[245] This type of qualitative data can help to optimize the testing equipment or to steer the direction of data analysis by asking the user for the reasons for his behavior during the test e.g., by open questions using text boxes (cf. section 5.2.1).

---

[241] However, not all of the returned 916 valid data sets could be used in every statistical test (e.g., because the data was not normally distributed). Therefore, the sample sizes in the result tables can vary. For example, only 876 data sets derived from the Access database provided by the IIA data Table 49 in the appendix. Furthermore, only 781 data sets were provided from the data loader of the IIA data analysis module after preprocessing and preparing the data for analysis from the log files presented at the end of Table 49.

[242] Additionally, the working council of Siemens interrupted the second online survey for four weeks because of the take-over of Siemens VDO until the statement of affairs with the working council of SV had been clarified and the second online survey was allowed again. This circumstance mostly has presumably decreased the return rate. Furthermore, parts of the study have also been stopped locally in several countries because of different laws independently from the decisions of the working council at SV in Germany.

[243] For more details, please refer to file "070207 Studienüberblick.xls" in the online appendix. It turns out that a period of 1-3 days for data collection after the write up e-mail was sufficient to obtain reasonable return rates. When getting a firmer grip approx. 1 week after the write up e-mail, the complete return quota increased by approx. 30% once again.

[244] High download times were notable in China because of networks with low transmission rates caused by backbones having low bandwidth: the backbone (technical connection) between Europe and Asia had a restricted transmission rate.

[245] Another reason not to do the tests in the second online study could be the general restructuring measures within the organization of Siemens VDO (from Siemens VDO to Siemens and from Siemens back to Siemens VDO). These things became more important than this study, which led to a context in which the dissertation project could not be finished as planned in September 2006. Furthermore, it also became increasingly difficult to recruit unbiased employees to participate over the years because they had already heard about this study.

Only complete and valid data sets were analyzed using the IIA data analysis module and the statistic program SPSS.[246] Table 22 gives an impression of the characterization of the test participants in the two online studies regarding the distribution of samples, nationality, test language, age, gender and experience with PC.[247]

Analysis of complete data sets

Characterization of test participants

Table 22: Characteristics of the test participants in the two online studies

Study	Sample Size	Test Language (C/G/E)	Nationality (Chinese/German/US/Canadian)	Age (<20,20-30, 30-40,>40)	Gender (m/f)	PC experience (no/beginner/ adv./exp.)
1	102	34 : 44 : 24	35 : 39 : 9 : 8	1 : 30 : 37 : 6	83 : 19	2 : 18 : 52 : 30
2	916	105 : 375 : 436	100 : 345 : 133 : 64	6 : 140 : 284 : 138	746 : 170	13 : 159 : 487 : 257

The randomly selected participants in the online studies at SV were employees locally situated in China, the USA, Canada, Germany, France, Romania, Mexico, Czech Republic, India and Brasil (most in Germany, the USA and in China).[248] Participants were matched as closely to the requirements stated in section 5.1.3 having some PC experience and a basic education level that matches the job requirements of SiemensVDO. About 18% were female, 82% male. Their age was between 18 and 64. They all shared the company culture of SiemensVDO.

Employees of Siemens VDO worldwide

To simplify things, it has been assumed that primary language (mother tongue) determines the main cultural background of the user because on average most users do not have experience abroad: therefore, the preferred language used in the IIA test indicated the culture of the user with which he is most familiar with.[249]

Assumption A3

Assumption A3 confirmed

---

[246] For using SPSS, cf. e.g., Kockläuner 2000.

[247] In the work report in section 10.3.3 there are the most important results from SPSS regarding the participants. Cf. also the output-files of SPSS in the online appendix (*.spo and *.spv). The most relevant results will be presented in this section in the work in hand.

[248] Due to the number of SV employees in Germany, the USA and China, it was assumed that most experimentees would be available in these countries, which was confirmed (cf. Figure 22 in section 6.4).

[249] This equals assumption 3 (A3) in section 4.3.1.

Assumption A3 could have been confirmed by the obtained data from the studies: the discrimination rate of classifying the users to their preferred test language (the selected test language from the set of available test languages) by the variables concerning the cultural background of the user's mother tongue, nationality, country of birth and primary residence is 83.3% for the first and 81.9% for the second study.[250]

High correlations between test language and nationality

Therefore, the differences in HCI in these studies were frequently analyzed in relation to three groups of test persons according to the selected test languages (Chinese (C), German (G) and English (E)) in order to reduce data analyzing costs. It is clear that language may not be mistaken for nationality or culture. However, due to the high correlation between test language and nationality, it was permitted to carry out the evaluation of the data sets using the test language for Chinese and German-speaking groups to distinguish the cultural differences at country level.[251]

However, this is not valid for the group of subjects who selected English as test language because this group contained not only one but many nationalities other than German and Chinese. Some tests (e.g., the VSM test) can be and are carried out only regarding the nationality, though (cf. e.g., section 6.4).

---

[250] The discrimination rate was calculated using a discriminance analysis (cross validated and grouped, Wilk's Lambda (cf. Bortz & Weber 2005) in study 1: $\lambda_{1-2}=0.072**$, $\lambda_2=0.568**$, Wilk's Lambda in study 2: $\lambda_{1-2}=0.192**$, $\lambda_2=0.513**$). The level of significance is referenced with asterisks in this work (* $p<0.05$; ** $p<0.01$). For further details, please refer to section 6.6.2, footnote 299 on page 205).

[251] However, even country level does not equal nationality level or level of first residence. This resembles the problem of capturing unambiguous and clear concepts in linguistics (cf. Cohen 1999). However, to be able to work without infinite discussion, one has to make a decision to agree on a certain concept to be used as working definition. The groups to classify in this case are described according to the selected test language.

In the following, the presentation concentrates on the more representative second main study, because about nine times more valid test data sets were available ($n_2 : n_1 = 916 : 102 = 8.98$). Furthermore, the second study mostly mirrored the results of the first study.[252] The differing results will be compared and discussed in detail in this work.[253] Table 23 presents the potential cultural interaction indicators (PCIIs) that have been investigated in the two online studies.[254]

Table 23: Potential Cultural Interaction Indicators (PCIIs) analyzed in the two online studies

Comparison of the Results of the Analyses of the First and the Second Data Collection												
Method	ONEWAY ANOVA						Kruskal-Wallis				Interpreta-tion	Conclusion
Data Collection (DC)	DC 1			DC 2			DC 1		DC 2		DC 1 / DC 2	DC 1 + DC 2
Potential Parameter (PCII)	F	p	h	F	p	h	χ^2	p	χ^2	p	Significant?	Significant Parameter (CII)
Informa-tion Speed Value	9.77	0.00	0.00	51.92	0.0	0.0	17.3	0.0	82.9	0.0	yes / yes	quantitatively
MG.Car Speed	8.86	0.00	0.06	17.58	0.0	0.0	13.1	0.0	29.0	0.0	yes / yes	quantitatively
MG.Messa	7.64	0.00	0.12	16.24	0.0	0.1	13.8	0.0	30.9	0.0	yes / yes	quantitatively

[252] This is discussed in detail in section 6.6.2. The exact values and detailed results of the first online study can be found in the work report in section 10.4 as well as in the files "84 Datensätze ergebnisse.txt", "84 Datensätze Ergebnis 1 Korrelationen.spo" and especially in file "060124 Most Discriminating Use Case Independent Cultural Interaction Indicators.spo" in the online appendix.

[253] A first comparison of the results of the two online studies has been presented in Heimgärtner 2007b.

[254] The resulting values are based on the SPSS files "070205 Auswertung beider IIA-Erhebungen OK.spo" and "070127 Alle Daten der Haupterhebungen.sav" in the online appendix containing data that was recorded in the Access databases during the IIA test session. Parts of their printed contents can be found in the work report in section 10.4 (cf. also file "070129 Vergleich 1. und 2. IIA-Online-Hauptstudie ok.xls" as well as the SPSS files in the online appendix just now mentioned). The results of the test of homogeneity of variances (h) indicate whether (p>.05) or not (p≤.05) the variables are distributed normally. "MG" means that the parameters were determined during the maneuver guidance test task (cf. Figure 13 in section 5.2.2). "MD" means that the parameters were determined during the map display test task (cf. Figure 12 in section 5.2.2). "Quantitatively" means: significant in both studies by comparing numbers, "qualitatively" means: significant in the second study by comparing numbers and by interpretation of qualitative studies, "borderlined" means: can be regarded as CII or not depending on the setting of limits for interpretation of the results in this work, "no" means: by no means significant in this work.

ge Distance													
Maximal Open Tasks	6.07	0.00	0.00	15.14	0.0	0.0	12.5	0.0	69.3	0.0	yes	yes	quantitatively
Number Of Chars	5.92	0.00	0.00	17.22	0.0	0.0	16.4	0.0	67.6	0.0	yes	yes	quantitatively
MD. Number Of POI	3.14	0.05	0.09	15.41	0.0	0.0	5.26	0.07	32.17	0.0	yes	yes	quantitatively
Uncertainty avoidance val.	5.16	0.01	0.00	8.47	0.0	0.0	5.30	0.0	26.2	0.0	no	yes	qualitatively
Maneuver	5.00	0.01	0.00	37.78	0.0	0.0	4.78	0.0	54.0	0.0	no	yes	qualitatively
Interaction exactness	2.34	0.10	0.72	8.96	0.0	0.0	5.05	0.0	24.1	0.0	no	yes	qualitatively
Exceptions	1.96	0.15	0.00	5.16	0.0	0.0	0.18	0.9	15.8	0.0	no	yes	qualitatively
Interaction speed value	1.80	0.17	0.28	16.25	0.0	0.0	3.42	0.1	29.0	0.0	no	yes	qualitatively
Interaction exactness value	2.69	0.07	0.46	25.21	0.0	0.0	4.03	0.1	40.8	0.0	no	yes	borderlined
Individual sport	2.67	0.07	0.34	7.53	0.0	0.1	5.16	0.0	14.3	0.0	no	yes	borderlined
Density value	2.66	0.07	0.00	2.38	0.0	0.0	5.16	0.08	4.66	0.1	no	no	borderlined
MG.Info Presentation Duration	2.60	0.08	0.81	1.77	0.1	0.0	5.31	0.07	4.48	0.1	no	no	borderlined
Color	1.85	0.16	0.85	2.13	0.1	0.0	6.53	0.04	3.60	0.17	no	no	borderlined
Mouse clicks	1.72	0.18	0.00	0.63	0.5	0.0	1.58	0.45	4.37	0.11	no	no	borderlined
SysMouse Keys Max Speed	1.65	0.20	0.00	4.23	0.0	0.0	3.25	0.20	6.01	0.05	no	yes	borderlined
Restaurants	1.26	0.29	0.32	8.24	0.0	0.0	3.68	0.16	19.21	0.00	no	yes	borderlined
Streets	0.98	0.38	1.00	11.59	0.0	0.0	2.25	0.32	18.81	0.00	no	yes	borderlined
Power distance	0.75	0.48	0.18	2.01	0.1	0.4	4.70	0.10	13.85	0.00	no	no	borderlined
Error clicks	0.35	0.71	0.65	12.40	0.0	0.0	2.50	0.29	9.77	0.01	no	yes	borderlined
Number of requiring help	0.33	0.72	0.22	3.73	0.0	0.0	0.04	0.98	1.62	0.45	no	yes	borderlined
Textures	0.20	0.82	0.42	2.50	0.0	0.3	0.26	0.88	5.79	0.06	no	no	borderlined
Street names	0.15	0.86	0.39	5.73	0.0	0.2	0.50	0.78	13.02	0.00	no	yes	borderlined

Group sport	0.04	0.96	0.84	4.75	0.0	0.0	0.08	0.96	8.66	0.01	no	yes	borderlined
All mouse clicks	0.02	0.98	0.41	5.76	0.0	0.6	0.06	0.97	15.24	0.00	no	yes	borderlined
System Mouse Speed	1.58	0.21	0.01	0.30	0.7	0.8	3.43	0.18	1.75	0.42	no	no	no

In both online studies, some values of the implemented variables in the IIA tool showed significant differences, which represent differences in user interaction according to the different cultural background of the users. Therefore, these variables can be called "cultural interaction indicators" (CIIs).

Cultural interaction indicators (CIIs)

Table 24 presents the most interesting cultural interaction indicators for intercultural HMI design because they represent direct visible and direct hidden cultural variables that can be derived from the quantitative results of the *two* online studies.[255]

CIIs relevant for HMI design represent direct visible and hidden cultural variables

---

[255] The variables in the valid test data sets are not distributed comparably between the first and the second online study. Therefore, in part, the same variables have been analyzed either by ANOVA or by Kruskal-Wallis-test (indicated with F or χ^2). To compare them exactly, both have been analyzed by ANOVA and by Kruskal-Wallis test (even if this is not really allowed in statistics). Nevertheless, all parameters are highly significant disregarding the method of statistical analysis and distribution, which mutually supports the correctness of the results (independent of the statistical method used) (cf. e.g., the files "070526 Proximity Matrix Of All Variables.spo", "070205 Auswertung beider IIA-Erhebungen OK.spo", "070309 Alle Daten der Hauptauswertung verknüpft 2.spo" and "070309 Logfileauswertung 1632.spo" in the online appendix using ANOVA, factor analysis, discriminance analysis, or analysis of the correlation matrix as well as descriptive and explorative statistics).

Table 24: Cultural Interaction Indicators (CIIs) found in both studies most relevant for intercultural HMI design (Source: section "Univariat Mittelwersanalyse ANOVA C-D-E" in file "070205 Auswertung beider IIA-Erhebungen OK.spo" in the online appendix)

Cultural Interaction Indicator (CII)	Type	First study	Second study
MG.Car Speed	NVIV	$F_{(2,102)}=8.857^{**}$	$\chi^2_{(2,916)}=29.090^{**}$
MG.Message Distance	NVIV	$F_{(2,102)}=7.645^{**}$	$F_{(2,916)}=16.241^{**}$
MD.Number Of POI	VIV	$F_{(2,102)}=3.143^{*}$	$\chi^2_{(2,916)}=32.170^{**}$
Maximal Open Tasks	VIV	$\chi^2_{(2,102)}=12.543^{**}$	$F_{(2,916)}=15.140^{**}$
Maximal Open Tasks Ratio (C,G,E)	Ratio	2.5 : 1.4 : 1	1.7 : 1.03 : 1
MG.Info Presentation Duration	NVIV	$\chi^2_{(2,102)}=17.354^{**}$	$\chi^2_{(2,916)}=82.944^{**}$
Number Of Characters[256]	VIV	$\chi^2_{(2,102)}=16.452^{**}$	$\chi^2_{(2,916)}=67.637^{**}$

Most significant CIIs from both studies

The significant cultural interaction indicators are the following: MG.Car Speed ($\chi^2 (2, 916) = 29.090^{**}$) means the driving speed of the simulated car in the "maneuver guidance test task" ((C) less than (G) and (E)). MG.Message Distance ($F (2, 916) = 16.241^{**}$) denotes the temporal distance of showing the maneuver advice messages in the maneuver guidance test task. (C) desired about 30% more pre-advice ("in x m turn right") than (G) or (E) before turning right. This can be an indication of the higher information speed and higher information density in China compared to Germany, for example. MD.Number of POI ($\chi^2 (2, 916) = 32.17^{**}$) counts the number of points of interest (POI) set by the user in the map display test task. Information density increases with the number of POI and is two times higher for (C) than for (G) or (E). Max Open Tasks ($F (2, 916) = 15.140^{**}$) represents the maximum number of open tasks in the working environment (i.e. running applications and icons in the Windows® task bar) during the test session with the IIA data collection module. (C) tend to work on more tasks simultaneously than (G) or (E) (ratio (C, G, E) = 1.7 : 1.03 : 1) which can be possibly explained by the way of work planning (poly-chronic vs. mono-chronic timing, cf. Hall 1976) or the kind of thinking (mono-causal (sequential) vs. multi-causal (parallel) logic, cf. Röse et al. 2001). MG.Info Presentation Duration ($\chi^2 (2) = 82.944^{**}$) represents the time the maneuver advice message is visible on the screen. (C) and (G) wanted the advice to be about 40% longer than (E), which was not expected (cf. DIP in Table 19 in section 4.5). Number of characters ($\chi^2 (2) = 67.637^{**}$) contains the number of characters entered by the user during the maneuver guidance and map display test tasks in answering open questions ((C) < (G) and (C) < (E)). This is explained by the fact that the Chinese language needs considerably fewer characters to represent words than English or German.

---

[256] The significant difference in the number of entered characters between (C) and (G) supports their different writing systems and confirms their cultural differences in this respect.

There are also possible cultural interaction indicators that are significant in the second study which is more representative than the first because of $n_2=916$ in comparison to $n_1=102$ and that are almost significant in the first study (cf. Table 25).

Table 25: Borderlined cultural interaction indicators when comparing the studies (Source: section "Univariat Mittelwersanalyse ANOVA C-D-E" in file "070205 Auswertung beider IIA-Erhebungen OK.spo" in the online appendix)[257]

Variables with borderline values	First study	Second study
IE.Interaction Exactness	F(2,102)=2.345 (p=0.101)	χ^2 (2,916)=24.106**
IS.Interaction Speed Value	F(2,102)=1.801 (p=0.170)	F(2,916)=16.246**
MG.Number Of Maneuver	χ^2 (2,102)=4.785 (p=0.091)	χ^2 (2,916)=54.051**
UV.Uncertainty Avoidance Value	χ^2 (2,102)=5.297 (p=0.071)	χ^2 (2,916)=26.239**
IS.Interaction Exactness Value	F(2,102)=2.698 (p=0.073)	χ^2 (2,916)=40.862**

IE.Interaction Exactness (χ^2 (2, 916) = 24.106**) measures the exactness in clicking on dots in the abstract test task of "clicking dots away". (G) clicked the dots away almost twice as exactly as (E) or (C). IS.Interaction Speed Value (F (2, 916) = 16.246**) measures the duration of the abstract test task of "clicking dots away". (C) clicked the dots away almost twice as fast as (E) or (G). The number of mouse clicks differs in both studies but with different significance values. For example, UV.Mouse Clicks counts the mouse clicks in the test task "uncertainty avoidance" and All Mouse Clicks (χ^2 (2, 916) = 15.235**) counts all mouse clicks done by the user in the complete IIA test session. (C) do more than (G) or (E) which possibly indicates that the desire of (C) to obtain an immediate system reaction according to their input requests (e.g., mouse clicks) is very high. This is also supported by the nearly twofold amount of Error Clicks by (C) in contrast to (G) or (E). Error Clicks (χ^2 (2, 916) = 9.771**) counts the mouse clicks, which do not have any function for a test task (and hence, which can e.g. be a cue for impatience).

[margin note:] CIIs with borderline values because only significant in second online study

---

[257] "IE" means that the parameters were determined during the interaction exactness test task (cf. screenshot of the use cases in the work report in section 10.3.4). "IS" means that the parameters were determined during the interaction speed test task (cf. Figure 15 in section 5.2.2). "UV" means that the parameters were determined during the uncertainty avoidance test task (cf. screenshot "Uncertainty Avoidance Test Task" in the work report in section 10.3.4).

Four best quantitatively
significant CIIs according
to log file analysis:

Mouse clicks

Mouse moves

Test duration

Key strokes

In addition, the analysis of the log files of the data collection from the second online study using 1632 valid data sets revealed the following four best quantitatively significant cultural interaction indicators.[258] *MouseLeft-Down_norm* (F (2, 916) = 28.84**) count the amount of mouse clicks with the left mouse key divided by the duration of the total test session. *Mouse-Move_norm* (F (2, 916) = 26.20**) is the number of mouse move event recorded during the complete test session divided by test duration, representing the amount of mouse movements by the user. (C) did about 40% more mouse clicks and mouse moves than (E) and (G) (cf. Table 49 in the appendix). At the same time, (G) took about 15% longer than (C) to do the test (*Test duration* (F (2, 916) = 11.53**, cf. variable "duration of test" in Table 49 in the appendix). *Key Downs_norm* (F (2, 916) = 27.31*) is the number of key pressed events during the complete test session representing the number of pressed keys on the keyboard by the user. (C) produced about 40% more key presses than (G) (cf. Key Downs_norm in Table 49 in the appendix).

Reduction to the most
discriminating CIIs

This is strongly supported by the results from factor analysis on the PCIIs. The emerging factor loadings (three components covering more than 97% of the total variance in the data set) seem to be identical with test duration, mouse moves and mouse clicks. In contrast to those CIIs, all other PCIIs do not matter. However, if analyzed without the mentioned three components, the classification rate of the remaining PCIIs is still useful because their group means are different enough to correctly classify to the different groups (G) and (C) with at least 80% certainty and F > 4 according to ANOVA.[259] Therefore, all derived CIIs from the log files of the online studies using the IIA tool are quantitatively significant (cf. Table 26).

<hr/>

[258] The files "070309 Logfileauswertung 1632.spo" and „070309 Logfileauswertung 1632.sav" in the online appendix contain the condensed data of the data stored in the log files recorded during the IIA test sessions and their analysis.

[259] Cf. file "070309 Logfileauswertung 1632.spo" in the online appendix). F expresses the ratio of explained to unexplained variance (cf. Bortz et al. 2006). A high value of F indicates a high probability that the mean values of two samples are different.

Table 26: Cultural interaction indicators derived from log files of the second online data collection

Cultural interaction indicators (CII) derived from log files of the second study						
df = 2	*Oneway ANOVA*			*Kruskal-Wallis*		*Interpretation*
Name of CII	*F*	*p*	*h*	*χ^2*	*p*	*CII is significant*
Test Duration	11.53	0.000	0.404	54.508	0.000	yes, quantitatively
MouseMoves_norm	26.20	0.000	0.225	57.900	0.000	yes, quantitatively
KeyDowns_norm	27.31	0.000	0.318	59.451	0.000	yes, quantitatively
LeftButtonDowns_norm	28.84	0.000	0.266	59.471	0.000	yes, quantitatively

The significant difference in the group means between (C), (G) and (E) can probably be explained by the fact that the interaction data from the user is logged permanently into a history file and therefore every small difference is recorded. The maximal possible range of values of the HMIDs could thereby be used to reveal any differences in interaction behavior of the user. This is also the reason, why, in contrast to the CIIs derived from information related HMIDs (e.g., DIP and ID), which are initiated by the system, the CIIs derived from interaction related HMIDs (e.g., INF and INS) that are initiated and directed by the user, are all highly significant. Therefore, in Table 26 only entries can be found, representing the best discriminating CIIs exhibiting differences in the group means of F > 11.

The studies with the IIA tool comparing Chinese and German speaking users revealed different interaction patterns according to the cultural background of the users that can be called "cultural interaction patterns" (CIPs). These patterns represent the individual interaction behavior of the user with the system over time formed by the agglomeration of the values of the CIIs (as presented in Figure 10 in section 5.2.2). The cultural interaction indicators can be used to recognize the cultural interaction behavior of the user and to relate the derived "cultural interaction patterns" (CIPs) to the characteristics of the user's culture.

Cultural interaction patterns (CIPs) according to cultural background

6.3   Influence of Disturbing Variables

One of the main objectives of this work is to reveal culture dependent differences in HCI. However, there are many variables involved in conducting cultural studies in HCI as indicated in Figure 9 in section 5.1.3. Therefore, it must be ensured that the differences found really depend on cultural aspects and not e.g., on demographic causes, the experience of the user with the computer, machine, environment or the methods and means used. Special techniques can be applied to avoid such problems, e.g., choosing reasonable

Ensuring to reveal culture dependent differences in HCI

samples, adjusting the collected data and using control variables. If the disturbing variables are known, they can be consciously observed and controlled as "controlled disturbing variables" in data processing. For example, age, gender and computer experience are all variables that can affect the results negatively. These variables compensate for the effect of recognizing cultural differences in HCI because they are already influenced by culture and hence, contain implicitly cultural aspects that decrease the variability of the culturally explainable part of the variance in the values of the CIIs.[260] Hence, ANOVA or Kruskal-Wallis-Test was done to determine the significance level of those variables. Due to the distribution in the data set of these variables, the results from ANOVA or Kruskal-Wallis-Test must be considered. The values valid to the corresponding statistical method are presented in Table 27.

Table 27: Significance of controlled disturbing variables

Comparison of the Results of the Analyses of the First and the Second Data Collection

Method	ONEWAY ANOVA						Kruskal-Wallis				Interpretation		Conclusion
Data Collection (DC)	DC 1			DC 2			DC 1		DC 2		DC 1	DC 2	DC 1 + DC 2
Disturbing variable	F	p	h	F	p	h	χ^2	p	χ^2	p	Significant?		Significant Parameter
Age	8.07	0.00	0.01	41.42	0.00	0.0	18.86	0.00	87.04	0.00	yes	yes	quantitatively
PC experience	1.57	0.21	0.02	8.02	0.00	0.0	4.06	0.13	16.47	0.00	no	yes	qualitatively
Gender	0.07	0.93	0.75	1.52	0.22	0.0	0.15	0.93	2.95	0.23	no	no	no

The results indicate that the variable "age" is a significant variable that contributes to the classification of users according to their test languages (cf. section 6.2). The influence of the disturbing variable of "age" on the validity and on the values of the cultural interaction indicators depend on the fact that the age of the test persons of the different countries was not distributed equally in the samples. For example, there were no Chinese test persons above the age

---

[260] Another interesting variable would be "experience with driver navigation systems". This variable was collected during the online studies. Unfortunately, the results have not been recorded by the test program, which was detected too late. Therefore, there are no values for this variable available. However, the high education level of the employees of SV who work with electronic devices lets one suppose that they have some idea about driver navigation systems. This variable should, therefore, not disturb the results significantly.

of 39 in the first online study (n=102) (cf. section 6.2).[261] However, the effect was lower using only test persons whose ages were distributed equally in the user groups ((C), (G) and (E), separated by the test languages) or by calculating partial correlations.[262] In addition, Pearson's correlation shows that the controlled disturbing variable "age" correlates only slightly with the selected test language by the user (cf. Table 28).[263]

Table 28: Relationship between test language and controlled disturbing variables

Pearson's correlation matrix[264]	First study (n=102)	Second study (n=916)
Controlled disturbing variable	Test language	Test language
Test language	1.000**	1.000**
Age	0.370**	0.161**
Gender	-0.038	-0.017
Computer experience	0.174	-0.048

Therefore, the disturbing influence of age on the CIIs is not as strong as expected at the first sight.[265] The influence of "age" is relativized even more by the fact that the variables "gender" and "computer experience" do not correlate significantly with the variable "test language" and variable "gender" does not disturb the results at all (because of correlation values near zero) (cf. Table

Disturbing variables

---

[261] Cf. file „051226 81 Datensätze ergebnisdaten.xls" in the online appendix, which contains the valid data sets of the first online data collection.

[262] Partial correlation measures the degree of the association between two random variables without the effect of other controlled random variables (cf. Bortz & Döring 2006). Cf. the SPSS files "070205 Auswertung beider IIA-Erhebungen OK.spo" and "070127 Alle Daten der Haupterhebungen.sav" as well as „070129 Auswertung beider IIA-Erhebungen OK.spo" in the online appendix. The classification rate increased up to 92% as it can be seen in section "Diskriminanzanalyse (CIIs 92,3% Alter>30 nur C und D) kreuzvalidiert" in file "070205 Auswertung beider IIA-Erhebungen OK.spo" in the online appendix.

[263] In the tests with the IIA tool, Chinese users mainly chose Chinese as test language and German users chose German. This is strongly supported by the high correlation of over 80% between cultural imprint (e.g., nationality, mother tongue and principal residence) and the selected test language calculating also the Pearson's correlation matrix (cf. section 6.2).

[264] The values represent the Pearson's correlation coefficients whose significance level is indicated by stars (* $p<0.05$; ** $p<0.01$).

[265] This conclusion has been confirmed by the collected data of the second online study: Pearson's correlation and the Kruskal-Wallis-test showed a lower correlation coefficient for the variable of "age" than in the first study (cf. Table 28). This phenomenon is mainly caused by the fact that the sample size of the second study (n=916) is about 9 times higher than those of the first study (n=102) which yields better results due to the "law of large numbers" in stochastics (cf. Brüggemann 2002 or Bauer 2002).

28). Gender does not have significant influence on the test language, which is possibly indebted to the fact that mostly male test persons took part in the tests (83 male and 19 female in the first (ratio (M:F) $_{Study\ 1}$ = 4.37), and 744 male and 168 female in the second online study (ratio (M:F) $_{Study\ 2}$ = 4.43)).

Furthermore, even if computer experience intuitively seems to be the most relevant variable directly connected to interaction behavior (e.g., to interaction speed and interaction frequency), it did not interfere significantly with the measuring process of the interaction behavior within the two online studies using the IIA tool. This can be explained by the fact that computer experience was almost equally distributed in the test data as well as in the test users at the worldwide locations of Siemens VDO: the link to the IIA tool had been sent by e-mail only to users who have Internet access and hence, who must have some (basic "interacting") experience with computers.

Analysis by FTE tests

However, the analysis by FTE tests revealed a strong connection between user experience and cultural imprint of the user (cf. Table 29).[266]

Connection between user experience and cultural imprint of user

Table 29: Classification results according to user culture and experience using the FTE tool

Experience	Real culture	Target value	Actual value	Recognized culture	Recognition result
Much	Chinese	1.00	1.00	Chinese	Correct
Much	German	0.25	0.75	Chinese	Wrong
Little	Chinese	0.75	0.25	German	Wrong
Little	German	0.00	0.00	German	Correct

User experience influences the classification rate when classifying the user according to his cultural membership. If there are many data sets from Chinese and German users that have very different interacting experience, then the classification output is arbitrarily, i.e. no national separation is possible because of the different user experiences (cf. the grey lines in Table 29). Probably, this effect can be attributed to the tiny sample size (only 25 valid datasets have been recorded at the FTE test).

A closer look on the relationship between experience and nationality relaxed this challenge tremendously. Table 30 shows the relationship between group

---

[266] "Fortuna Trace Evaluation" (FTE) means the analysis of the data from the log file produced by the FTE tests using the data generated with the CAHMI demonstrator (cf. section 7.3) using the FTE tool (integrated into the IIA data evaluation module) containing neural networks (cf. section 5.4). The output of the neural network in the FTE tool shows a value between 0 and 1. [0;1] represents the "cultural index" (c-value) as used in the CAHMI demonstrator [0=0%; 1=100%]. For example, if c-value = 0.75, then the user is classified with 75% probability to have a Chinese cultural background.

variables, classification rates and most discriminating cultural interaction indicators to classify the cases successfully according to group variables.

Table 30: Relationship between group variables, classification quotes and most discriminating cultural interaction indicators (Source: file "070205 Auswertung beider IIA-Erhebungen OK.spo" in the online appendix)

| Group variable | Degree of freedom (df) | Classification Quote [%] | | Most discriminating cultural interaction indicators to classify the cases successfully according to the group variable |
		Without disturbing variables (excluded)	With disturbing variables (included)	
Test language	2	60	65	**Information presentation speed value (~DIP)**, uncertainty avoidance value, speed (MG), interaction exactness value, **number of maneuvers, POI, restaurants, streets,** characters, maximal open tasks
Age	46	10	10	**Number of help requests, error clicks,** exceptions, mouse clicks, characters, **interaction exactness value**
Gender	1	82	82	**Speed (MG)**[267], **message distance,** number of help, mouse clicks, characters, street names, maximal open tasks
Computer experience	3	53	54	**Interaction speed, uncertainty avoidance value,** number of mouse clicks, open tasks before test
Nationality	10	42	69	**Information presentation speed value (~DIP),** **interaction exactness value, total dialog time, speed (MG),** number of help, exceptions, **maneuvers,** error clicks, **POI, streets, maximal open tasks**

The low discrimination rate for the group variable "nationality" excluding the controlled disturbing variables (42%, cf. Table 30) comes from the fact that the discrimination rate decreases with the degree of freedom (DF) of the group variable. For example, "gender" (DF $_{gender}$ = 1) discriminates with 82% in comparison to "age" (DF $_{age}$ = 46) with only 10%. Hence, if we reduce DF $_{nationality}$ from 10 to 1 (e.g., regarding only Chinese and German nationalities), the discrimination rate increases tremendously from 42% up to over 80% similar to the discrimination rate of the group variable "gender" (cf. Table 30).[268]

Reducing degrees of freedom increases discrimination rates

---

[267] Speed (MG) means the speed of the simulated car in the MG test task.

[268] The classification rate for correctly classifying the users to their nationality including or excluding the disturbing variables is 91% or 68% (cf. esp. the sections "Diskriminanzanalyse (Analyse der CIIs nach Nationalität mit Störvariablen und Nationalitäten China, Deutschland und USA => 91%)" and "Diskriminanzanalyse (Analyse der CIIs nach Nationalität ohne Störvariablen und nur Chinesische, Deutsche und USA-Nationalitäten => 68%)" as well as the other sections in file "070205 Auswertung beider IIA-Erhebungen OK.spo" in the online appendix).

Right combination of CIIs describes culturally imprinted interaction differences	This means that the classification power of "nationality" is as good as the classification power of the controlled disturbing variables (at least as long as $DF_{nationality} = 1$), which proves that real cultural classification works because the variables (CIIs) can be selected according to the expected definition of culture (e.g., nationality).[269] This means that with the right combination of CIIs it is possible to capture interaction differences that are almost purely culturally imprinted.
Nearly same HCI characteristics for groups formed by test language or nationality	The users grouped by test language or nationality exhibit almost the same HCI characteristics (mirrored mostly by the same high discriminating cultural interaction indicators). In contrast, other cultural interaction indicators characterize the users grouped by age, gender or computer experience. For example, number of help requests and number of error clicks as well as interaction exactness value classify users of different ages. Interaction speed,
Combination of CIIs characterize user groups by age, gender or computer experience	uncertainty avoidance value, the number of mouse clicks and the number of open tasks before doing the test can be used to recognize best the experience of the users. Furthermore, it seems that the combination of the most discriminating cultural interaction indicators point to the characteristics of the group variables. Hence, according to Table 30, classification of the user interaction behavior to his cultural background needs the combination of more cultural interaction indicators than those, which are sufficient to classify the user interaction behavior in respect of age, gender and computer experience.
Most discriminating CIIs for nationality	Therefore, the most discriminating cultural interaction indicators for nationality, which do not significantly classify disturbing variables at the same time, are information speed value, number of maneuvers, number of POI as well as total dialog time (bold in Table 30).
Weighting the CIIs	To weaken the classification problem that has been raised by the FTE study (cf. Table 29), the CIIs can be weighted according to classification objective or only those CIIs are used in discriminance analysis that are relevant for the desired variable for which the classification rate is desired (cf. Table 30). For example, if the users are to be classified according to their nationality, only those CIIs should be used that best classify the group variable "nationality". If we want to check the PC experience of the user, only the CIIs for computer experience should be taken into account. This solution solves the methodological problem raised by the FTE study.

---

[269] For detailed information about the classification of the user according to their nationality, please refer to file "070205 Auswertung beider IIA-Erhebungen OK.spo" in the online appendix.

This also means that the influence of disturbing variables for classification can be controlled and even eliminated simply by using the adequate collection of cultural interaction indicators (CIIs). Thereby, the CIIs serve to determine cultural imprint along with computer experience, age, gender etc., which are most relevant for building the working user models necessary for adaptive systems.

Influence of disturbing variables on classification can be controlled using adequate collection of CIIs

Furthermore, some of the variables are represented in more than only one group. Therefore, according to the high correlation of nationality and test language (cf. section 6.6.2), it is reasonable also to pick out those CIIs forming the group variable "test language" and which do not form the group variables age, gender and computer experience at the same time (bold in Table 30). This means, even if experience and cultural imprint are mutually influenced, those CIIs can be picked out that are least influenced preserving the most possible variance in the data necessary to classify the desired variable (culture or experience related). This seems to be a very smart way to overcome the mentioned methodological problems regarding the improvement of classification power (cf. also the leveling effect mentioned in section 8.1).

Exact related variables help to overcome methodological problems

Finally, remaining inferences can be eliminated by reasonable methodological strategies (e.g., selecting most appropriate CIIs). Hence, in both studies, the statistical methods justified the assumption that the results of the studies are correct and representative for employees of Siemens VDO in China and Germany.[270] Furthermore, none of the controlled disturbing variables influenced the CIIs in a way that they cannot be called "cultural interaction indicators". This shows that the results are stable and there is high test reliability, which indicates that the data collection and the data analysis methods are correct (cf. also section 6.6.3). This is also supported by the high correspondence between the cultural interaction indicators found by one-way ANOVA and the Kruskal-Wallis-Test respectively on the one hand and the high classification quotes by discriminance analysis on the other hand as presented in section 6.6 where the results of the two online studies will be discussed in detail.

Correct results

No decisive influence of controlled disturbing variables on CIIs

Correspondence of combination of CIIs and classification quotas

6.4 Cultural Imprint of the Test Participants

The cultural characterization of the test participants was obtained from the two online studies by using the VSM94 questionnaire according to Hofstede

Analyzing cultural characterization

---

[270] Probably also for the USA and Canada (cf. file "070205 Auswertung beider IIA-Erhebungen OK.spo" in the online appendix). However, this needs further research.

1994.[271] The values of the VSM data collection in this work are acceptable because the sample size in the second online study is greater than twenty participants per question as required by the VSM test of Hofstede 1994 indicated in Figure 22.[272]

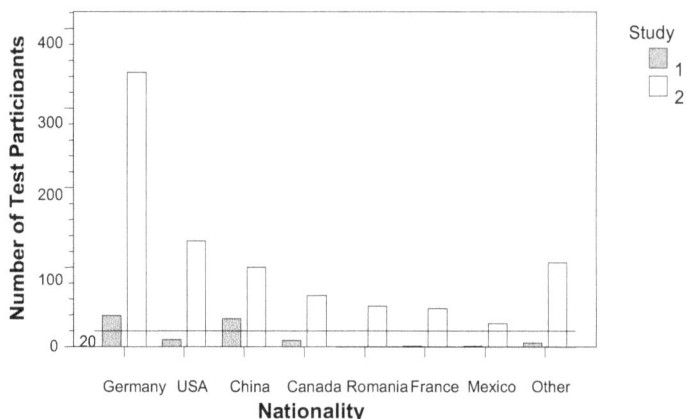

Figure 22: Sample sizes according to country (dark grey = first online study, white = second online study)[273]

Significant differences between China and Germany except for MAS

Figure 23 illustrates the cultural behavior differences according to Hofstede for the countries most relevant in this work according to sample size: Germany and China (cf. Figure 22). It is clearly visible that there are significant differences between those two countries except for MAS.[274] In contrast, Figure 24 shows the indices obtained by the second online study in this work supporting considerably fewer differences.[275] Furthermore, obviously the Chinese users at

---

[271] Cf. Figure 19 in section 5.3 as well as the questionnaire implemented in the IIA tool documented in the work report in section 10.2.7.

[272] For Chinese and German test participants in both studies.

[273] Source: files "070428 VSM Auswertung exakt.xls" as well as "041213 Modell interkultureller Variable55 überarbeitet am 08-01-2009_pres.xls" in the online appendix.

[274] MAS China = MAS Germany = 66 (cf. Table 50 in the appendix). The reliability of the VSM results will be discussed explicitly in section 6.6.3.

[275] The exact values from the studies can be found in file "041213 Modell interkultureller Variable55 überarbeitet am 08-01-2009_pres.xls" in the online appendix.

SV adopted the cultural imprint of German and US-American users at SV, which represent the culture of the parent company of Siemens VDO.[276]

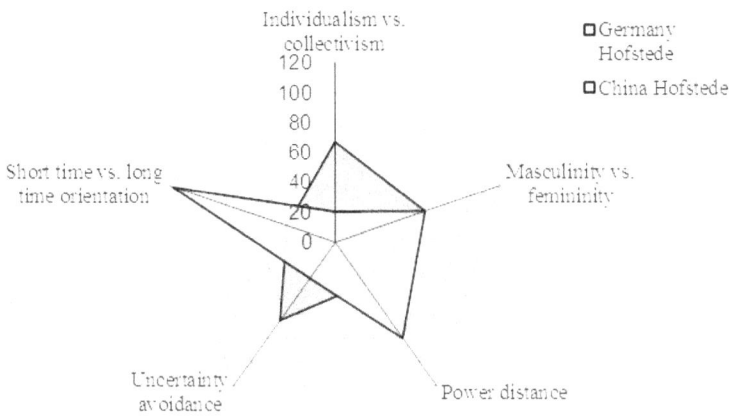

Figure 23: Different indices for China and Germany according to Hofstede

---

[276] For further details concerning method of data collection, analysis and results, please refer to section 6.4 in the work report.

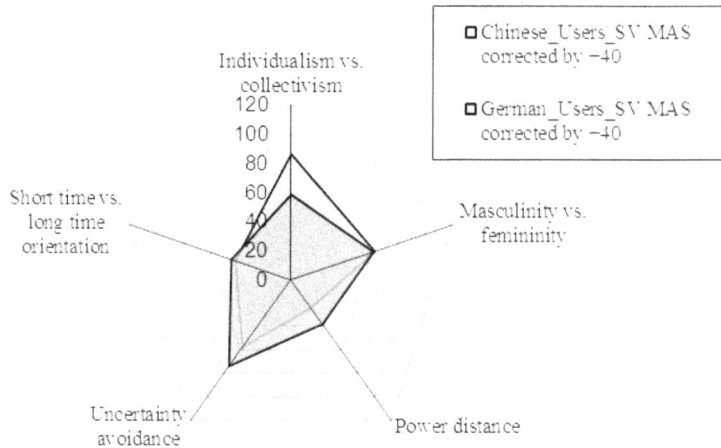

Figure 24: Cultural dimensions an their peculiarities for China and Germany according to the results of the second online study of this work

Correct data collection and results

Figure 25 shows the differences of Hofstede's scores and the averaged scores gathered by the two online studies in this work.[277] The biggest deviations have been found regarding the PDI, IDV and LTO scores for China.[278] The merely slight differences in the values for Germany and USA prove the plausibility of the results received from the VSM survey indicating that the findings are cor-

---

[277] The scores of the second study weigh about 9 times more than those from the first study because of the sample ratio of 8.98 (cf. section 6.6.2).

[278] The shapes of the "cultural HCI fingerprints" as demonstrated in Figure 29 in section 6.6.3 can be seen also in Figures 24–28 in section 6.4 in the work report regarding the VSM results.

rect.

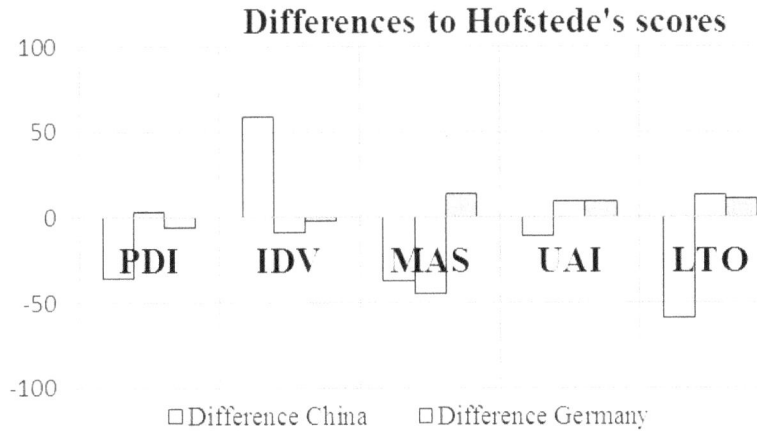

Differences to Hofstede's scores

Figure 25: Difference of Hofstede's scores and the averaged scores gathered by the two online studies in this work (the darkest bars indicate the differences regarding USA)

The direct comparison of the differences in the VSM results of the study presented in this work to the estimated indecies by Hofstede for China and those of the study of Komischke et al. 2003 show that there are differences between Hofstede's estimations for China and the empirically obtained values for China from this work and the work of Komischke et al. 2003. In contrast, the differences between the results of Komischke et al. 2003 and those of the work in hand are very slight, because IDV, MAS, UAI and LTO are very similar to the scores found by Komischke et al. 2003, which also indicates high retest reliability.[279]

Differences between the results of this work and Hofstede's regarding China

Similar results to related work

6.5   Verifying the Empirical Hypotheses

In this section, the postulated hypotheses of this dissertation project will be verified. Most of the hypotheses can be confirmed according to the values in Table 49 in the appendix and Table 23 in section 6.2, based on the test system

Verifying the results

---

[279] Cf. section 6.6.3 in the work report for reliability studies taking into account related work.

described in section 5.1.1. In the following, additional explanations will be given for the hypotheses, variables and values where necessary.[280]

According to the data in Tables 22 – Table 26 as well as the explanations of the derived results in the last section, some of the test hypotheses can be confirmed. The doubled underlined hypotheses have been confirmed (H_0 is rejected and H_1 is accepted) in both studies, those underlined were confirmed only in the first study, and the stricken hypotheses were rejected in the second study (H_0 is accepted and H_1 is rejected).

The test hypotheses (TH) that are not marked were not verifiable due to a lack of data or data analysis:[281]

TH_{15}: ~~H_0: $\mu DIP_C \geq \mu DIP_G$~~ — ~~H_1: $\mu DIP_C < \mu DIP_G$~~

TH_{14}: H_0: $\mu NIT_C \leq \mu NIT_G$ H_1: $\mu NIT_C > \mu NIT_G$

TH_{13}: H_0: $\mu FI_C \leq \mu FI_G$ H_1: $\mu FI_C > \mu FI_G$

TH_{12}: H_0: $\mu KS_C \leq \mu KS_G$ H_1: $\mu KS_C > \mu KS_G$

TH_{11}: ~~H_0: $\mu HI_C \geq \mu HI_G$~~ — ~~H_1: $\mu HI_C < \mu HI_G$~~

TH_{10}: H_0: $\mu LMT_C \leq \mu LMT_G$ H_1: $\mu LMT_C > \mu LMT_G$

TH_9: H_0: $\mu NIN_C \leq \mu NIN_G$ H_1: $\mu NIN_C > \mu NIN_G$

TH_8: H_0: $\mu TDA_C \leq \mu TDA_G$ H_1: $\mu TDA_C > \mu TDA_G$

TH_7: H_0: $\mu RM_C \leq \mu RM_G$ H_1: $\mu RM_C > \mu RM_G$

TH_6: H_0: $\mu EC_C \leq \mu EC_G$ H_1: $\mu EC_C > \mu EC_G$

TH_5: H_0: $\mu PT_C \leq \mu PT_G$ H_1: $\mu PT_C > \mu PT_G$

TH_4: H_0: $\mu MMS_C \leq \mu MMS_G$ H_1: $\mu MMS_C > \mu MMS_G$

TH_3: H_0: $\mu MC_C \leq \mu MC_G$ H_1: $\mu MC_C > \mu MC_G$

TH_2: H_0: $\mu POI_C \leq \mu POI_G$ H_1: $\mu POI_C > \mu POI_G$

TH_1: H_0: $\mu IN_C \leq \mu IN_G$ H_1: $\mu IN_C > \mu IN_G$

---

[280] The verification of the hypotheses in this work is based on the files "060901 Argumentations-gang Hypothesenauswertung.spo" (using the data in "060124 Datensätze.sav") available in the online appendix.

[281] H1 is constituted by other hypotheses. Therefore, first, the constituents of H1 must be verified before H1 itself can be verified. Therefore, the order of verifying the hypotheses is reversed.

According to the verification of the test hypothesis (TH), the statistical hypotheses (SH) are confirmed or not according to Table 49 depicted in the appendix.

$$SH_{15}: \quad \mu DIP_C > \mu DIP_G \qquad \leftrightarrow \qquad \mu DIP_C - \mu DIP_G > 0$$

The average value of "duration of information presentation" (DIP) is significantly lower for the group of persons assigned to be of Chinese culture than of German culture represented by the variable "Display Duration". This variable expresses the duration of presenting the MG announcement message on the screen in the MG test task (cf. section 5.2.2). SH_{15} must be rejected based on rejection of TH_{15}: $\mu DIP_{(C)}$ (2351) < $\mu DIP_{(G)}$ (2285) is false.[282]

$$SH_{14}: \quad \mu NIT_C > \mu NIT_G \qquad \leftrightarrow \qquad \mu NIT_C - \mu NIT_G \geq 0$$

The average value of "number of presented pieces of information per time unit" (NIT) is significantly higher for the group of persons assigned to be of Chinese culture than of German culture represented by the variable "Message Distance". This variable represents the distance between two visually presented MG announcements in the MG test task (cf. section 5.2.2). To obtain the corresponding variable representing the number of presented pieces of information per time unit, the reciprocal value of "Message Distance" has to be used: Message Distance for (C) is 112.68 and for (G) it is 141.05. Therefore, the reciprocal values are 0.0089 for (C) and 0.0071 for (G). Hence, SH_{14} can be confirmed based on acceptance of TH_{14} because of $\mu NIT_{(C)}$ (0.0089) > $\mu NIT_{(G)}$ (0.0071). The confirmation of SH_{14} is also supported by the variable "Speed" ($\mu NIT_{(C)}$ (43.66) > $\mu NIT_{(G)}$ (27.41)) representing the speed of the simulated car in the MG test task. Obviously, (C) expect to receive information more quickly than (G). This is also backed up by the impressions of the author from the qualitative studies conducted with Chinese test persons (cf. section 6.1).

$$SH_{13}: \quad \mu FI_C > \mu FI_G \qquad \leftrightarrow \qquad \mu FI_C - \mu FI_G \geq 0$$

The average value of "functional initiations" (FI) is significantly higher for the group of persons assigned to be of Chinese culture than of German culture represented by the variable "Sems_norm" in Table 49. This variable expresses the number of user interactions with semantic meaning effecting in system reactions, e.g., pressing an "ok"-button, clicking on a link, or selecting a menu item with the mouse. Hence, SH_{13} is confirmed based on acceptance of TH_{13} because $\mu FI_{(C)}$ (1036) > $\mu FI_{(G)}$ (735) is true.

$$SH_{12}: \quad \mu KS_C > \mu KS_G \qquad \leftrightarrow \qquad \mu KS_C - \mu KS_G \geq 0$$

---

[282] The values can be looked up in Table 49.

The average value of "keyboard strokes" (KS) is significantly higher for the group of persons assigned to be of Chinese culture than of German culture indicated by "KeyDowns_norm" ($\mu KS_{(C)}$ (477) > $\mu KS_{(G)}$ (340)) and "KeyUps_norm" ($\mu KS_{(C)}$ (127) > $\mu KS_{(G)}$ (88)), which represent the number of key presses over the whole test session divided by the test session duration. Hence, SH_{12} is confirmed because of acceptance of TH_{12}: $\mu KS_C > \mu KS_G$ is true. The difference between the number of input characters and the number of key strokes can be explained by the fact that (C) exhibit high interaction frequency and in parallel need not input as many characters as (G) to express words because of a different writing system (and not be forced to use input method editors) (cf. section 6.2).

SH_{11}: $\mu HI_G > \mu HI_C$ ⟷ $\mu HI_G - \mu HI_C > 0$

The average value of "number of help initiations" (HI) is significantly lower for the group of persons assigned to be of Chinese culture than of German culture by the variable "Number Of Help Initiations" ($\mu HI_{(C)}$ (0.61) < $\mu HI_{(G)}$ (0.09) is false). Therefore, this hypothesis must be rejected. This result is contrary to the expected result according to literature (cf. hypothesis INH11 in section 4.3.3). However, this result is unsurprising because the Chinese employees had assimilated company culture at Siemens VDO, which is mainly imprinted by Germany and the USA (as explained in detail in section 6.4 in the work report).

SH_{10}: $\mu LMT_C > \mu LMT_G$ ⟷ $\mu LMT_C - \mu LMT_G > 0$

The average value of "length of mouse tracks" (LMT) is significantly higher for the group of persons assigned to be of Chinese culture rather than of German culture. This hypothesis could not be verified because the parameter providing this value was not evaluated because of time restrictions.

SH_9: $\mu NIN_C > \mu NIN_G$ ⟷ $\mu NIN_C - \mu NIN_G > 0$

The average value of "number of non-verbal interactions with the system per time unit" (NIN) is significantly higher for the group of persons assigned to be of Chinese culture rather than of German culture. This hypothesis could not be tested as adequate parameter indexes were not implemented in the IIA tool because of time restrictions.

SH_8: $\mu TDA_C > \mu TDA_G$ ⟷ $\mu TDA_C - \mu TDA_G > 0$

The average value of "time to disable virtual agents" (TDA) is significantly higher for the group of persons assigned to be of Chinese culture rather than of German culture. The reference value for TDA obtained by the IIA analysis module is 2.5 for (G) and 26 for (C), i.e., $\mu TDA_{(C)}$ (26) > $\mu TDA_{(G)}$ (2.5) is true. Therefore, SH_8 can be confirmed.[283]

SH_7: $\mu RM_C > \mu RM_G$ $\leftrightarrow$ $\mu RM_C - \mu RM_G \geq 0$

The average value of "number of refused system messages" (RM) is significantly higher for the group of persons assigned to be of Chinese culture rather than of German culture represented by the variable "Refused Messages". $\mu RM_{(C)}$ (0.75) > $\mu RM_{(G)}$ (0.57) is true. Therefore, SH_7 can be confirmed.

SH_6: $\mu EC_C > \mu EC_G$ $\leftrightarrow$ $\mu EC_C - \mu EC_G \geq 0$

The average value of "number of error clicks" (ET) is significantly higher for the group of persons assigned to be of Chinese culture rather than of German culture represented by Error Clicks ($\mu EC_{(C)}$ (0.96) > $\mu EC_{(G)}$ (0.34) is true). Therefore, SH_6 can be confirmed.

SH_5: $\mu PT_C > \mu PT_G$ $\leftrightarrow$ $\mu PT_C - \mu PT_G \geq 0$

The average value of "number of parallel tasks in task bar" (PT) is significantly higher for the group of persons assigned to be of Chinese culture rather than of German culture represented by Maximal Open Tasks ($\mu PT_{(C)}$ (4.64) > $\mu PT_{(G)}$ (2.87) is true). Therefore, SH_5 can be confirmed.

SH_4: $\mu MMS_C > \mu MMS_G$ $\leftrightarrow$ $\mu MMS_C - \mu MMS_G \geq 0$

The average value of "mouse movement speed" (MMS) is significantly higher for the group of persons assigned to be of Chinese culture rather than of German culture. No explicit parameter providing this value had been developed in the data analysis phase because of time restrictions. However, $\neg IN <$ 1ms counts the amount of mouse moves (MM) per time unit (1ms), which captures and represents directly the speed of mouse movement (MMS). Thereby, this hypothesis can be confirmed because of the results obtained by the two online studies: $\mu MM_{(C)}$ (10566) > $\mu MM_{(G)}$ (7529) is true. Furthermore, the results of the tests with the CAHMI demonstrator are similar: $\neg IN < 1ms_{(C)}$ (7.6) > $\neg IN < 1ms_{(G)}$ (4.6) is true (cf. Table 44, in section 7.3). Therefore, SH4 can be accepted.

SH_3: $\mu MC_C > \mu MC_G$ $\leftrightarrow$ $\mu MC_C - \mu MC_G \geq 0$

---

[283] The analysis of the data of the first study is stored in file "070309 Alle Daten der Hauptauswertung verknüpft 2.spo" based on the data in file "070309 Alle Daten der Hauptauswertung verknüpft.sav" in the online appendix. To have a look into the *.sav-files, the statistic tool SPSS is necessary. Therefore, for convenience, some example data can be viewed in files "061226 Datenauszug.xls", "051226 81 Datensätze ergebnisdaten.xls" and "Logfile-Ergebnisse.xls".

The average value of "number of mouse clicks per time unit" (MC) is significantly higher for the group of persons assigned to be of Chinese culture rather than of German culture represented by L_BUTTON_DOWNS ($\mu MC_{(C)}$ (301807) > $\mu MC_{(G)}$ (259875) is true, L_BUTTON_UPS ($\mu MC_{(C)}$ (230001) > $\mu MC_{(G)}$ (198155) is true, L_Button_Ups_norm ($\mu MC_{(C)}$ (92.40) > $\mu MC_{(G)}$ (65.38) is true) and L_Button_Downs_norm ($\mu MC_{(C)}$ (121.23) > $\mu MC_{(G)}$ (85.75) is true). Therefore, SH$_3$ can be accepted.

SH$_2$: $\mu POI_C > \mu POI_G$ $\leftrightarrow$ $\mu POI_C - \mu POI_G \geq 0$

The average value of "number of points of interest in the map display" (POI) is significantly higher for the group of persons assigned to be of Chinese culture rather than of German culture represented by POI ($\mu MC_{(C)}$ (35.26) > $\mu MC_{(G)}$ (19.91) is true). Furthermore, also other related variables representing the information amount (POI) expose a similar tendency (e.g. number of restaurants: $\mu MC_{(C)}$ (49.34) > $\mu MC_{(G}$ (35.30) is true as well as number of graphical features: $\mu MC_{(C)}$ (50.78) > $\mu MC_{(G)}$ (46.82) is true). Therefore, SH$_2$ can be accepted.

SH$_1$: $\mu IN_C > \mu IN_G$ $\leftrightarrow$ $\mu IN_C - \mu IN_G \geq 0$

The average value of "number of interactions with the system per time unit" (IN) is significantly higher for the group of persons assigned to be of Chinese culture rather than of German culture. The factor "number of interactions with the system per time unit" (IN) is represented by the following measurement variables per time unit: number of mouse clicks (MC), number of key strokes (KS), number of mouse moves (MM), number of dialog/function initiations (FI), number of help initiations (HI) and number of nonverbal interaction (NVIN).[284] Hence, this hypothesis can be accepted because the concerned statistical hypotheses have been confirmed above (except NVIN).[285] Furthermore, all available measurement variables relevant for interaction amount (e.g. the number of mouse moves per time unit or the number of mouse clicks per time unit represented by Mouse_moves, Mouse_moves_norm, Mouse_Clicks, L_Button_Downs,   L_Button_Ups,   L_Button_Ups_norm   and L_Button_Downs_norm) are significantly greater for (C) than for (G) (cf. Table 49 in the appendix as well as Table 23).

---

[284] NVIN is excluded (because of missing data).

[285] Also the number of help initiations (HI) as well as the number of function initiations (FI) supports the high interaction frequency (INF) of (C) because HI$_C$ (0.60) > HI$_G$ (0.09) and of FI$_C$ (1036) > FI$_G$ (735) (cf. Table 49).

The empirical hypotheses (EH) were generated in chapter 4 and are described in detail in section 4.3.3. According to the confirmed and rejected statistical hypotheses as well as the results of comparing the group means of the PCIIs using ANOVA or Kruskal-Wallis-Test in section 6.2, Table 31 shows the confirmed and rejected empirical hypotheses (EH) from the results of the online studies elaborated in this work. Table 31 also contains the hypotheses that have not been investigated empirically because of a lack of operational variables. In addition, some hypotheses in Table 31 could not be adequately verified in this work.[286]

Overview of confirmed or rejected empirical hypotheses:
⇨   5 confirmed
⇨   1 rejected
⇨   3 not investigated

---

[286] This is at least because one of the following reasons: methodologically difficult to verify, cannot be supported very well by the developed test equipment, the collected data have not been analyzed yet because of time restrictions or the hypotheses were generated to late in an iterative development step. This is the tribute that is paid for the iterative development methods (e.g., some hypotheses are generated later in development phase according to "Grounded Theory", cf. section 3.3.1).

Table 31: Empirically confirmed, rejected and not investigated empirical hypotheses (EH) in the studies in this dissertation project because of lack of operational variables or resources to analyze the empirical results

Hypo-thesis	Cultural dimension	Ger-many	Chi-na	HMI dimension	Operalization / Variable	Ger-many	Chi-na	Short name	Empirical Result
IH0	low vs. high context orientation	low	high	information redundancy	number of redundant pieces of information (e.g. at the map display)	low	high	-	not investigated
IH1a	mono-chronic vs. poly-chronic time orientation	mono	poly	information frequency	time between the presentation of two pieces of information by the system	low	high	TPI	confirmed
IH1b1	communication network density	low	high	information density (spatially)	number of parallel presented pieces of information (e.g. at the map display)	low	high	PT, POI	confirmed
IH1b2	communication network density	low	high	information density (temporally)	number of pieces of information presented by the system per time unit	low	high	NIT	confirmed
IH1c	communication speed	low	high	information frequency	number of pieces of information presented by the system per time unit	low	high	NIT	confirmed
INH1c1	communication speed	low	high	interaction frequency	number of interactions with the system per time unit (e.g. mouse clicks)	low	high	IN	confirmed
INH1c2	communication speed	low	high	interaction speed	speed of interactions with the system (e.g. mouse movement speed)	low	high	INS, MMS	confirmed
IH1d	mono-chronic vs. poly-chronic time orientation	mono	poly	information sequentiality	number of parallel tasks in task bar	low	high	PT	confirmed
INH1d	mono-chronic vs. poly-chronic	mono	poly	interaction sequentiality	point clicking sequence	mono / linear	poly / non-	PT MMLMT	not verified

	time orientation						linear		
IH5	communication network density	low	high	information frequency	number of pieces of information presented by the system per time unit, number of error clicks	low	high	NIT, EC	confirmed
INH5	communication network density	low	high	interaction frequency	number of interactions with the system per time unit	low	high	IN	confirmed
IH6a	uncertainty avoidance	high	low	information sequentiality	number of parallel tasks in task bar	low	high	PT	confirmed
IH6b	uncertainty avoidance	high	low	information tolerance	number of refused system messages, number of error clicks	low	high	RM, EC	confirmed
INH6b	uncertainty avoidance	high	low	interaction tolerance	time to disable virtual agents	low	high	TDA	confirmed
IH7	relationship vs. task orientation & low vs. high context	low	high	information transmission	number of non verbal interactions with the system per time unit	low	high	-	not investigated
INH7	relationship vs. task orientation & low vs. high context	low	high	interaction complexity	(number of long mouse tracks) length of mouse track	low	high	LMT	not verified
IH8	task vs. relationship orientation	low	high	information frequency	number of interactions with the system per time unit	low	high	IN	confirmed
INH8	task vs. relationship orientation	low	high	interaction frequency	number of interactions with the system per time unit	low	high	IN	confirmed
IH9	low vs. high context orientation	low	high	information transmission	number of non verbal interactions with the system per time unit, number of error clicks	low	high	EC	confirmed
IH10	task vs. relationship orientation	low	high	information transmission	number of non verbal interactions with the	low	high	-	not investigated

					system per time unit				
INH10	task vs. relationship orientation	low	high	interaction device	mouse, touch screen, speech, menu control button, keyboard	mouse, control button	touch screen	-	Not investigated
INH11	face saving	low	high	interaction frequency	number of help initiations per time unit	low	high	HI	rejected
INH12	task vs. relationship orientation	low	high	Information pres.speed	duration of information presentation	long	short	DIP	rejected

Different cultural explanations are possible for the same interaction behavior

The results of the empirically confirmed hypotheses show that there are several possible explanations for the same cultural interaction differences in HCI. For example, high vs. low information frequency for (C) vs. (G) can be explained by poly-chronic vs. mono-chronic time orientation (IH1a) or by high vs. low communication speed (IH1c) or by high vs. low communication network density (IH5) or by high vs. low relationship orientation (IH8).

Further and more detailed studies necessary

Hence, empirical research supported the fact that it is not trivial (methodologically easy) to determine the right and distinct explanation for the differences in information frequency for users with different cultural imprint. Therefore, further and essentially more detailed studies must show the real (even another) reason for the high vs. low information frequency. In this respect, also the other hypotheses of this work should be tested in future.

Cultural differences in HCI regarding interaction speed and frequency

Nevertheless, the results of this work proved that there are cultural differences in HCI regarding interaction speed and frequency. Therefore, the empirical results identified so far by this work can be considered to represent the first step towards reasonable explanation models for cultural differences in HCI regarding the interaction level. Moreover, the approach and model used in this work, which underlies this interrelationship, is worth being researched and optimized in the future.

Real ratios of the values of the measurement variables in contrast to the postulated ratios

Figure 26 shows the differences in the empirically gathered ratios of the values of the measurement variables in contrast to the postulated ratios of the values of the variables originally assumed in the confirmed hypotheses. For example, it has been postulated that the number of interactions with the system per time unit (IH1a) of Chinese users is about four times higher than that of German users (0.8 : 0.2 = 4), as shown in Figure 19 in section 4.5 and indicated in Figure 26 by the white bars.

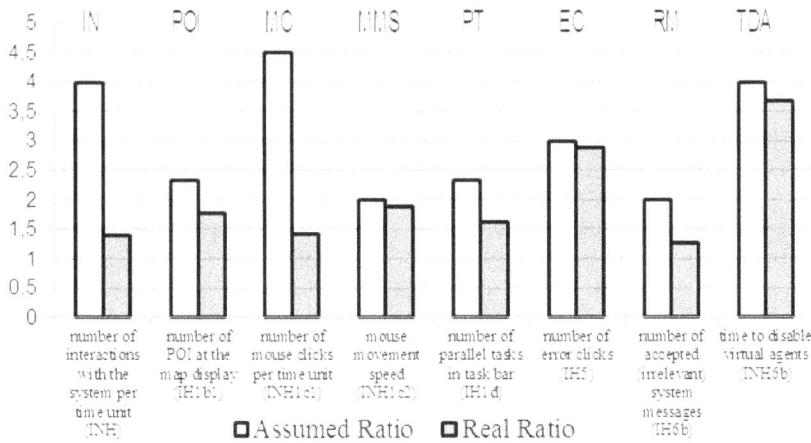

Figure 26: Ratio of postulated and real values of Cultural Interaction Indicators (CIIs) regarding Chinese speaking users in comparison to German speaking users (Source: "071115 Empirische Hypothesen der Dissertation pres.xlsx")

However, in reality the ratio is only 1.4, e.g., regarding the number of average mouse moves within one test session (10566:7529).[287] The ratios of the postulated to the real values of the measurement variables can be considered as indicators for the confirmation strength of the hypotheses. Even if the postulated ratio could not be matched exactly, most of the content of the postulated hypotheses could be confirmed successfully: the ratios of six out of the eight (confirmed) partial hypotheses (from the EHs) were estimated *a priori* almost correctly (except for INH and INH1c1) and all eight hypotheses have been confirmed *a posteriori* by the two online studies in this dissertation project (cf. Figure 26). In addition, even if the ratio of IN and MC have not been correctly estimated *a priori*, they have been confirmed *a posteriori*, which proved that also the hypotheses IN and MC are reasonable.[288]

Strong confirmation of 5 from 9 empirical hypotheses (EH)

---

[287] The operationalization of the hypothesis IH1a was carried out using the factor "number of interactions with the system per time unit" which is represented by several measurement variables per time unit (cf. section 4.5). Vagueness therefore arose in the hypothesis, which was reflected in the differences of the assumed to the real relationship of the values of the cultural interaction indicators.

[288] One reason for the relatively big difference in the relationship between the assumed and real ratio of the number of mouse clicks could be that mouse clicks are executed not unconsciously but usually for a specific task, unlike mouse movements. Mouse clicks are therefore possibly more dependent on the application and on the functionality the user demands than on the cultural imprint of the user as the author postulated.

Plausible and correct results

Thereby, the results presented in Figure 26 indicate that the analytical reflections, the methods used and the conducted studies in this work were done well and the results can be regarded as plausible and correct.[289]

Evaluation of measurement variables

Therefore, according to the verified hypotheses, most of the potential cultural interaction indicators (PCIIs) presented in section 4.5 could have been confirmed to be meaningful and useful. These are marked with "✓" in Table 32, if confirmed by the results of both online studies, and "✓1.study", if confirmed only by the results of study 1. They can be called cultural interaction indicators (CIIs). PCIIs that have not been investigated are marked with "not inv.". PCIIs that cannot be considered to be CIIs are marked with "rejected". Some hypotheses (e.g., IH7 (NVIN) and INH7 (LMT)) could not be verified because of missing parameters or data. Furthermore, the hypothesis INH11 (number of help calls (HI, SH_{11})) as well as hypothesis IH12 (duration of information presentation (DIP, SH_{15})) had to be rejected (cf. Table 31 and Table 49).

Table 32: Evaluation of measurement variables (marked with "✓" when confirmed in both studies; "✓1.study" when confirmed only in the first study; "rejected" when rejected; "not inv." when not investigated)

Measurement variable (operationalized according to hypothesis)	Germany	China	Short name of measurement variable	Evaluation
Information speed (time between two sequentially presented information units) (IH1a)	low	high	TPI	✓
Number of long interaction breaks (¬INH1a)	high	low	¬IN	✓
Number of POI in the map display (IH1b1)	low	high	POI	✓
Number pieces of information presented by the system per time unit (IH1b2)	low	high	IN	✓
Number of interactions with the system per time unit (IH1c)	low	high	IN	✓
Number of mouse clicks per time unit (INH1c1)	low	high	MC	✓
Mouse movement speed (INH1c2)	low	high	MMS	✓
Number of mouse moves per time unit (INH1c3)	low	high	MM	✓

---

[289] In section 6.6.3, the reliability of the results in this work will be discussed in detail.

Number of parallel tasks in task bar (IH1d)	low	high	PT	✓
Number of pieces of information presented by the system per time unit (IH5)	low	high	NIT	✓
Number of interactions with the system per time unit (INH5)	low	high	IN	✓
Number of parallel tasks in task bar (IH6a)	low	high	PT	✓
Number of error clicks (IH6b)	low	high	EC	✓
Number of refused system messages (IH6b)	low	high	RM	✓ 1.study
Time to disable virtual agents (INH6b)	low	high	TDA	✓ 1.study
Number of non verbal interactions with the system per time unit (IH7)	low	high	NVIN	not inv.
Number of long mouse tracks / length of mouse track (INH7)	low	high	LMT	not inv.
Number of interactions with the system per time unit (IH8)	low	high	IN	✓
Number of interactions with the system per time unit (INH8)	low	high	IN	✓
Number of non verbal communication and interactions with the system per time unit (IH9, IH10)	low	high	NVIN	not inv.
Number of function initiations per time unit (INH10)	low	high	FI	not inv.
Number of help initiations by the user per time unit (INH11)	high	low	HI	rejected
Duration of information presentation (IH12)	long	short	DIP	rejected

The very interesting individual values of the cultural interaction indicators from these results can only be topped by the general impression that there are actually differences in the interaction behavior between Chinese and German users due to their cultural imprint, which are ascertainable purely quantitatively. This indicates that it is possible to confirm the methodological hypotheses MHCV1 and MHCV2 (postulated in section 4.3.2). In fact, the methodological hypotheses will be verified after testing the CAHMI principle in chapter 7. Thereby, some of the measurement variables (PCIIs) that turned out statistically to be CIIs (marked with "✓" in Table 32) will be applied to reality by implementing them in a CAHMI demonstrator based on a real mobile driver navigation system to prove that they also work in reality and not only statistically. Before that, the results presented will be discussed.

6.6   Discussing the Results

In this section, the most salient results of the two online studies presented in section 6.2 will be discussed. The disturbing variables, the classification power of the cultural interaction indicators, the cultural user characteristics and the reliability of the IIA tool will be discussed to argue for and to underline the plausibility of the results as well as the justification of the postulated HMI dimensions (section 6.6.1), the classification power of the cultural interaction indicators and their generalization (section 6.6.2) as well as the reliability of the results supported by this and related work (section 6.6.3).

6.6.1   Statistical Confirmation of the HMI Dimensions (HMIDs)

HMI dimensions as main factors relevant for HMI design

HMI dimensions (HMIDs) represent the classes of cultural interaction indicators identified in this work. In this sense, HMI dimensions can be regarded as main factors relevant for HMI design. For example, the CII "number of information units per *space* unit" belongs to the HMI dimension "information density" and can be expressed e.g., by the number of POI displayed on a screen. Another HMI dimension (HMID) is "interaction frequency". This class contains e.g., the number of interactions per time unit (e.g., represented by the number of mouse clicks per second). Support for the correctness of the HMIDs in this work comes from the application of factor analysis methods.

Factor analysis methods

Correlation and component matrices

Explorative factor analysis served to derive HMI dimensions by grouping the potential variables to factors (component matrix) according to the strength of their correlation (correlation matrix).[290] Table 33 shows the component matrix extracted by main component analysis taking into account 19 measurement parameters. It describes the contents of the main constituents of the four main components using analytical interpretation (indicated by the different shadings).

---

[290] The correlation matrix for the parameters used in the first online study can be found in file "Korrelationen.spo" in the online appendix.

Table 33: Four main components found by explorative factorial analysis of the data of the first data collection (Source: file "IIA Faktorenanalyse Demo.spo" in the online appendix) (bold: interaction behavior, italicized and very lightly greyed: information reception (information density and order), light grey: information speed, dark grey: power distance)

Measurement parameters	Component			
	1	2	3	4
	Interaction behavior	*Information reception*	Information speed	Gender/Power distance
Age	0.650	-0.414	0.423	-0.080
Duration abroad	0.789	-0.153	-0.146	-0.577
PC experience	0.905	0.297	0.045	0.230
Order index	-0.495	*0.640*	0.585	0.038
Number index	-0.524	*0.726*	0.444	0.028
Density index	-0.642	*0.635*	0.430	0.005
Size index	0.699	-0.573	-0.423	0.067
Result index	0.834	-0.222	0.459	0.130
Task orientation index	0.834	-0.222	0.459	0.130
Time interval	0.782	0.056	0.564	-0.181
Gender	0.017	0.590	-0.481	0.608
Information density index	0.379	*0.908*	0.093	-0.098
Information speed index	0.362	0.475	-0.746	0.038
Information order index	0.614	*0.771*	0.070	-0.082
Interaction exactness index	0.955	0.259	0.098	-0.007
Interaction speed index	0.857	0.437	-0.227	-0.100
Uncertainty avoidance index	0.538	*0.644*	-0.033	-0.255
Power distance index	0.615	0.102	-0.201	0.664
Number of help calls	-0.188	0.416	-0.685	-0.514

Style of user interaction behavior (expressed by interaction speed index and interaction exactness index) is influenced by age, time abroad and experience in the usage of computers as well as task orientation of the user (bold). Information reception (represented by information density, number and order index) varies because of the influence of uncertainty avoidance (italicized). Information speed (represented by information speed index) correlates obviously with help usage (represented by the number of help calls) (light grey).

Mutually influenced components

Furthermore, gender and power distance indices seem to be correlated (dark grey). The indexes in Table 33 are computed partly according to the formulae presented in section 10.6.3 in the work report. Their meaning is compatible with the meanings of the variables explained in section 6.2.

Correlation of gender and power distance

Table 34 depicts the four main factor loadings ("components") derived from the data of the first data collection that explain nearly 95% of the variance of the 19 measurement parameters (as seen in Table 33).[291]

Four main components of first data collection
⇨ Interaction style
⇨ Information reception
⇨ Information speed
⇨ Gender / power distance

Table 34: Variance explained by four main components found by explorative factorial analysis of the data of the first data collection (Source: file "IIA Faktorenanalyse Demo.spo" in the online appendix)

Com-ponent #	Beginning Eigenwerte using the extracting method of main component analysis			Sums of quadratic factor loads for extraction		
(n of 19)	Total	% of variance	cumulated %	Total	% of variance	cumulated %
1	8.289	43.628	43.628	8.289	43.628	43.628
2	4.902	25.799	69.428	4.902	25.799	69.428
3	3.219	16.941	86.368	3.219	16.941	86.368
4	1.633	8.597	94.965	1.633	8.597	94.965

Overlapping components

⇨ Need for extended factor analysis

The remaining 15 components in total explain only 5% of the variance of the 19 measurement parameters. This analysis is clear if also not very meaningful because the variables constituting the components partly overlap. Therefore, an "extended" factor analysis has been carried out.

Table 35 presents the seven main components extracted by the extended factor analysis from the correlation matrix explaining cultural and HMI relevant aspects as expected by the theoretical part of this work. The postulated hypotheses represented by the first 7 components explain 36.4% of the total variance, i.e. at least 36% of the effect is explained by the test setting. Nineteen components explain around 66% and 45 components explain 100% of the total variance. This indicates that the study is influenced by many factors. The extended (more detailed) factor analysis revealed that component #1 (interaction behavior) in the "simple" factor analysis (cf. Table 34) can be split up into the two components "primary cultural imprint" and "interactional behavior" or "HMI style".

Largest components concern HMI and cultural aspects

The fact that the largest components concern HMI and cultural aspects (as expected by the test setting) points to the correctness of the research strategy in this work.

---

[291] Even if the data collected in the studies contain much more information than interpreted until now, the work project to extract more detailed information must remain for the future because of the limited time resources of this work. In addition, verifying the HMIDs by doing an explorative factor analysis with the data from the second online study to enhance the separation effect and discriminatory power of the HMI dimensions also remains a task for the future.

Table 35: The seven most important components extracted from the results of the first online study by the "extended" explorative factor analysis (Source: file "070526 Proximity Matrix Of All Variables.spo" in the online appendix)

Compo- nent #	Meaning of the Component	Aspects (measured parameters)	Explanation share	Explanation total
1	Primary cultural imprint	Nationality, primary residence, country of birth, cultural origin	8.5%	8.5%
2	Interaction behavior/style (IN)	Speed, Exactness, [age], [language]292	6.5%	15%
3	Information density (ID)	Number of presented information units	5.5%	20.5%
4	Information speed (IS/TPI/DIP)	Presentation frequency and presentation duration of presented information units	5%	25.5%
5	Secondary cultural imprint	Second nationality, secondary residence [mouse clicks]	3.8%	29.3%
6	Relationship- orientation	[Sense of community], [femininity vs. masculinity], [open tasks], [mouse clicks]	3.6%	32.9%
7	Parallel work method	[Poly-chronic vs. mono-chronic?], [femininity vs. masculinity], [PC-experience?]	3.5%	36.4%

The components marked in light grey are informational explanations for the differences in HMI (17%). The components marked in dark grey explain the differences in HMI between the test persons by cultural reasons (12.3%). This constitutes the statistical proof from empirically obtained data to the effect that culture influences the user interaction with the system.[293] Nevertheless, explorative factor analysis must be done again in future studies without the parameters contributing to cultural imprinting (components number one and five) to concentrate more on the separation effect and discriminatory power of the components, i.e. the HMI dimensions (HMIDs). This is a chance to differentiate further the HMI variables (describing single objects) into HMI parameters (describing the whole population). Even if, until now, only the components #2 (interaction behavior/style (IN)), #3 (information density (ID)) and #4 (information speed (TPI + DIP)) could have been proven empirically by the analysis done in this work, progress in intercultural HMI research increased because the loadings of the HMI dimensions are also supported by the empirical results of this work presented in section 6.2.

Statistical proof of culturally influenced user interaction

Need for future studies on separation effect and discriminatory power

From HMI variables to HMI parameters

Progress in intercultural HMI research

---

[292] The variables in square brackets correspond to the correlations marked dark green (positive) or red (negative) in Table 21 in section 6.6.1 in the work report.

[293] These results have also been supported by multidimensional scaling (cf. section 6.6.1 in the work report).

Even if the HMI related components, which represent the HMI dimensions, are still very fuzzy and partly overlapping,[294] the HMIDs found by this method are separated clearly from each other. For example, clusters 2, 3 and 4 clearly represent interaction exactness and information density as well as information- and interaction speed in accordance with results of factor analysis presented in Table 35. These clusters (relevant for HMI design) appear throughout this work, which supports the empirical correctness as well as the factual existence of the assumed HMI dimensions like information and interaction speed, information and interaction frequency as well as information density and interaction exactness that all depend significantly on cultural aspects support-ing the results presented in section 6.2.

6.6.2   Classification Power of CIIs and CIPs

The discriminatory power of the cultural interaction indicators has been calculated using discriminance analysis. There are many combinations of such indicators (cf. section 6.2), which contribute positively to a high discrimination rate in assigning users to their test language or nationality without knowing their nationality or cultural background – only the interaction patterns within the use cases or applications are known.

Jackknife-Method" (Step-by-Step analysis) = iterative analysis

"Step-by-step" discrimination analysis ("Jackknife-Method") offers iterative analysis of the best discriminating cultural interaction indicators automatically out of a given set of potential ones.

The best discriminating cultural interaction indicators of the 118 parameters implemented into the IIA tool (cf. Table 20 in section 5.2.2) identified by the first study are presented in Table 36.[295]

---

[294] They also depend on disturbing variables (e.g., component #5) even if not significantly (cf. section 6.3). Furthermore, component #5 regarding cultural behavior (expressed by uncertain-ty avoidance, parallel working, open tasks, mouse clicks) and component #7 regarding expe-rience (embracing pc experience, gender, parallel working (error clicks, help initiations)) are semantically very similar, because they appear side by side in the resulting diagram by multi-dimensional scaling, which is represented visually in Figure 31 in section 6.6.1 in the work report.

[295] The data are from the files "060124 Most Discriminating Use Case Independent Cultural Interaction Indicators.spo" and "060103 84 Datensätze.sav" in the online appendix generated after the data collection of the first study in 2006 containing all implemented variables in the IIA tool. "IH" represents the test task for information hierarchy. "CS" means the comic strip test task. "AP" refers to the abstract picture test. The screens of those tests can be seen in the work report in section 10.3.4.

Table 36: Best discriminating Cultural Interaction Indicators (CIIs) of the implemented parameters in the IIA tool (from the first online study including the CIIs from log files) (Source: files "070411 Results for IWIPS 2007.spo" and„070127 Alle Daten der Haupterhebungen.sav" in the online appendix)

Cultural Interaction Indicator (CII)	Short name of measurement variable	Standard Coefficients of the Canonical Discriminance Function	
		1	2
MD.Number Of Maneuvers	(POI)[296]	0.478	-0.486
MG.Mouse Clicks	MC	0.242	0.387
MG.Info Presentation Duration	DIP	0.292	-0.404
Yes Counter	AM	0.557	0.925
No Counter	RM	1.442	-0.164
MD.Number Of Restaurants	(POI)	0.152	0.573
CS.Mouse Clicks	MC	0.519	-0.100
IH.Number(Of List Entries)	(POI)	-0.243	-0.556
AP.Covering Coefficient	(POI)	-0.660	0.325
Break0ms	(¬IN)	0.363	0.074
Break10s_norm	(¬IN)	-0.475	0.324
Refuse Message_norm	(¬IN)	-1.551	-0.916
Move Agent_norm	TDA	0.971	0.183
Error Clicks	EC	0.371	-0.025

In Figure 27, the proper distribution of the data points according to the classified test languages can be seen very well. This is supported by the high cross-validated classification rate of 88.7% shown in Table 37, which represents the classification quotes of the best discriminating CIIs. Some CIIs derived from the log file (test duration, mouse moves and key presses) together classify the user correctly to their selected test language in about 88% of the cases.[297] The CII "mouse moves" alone classifies about 77% of the cases correctly.

High classification rate of 88%

CII "mouse moves" alone has 77% classification rate

Table 37: Classification quotes of the best discriminating Cultural Interaction Indicators (CIIs) of the implemented parameters in the IIA tool (from the first online study including the CIIs from log

---

[296] Short names in brackets indicate that they combine more than one variables (e.g., (POI) is composed of four variables and (¬IN) is composed of three variables).

[297] Cf. files "070309 Logfileauswertung 1632.spo" and „070309 Logfileauswertung 1632.sav" in the online appendix.

files) (Source: files „070411 Results for IWIPS 2007.spo" and "070127 Alle Daten der Haupter-hebungen.sav" in the online appendix)

Classification Results [b,c]		Language_num	Predicted Group Membership			Total
			1	2	3	
Original	Count	1	31	0	0	31
		2	1	36	3	40
		3	2	3	21	26
	%	1	100.0	0.0	0.0	100.0
		2	2.5	90.0	7.5	100.0
		3	7.7	11.5	80.8	100.0
Cross-val. [a]	Count	1	30	0	1	31
		2	2	35	3	40
		3	2	3	21	26
	%	1	96.8	0.0	3.2	100.0
		2	5.0	87.5	7.5	100.0
		3	7.7	11.5	80.8	100.0

a) Cross validation is done only for those cases in the analysis. In cross validation, each case is classified by the functions derived from all cases other than that case.

b) 90.7% of original grouped cases correctly classified.

c) 88.7% of cross-validated grouped cases correctly classified.

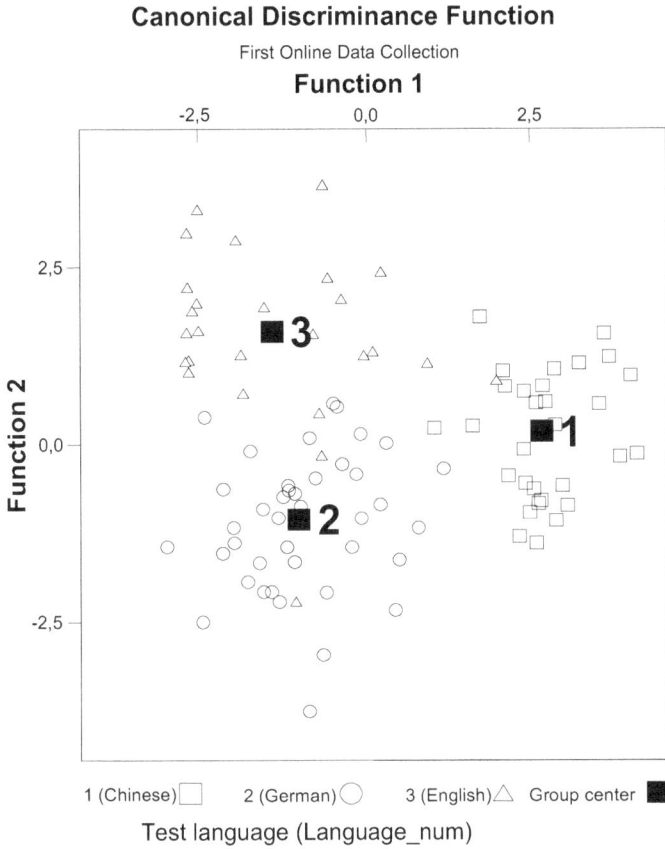

Canonical Discriminance Function

First Online Data Collection

1 (Chinese) □   2 (German) ○   3 (English) △   Group center ■

Test language (Language_num)

Figure 27: Visual presentation of the classification results of the combination of the cultural interaction indicators (CIIs) found by the first study presented in Table 36 (Source: files "070411 Results for IWIPS 2007.spo; database: 070127 Alle Daten der Haupterhebungen.sav" in the online appendix)

The differences are also qualitatively confirmed by the impressions of the author obtained whilst conducting interviews and participatory observation for the qualitative studies done in China and Germany (cf. section 6.1). Chinese users interact in a more emotional manner than German users and this is represented by a higher interaction frequency, i.e. in the greater number of mouse clicks and mouse moves per time unit as well as in shorter test duration.

User interaction can be quantitatively described with only a few discriminative intercultural variables

The resulting discrimination rate by the 13 most discriminating cultural interaction indicators of the second online study (cf. Table 38)[298] for classifying all test users to their selected test languages simultaneously and correctly is 59.9% (cf. Figure 28).[299]

Table 38: The most discriminating Cultural Interaction Indicators (CIIs) according to "step-by-step" discriminance analysis in the second online study (without CIIs from log files)

Discrimination coefficients Cultural Interaction Indicator	Short name of measurement variavle	Function 1	2
Information Speed	IS, (TPI)	0.487	0.273
Uncertainty Avoidance	UV	0.197	-0.208
Wave Volume Init Position	-	0.226	0.188
Number Of Maneuvers	(POI)	0.203	-0.665
Number Of Characters	KS	0.183	0.169
Reference Measure Value	-	-0.190	0.444
Interaction Exactness	INE	0.402	-0.142
System Mouse Keys Max Speed	(MMS)	0.147	0.177
Number Of Maximal Open Tasks	PT	-0.198	-0.201
Number Of POI	POI	-0.248	-0.155
Number Of Streets	(POI)	0.312	0.047
Number Of Restaurants	(POI)	-0.212	0.298
Maneuver Guidance Speed	(TPI)	-0.189	0.171

---

[298] Cf. files „*.spo" in the online appendix (e.g., „070117 Auswertung der zweiten IIA-Online-Haupterhebung.spo"). The most relevant CIIs in this table have been already explained in section 6.2. For a description of the remaining CIIs, please refer to page 17 seqq. in file "060906 Argumentationsgang Dissertation.doc" in the online appendix.

[299] Cross-validated and grouped (cf. Backhaus et al. 2006), ($p_{inclusion}=0.05$; $p_{exclusion}=0.1$; Wilk's: $\lambda_{1-2}=0.649**$; $\lambda_2=0.850**$). Classifying to nationality results in a higher classification rate of 96,8% than classifying to test language with 81.9% (cf. section 6.2 as well as file "070428 Hofstedes Indices vs. CIIs (100% vs. 92%).spo" in the online appendix). Furthermore, the calculation of this classification rate did not include the CIIs from log files. It can be supposed that the classification rate is even higher when also considering the CIIs from log files because then there are better cultural indicators narrowing the window of potential interaction behavior assigned to a user with a special cultural background. The verification of this assumption remains for future work as well as the additional profound and far-reaching discussion of the CIIs found (because of time restrictions in this work).

Canonical Discriminance Function

Second Online Data Collection

Test language

1 (Chinese)   2 (German)   3 (English)   Group Centers ■

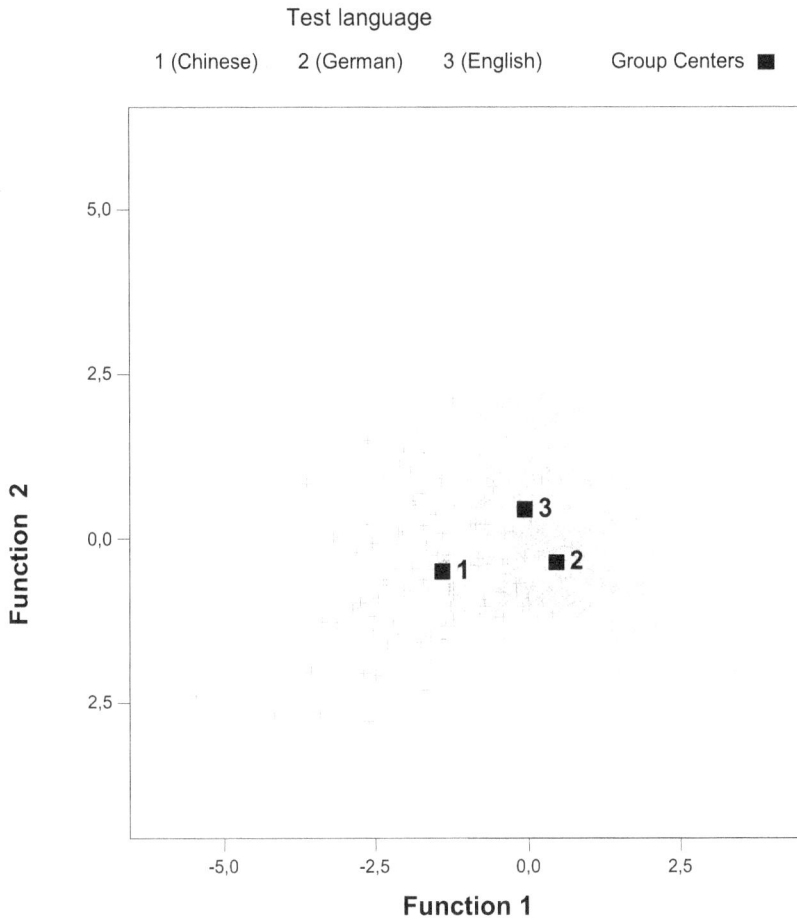

Figure 28: The distribution of classified cases according to test language in the second online study (Source: file „070411 Results for IWIPS 2007.spo" based on database in file „070127 Alle Daten der Haupterhebungen.sav" in the online appendix)

The resulting discrimination rate for classifying all test users simultaneously and correctly to their selected test languages (i.e. to the groups (C), (E) and (G)) is 59.9% for the second and 60.8% for the first study (without CIIs from log files). This indicates a strong similarity of the collected data as well as the correctness of the methodology and the results of the studies (cf. Table 39).

Similarity of collected data

Hence, assumption A2 (cf. section 4.3.1) is fulfilled: for the automatic identification of the user culture and the automatic adaptation of the system to this user culture at runtime, only a few discriminative intercultural variables suffice to include and describe the user and his interaction with the system quantitatively.

Table 39: Comparison of the classification power of the Cultural Interaction Indicators (CIIs) according to test language between the first and the second online study (without CIIs from log files)[300]

Discriminance analysis			Predicted group membership		
Study	Classification rate [%]	Test language	Chinese	German	English
1	Cross validated total: 60.80	Chinese	**58.82**	29.41	11.76
	Wilk's λ_{1-2}=0.574**, λ_2=0.855**	German	9.09	**70.45**	20.45
	$p_{inclusion}$=0.05; $p_{exclusion}$=0.1	English	29.17	25.00	**45.83**
2	Cross validated total: 59.90	Chinese	**35.58**	23.08	*41.35*
	Wilk's λ_{1-2}=0.649**, λ_2=0.850**	German	4.55	**61.76**	33.69
	$p_{inclusion}$=0.05; $p_{exclusion}$=0.1	English	6.45	29.49	**64.06**

However, the Chinese interaction behavior is not classified very clearly in the second study (35.58%, cf. Table 39), which indicates that in this case disturbing variables influence the classification power of the cultural interaction indicators. One possible explanation for this is the difference in the sample sizes of the second online data collection: the sample size of (E) is three and those of (G) is six times higher than for (C) (n $_{(C)}$ = 1500, n $_{(E)}$ = 4500, n $_{(G)}$ = 8500). Probably there are too few complete and valid Chinese data sets to reasonably conduct discriminance analysis for classification to all three groups simultaneously. This aspect required a deeper analysis. Hence, in applying the same method of discriminance analysis, but classifying the cases into two groups (instead of three groups at the same time), the discrimination rate increased tremendously: it went up to 70.4% for (G) and (E) and was even 85.4% for (C) and (G). These results indicate that the results presented in Table 39 can also be taken as plausible and correct.

---

[300] In file "070205 Auswertung beider IIA-Erhebungen OK.spo" in the online appendix there are additional calculations by discrimination analysis concerning test language as well as nationality in different combinations. All computations confirm the strong correlation of test language and nationality but also the light influence of the disturbing variables on the classification rate. Furthermore, the classification quote of the CIIs is higher than those of the disturbing variables.

6.6.3   Reliability of the Results Supported by this and Related Work

Despite the presented methodological challenges, the high discrimination rate of over 80% and the high correspondence between the cultural interaction indicators found by one-way ANOVA and the Kruskal-Wallis-Test (cf. sections 6.2 and 6.6.2) in conjunction with the weak influence of disturbing variables (cf. section 6.3) support the high reliability and criteria validity of the statistical results received in these studies as well as the functional correctness, appropriateness and reliability of the IIA tool (cf. section 5.2). In addition, this is fostered by the results of the evaluation of the functionality of the CAHMI demonstrator using the FTE tool implemented in the IIA data evaluation module applying neural networks.[301] Especially the high classification quote of about 80% caused by the two CIIs ("Nb Of Scrolls Shorter Than 1ms" and "Mouse Up") (cf. section 7.3) can be taken into account to prove and enhance the plausibility of the quantitative results of this work. Moreover, this discriminating rate is still higher (up to 97%) when using mouse and keyboard events on a PC as shown in section 7.5.

Reliability of IIA tool

Discrimination rate of over 80%

High accordance of CIIs

Weak influence of disturbing variables

Functionality of CAHMI demonstrator

Cronbach's Alpha is a coefficient expressing the internal consistency of psychometric instruments (cf. Cronbach 1951). It slightly exceeds the value of 0.7 for the implemented complete PUMTM in the IIA data collection module (cf. section 5.2.2), which justifies using the developed test setting using the potential usability metric trace model.[302] This value is even higher for semantically clustered groups of CIIs according to the determined HMI dimensions. For example, Cronbach's Alpha for the inner consistency of the items ("number of POI", "number of roads", "number of road names", "number of textures", "number of restaurants" and "number of maneuvers") used to represent information density is 0.736.[303] Cronbach's Alpha for the "interaction" cluster regarding the mouse clicks is even 0.788, which supports the high discrimination power of CIIs from log files (cf. sections 6.6.2 and 7.5). This overall

Cronbach's Alpha > 0.7

---

[301] Cf. section 5.4 as well as section 10.2.1 in the work report.

[302] It is commonly accepted that values of Cronbach's Alpha greater 0.7 justifies the usage of the tested psychometric instrument (cf. Bortz et al. 2006). Furthermore Kendall's value for two "quantitative estimators" can be used to compare the two timely separated online studies in 2006 and 2007. However, this analysis remains for the future. The exact values of Cronbach's Alpha depend on the item groups and can be found in file "060917 97 DS Testvalidierung4.spo" in the online appendix. They range between 0.7 and 0.8.

[303] Please refer to file "060917 97 DS Testvalidierung4.spo" in the online appendix for looking up Cronbach's Alpha of this and other CII clusters not explicitly mentioned here.

outcome proves the high reliability of the results and justifies the usage of the IIA tool.

Results confirmed by
related work

Furthermore, many aspects have been confirmed by qualitative studies from related work e.g., by Lewandowitz et al. 2006, Kralisch 2006 and Kamentz 2006 or Brunner 2005. For example, Brunner 2005 checked three assumptions stated by the author (cf. Heimgärtner 2005), which are also examined in this dissertation project. The results confirmed each other: the Chinese users cope very well with high information density as well as with more simultaneous tasks and additional information (cf. section 6.2).

Information density

Layout

Another confirmed aspect is that Chinese users expect a different layout (arrangement of widgets) than German users. The arrangement of the widgets by Chinese and German users differs mainly in two aspects:

- Back ("zurück") and forward ("vor") buttons for navigation are reversed, i.e. (C) placed the buttons in the back-forward order, (G) placed them in forward-back order.
- The position of the status bar is different: (C) top, (G) bottom.

This aspect has also been researched qualitatively by Röse et al. 2001. Chinese users like to see the most important information in the left bottom area of the screen in contrast to German users. The latter expect the most interesting information to be on the right top of the screen (cf. also Röse et al. 2001), which supports the results from the URD test task of this work.[304] The German users prefer less important information like time and date to be displayed in the status line in the lower area of the screen.

Qualitative studies in this work brought to light some results concerning the direct visible cultural variables (cf. section 6.1). However, the sample sizes of the qualitative studies done in this work were very small and hence, these results can only provide new hints instead of being precise guidelines for the future.

Nevertheless, even the reliability of the qualitative studies is given by the fact that the results (cf. section 6.1) do not contradict to the results of the quantitative studies (cf. section 6.2) in general.

Figure 29 shows the values of the quantitatively significant cultural interaction indicators (CIIs) derived from the log files of the second study according to the

---

[304] Similarly, Dong & Salvendy 1999 came to the recommendation that English-speaking software for Chinese users should have horizontal menus. Chinese-speaking software should be offered with a vertical menu order.

nationality of the test persons.[305] These are normalized mouse moves (continuous black line), mean of normalized key downs (chained-dotted line) and
mean of normalized left mouse button downs (short-dotted line). All three CIIs
belong to the set of CIIs that represent interaction frequency because of their
strong mutual correlation.

It is remarkable that all three CIIs concerning the kind of interaction behavior
of the users are shaped in a similar way according to the nationality of the test
participants indicating that the interaction style is clearly different between
nations (cf. Figure 29).

Different interaction behavior across nations

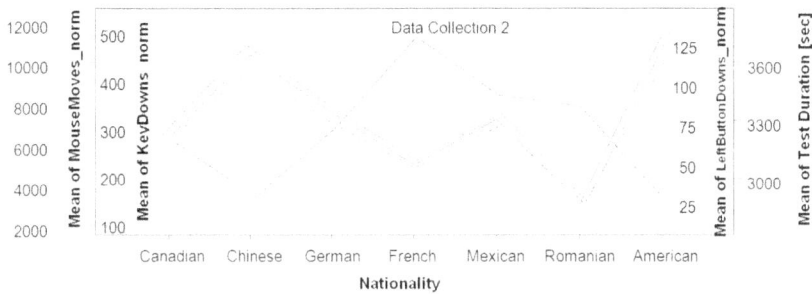

Figure 29: Quantitatively significant Cultural Interaction Indicators (CIIs) derived from the log files of the second online study according to the nationality of the test persons (Source: file "070306 Logfileauswertung zweite iia online haupterhebung.spo" in the online appendix)

The agreement of the shapes in Figure 29 underlines the plausibility and
cultural dependence of the cultural interaction indicators, the correctness of the
measurement and the test setup of the study as well as the study results. The
course of "test duration" (long-dotted line in Figure 29) is almost reversed for
Chinese, French, Romanian and US-American users. This is the case particularly with Chinese and US-American users. This phenomenon cannot be
attributed to the fact that their measured IDV is similar (cf. section 6.4)
because this is in contrast to the fact that the interaction behavior of Chinese
and US-American users is approximately the same regarding the measured
mouse and keyboard events.

Agreement of shapes indicates reliability of method, test setting and results

The (potential) cultural interaction indicators can be visualized by applying the
IIA data analysis tool to plot "(potential) cultural HCI fingerprints" (in the
style suggested by Smith & Chang 2003) which represent the cultural differ-

---

[305] Cf. file "Logfile-Ergebnisse.xls" in the online appendix.

ences in HCI in respect to several variables for HCI design (Figure 30).[306] This visual representation of the CIIs helps to ease information reception and improves comparative understanding of the cultural differences in HCI.

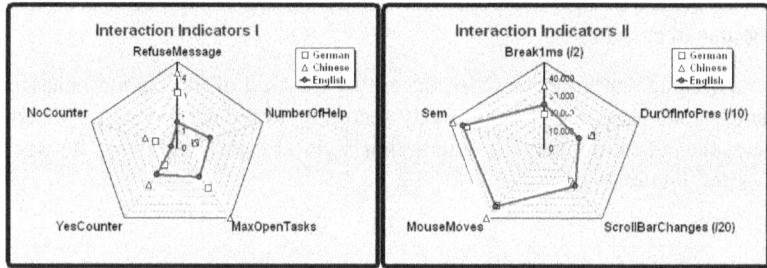

Figure 30: "Cultural HCI Fingerprints"(different peculiarities of the (Potential) Cultural Interaction Indicators ((P)CIIs) according to test language) plot by the IIA data analysis module

Differences in specific values of CIIs

Correct test equipment

More importantly, the way of presenting information in Figure 30 allows confirming two aspects: First, the picture on the left hand side shows that there are differences in the specific values of the (P)CIIs. Second, the right hand side picture indicates that the test equipment is correct because of similar pentagonal shapes in the graph.

The results are reliable because they are traceable and reproducible by the two online studies, finally, yet importantly, because of the high sample size of the second online study.

In sum, discussing the results showed that they are correct and the method used to secure them is plausible.[307]

---

[306] Please refer to section 10.4.1 in the work report for further cultural HCI fingerprints.

[307] For additional support, please refer to section 6.6.3 in the work report and to the online appendix.

7 Culturally Adaptive HMI Demonstrator

"Teuer zu verkaufen ist keine Sünde, wohl aber falsch zu messen."
(Old German proverb)[308]

The strong statistically discriminating cultural interaction indicators identified by the two online studies in this work motivated the author to demonstrate that they also work in a real environment (cf. section 7.3). By means of a demonstrator (sections 7.1 and 7.2), some important cultural variables as well as the principle of CAHMI (cf. section 3.2.1) are demonstrated as an example to support the following argumentation: If the CAHMI demonstrator is capable of classifying the user according to his interaction with the system and correctly identifying his cultural characteristics, then there is empirical proof that parts of the interrelationship between the HMI dimensions relevant for HMI design and the cultural dimensions postulated in the hypotheses of this work in section 4.3.3 are correct. A demonstrator regarding culturally adaptive HMI requires the following properties to show the correctness of the postulated models and guidelines as well as the principle of CAHMI:

Empirical proof by CAHMI demonstrator

- Parameterization with cultural properties for different cultural groups
- Recognition of the specific values of the intercultural variables by user monitoring
- Automatic adaption of the HMI to the cultural needs of the user (= CAHMI).

Properties of the CAHMI demonstrator

This "CAHMI functionality" has been integrated in a portable navigation system by Siemens VDO called "CAHMI demonstrator" (cf. Figure 31).

---

[308] "It is no sin to sell something expensively, but it is a sin to measure wrongly." (cf. footnote 1 on page 1 and file "Sprichwörter mit messen.txt" in the online appendix).

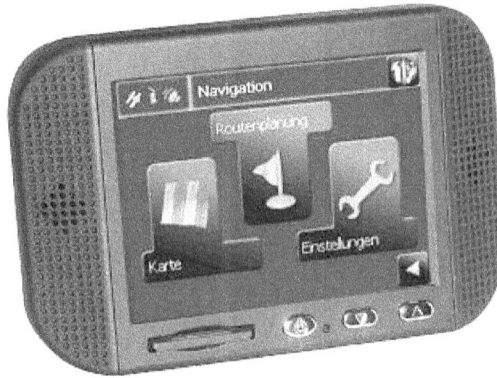

Figure 31: The CAHMI demonstrator based on a mobile driver navigation system by Siemens VDO

"Arriba Mobile WinCE navigation platform"

The CAHMI demonstrator runs on the "Arriba Mobile WinCE navigation platform", which is a basic navigation core for navigation systems developed by Siemens VDO. It is equipped with a touch screen, three hardware buttons (up, down, on/off) as well as a slot for SD memory cards containing the navigation database.[309] The software architecture uses classes and libraries from the Microsoft Foundation Classes (MFC) (cf. Prosise 1999). It is based on the operating system "Microsoft Windows CE" (cf. Boling 2008) and programmed in "VC++ Embedded" (cf. Boling 2008).

7.1   Implementation of Cultural Interaction Indicators and Use Cases

Types of interaction means in driver navigation systems

To transmit the PUMTM for computers to driver navigation systems, it is necessary to think about the interaction means between user and driver navigation systems. The most important types of interaction means in driver navigation systems are shown in Table 40.

---

[309] The SD memory card (Secure Digital Memory Card) serves to store data in a flash memory.

Table 40: Relevant types of interaction means for driver navigation systems

Interface	Interaction means	Available in driver navigation systems	Relevant for driver navigation systems
GUI	Soft key	no	yes (if using a touch screen)
GUI	Hard key	yes	yes
GUI	Touchpad	yes	yes
GUI	Control button	yes	yes
GUI	Touch screen	yes	yes
GUI	Mouse	no	yes (if using a touch screen)
GUI	Keyboard	no	yes (if using a software keyboard)
SUI	Natural Speech	yes	yes

Some interface technologies can only be used in PCs because the number of usable interface techniques in embedded systems like driver navigation systems is limited by space, memory and processor performance restrictions. In addition, only interface techniques can be used that do not disturb driving tasks or distract the driver from traffic. In this sense, for example, situating a map display at the center of a console is not very reasonable. It is better to use a head up display in the front window or even avoid visual interaction with devices for secondary driving tasks completely. However, to avoid costs and exploit resources, a mobile driver navigation system has been used.

Restrictions for interface technologies in embedded systems

According to the results from the two online studies (section 6.2) supported by the resulting tendencies of the pre-studies (section 6.1), the most important variables, which categorize best the HMI style by people of different cultures, encompass the following cultural interaction indicators (cf. section 6.6.2):

- Number of all mouse clicks (MC)
- Error clicks (clicks without initiating any functionality, e.g., click on the background of a menu) (EC)
- Number of breaks between 2 input events, longer than 10s ($\neg$IN)
- Number of breaks between 2 input events, shorter than 10s and longer than 1s ($\neg$IN)
- Number of breaks between 2 input events, shorter than 1s and longer than 1ms ($\neg$IN)
- Number of breaks between 2 input events, shorter than 1ms ($\neg$IN)
- Speed of moving the mouse (MMS)
- Number of refused system messages (RM)
- Number of accepted system messages (AM)
- Time, how long a system message is viewed (DIP)
- Number of open tasks during running the driver navigation application (PT).

Cultural interaction indicators

The most important aspects that should be adapted according to the results in section 6.2 as well as to the requirement for I18N/L10N in section 2.3.5 are:

Most important aspects to be adapted

- Number of information pieces presented simultaneously, e.g., number of POI on map display (POI)
- Information presentation frequency, e.g., number of maneuver announcements per time unit (NIT)
- Time between two spoken words by text-to-speech engine, e.g., speed of speech output (TPI)
- Scrolling speed of list entries and the map content (IN)
- Size and arrangement of input- and output elements (layout)
- Language
- Font and writing direction
- Colors.

Traceable variables implemented into the CAHMI demonstrator

All these variables had to be included in the system of an existing driver navigation software project to show that the CAHMI principle works in a real system – and not only statistically. However, it was not possible to implement the functionality for all variables because of code, architecture and time restrictions within embedded mobile systems. In the end the following traceable variables were implemented in the CAHMI demonstrator (cf. Table 41).

Table 41: Implemented measurement variables in the CAHMI demonstrator

Variable	Description of variable (PUMTM-Parameter)	Short name	Kind of variable	Data type
ScrollMapl1ms	Number of mouse moves in map shorter than 1ms	MMS, ¬IN	Counter	integer
Scroll-Mapm1ms	Number of mouse moves in map longer than 1ms	MMS, ¬IN	Counter	integer
ScrollMapl1s	Number of mouse moves in map shorter than 1s	MMS	Counter	integer
ScrollMapm1s	Number of mouse moves in map longer than 1s	MMS, ¬IN	Counter	integer
ScrollCounter	Number of mouse move actions on the map	MM	Counter	integer
IOBreakl1ms	Number of breaks between two I/O-events shorter than 1ms	¬IN	Counter	integer
IOBreakl1s	Number of breaks between two I/O-events shorter than 1s	¬IN	Counter	integer
IOBreakm1s	Number of breaks between two I/O-events longer than 1s	¬IN	Counter	integer
IOBreak10s	Number of breaks between two I/O-events longer than 10s	¬IN	Counter	integer
Movecounter	Number of mouse move events occurring since the last mouse move action of the user	MM, IN	Counter	integer
MC_all	Number of all mouse clicks	MC	Counter	integer
EC_all	Number of all error clicks	EC	Counter	integer
MC_drive	Number of mouse clicks during an active maneuver guidance	MC	Counter	integer
ChangeDest	Number of destination changes after starting guidance	FI	Counter	integer
SemEvent	Number of inputs from the user initiating a function	FI	Counter	integer
NrDelete	Number of input corrections	FI	Counter	integer
NrOppZoom	Number of opposite zoom events	IN	Counter	integer
ScrollMap Time1ms	Whole time scrolled on the map (in milliseconds)	IN	Time	long
Disclaimer Duration	Time range for displaying the Disclaimer Dialog (in milliseconds)	DIP	Time	long
ScrollNon Linearity Average	Indication of how linear the mouse moves of the user were on average. 0 means 100% linear, the larger the less linear.	LMT	Coefficient	integer
Scrolling NonLinearity (Coefficient)	Indicates how linear the mouse moves of the user were over the whole measurement period. 0 means 100% linear, the larger the less linear.	LMT	Coefficient	integer

The following aspects can be adapted within the CAHMI demonstrator: *Adaptable aspects*

- Color scheme of the map display
- How often a voice output will be automatically repeated (NIT)
- Speed of the voice output (TPI)
- Number of displayed road names (~POI)
- Number of buttons and configuration possibilities in menus (~POI)
- Number of POI (POI)
- Language.

7.2   Setup, Runtime and Using the CAHMI Demonstrator

Modules for
⇨   Monitoring
⇨   Analysis
⇨   Adaptation

CAHMI functionality can
be switched on/off

The CAHMI demonstrator consists of three modules according to the three main parts of the principle of culturally adaptive HMI (cf. section 3.2.1): a monitoring module, an analysis module and an adaptation module. Every module of the demonstrator (recording the trace data into memory and into a log file, analyzing, adapting) can be switched on or off according to the needs of the experimental presenter. The demonstrator functionality can also be switched on or off completely (cf. Figure 32).

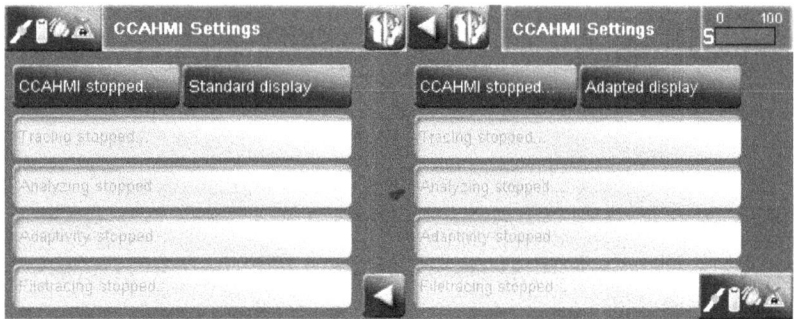

Figure 32: Adaptability can be switched off (left) or on (right) in the CAHMI settings dialog in the CAHMI demonstrator

Implementation of five
adaptation levels

No fuzzy, but only five-adaptation levels have been implemented in the demonstrator because of cost and system performance restrictions by embedded technology. C-value is the cultural index, which expresses the assumption strength in percent that the user is a Chinese user (calculated by the system), i.e. if the C-value is 100, the system recognized a Chinese user; if the C-value is 0 the system recognized a German user. MD indicates that the adapted aspect is mostly relevant for the use case of presenting information on a map display. MG indicates the "maneuver guidance use case".

Possible adaptation levels
and parameters within the
CAHMI demonstrator

Figure 32 gives an overview regarding some aspects of the possible adaptation levels and parameters within the CAHMI demonstrator for the adaptation of the HMI.[310]

---

[310] According to the estimations by the author drawn from the preliminary Chinese user expectations obtained by the qualitative survey with 20 Chinese students in Hangzhou (cf.

Table 42: Adaptation levels provided by the CAHMI demonstrator

Adap-tation level	Number of POI (MD) [POI]	Highway color (MD)	Route color (MD)	Number of Announcements (MG) [NIT]	Voice speed (MG) (Words per second) [DIP]	C-value [%]
1	40	Blue	Light blue	1	50	0-20
2	80	Light blue	Light violet	2	100	20-40
3	120	Turquoise	Violet	3	150	40-60
4	160	Light turquoise	Light red	4	200	60-80
5	200	Green	Red	5	250	80-100

According to the levels of adaptation, the look and feel of the HMI of the demonstrator differs. For example, Chinese users prefer the most important information to be on the left top (vs. least important information on the right bottom).[311] If the system recognizes that the user behaves like a Chinese user, it adapts the HMI to the Chinese settings according to the content of the C-value. In the advanced settings menu, the CAHMI trace information (i.e. the values of the discriminating cultural interaction indicators) can be inspected (cf. Figure 33).

Demonstrator changes its user interface according to levels of adaptation

---

section 6.1). Cf. also section 6.1 in the work report as well as file "060519 China Auswertung HMI-Design-Regeln konkret.xls" in the online appendix.

[311] Cf. the results from the URD test task and other studies presented in sections 6.1 and 6.6.3.

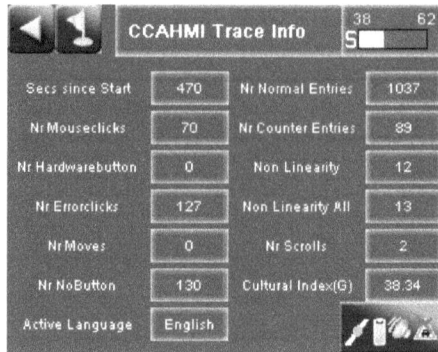

Figure 33: Presentation of the current values of the Cultural Interaction Indicators (CIIs) in the "CAHMI Trace Info Dialog"[312]

Many more elements can be considered in intercultural HMI design as can be seen in the map display-setting screen (cf. Figure 34). Icons and symbols, design, layout, language, text size, format, units, street names, etc. could also be adapted (cf. section 2.3.5).

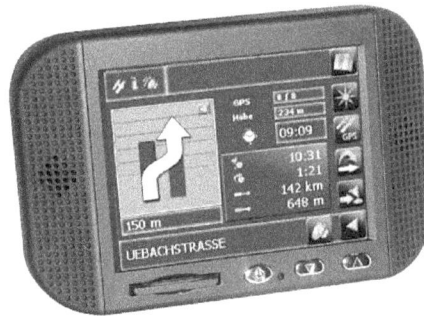

Figure 34: Map display setting screen

The CAHMI demonstrator developed and presented by the author in this section should only indicate some aspects that can be changed within intercultural HMI design.

---

[312] In this info menu, instead of C-value the G-value is displayed. G-value = 100 – C-value. It is the cultural index, which expresses the assumption strength of the system in percent that the user is a German user, i.e. if the G-value is 100, the system recognized a German user; if the G-value is 0 the system recognized a Chinese user.

However, the main objective of using the CAHMI demonstrator is to show that the principle of CAHMI works in reality (cf. section 7.3), i.e. that HMI (e.g., colors or layout) changes according to the interaction behavior of culturally different users as well as to verify the methodological hypothesis (MH) of this work by the results emerging from this chapter in section 7.6.[313]

Main objectives of using the CAHMI demonstrator

7.3   Testing the CAHMI Principle

The functional test presented in this section served to prove the classification correctness and the proper functionality of the CAHMI principle, i.e. that the basic principles of cultural adaptivity (monitoring, analyzing and adapting) work. To verify the CAHMI principle, a test scenario was developed to record the user interaction behavior of Chinese and German students at the university of Aachen[314] and employees of SV in Regensburg while doing some special test tasks with the CAHMI demonstrator. In addition, the users were interviewed afterwards regarding the usability of the device. Tests were conducted using the FUPA procedure (cf. Table 43).[315]

---

[313] Hence, to localize and internationalize driver navigation systems in total remains a task for professional software developers and HMI designers in industry, who will hopefully be using the design recommendations formulated in this work (cf. section 8.3).

[314] Most of the Chinese students studying in Germany are matriculated at Rheinisch-Westfälische Technische Hochschule (RWTH) in Aachen. Therefore, the probability of rapidly finding enough adequate test persons was high, which saved time resources.

[315] "FUPA" is the short form for "Fortuna User Preference Analysis". This method includes "Fortuna Usability Evaluation" (FTE) and "User Preference Analysis" (cf. also FTE-screenshot in the work report in sections 10.2.1 and 10.5.7). "Fortuna" was the project name of the development project for mobile driver navigation systems at Siemens VDO, which was later renamed "Waytona".

Table 43: "Fortuna" User Preference Analysis (FUPA) Procedure

Action item	Description	Estimated duration time [min]
1	Warming up (Recording session with Webcam, test preparation, etc.)	5
2	Do the use case with the users using "Fortuna" on a Laptop (logging data used for the functional test)	10
3	Ask the qualitative post-test-questions (debriefing)	10
4	Do the use case with the users using "Fortuna" on a Pocket-PC (logging data used for the functional test)	5
5	Ask the qualitative post-test-questions (debriefing)	5
6	Show the user the HMI-Screens to evaluate them	10
7	Closing	5

Test tasks

Twenty-five (13 Chinese and 12 German) users were requested to do the following test tasks with the CAHMI demonstrator:

1. Assume you want to go to Berlin taking the most effective path. Please, input the destination and let the system guide you (by starting the simulation) until you reach the highway (to start the simulation use the button with the bow and arrow icon).
2. Please, adjust the map display optimally according to your preferences (zoom, driving direction, perspective).
3. Set volume to 40%.
4. If you have completed all tasks, close the program.

All tasks were required to be done as quickly as possible. Questions could be posed to the test leader. For evaluation at the time, two groups from different cultures again with similar conditions regarding use case, education, profession, age and gender were built. Interaction data that emerged during the interaction of the user with the CAHMI demonstrator was recorded by the logging module of the demonstrator.

"Fortuna" Trace Evaluation (FTE) tool

Using neural network

The data was analyzed using the "Fortuna" Trace Evaluation (FTE) tool as part of the IIA data evaluation module using a neural network as described in section 5.4. The results of the analyses with the FTE tool led to the following statements:[316]

- The amount of total entries in the log file (representing the amount of user interaction), error clicks and mouse moves classified very well.

---

[316] Cf. files "060613 25 Datensätze.sav" and "060906 ANOVA auf FTE.spo" in the online appendix. The analysis with the FTE tool is described in sections 7.3 and 7.4 (cf. also section 6.3).

- The more frequent the interaction breaks > 10s, the less experienced or trained the user is to handle the application – a higher cognitive processing time of the user could also be a reason to explain this fact – or the user is Chinese.
- The longer the test duration, the more exact or less experienced is the test person.
- The more interaction breaks < 1ms (equals the number of scrolls < 1ms, i.e. moves with the finger on the touch screen, i.e. "mouse moves", i.e. MM and derived mouse move speed (MMS)), the less experienced the user is in dealing with use cases of driver navigation systems or the user is very hasty or Chinese.
- Interaction breaks (<1ms and >10s) classify well, being cross-validated between Chinese and German users up to 72%. Additionally, using the third parameter "test duration" within discriminance analysis, the classification rate reaches 74%.

It turned out that there are interaction differences between Chinese and German users. The averaged values of the culturally different groups tend always to be in one direction, which indicates a trend regarding cultural interaction patterns as shown in Table 44. The weights are estimated subjectively by the author according to the values in the log files of the CAHMI demonstrator as well as according to the classification power of the CIIs based on the results of the two online studies presented in section 6.2.

CIIs implemented in CAHMI demonstrator
⇨ Classifying cultural imprint of user

Table 44: Applied Cultural Interaction Indicators (CIIs) in the CAHMI demonstrator and binary limiting values of the CIIs to differentiate the cultural imprint of the user automatically by user interaction analysis at runtime

Cultural interaction indicator (CII) / Measurement variable	Type	Averaged value (12 German users)	Binary limiting value between Chinese and German users[317]	Averaged value (13 Chinese users)	Weighting / significance of CII	Measured averaged value of a test user	Culturally imprinted interaction behavior / pattern (Chinese)	Culturally imprinted interaction behavior / pattern (German)
Total entries	IN	44	49.5	55	1	66	100	0
Break < 1ms	¬IN	4.6	6.1	7.6	1	8	100	0
Break > 1s	¬IN	7.9	8.8	9.7	1	9	61.11	38.89
Break > 10s	¬IN	1	1.15	1.3	1	1.3	100	0
Counter entries	IN	16.8	18.9	21	2	34	100	0
Normal entries	IN	27	31	35	1	31	50	50
Mouse Up	MC	12	13.5	15	2	45	100	0
Mouse Down	MC	12	13	14	2	13	50	50
No Button	EC	6.7	8.65	10.6	2	9	58.97	41.03
Error Up	EC	1.1	1.55	2	1	2	100	0
Error Down	EC	1.1	1.5	1.9	1	2	100	0
All mouse clicks	MC	10.5	11.5	12.5	1	13	100	0
All error clicks	MC	1.1	1.5	1.9	1.5	1	0	100
Last Disclaimer Presentation Duration	DIP	79	86	93	1	85	42.86	57.14
Kind of interaction behavior of the test user in [%] (cultural index)							74.16 % (C-value)	25.84 % (G-value)

The results of the implemented cultural interaction indicators in the CAHMI demonstrator can be used to correct the estimated weights in Table 44 as presented in Table 47. In the future, weights can be used that are more exact in accordance to the significant coefficients from SPSS.

Two best CIIs: MC (mouse clicks) and MM (mouse moves)

From the 25 data sets nine were analyzable by discriminance analysis to calculate the statistical classification power of the CIIs used in the CAHMI demonstrator. Out of the implemented cultural indicators in the CAHMI demonstrator, two CIIs "mouse-up" and "scrolls<1ms" (cf. Table 45) classified (cross-validated) 80% of the user's correctly to their cultural background

---

[317] The binary limiting values resulted from explorative data analysis in file „060830 Fortuna Ergebnisse Mittelwertvergleiche.spo" in the online appendix.

(Chinese or German) as indicated in Table 46.[318] "Mouse-Up" represents the measurement variable "mouse clicks" (MC) and "Scrolls<1ms" measures the number of interaction breaks < 1ms, which represents "mouse movements" (MM) that correlates to "mouse movement speed" (MMS) (= ¬IN <1ms).[319]

Table 45: Two of the best classifying Cultural Interaction Indicators (CIIs) identified using the CAHMI demonstrator

Step	Variables in the analysis	Tolerance	F to remove	Wilks' Lambda	Classification function coefficients for nationality_num	
1	Mouse Up_NORM	1.000	4.573		0.00	1.00
2	Mouse Up_NORM	0.459	13.828	0.853	5.164	7.102
	Nr Of Scrolls Shorter Than 1ms	0.459	8.065	0.605	-1.307	-1.977
	Fisher's linear discriminant functions (Constant)				-31.167	-58.004

Table 46: 80% of the user's were classified correctly to their cultural background (Chinese or German) in the test with the CAHMI demonstrator using the Cultural Interaction Indicators (CIIs) "Mouse Up_NORM" (MC) and "Scrolls<1ms" (MM, ¬IN, MMS)

Classification matrix

rows: observed classifications, columns: forecast classifications

	Percent correct	German - p=0.48000	Chinese - p=0.52000
German	83.33334	10	2
Chinese	76.92308	3	10
Total	80.00000	13	12

Surely, these results depend on the small sample size as well as on several statistical settings, e.g., how many and which variables are in the set applying discriminance analysis or what including and excluding statistical limits are set. However, there are classification quotes significantly over 50%, which proves that the results have not been found randomly, but support themselves mutually as have been shown in detail in the discussion of the results in section 6.6.

(margin notes) Results depend on the small sample size and on several statistical settings

Classification quotes over 50% up to 80%

---

[318] A list of all implemented and calculated cultural interaction indicators in the CAHMI demonstrator can be found in the work report in section 10.5.6. The classification power of the CIIs is based on the data in file "060613 25 Datensätze.sav" in the online appendix.

[319] The measurement variables and potential cultural interaction indicators (PCIIs) and their naming are explained in detail in sections 4.5, 5.1.1 and 6.2.

CAHMI demonstrator classifies nationality correctly with respect to interaction behavior with ca. 80% certainty using the CIIs
⇨   "Mouse Clicks"
⇨   Interaction breaks

Thus, it can be proven that the CAHMI demonstrator classifies the nationality of the test user correctly with respect to the interaction behavior of the test user. For example, "CIIs Nr_Of_Scrolls_Shorter_Than_1ms", "Breaks_Greater_Than_10s" and "Nr_Of_Scrolls_Over_1ms", which represent interaction breaks using a touch screen as well as "Mouse Up" and "Counter Entries", assign the nationality up to 80% correctly with respect to the interaction of the test user.[320] Table 47 shows a ranking of the excellence of the cultural interaction indicators used in the CAHMI demonstrator.

---

[320] The probability values of the classification regarding the single data sets can be found in the work report in section 10.5.3. Cf. also the files "060613 Ergebnis SPSS FTE.spo" and "060613 Auswertung SPSS 4 mit 25 DS.spo" in the online appendix.

Table 47: Cultural Interaction Indicators (CIIs) used in the CAHMI demonstrator[321]

Cultural Interaction Indicator	Weight in %	F-Value	Signifi-cance	Homogenity of variances [h]	Weight [0;1]	Ran-king
Nr Of IO Breaks Over 10s_NORM	**100**	**9.06**	**0.006**	**0.539**	**1.000000000**	**1**
Mouse Up_NORM	*59*	*5.353*	*0.03*	*0.867*	*0.5908388521*	*2*
Counter Entries_NORM	*49*	*4.478*	*0.045*	*0.947*	*0.4942604857*	*3*
Total Entries_NORM	*48*	*4.382*	*0.048*	*0.82*	*0.483664459*	*4*
Mouse Down_NORM	46	4.141	0.054	0.722	0.4570640177	5
Nr Of IO Breaks Over 1s_NORM	41	3.69	0.067	0.571	0.407284768	6
Mouse Up_Error Click_NORM	40	3.629	0.069	0.111	0.4005518764	7
Mouse Down_Error Click_NORM	40	3.619	0.07	0.053	0.3994481236	8
Nr Of Error Clicks_all_NORM	40	3.619	0.07	0.53	0.3994481236	9
Normal Entries_NORM	39	3.519	0.073	0.769	0.3884105960	10
Nr Of IO Breaks Shorter Than 1ms_NORM	34	3.091	0.092	0.053	0.341169977	11
Nr Of Mouse Clicks_all_NORM	27	2.436	0.132	0.512	0.2688741722	12
Keyboard Button_NORM	22	2.007	0.17	0.674	0.2215231788	13
No Button_NORM	16	1.472	0.237	0.969	0.1624724062	14
Nr Of Mouse Clicks_Since Start Driving_NORM	11	0.976	0.333	0.643	0.1077262693	15
Whole Scrolling Time_NORM	7	0.617	0.44	0.098	0.0681015453	16
Average Scrolling Time_NORM	6	0.54	0.47	0.113	0.0596026490	17
Duration Of Test In Min	3	0.263	0.613	0.047	0.029028697	18
Nr Of Scrolls_NORM	2	0.189	0.668	0.49	0.0208609272	19
Nr Of IO Breaks Shorter Than 1s_NORM	2	0.158	0.694	0.332	0.017439293	20
Legend:						
Best variable with best significance and very high F-value	**100**	**9.06**	**p=0.006**	**h=0.047**	**Ref.: 1.00 = 100% of F max (9.06)**	**1**
Very good variable with significance p < 0.05 and very high F-value	*48-59 (100)*	*4.382-9.06*	*p < 0.05*			
Good variable with significance p < 0.1 and high F-value	34-46	3.091-4.141	p < 0.1			
Bad variable without significance and very low F-value	2-27	0.158-2.436	p > 0.2			
Worst variable with worst significance and very low F-value	2	0.158	p=0.694	h=0.969	0.017439293	20

ONE-WAY ANOVA showed that the cultural interaction indicators presented bold and italic in Table 47 work very well: their discrimination power is high,

CAHMI principle works statistically and in a real system

---

[321] Basis of these results is the data in "060613 25 Datensätze.sav" and the analysis done with SPSS in "060906 ANOVA auf FTE.spo". Both files are available in the online appendix.

and hence, their weight within the adaptivity algorithm implemented in the CAHMI demonstrator using production rules is also high. These results prove that the CAHMI principle works not only statistically, but also within a real system exemplified by a mobile driver navigation system of SV.

The results obtained, using the CAHMI demonstrator, justify the direction of research in this work that motivates further studies, e.g., to augment the exactness and the completeness of the results as well as the discrimination power and separation effect of the CIIs. Furthermore, the results contribute to the confirmation of some of the basic methodological hypotheses (MH) (cf. section 7.6).

7.4   Classification Method and Adaptation Rules

Cross validation test

In addition to discriminance analysis, a tenfold cross validation test has also been applied (recommended e.g. by Mandl 2005) using the IIA data evaluation tool employing split data sets for the training of neural networks (cf. section 5.4). The IIA data evaluation module mainly served to show the plausibility of the quantitative results. To verify the discriminating quote and to show individual classification (i.e. according to the cultural characteristics of one single user), a back propagation network was implemented in the IIA data evaluation module. From the data collection of the first online study, 77 data sets were randomly selected (out of 97 complete and valid in total) and are used as training data. Ten data sets are used for validation and the remaining 10 data sets served as test data. All values of all data sets for the potential cultural interaction indicators implemented in the IIA tool have been z-transformed and thereby normalized to the range of [0;1] to feed the input neurons with comparable data.[322] Three output neurons indicated the test languages Chinese, German and English. According to the network topology and learning rate, the discrimination rate varied, but it reached up to 80% for correctly associating the users with the selected test language.[323] This discrim-

Back propagation network

Z-transformation

Discrimination rate up to 80%

---

[322] Z-transformation means the conversion of original values to a normalized range of [0;1] to enhance comparing convenience and usage of special statistical methods (e.g. cluster analysis) by balancing different levels of scales. The Z-score is calculated by the quotient of the difference of the original score and the mean of the standard deviation (cf. Backhaus et al. 2006: 537 seq.).

[323] Different topologies of the neural networks as well as anonymized data used for training and evaluation are stored in the files "daten.xls", "zdaten.xls" and "nn_83 Prozent.txt" in the online appendix.

ination rate has been calculated by cross-validated checking of samples using the application of repeated rotation of the training data. Each time the classification rate was similar which points to correct results. This is another cue for the reliability of the methodology used and of the correctness of the results (cf. section 6.6.3).

The interaction of the user with the system is recorded and analyzed according to the interaction indicators found in the empirical studies in this work (cf. chapter 6). The system adapts its behavior to the peculiarities of the cultural interaction indicators (derived in the design phase) to imitate the interaction behavior of the user. The adaptation rules express the connection between user interaction behavior, culture and system interaction behavior:

The look and feel of the user interface is adapted correspondingly to the user needs (adaptation objective – to adapt HMI to cultural needs) by retrieving the adaption means (values of the HMIDs (like INF, INS, INP, ¬IN, etc.)) corresponding to the aspects of HMI that can be adapted (adaptation information – HMI aspects related to HMIDs like layout, color scheme, or the values of HMIDs (like IF, TPI, NIT, DIP, ID, IS, etc.), cf. e.g., Table 42 in section 7.2) retrieved from a look-up table stored in a database (researched in the design phase). *User interface is adapted to user needs*

The adaptation rules used in the CAHMI demonstrator are implicitly presented in several tables (Table 42, Table 44, Table 47 and Table 48). For example, in Table 44 the strongest indicators are weighted most according to the results presented in Table 47. The binary limiting value is used to separate the measured values of the corresponding indicators to German and Chinese user groups. However, these rules have not been verified in detail because of time restrictions. Therefore, they cannot be shifted into the focus of this work. *Adaptation rules*

Even if this rudimentary first approach to acquire explicit and clearly separated adaptation rules represents the basis for further optimizations, much research needs to be done to on them in the future to obtain complete and reliable explicit formulae expressing adequate rules regarding the connection between cultural aspects and HMI dimensions as indicated in section 6.6.1.[324]

The adaptation decision component can use the adaptation rules provided by interaction analysis and the results of learning components. Finally, the HMI adaptation component adapts HMI to the culturally imprinted needs of the individual user.

---

[324] The meanings of the adaptation rules are compatible with the meanings of the variables explained in section 6.2. First trials of formulae can be found in the work report in section 10.6.3.

7.5   Bootstrapping Problem

Additional empirical study

The classification power of the CIIs can also be supported by the results from an empirical study done in September 2008 by the author where not only the classification of the interaction behavior of the user but thereby also the identification of the user by analyzing the interaction behavior was investigated (cf. Heimgärtner 2009b). This study extends the study of Bartmann et al. 2007 regarding user identification by keyboard usage through analysis of mouse usage: Also here the values of some of the most significant "cultural interaction indicators" have been recorded and analyzed. For example, regarding mouse usage, the following parameters have been used: number of mouse moves and mouse clicks as well as number of times using the mouse wheel and number of keystrokes.

Extending research of Bartmann 2007 by mouse device

Test program in C#

To record the user interaction behavior during interaction with the computer, a test program in C# was developed by the author. Several working sessions of a Chinese and a German software developer have been recorded.[325] To begin a session, the user had to register with the system using a login procedure by specifying user name and password. In the learning stage, this allows the system to know which user is currently interacting with the system. During the user interaction with the system, the mentioned events were recorded and sequentially stored in a history file including date and time stamp.[326]

Test setting

For the interaction analysis, 12 computed parameters out of the collected data set regarding mouse and keyboard events were used. The data analysis was carried out manually using the statistic-tools SPSS 16.0 and Statistica 8.5 applying the statistical methods "Jack-Knife" (discriminance analysis) and ANOVA.[327]

Up to 97% correct user identification

The users could be identified up to 97% correctly just by analyzing the data of one working session. Since not all interaction parameters classify similarly well, mutual "disturbances" can arise in the context of the calculation of the classification quote. Although the classification rate of approx. 97% is very

---

[325] I thank Mr. Xuhui Wen very much for participating in this study. The other participant was the author himself.

[326] Examples of the collected data can be found in the online appendix in files "BP1.txt" and "BP2.txt".

[327] For a more detailed description of the study, please refer to Heimgärtner 2009b. The data and the detailed statistical analysis can be found in files "user identification mittelwerte.xls", "UserLock6 - ohne Interaktionspausen.spv", "UserLock6a - nur Interaktionspausen.spv", "UserLock.spv" and "user lock test.spf" in the online appendix.

good, an increase can still be expected using additional well classifying cultural interaction indicators. Hence, even more and relevant parameters must be researched to acquire proper information about the user's behavior and to obtain information that is more suitable to classify the user. This is especially necessary for early cultural recognition, i.e. that the user can be recognized at best immediately after beginning the session to avoid the bootstrapping problem (cf. section 2.4.3). The learning curve until the user can be identified is shown in Figure 35.

The analysis of the measured data shows a recognition precision of approximately 97% after a learning phase of about 2.5 hours. In Figure 35 it can be seen that the learning stage could have ended after a considerably shorter time. Already, shortly after the beginning of the session, the course of the curves for user 1 is higher for every point of the curves than the course of the curves for user 2 except for mouse moves per second and both curves represent approximately the same trend of the distances of the mean average values for the complete session. At approx. 0.25 to 0.5 hours, all mean average values already intersect the curves of the users at the right distance from each other. Therefore, it can be assumed that the learning stage can be shortened correspondingly from approx. 2.5 to approx. 0.5 hours.

Recognition precision of 97% after a learning stage of 2,5 hours

Learning stage can be shortened

The fact that user identification is possible by analyzing the user interaction behavior with the computer system using relevant cultural interaction indicators with classification rates of more than 97% from data captured within 2.5 hours substantiates the high classification quality of the cultural interaction indicators obtained by this dissertation project.

High classification quality of the cultural interaction indicators

However, the learning curve shows that the interaction differences between the users become smaller with increasing time. Therefore, further studies must reveal if in the long run over many sessions, the differences still clearly exist or if they will disappear (cf. leveling effect described in section 8.1).

Leveling effect

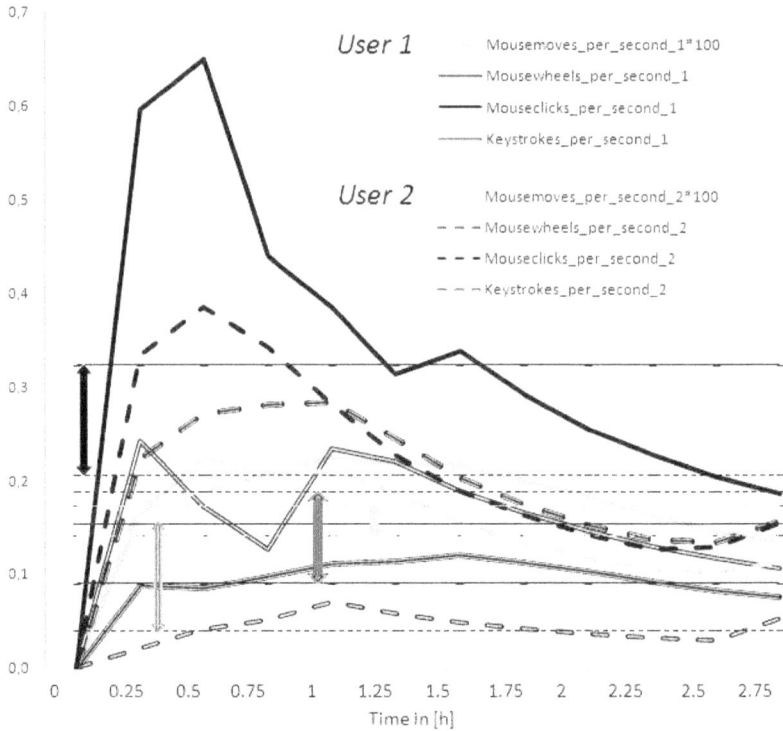

Figure 35: Learning curve of the user profile for some Cultural Interaction Indicators (CIIs) as well as the duration until the user can be identified (indicated by the similar course of the learning curves of both users after about 2.5 hours) (Source: Figure 1 from Heimgärtner 2009b, extended by the author).

Need for same test conditions in future studies

Furthermore, after system start (in the 0.25 to 0.5 hour time period), the applications currently executed by the users could have been different which probably caused different interaction behavior. This effect must be eliminated in future studies by ensuring that the users work with the same application and monitoring this by the method of observational participation (cf. section 6.1).

7.6   Verifying the Methodological Hypotheses

Both methodological hypotheses generated in section 4.3.2 that concern the determination of cultural variables can be confirmed because the results obtained in section 6.2 have been determined purely quantitatively by quantitative (statistical) analysis of the log files and quantitative data from the interaction of the user with the system:

(MHCV1) Methodological hypothesis concerning cultural variables #1: Intercultural variables can be determined purely quantitatively by analysis of the interaction of the user with the system (considering only the interaction tracing log file of the system).

MHCV1 confirmed: Intercultural variables can be determined purely quantitatively

(MHCV2) Methodological hypothesis concerning cultural variables #2: The values of the intercultural variables can be determined purely quantitatively by analysis of the interaction of the user with the system (considering only the interaction tracing log file of the system).

MHCV2 confirmed: values of intercultural variables can be determined purely quantitatively

Second, the methodological hypotheses regarding culture were confirmed too: In this work, groups were employed that chose Chinese (C), German (G) and English (E) as their test language. The interaction differences between (C) and (G) respectively (E) are greater than those between (G) and (E) according to the cultural distances between these groups (cf. sections 6.2 and 6.6.2). Hence, the cultural differences in HCI are the greater, the greater the cultural distance is, which contributes to the reconfirmation of P2 to P4 in section 4.3.1. The interaction behavior of the users of different nationalities is different, too, as shown in section 6.2.[328] Hence, MHC1 is confirmed, which also substantiates the confirmation of MHC2:

(MHC1) Methodological hypothesis concerning culture #1: The difference in the kind of interactions of humans with a system (computer, machine, navigation system, etc.) is the greater, the greater the cultural distance is, which confirms assumption A4 (cf. section 4.1).

MHC1 confirmed: Cultural differences in HCI increase with cultural distance

(MHC2) Methodological hypothesis concerning culture #2: It is possible to determine the culturally imprinted characteristics of the user by analyzing the interaction of the user with the system.

MHC2 confirmed: Determination of cultural imprint by analyzing interaction

Furthermore, all three postulated main methodological hypotheses regarding CAHMI (indicated by MMH) that form the most abstract hypotheses of this work (cf. section 4.3.2) can be confirmed because within this dissertation project it has been statistically proven that there are significant cultural differences in the interaction behavior of the user with the system (using the IIA tool and SPSS) (cf. sections 6.2 and 6.6.2). The combination of these cultural differences represented by CIIs form cultural interaction patterns (CIPs) according to the cultural imprint of the user, which confirms MMH1:

---

[328] A detailed discussion regarding the classification according to test language or nationality is presented in sections 6.3 and 6.6.2 (cf. also footnote 299 on page 202).

MMH1 confirmed:
User interaction depends
on his cultural
background

(MMH1) Main methodological hypothesis #1: There are significantly different patterns of interaction in HMI according to culture (composed of combinations of cultural interaction indicators) depending on the cultural imprint of the user, i.e. the interaction of the user with the system depends on his cultural background.

Furthermore, the cultural interaction differences of the users with the system have been identified quantitatively and not qualitatively (e.g., using interaction times or number of interactions): they can be statistically recognized and measured by a computer system (using the IIA tool and the CAHMI demonstrator) (cf. sections 5.3 and 7.3), which confirms MMH2:

MMH2 confirmed:
Cultural interaction
differences in HMI can be
recognized and measured
quantitatively

(MMH2) Main methodological hypothesis #2: Cultural interaction differences in HMI can be recognized and measured quantitatively by a computer system (only by monitoring and analyzing the interaction of the user with the system quantitatively, resulting in adequate culturally dependent values of the intercultural variables).

Adaptive systems need a
quantitative "apparatus of
recognition"

Presumption P1 fulfilled

Thereby, the constraint represented by presumption P1 that adaptive systems need a quantitative "apparatus of recognition" (cf. section 4.3.1) is fulfilled. Furthermore, this in turn implies that MMH3 can be considered to be correct (empirically confirmed by the results using the CAHMI demonstrator in chapter 7.3):

MMH3 confirmed:
Systems with culturally
adaptive HMI are possible

(MMH3) Main methodological hypothesis #3: Systems with culturally adaptive HMI are possible (the HMI can be automatically adapted by the system to the culturally dependent interaction characteristics of the user), i.e. the postulated principle of culturally adaptive HMI (in section 3.2.1) works.

Assumptions A1 to A4
fulfilled

In addition, the assumptions A1 to A4 are turned out to be plausible in the face of the results in this work:

- Assumption 1 (A1): Interruption tolerance of Chinese users is higher than those of German users (cf. section 4.2).
- Assumption 2 (A2): For the automatic identification of the user culture and the automatic adaptation of the system to this user culture at runtime, a few discriminative intercultural variables suffice, which can quantitatively include and describe the user and his interaction with the system (cf. section 4.4).
- Assumption 3 (A3): The preferred language used in the IIA test indicated the culture of the user with which he is most familiar (cf. section 6.2).
- Assumption 4 (A4): The differences in the behavior in relationship-oriented cultures to task-oriented cultures are larger than the difference in the behavior within relationship-oriented cultures or task-oriented cultures (cf. section 4.1).

8   Discussion, Implications and Suggestions

„Jak kdo merí, tak se mu odmeruje.“
(Czech saying)[329]

In this chapter, the methods used in this work (section 8.1) as well as the implications of the results yielded from the empirical research will be reflected on. In section 8.2, the outcome of this work regarding the interaction characteristics based on the dimensions "information" and "interaction" relevant for HCI analysis and HMI design will be reflected on to develop a confirmed practical model for intercultural HMI design (MICHMID). Furthermore, the results are made available for recommendations concerning intercultural HMI design (section 8.3), revising the principle of culturally adaptive HMI (section 8.4) as well as enhancing the culturally adaptive interface-agent architecture (section 8.5).[330]

8.1   Methodological Challenges

The methodological objection against using explorative factor analysis for the support of the statistical results is that this method depends on the theory it wants to prove. However, the results determined by explorative factor analysis in this work (cf. section 6.6.1) confirm the empirical results obtained by the online studies, which in turn support the assumed theory behind the method of explorative factor analysis.

Methods depend on theory

---

[329] "How you measure, you will be measured." (cf. footnote 1 on page 1 and file "Sprichwörter mit messen.txt" in the online appendix).

[330] Open items and tasks for future research will be mentioned in chapter 9 and discussed in detail in the work report in section 8.6.

Leveling effect:
more difference at the
personal level, less
differences at country
level

In addition, there is the problem of equalizing the personal preferences in doing complete data collection from all persons of a cultural group (e.g., the more different preferences at personal level are collected the less are the differences in the common cultural imprinted preferences at country level). This problematic aspect is illustrated in Figure 35 in section 7.5.

CIIs do not culturally
classify by themselves

Enhanced statistical
methods necessary

Cultural indicators (CIIs) – as the study's results confirm – describe the differences in interaction behavior but still do not culturally classify by themselves: To recognize general classification patterns, additional methods are necessary. For this purpose, enhanced statistical methods like discriminance analysis or neural networks have been used in this work, which delivered some classification answers (cf. sections 6.6.2, 7.3, 7.4 and 7.5).

Differences in the
processing speed of the
computer hardware

There may be differences in the processing speed of the computer hardware, because the reference measurement value is different for (C) and (G). This possibly decreases the plausibility of the results regarding interaction speed. However, the interaction speeds of (C) are higher than those of (G) even if the processors speed of the computers used by (C) are slower than those used by (G) (CPU Norm Freq $_{(C)}$ (2184) < CPU Norm Freq $_{(G)}$ (2426), cf. Table 49 in the appendix). This indicates that the results are correct regardless of the problematic aspect just mentioned.

Partial difference in
results of quantitative and
qualitative studies

On the one hand, the results of the quantitative studies of this work partly diverge from the results of qualitative studies from other authors (e.g., Knapp 2007)[331] because of the test setting, which can be still improved (cf. section 5.1.1) or because of a lack of implemented potential cultural interaction indicators in the IIA tool (cf. Table 32 in section 6.5). On the other hand, the results from Knapp 2007 that the Chinese user group's performance and the German user group's perceived attractiveness of a driver navigation system is negatively affected if the system is based on the other group's mental model (cf. also Honold 2000) support the results of the work in hand (cf. e.g., section 6.1).

VSM studies' results
expose cultural
differences at country
level, not at the culture of
a company

Another problem poses a main statistical question: Can the parent populations concerning the VSM survey be compared? Hofstede did the main VSM survey at IBM in 1974. The author of this work did the VSM survey at Siemens VDO in 2006. Therefore, there are differences in company philosophy, propositional attitudes, time and therefore, probably in culture.[332] However, according to

---

[331] For example, according to Knapp 2007 the handling of the problems caused by the primary driving task influences the usage of driving navigation systems more than cultural aspects even if the latter also cause interaction differences as shown in this work in sections 6.2 and 6.5.

[332] Cf. the discussion in section 8.18.1 in the work report.

Hofstede 1984 or Podsiadlowski 2002: 44, the cultural influences measured within the VSM studies can mainly be traced back to the investigated nations and not to the culture of the company which increases the probability of getting results exposing cultural differences at a country level rather than other differences. Hence, the VSM research focused only on the differences at country level.

However, it is an open question whether the cultural differences are even larger within a culture (e.g., within a country) than between cultures (e.g., between several countries or companies). This would also demand that the originally postulated approaches in this work concentrating on national level (cf. section 3.2) must be changed (cf. sections 8.4 and 8.5).

Are cultural differences larger within a culture or between cultures?

Therefore, the character and the deep cultural stamp of the test participants are not known in advance in online studies. Only quantitative aspects like nationality, mother tongue, or time abroad can be collected to gain an impression of the cultural imprint of the user as done in this work (cf. section 6.2).

Impression of cultural imprint by collection of quantitative aspects

Qualitative studies of reference persons can reveal cultural information e.g., by means of interviews or focus groups. Hence, investigative qualitative interviews would be necessary in this case to illuminate these aspects in order to select the right test persons before the data collection. Furthermore, the test leader can control the test environment or do participatory observation (i.e. observing the test persons during the test session). In a pure online survey this is not possible because the test conductor is not personally on the spot locally.[333]

Qualitative studies for selecting the right test persons

However, qualitative research is methodologically more problematic than quantitative research for the following reasons:

- It is very difficult to select and recruit the correct reference persons.
- There is the need for high interpretation efforts by the test leader.
- In focus groups, mutual influencing of test persons and test leader is possible.
- The tester or interviewer is necessarily subjective, and therefore manipulative, which makes purely objective science impossible (cf. Husserl & Lohmar 2003).
- The answers of the test persons are subjective and can be dishonest.
- Unconscious manipulation cannot be excluded.

---

[333] It surely would be possible to use video conferences. However, not all communicative signals are transmitted through this medium. Hence, the general impression is distorted (e.g., no smell, poor simultaneous detection of facial expression and gestures, environmental conditions (light, temperature and air pressure), mood, ambience, etc.).

Test language English,
not mother tongue

In addition, without native test leaders, the author conducted the qualitative studies locally in the English language. The results of the qualitative studies would probably have been better if the test were carried out by a test leader speaking the mother tongue of the desired test participants (cf. Vatrapu & Pérez-Quiñones 2006).[334]

Spongy character of
qualitative studies for
interaction analysis

In addition, the qualitative studies for interaction analysis (cf. section 6.1) have a spongy character. Very dynamic phenomena (like interaction and information frequency or speed) cannot be observed by human beings without the support of special tools (like the IIA tool, cf. section 5.2). Therefore, the qualitative studies done in this work (esp. without using the IIA tool) did not reveal useful design recommendations.

Need for measuring
dynamic aspects in HCI
⇨ Only possible over
     time
⇨ Using quantitative
     methods & tools

Furthermore, to analyze the interaction of the user with the system, which is the main objective in this work, it is necessary to measure dynamic aspects in HCI depending on time, which is only achieved by observing the user behavior chronologically without a gap. Hence, the preferred means are quantitative methods. Quantitative surveys by means of usability tests and questionnaires by the use of the IIA tool are very reasonable for this purpose.

Collected data restricted
to use cases of driver
navigation systems

No explicit design rules

Design recommendations
for intercultural HMI
design allowed

Another general objection to the application of the results yielded by the research of this dissertation project could concern the fact that the collected data are selective samples because they are restricted to use cases of driver navigation systems. Hence, it is problematic to generalize the CIIs because they are very concrete and restricted to a certain sample and it is not permitted to generalize the results for all applications and use cases. However, there abstract use cases have also been researched that are outside the context of actually using a car as a real navigation task nevertheless exhibiting similar properties and providing similar results. Hence, there is an indication, that some of the CIIs can also be used independently of applications (cf. section 7.5). Furthermore, even if it is prohibited methodologically to extract general rules for intercultural HMI design from the CIIs, it is permissible and reasonable to give some design recommendations (cf. section 8.3).

---

[334] Vatrapu & Suthers 2007 present a review of the concept of culture and the implications for intercultural collaborative online learning. Probably it is possible to avoid the influences of different test languages on the test setting by doing the tests with the IIA tool only with one test language for all test persons (e.g., English) to minimize language side effects, i.e. to reduce them to only one disturbing variable concerning language, namely the differences in the understanding the test language. However, then the question arises how to compare the results.

Also the other way around: the interaction patterns determined by the IIA tool on a PC do not (necessarily) have to be similar to the interaction patterns arising from the interaction with driver navigation systems. Hence, it is problematic to transfer all the results of this work to driver navigation systems because of different environmental conditions for the use cases (situations and context). Nevertheless, the proof of concept with the CAHMI demonstrator supported that at least some results can be applied in developing driver navigation systems (cf. section 7.3). The tests with the CAHMI demonstrator also showed that some of the cultural interaction indicators work in real driver navigation systems and not only statistically but "in reality".

Collected data with IIA tool restricted to PCs

Some of the CIIs work in real driver navigation systems

Furthermore, the collected samples are restricted to users from SV. Therefore, strictly speaking, the results are only representative for the employees of SV that have been tested with the IIA tool. Nevertheless, it seems that the step to transfer the results of employees of SiemensVDO to all users in China and in Germany is justified, because despite similar cultural VSM values consciously delivered by the users (cf. Figure 23 and Figure 24 in section 6.2), the (un-)conscious) interaction in HMI between Chinese and German users is different (cf. sections 6.2 and 6.4) and the results with a sample size above 900 are statistically relevant.[335] Therefore, it is permissible and even reasonably encouraged to use the results and recommendations obtained in this work for Chinese and German users for further intercultural HMI research (e.g., to create new hypotheses). However, these recommendations cannot substitute for further research and additional studies also for other application contexts.

Test persons restricted to employees of Siemens VDO

Transferring results to all users in China and Germany is justified

In addition, some disturbing variables seemed to influence the results slightly (e.g., age and PC experience). There is a close relation between culture and experience. It is difficult to separate cultural influences from experience (because experience is culturally imprinted). In any case, it must be checked if user experience plays a decisive role within analysis (especially for the training and the classification possibilities when using neural networks) (cf. section 6.3).

Disturbing variables "Age" and "PC experience"

Furthermore, not all possible control variables could be treated in detail in data analysis (cf. sections 5.1.1). Hence, the results could differ (better or worse) from the real results.[336] However, this negative aspect is less problematic due

Lack of analysis for all possible control variables

---

[335] Furthermore, Hofstede's results have also been transferred from IBM employees to whole nations.

[336] For example, it can be supposed that the study would have yielded even more discriminating cultural differences in HMI if the time of being abroad of a test participant had been analyzed because the participants were additionally culturally marked by a longer stay in another culture. However, this analysis was left out because of time restrictions.

to the high sample size with more than 900 valid data sets (cf. section 6.2): According to the law of the "law of the large numbers" the results should be plausible as discussed in detail in section 6.3.[337]

Idiosyncrasies of CIIs

A weak point of the test setting concerns the idiosyncrasies of the cultural interaction indicators. They are partly computed only from one single measurement variable. Therefore, the reliability of the results of those indicators is low. Even if it seems that their reliability rises with every additional significant measurement variable (cf. section 6.6.2), their separation power and many more CIIs must be determined by future research. However, it is recognizable that the trend of the results obtained in this work always remains the same (cf. Figure 26 in section 6.5) because several indicators and much data were exploited and the analysis of the data using different statistical methods confirmed the same trend in the results (cf. section 6.6), which substantiates the methodological correctness of the studies in this work.

Test setting with CAHMI demonstrator too insignificant

Nevertheless, the reliability of the classification ability of the identified cultural interaction indicators using the CAHMI demonstrator should be enhanced by further studies because of the probability that the use cases and the conducted tests with the CAHMI demonstrator were too insignificant. Furthermore, the amount of use cases applied in the CAHMI demonstrator might have been too low. Therefore, the recorded log files could have been too short to provide adequate data allowing correct data analysis and hence, obtaining sacrosanct results (cf. the discussion regarding FTE in section 6.3) as well as the short time for recognition (bootstrapping problem) of about 0.25 to 0.5 hours (in this first research phase), which would imply that the verification of some of the methodological hypotheses (namely MMH2 and MMH3) are not justified but must be verified again in new and detailed research. Nevertheless, the results gave useful hints for further research. And finally, the collected

Results useful for further research

data by quantitative means have been sufficient to recognize culturally caused differences in HCI (cf. sections 6.2, 6.3 and 6.6.2).

Methodological variability in measuring cultural differences

Moreover, the methodological variability in measuring cultural differences challenges the reliability as well as the deployment of cultural dimensions for culturally adaptive systems. Studies regarding the determination of the values of the cultural dimensions are an example for the variability in methodology and the influence of time and situational aspects on research. This points to the fact that perspective and time aspects (domain and scope) decisively influence research.

---

[337] For details about the "law of large numbers" in stochastics, please refer to Brüggemann 2002 or Bauer 2002.

For instance, one of the latest and largest studies analogous to those of Hofstedes' is the GLOBE study, which has been extended by the use of additional well known cultural models (cf. House et al. 2002). However, Hofstede's indices and the results of the Globe study are controversial because of methodological variability in measuring cultural differences.[338]

GLOBE study

In addition, it is possible that the values of cultural dimensions change over time and according to the situation (cf. sections 6.2 and 6.4) concerning the cultural imprint of the test participants.[339] This is also strongly supported by Kralisch 2006: "Culturally determined behavior (in contrast to values) is therefore not absolute, but should be primordially understood as a comparative measure: if fast walking at a speed of 5 km/h was found to be a characteristic of highly individualistic countries (Levine & Norenzayan, 1999), the speed that is perceived as fast today could be characteristic of low individualistic/collectivistic countries in a couple of years. [..]"(Kralisch 2006: 21, emphasis in original).[340] Furthermore, Kralisch argues that "stability in Hofstede's paradigm is not absolute: the impact of socio-economic variables – even if identical for each cultural group – makes the impact of cultural variables on group characteristic behavior relative. A broadening of Hofstede's concept should therefore be considered." (Kralisch 2006: 20).[341]

Values of cultural dimensions possibly change over time

---

[338] Cf. section 8.1 in the work report for details. This methodological variability is supported by the philosopher Edmund Husserl who claimed that science cannot be objective in the strong sense because in any case it is driven by a human being that is forced to interpret subjectively (cf. Husserl & Lohmar 2003).

[339] This also supports the dynamic test methodology applied in this work: along "static" questionnaires also "dynamic" interaction tests have been used to minimize the conscious influence of the test setting by the test subjects (as in the MG test task, cf. section 5.2.2). Furthermore, cultures behave similarly to dynamical systems (cf. Latane 1996). Even if they can be computed, calculated and predicted in advance, they can behave differently (cf. Haken 1983, Bossel 1992). For the description of the usage of dynamical systems relevant for the representations necessary in communication as the main constituent of culture (cf. section 2.2.4), please refer to Heimgärtner 2002.

[340] This is also supported by Levine & Norenzayan 1999 who investigated the time behavior according to Hall 1959 in several countries confirming the mono-chronic and poly-chronic time orientation of different cultures (cf. also Levine 2007).

[341] This aspect is discussed in detail in sections 8.4 and 8.5 as well as in section 8.1 in the work report.

Hofstede's indices not applicable in culturally adaptive systems

Moreover, Hofstede's indices can only be generated with at least 20 group members.[342] It is not possible to obtain valid values by examining a single person or user. Therefore, those indices cannot be updated by a single user in front of a machine and hence the values cannot be up to date at runtime at all (without asking a group of 20 users of the same culture, i.e. permanently running online questionnaires). In addition, asking a user at runtime completely contradicts the idea of adaptive systems (cf. section 2.4.1) as well as the principle of CAHMI (cf. section 3.2.1). Admittedly, even if the user would be asked at runtime, further questions would arise, e.g., what kind of users should be asked? How does the system know in advance, which users belong to the same cultural group? Otherwise, the system must ask many more users than only 20. In sum, using Hofstede's indices in culturally adaptive systems at runtime is not reasonably applicable.

8.2   Model for Intercultural HMI Design

FAH confirmed: HMI is culturally imprinted

The reliability of the results summarized in section 6.6.3 justifies the verification of the models. The course and the outcome of this work that is in favor of culturally imprinted user interaction confirms analytically as well as empirically the fundamental abstract hypothesis (FAH) that HMI is culturally imprinted because the user moves about in a cultural surrounding (cf. section 2.3.1). Therefore, FAH can be considered to be reconfirmed by the results of this work in addition to the already existing proof for the confirmation of FAH in literature (cf. section 2.3.1). Thereby, the presumptions (P6) and (P7) in section 4.3.1 are also fulfilled. In addition, several CIIs represent differences in user interaction according to the different cultural background of the users (cf. Table 24 in section 6.2).

Cultural Interaction Indicators (CIIs) represent culturally imprinted user interaction

Explorative factor analysis and multi-dimensional scaling

This is strongly supported by the results obtained by the application of explorative factor analysis and multidimensional scaling on the cultural interaction indicators: Cultural as well as interaction differences have been found (indicated by factor loadings semantically corresponding to the HMIDs) (cf. section 6.6.1). The emerging factor loadings (three components covering more than 97% of the total variance in the data set) seem to be identical with test duration, mouse moves and mouse clicks, which proves that there are culturally influenced differences in HCI regarding interaction speed and frequency. In addition, support that the obtained differences are culturally

Proof of cultural differences in HCI

---

[342] As it is required by Hofstede 1994.

imprinted yields the fact that despite the same IDV values of the users their interaction is different (cf. sections 6.2 and 8.1).

There are culture dependent perspectives and views of the users about the product, which represent cultural differences relevant for HMI design (cf. section 2.3.6). Using HMI depends on many parameters relating to situation; context, user preferences and world knowledge (cf. sections 2.1 and 6.6). Since the view of space, time and mental aspects are strongly culture dependent and HMI involves mental aspects concerning space and time, HMI is also culture dependent (cf. sections 2.2, 2.3 and 6.6). In addition, interaction behavior is imprinted by culture over time (cf. sections 6.4 and 8.1). Last but not least, most of the postulated empirical and methodological hypotheses have been confirmed in this work (cf. sections 6.5 and 7.6), clearly stating that there are culture dependent differences in HMI which can be determined quantitatively: HMI is culturally influenced, i.e. the interaction of the user with the system is culturally influenced by the cultural imprint of the user.

Confirmed hypotheses: quantitative determination of culture dependent differences in HMI possible

The potential model for intercultural HMI design (PMICHMID) consists of more than 300 mostly quantitative potential parameters relevant for intercultural HMI design that have been analytically determined as depending on culture by research literature and reflection (cf. section 4.4). 118 quantitative aspects have been implemented in the IIA tool (cf. chapter 5) and empirically tested (cf. chapter 6).

PMICHMID: more than 300 potentially mostly quantitative parameters relevant for intercultural HMI design

The quantitative data collection of the user preferences and their analysis revealed significant differences in HCI between Chinese (n=97) and German (n=359) speaking employees of Siemens VDO in accordance to the great cultural distance (primary culturally imprinting) between China and Germany as stated in literature (cf. section 2.2.3, P4 fulfilled).

Presumption P4 fulfilled

Thereby, most differences found in the values of the interaction parameters can be taken and verified as culturally influenced and hence, can be confirmed as actual cultural interaction indicators (cf. Table 24 in section 6.2 as well as section 6.6). The CIIs exposing the best classifying quota regarding the cultural preferences of the users derived from the data sets of both online studies (cf. section 6.6.2) could be incorporated into the model for intercultural HMI design (MICHMID).

Differences confirmed using CIIs

As shown in section 6.6.1, the cultural interaction indicators can be classified for HMI dimensions (HMIDs). The specific values of the HMI dimensions sensitive to culture are the cultural interaction indicators (CIIs). In addition to the CIIs, the HMIDs can be considered to be another confirmed part of the potential model for intercultural HMI design integrated in the verified model for intercultural HMI design. The most significant HMI dimensions (HMIDs) found in this work relevant for intercultural HMI design have been identified

Classification of CIIs according to HMIDs

Most relevant HMI dimensions confirmed part of PMICHMID

as depending on culture based on the CIIs found as presented in Table 32 in section 6.5.[343]

Real values still must be calculated

The real values of the relevant HMI dimensions for intercultural HMI design must be still calculated. This was not already done while creating the test setting because these parameters had not been known at that time (cf. iterative research based on grounded theory as explained in section 3.3.1).

HMI dimensions can be represented by CIIs

Not until finishing the empirical data collection and analysis, did it became clear that there are HMI dimensions that can be represented by CIIs. From now on these CIIs have to be investigated in such detail as to enrich UMTM so that it does not only contain ordinary, but also interval scaled variables. For example, POI can be divided by a forth of the screen size (i.e. screen height multiplied by screen width divided by 4). (C) used monitors with a screen resolution of 1024x800 on average and (G) 1200x1024, i.e. the effect is even greater (because (G) used less information units and higher resolution than (C) at the same time and vice versa). Another example is duration of information presentation (DIP) that may well contradict the hypotheses because of a bad test setting or a poor use case or because it is actually that way.[344] The interaction style is compiled from interaction patterns integrated over time containing all attributes of the user interaction like INS, INF, ¬IN, etc. (similar to the CIPs that are composed of CIIs, cf. Figure 10 in section 5.2.2 as well as sections 6.2 and 6.6.2) concerning different interaction devices like mouse, keyboard, menu control button, or touch screen.

The studies in this work reveal that there are cultural differences in HCI and that there is a metric, which is adequate to measure cross-cultural HCI. This model also includes the usability metric trace model (UMTM) containing the empirically confirmed variables for intercultural HMI design obtained in this work (i.e., the cultural interaction indicators (CIIs)), the relating HMI dimensions (HMIDs) as well as the relationship to culture represented by the verified hypotheses postulated in this work.

In sum, the confirmed results of this work are integrated in the confirmed model for intercultural HMI design (MICHMID) presented in Table 48, which should underline that by observation of the combinations of those cultural interaction indicators, different cultural interaction patterns can be identified, which are quantitatively measurable by a computer system depending on the

---

[343] The values presented in Table 48 for value (G) and value (C) are indexes from Table 49 in the appendix. A detailed explanation of postulated and real values as well as of postulated and real ratios is given in section 6.5 (cf. esp. Figure 26).

[344] This phenomenon must be further researched in future studies.

interaction behavior imprinted by the culture of the user, i.e. using (a set of) cultural interaction indicators, cultural differences in HMI can be measured (quantitatively).[345]

Table 48: Verified model for intercultural HMI design (MICHMID) containing the most significant HMI dimensions (HMIDs) found in this work relevant for intercultural HMI design based on the Cultural Interaction Indicators (CIIs) confirming the hypotheses postulated in this work

Measurement Variable (operationalized according to hypotheses IH or INH represented in UMTM)	Short name	Variable (CII)	Value (G)	Value (C)	HMID	Short name	Description of Parameter in Dataset	Formula	Desired unit	Basic physical dimension	Sign
Information frequency (expressed by the number of pieces of information presented by the system per time unit) (IH1a, IH1b2, IH5)	NIT	MG message distance	141	112	Information density (temporally, ID_{TIME}) (= information frequency (IF))	IF_{User} $ID-TIME_{(NIT)}$ $IF_{(NIT)}$	Number of adjusted MG messages within MG test task	n/t	Information units (IU) /s [IU/min]	Frequency	f
Number of POI in the map display (IH1b1)	POI	POI index	20	35	Information density (spatially, ID_{SPACE})	$ID_{S-PACE(POI)}$	Number of POI per area	n/a	1 / m²	Density	ρ
Number of interactions with the system per time unit (IH1c, INH5, IH8, INH8)	IN	IN represented by SEMS and duration of test (DT) (=SEMS_norm index)	735	1036	Interaction frequency (INF)	INF_S	Number of interaction cycles per session	n/t	Hz (1/s)	Frequency	f
Number of mouse clicks per time unit	MC	MC : DT represented by L_Button_	85	121	Interaction frequency	$INF_{(MC)}$	Number of mouse clicks per	n/t	Hz (1/s)	Frequency	f

[345] Table 48 also shows the parameters that can be calculated from the data obtained by the online studies presented in section 6.2. At the moment, this verified content of MICHMID is a compilation of the results obtained in this work, which is a good start for explanatory research but needs improvement because of its first publication. With further detailed research, the connections and relationships of the entities used within MICHMID become clearer and stronger and therefore, its presentation will become more precise in future publications.

(INH1c1)		Downs_norm index					session				
Mouse movement speed (INH1c2)	MMS	LMT roughly represented by the number of mouse move events per session, (=Mouse moves norm index)	7529	10566	Interaction speed (INS)	INS$_{(MM)}$	Length of mouse track per second	s/t	mm/s	Speed	v
Number of mouse moves per time unit (INH1c3)	MM	Mouse moves norm	7529	10566	Interaction frequency	INF$_{(MM)}$	Number of mouse movements per session (test duration)	n/t	Hz (1/s)	Frequency	f
Number of parallel tasks in task bar (IH1d, IH6a)	PT	Maximal Open Tasks	2.87	4.64	Interaction parallelism (INP)	INPmax	Maximal number of parallel tasks in task bar during the complete test session	n	-	Dimensionless	-
Number of error clicks (IH6b) (per time unit)	EC	Error Clicks index, Mouse Clicks (MC)	0.335	0.958	Interaction efficiency, Interaction speed	IN-EFI((MC-EC):MC), INS$_{(EC)}$	Number of error clicks within the complete test session	n/t	Hz	Frequency	f
Number of refused system messages (IH6b) (per time unit)	RM	RM	1.77	1.33	Interruption tolerance (INT)	INT$_{(RM)}$	Number of refused system messages during the complete session	n/t	Hz	Frequency	f
Time to disable virtual agents (INH6b)	TDA	TDA	2.5	26	Interruption tolerance	INT$_{(TDA)}$	Time to disable "Merlin" (cf. section 5.2.2)	t	s	Time	T

8.3 Recommendations for Intercultural HMI Design

It is difficult to derive generally valid guidelines for intercultural HMI design (as exemplified in section 2.3) from the results obtained in this work because of the methodological problems discussed in section 8.1. For example, only four cultural interaction indicators expose very high selectivity power (cf. sections 7.3, 6.6.2 and 7.5) and most of the best classifying CIIs are represented only by one measurement variable. Furthermore, a good deal of interpretation effort in qualitative as well in quantitative studies is necessary to obtain any recommendations at all.

Difficult task to acquire general design rules

Nevertheless, the confirmed hypotheses in this work serve at least as a basis and the results of this work revealed some proven facts that are usable to formulate recommendations for intercultural HMI design in general and for culturally adaptive systems in special. In addition, it is very reasonable for further development and research to take some rules of thumb into account even if they must be regarded as preliminary and handled with care.

Confirmed hypotheses basis to formulate recommendations for intercultural HMI design and for culturally adaptive systems

Furthermore, it can be stated from section 6.3 that interaction of the user with the system in HMI is influenced by static aspects (preferences) stemming from the cultural imprint of the user and his experience with the system as well as by dynamic aspects resulting from the concrete situation. Therefore, the following recommendation for system and architectural design can be given:

HMI influenced by static and dynamic aspects

The kind of interaction of the computer with the user within HMI must be adjustable, because the system must cope with the user's interaction needs that vary from the user's cultural imprint as well as experience and situation (cf. sections 6.3 and 6.4). This requires changing the adaptation parameters according to the specific values of the cultural interaction indicators and the HMI dimensions for intercultural HMI design (cf. section 6.6.1).

Adjust interaction of computer with user

Change adaptation parameters according to values of CIIs and HMIDs

In addition, the results in this work show, that the specific values of the following variables are significantly higher for Chinese than for German speaking users:[346]

---

[346] Cf. section 6.2 for further information.

- Information frequency (TDA): e.g., (G) users switch the virtual agent off very early in contrast to (C)
- Information density (ID): e.g., (G) desire 25% more entries than (C); (C) desired about 30% more advice than (G); number of information units (e.g., POI) was three times higher for (C) than for (G)
- Information processing parallelism (PT) / Interaction parallelism (quasi parallel processing): e.g., (C) tend to work on 80% more tasks simultaneously (ratio of max. open tasks during the test session for (C):(G) = 1.8:1)
- Interaction speed (INS): e.g., (C) did 100% more error clicks (EC) than (G);[347] speed of mouse movements is 60% higher for (C) than for (G)[348]
- Interaction frequency (INF): e.g., (C) moved the mouse 30% more often than (G); (C) did 20% more left mouse clicks than (G); ratio for interaction breaks (¬IN) with mouse > 10s for the three groups is (C):(G) = 1:1.22 showing that (C) exhibit higher interaction frequency doing fewer long interaction breaks
- Interaction style: e.g., (C) pressed "no" 50% more often than (G) concerning (RM); (C) said "yes" more often than (G) concerning (AM).

Cultural differences in HCI also concerned use cases of navigation systems

The cultural differences in HCI also concerned use cases of navigation systems. These aspects have to be taken into account for designing intercultural user interfaces in driver navigation systems for the global market. The use cases from driver navigation systems done in the tests with the IIA tool (cf Figure 12 and Figure 13 in section 5.2) showed differences in the interaction behavior as well as information processing of the users according to their cultural background (cf. section 6.2).

---

[347] This can probably be explained by the users' instinctive behavior of trying to request system reactions if the system response time is too high. Furthermore, as interaction speed (INS) and interaction frequency (INF) correlate with uncertainty avoidance (UV) as assumed in INH6b (cf. section 4.5) and as confirmed with SH_6 with high confirmation strength of the hypothesis (cf. section 6.5), these effects are reasonable because of the low UAI of (C) in contrast to (G) (cf. Hofstedes UAI values in Figure 2 in section 2.2.3, or in the VSM scores in Table 50 in the appendix). However, it must be clarified in future work, which CIIs in addition to EC contribute to support or reject INH6b, especially because the UAI values obtained in the online studies for the Chinese and German SV employees are very similar (cf. section 6.4). Furthermore, IS and IF derived from the cultural dimensions of Hall (cf. section 4.3.3) better explain the high EC rate for (C) in contrast to (G) than the cultural dimensions of Hofstede (as the overall outcome of this work suggests, cf. sections 6.5, 7.6 and 8.2 as well as the methodological discussion in section 8.1).

[348] However, another result contradicts higher IS for (C) than for (G): (G) clicked the dots away almost twice as fast as (C) as well as unexpected duration of information presentation (DIP) according to the hypotheses postulated: (C) and (G) wanted the advice to be about 40% longer than (E) (cf. rejected SH_{15} in section 6.5).

However, the derived recommendations for intercultural HMI design regarding driver navigation systems from these results cannot be strict guidelines as well because they have been obtained by simulating the use cases within the IIA tool using PCs and not by using driver navigation systems in real field tests. Nevertheless, with regard to additional parameters for adjusting HCI according to the cultural needs of the user in order to provide and handle adequate slots for the cultural interaction indicators presented in this work (cf. section 6.2), at least the following aspects should be considered very carefully when designing new architectures of driver navigation systems or extending existing systems:

- The number of information units presented simultaneously (e.g., points of interest in the map display) should be lower for German than for Chinese users.
- Number, duration and frequency of information units presented sequentially (e.g., (system) messages or maneuver advice in maneuver guidance) should be less for German than for Chinese users.
- Consider when designing information systems that frequency and speed of using interaction devices e.g., touch screen, hard keys and mouse is almost twice as frequent and fast as well as less exact for Chinese than for German users.

These design recommendations require that e.g., additional fields in the database of the driver navigation system have to be added in which the parameters according to different cultures can be stored (e.g., the default number of POI displayed on the map). Furthermore, the software regulating HMI has to be modified such that it is able to represent and display the specifics of different parameters (e.g., numbers of POI) due to the user's needs. Additional cultural parameters can be the color of the streets and routes, kind of voice (speaking speed and voice height), frequency of speech output and color style in general (cf. section 7.1).

Design recommendations require additional fields in the database and modifying the software regulating HMI

Furthermore, it is necessary to apply adaptivity in driver navigation systems because it is hard or even impossible for the driver to handle the functional and informational complexity of such systems in extreme driving situations: the mental workload, resulting from visible, audible, haptic, etc. information coming from all possible senses simply exceeds the mental capacity of the driver. Hence, HMI designers should consider that:

Applying adaptivity to avoid mental workload

- The mental workload should be maintained within acceptable limits in dangerous driving situations if the system adapts the information flow to the user automatically (cf. Piechulla et al. 2003). Concepts for adaptive HMI also have to take into account external input sources, e.g., signals from odometer (speed) or pre-crash sensors (lateral and longitudinal acceleration).

- The output modality of the system has to be adapted automatically to achieve the most adequate workload for the driver (e.g., using head-up displays (graphics) or loudspeaker (speech), cf. e.g., Salmen 2002).

Construction principles   Furthermore, to design culturally adaptive systems, some construction principles in the vehicle context have to be taken into account (cf. Kolrep & Jürgensohn 2003, Kobsa 1990):

- The distraction potential (the mental, visual and audio workload) of the driver must be maintained as low as possible (cf. De Waard 1996).[349]
- The HMI must be simple and safe in order not to reduce the driving safety (cf. Röse & Heimgärtner 2008).
- The reason for the adaptation (e.g., the current driving situation) and the kind of adaptation (e.g., structuring menus or renaming soft keys etc.) must be comprehensible for the driver at all times. Therefore, altering the frame of reference too strongly is not allowed (cf. Malinowski & Obermaier 1993). This means that the frequency of the adaptation has to be kept as low as possible (cf. Kobsa et al. 1989).
- Multi-modal dialog design requires that the driver can choose the modality freely at anytime (cf. Dieterich et al. 1993).
- The possibility that all haptically usable interaction elements can be accompanied by verbal output has to be guaranteed applying the motto "speak what you see".[350]
- The interruption and resumption of dialogs and interactions has to be possible (cf. Zeidler & Zellner 1992, Hof 2007).
- Adaptivity functionality to be switched off
- It must be possible for the driver to switch off the adaptivity functionality (cf. Kobsa 1990, Shneiderman 2009).
- To improve the usability, it is necessary to internationalize and to localize the system, i.e. to consider intercultural variables within the process of product design (cf. Vöhringer-Kuhnt 2002).

---

[349] In my view, it must be as balanced as possible. If the drivers attraction potential is too low (mental, visual and audio workload), the driver falls asleep which is not reasonable in traffic.

[350] From personal interviews with participants of the CHARISMA project at Siemens AG (cf. e.g., also Tonnis et al. 2008).

Finally, some results of this work can be expected to be valid for HCI design in general because there are culturally sensitive variables that can be used to measure cultural differences in HCI simply by counting certain interaction events without the necessity of knowing the semantic relations to the application. Surely, all those indicators can also be connected semantically to the use cases of applications running on the system. Such indicators are e.g., number of mouse moves (MM), breaks in the mouse moves ($\neg IN_{MM}$), speed of mouse moves (MMS), mouse clicks (MC), and interaction breaks in general ($\neg IN$). The values of the cultural interaction indicators change in a similar way even if different use cases and test tasks are applied. Hence, those CIIs can be called "general cultural interaction indicators" (GCIIs).

Some cultural interaction indicators (CIIs) useful for HCI design in general

⇨ Mouse moves
⇨ Mouse move speed
⇨ Mouse clicks
⇨ Interaction breaks

General cultural interaction indicators (GCIIs)

8.4   Revised Principle of Culturally Adaptive HMI

The methodological discussion (cf. section 8.1), the discussion of the results (cf. section 6.6), as well as the verification of the MICHIMID (cf. section 8.2) by the results obtained in this work evoked new reflections on the principle of culturally adaptive HMI (CAHMI) originally presented in section 3.2.1. Many of the aspects mentioned there imply the need to change the CAHMI approach in this work: the principle of CAHMI must be reviewed, adapted and optimized according the new findings obtained in the run of this dissertation project. Based on this, the path from the CAHMI principle to the general principle of adaptive HMI will be presented.

Changing the CAHMI approach

Cultural dimensions can be defined for every nation with different idiosyncrasies and values (cf. Hofstede 1991, cf. also section 2.2.3). However, there are no strict boundaries between the properties of different cultures (cf. Kralisch 2006, cf. also section 6.4). Therefore, there should be no sharp cultural classification (cf. Reinecke & Bernstein 2008, cf. also sections 6.6.1 and 8.5 as well as section 8.5.2 in the work report). It is not reasonable to apply culturally adaptive systems that make hard and sharp decisions. Rather, fuzzy grading of user interaction and the cultural parameters is advantageous. Therefore, in general, the assignment of users to a country or nationality using the adaptive system should be avoided (to prevent discrimination and to cover fast changing cultures).

No strict cultural classification

No assignment of users to country or nationality

No use of Hofstede's
indices because not
applicable at runtime

In addition, several reasons have been brought forward for not applying Hofstede's indices in intercultural HMI design especially for culturally adaptive systems at runtime (cf. section 8.1). Probably it is slightly better to relate the interaction behavior of the users to the cultural styles of Galtung 1981 (e.g. Teutonic, Nipponese or Gallic).[351] Thereby, at least the problem of wrongly classifying the interaction behavior of Chinese users to Germans users at country level and vice versa can be avoided (because Chinese users may behave in some respects like German users and vice versa because of their knowledge about the other culture and the acculturation processes resulting from it (cf. Thomas 1996)). However, using the classification of Galtung, even more countries are tossed into one pot (e.g., all countries of Teutonic origin), which makes it even more difficult to take into account the cultural imprint of the individual user (as required from the discussion in section 8.1) as presupposition for adaptive systems to know to which user it should adapt.

Cultural styles of Galtung
"too wide ranged"

Possibility of
classification users to
culturally imprinted
interaction and
information style

According to the results of this work driving the methodological discussion (section 8.1) and finally the change of the approach regarding culturally adaptive systems (cf. sections 8.4 and 8.5), it is not the objective to classify the user according to nationality or culture but to interaction and information processing style (i.e. to the specific values of the HMI dimensions) that is culturally imprinted. Hence, cultural classification can also be possible in this sense is (cf. section 6.6.2).

Classification into pure
interaction behavior, later
relating cultural
characteristics to
individual interaction
patterns

Automatic adaptation of
system to user's
interaction behavior

Therefore, the best solution is to classify according to kinds of pure interaction behavior and to relate cultural characteristics to the individual interaction patterns later. Consequently, it is not necessary for the system to "know" exactly under which cultural dimensions, culture or (even worse in regard to ethnical discrimination) nationality the user in front of the system should be classified. The assignment of the culture to the behavior is known from the results of studies at the design phase (cf. sections 3.3 and 6.6). The system should automatically adapt itself most adequately to the interaction behavior of the user by recognizing interaction patterns and by concluding the values of the HMIDs which are connected to cultural variables for HMI design (cf. model for intercultural HMI design in section 8.2).

---

[351] In Galtung 1981, these cultural styles are discussed in detail (cf. also Galtung 1985 as well as Wierlacher & Bogner 2003).

Therefore, it is an advantage, if the system knows as much as possible about the culturally imprinted interaction behavior of the user. This also reconciles the internal model of the system better with the user's expectations, which results in reducing the level of surprise that the user has in terms of system behavior (cf. Evers 2003). Therefore, it is reasonable to replace the cultural dimension and its values by HMI dimensions and their values, which are culturally imprinted (determined at the design phase).

Cultural imprinted interaction behavior must be known by system

Replacing cultural dimensions by culturally imprinted HMI dimensions

Figure 36 presents the revised principle for culturally adaptive HMI. The revisions are marked grey in contrast to the principle for culturally adaptive HMI firstly assumed and postulated by the pure study of literature presented in Figure 4 in section 3.2.

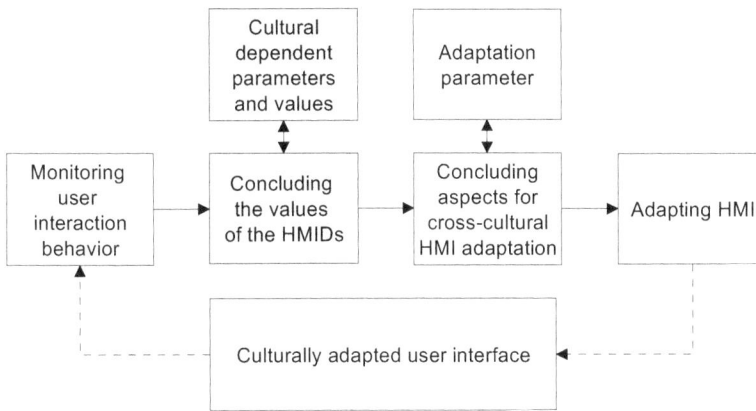

Figure 36: Revised principle of Culturally Adaptive HMI

In addition, the classification approach using the values of HMI dimensions representing the HMI style of the user is much more efficient and exact because the peculiarities of the interaction characteristics like interaction frequency or the information processing style regarding e.g., information density, are used instead of the culture related parameters like the values of the different cultural dimensions (e.g., uncertainty avoidance or individualism index) or even variables like nationality, country of birth, etc. which is methodologically very difficult and not applicable for adaptive systems at runtime as shown in section 8.1.

Efficiency of classification approach using the values of HMI dimensions

No cultural dimension but interaction behavior

General principle of CAHMI: eliminating the aspects related to cultural analysis
⇨   No problem with classifying user to culture

No analysis of cultural aspects, just culturally imprinted interaction of user behavior (HMI style)

Culturally imprinted HMI dimensions

Analyzing the interaction behavior of the user

Therefore, no cultural dimension will be used to relate the interaction of the user with the system to a certain culture. Only the interaction behavior itself will be classified according to the HMI dimensions regarding the HMI style of the user whose specific values depend on the cultural imprint of the user. Hence, it is not necessary to classify the user to a certain culture, but to the kind of interaction behavior while using the interface by the user (HMI style or characteristics, cf. section 4.2) from which is known, what cultural settings the user presumably prefers.[352]

Thereby, the system must only observe the most relevant and direct variables concerning aspects for HMI (i.e. the HMI dimensions) within the interaction behavior of the user and not conclude the values of the cultural variables indirectly related to HMI design at runtime which is a very difficult task even for cultural scientists at the "design phase" (as shown in section 8.1). Furthermore, it is very difficult and problematic to explain the cultural differences in the user interaction with a computer or machine using cultural models as shown throughout this work.[353]

The values of the HMI dimensions are culturally imprinted inherently because the user interaction behavior is influenced by his cultural surroundings.[354] Therefore, automatically all cultural aspects are covered implicitly by the analysis of the user interaction with the system. Furthermore, this approach takes the cultural influences into account very exactly simply by analyzing the interaction behavior of the user. For example, if the user interacts very rapidly with the system, the system should also provide information to the user in short time intervals. This can affect e.g., the system response time as well as the time before the information is actually presented to the user (e.g., processing time). Hence, this approach is very efficient because there is no need for a detour via the analysis of cultural aspects but only the need for

---

[352] Cf. also section 4.2 in the work report.

[353] This is also supported by Jagne & Smith-Atakan 2006 and explains why this basic work in hand is descriptive regarding the cultural differences in HCI and CAHMI rather than explanatory in the first place (cf. also the methodological challenges in section 8.1): most resources were necessary to secure empirically quantitative cultural differences in HCI and describe them first. Hence, to explain these observed differences in detail remains a goal for future research.

[354] Cf. the newly confirmed FAH in several sections (formally confirmed finally in section 8.2).

exactly measuring the culturally imprinted interaction behavior (HMI style) of the user.[355]

8.5   Culturally Adaptive Interface-Agent Architecture

From knowledge of the association of the recognized interaction behavior to the cultural characteristics of the user, appropriate implications regarding the user interface design and the adaptation of the HMI can be derived. This concept should allow adaptation to every culture and user simply by changing some default parameters without modifying software architecture and/or source code. The default parameters should be revealed by scientific research based on cultural psychology using empirical studies like those described in chapter 6 of this work. Furthermore, if no reasonable default parameters for the desired culture are provided, the system should be able to adapt itself to the culture of the user (even if the adaptation process takes much more time because the system must learn the behavior of the user and create a user model using learning algorithms).

Deriving implications regarding user interface design and adaptation of the HMI

⇨   *Adaptation by changing default parameters*

Scientific research for revealing default parameters

All these aspects can be regarded in the structure of a culturally adaptive interface-agent-architecture (CAIAA), which consists of several components, each of them fulfilling a special sub task (cf. Figure 37).[356]

Structure of CAIAA

---

[355] Further information about the CAHMI approach using the revised principle of CAHMI and extending it to a general one can be found and are discussed in sections 8.4 and 8.5 in the work report. However, these tasks remain for further research.

[356] The objective of automotive suppliers today is to generate no emissions, no accidents and no failures caused by their products including HMI. Hence, the software architecture of interior systems in cars has to be designed considering these requirements (cf. e.g., the figures in Würtenberger et al. 2003: 525-544 as well as Röse & Heimgärtner 2008), which is an USP for the OEMs. Hence, further information on the relevant parts of the CAIAA, which are used in GAF for driver navigation systems are described in detail only in documents for Siemens VDO, which may not be published.

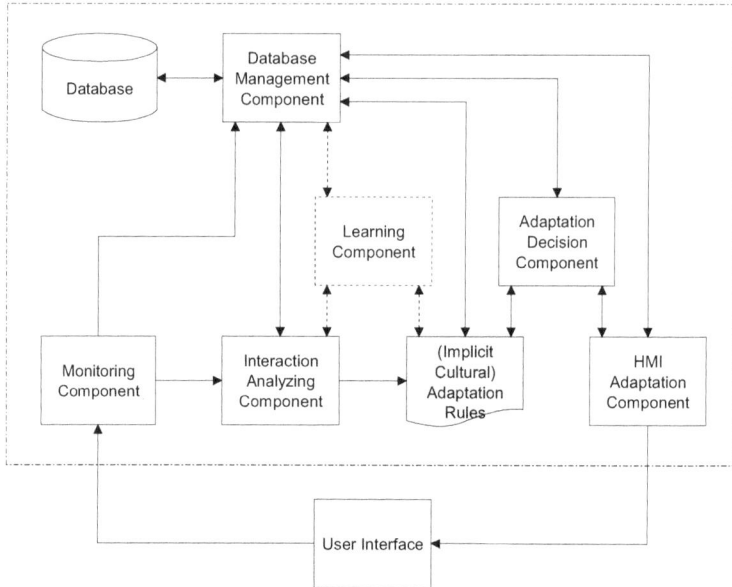

Figure 37: Structure of the Culturally Adaptive Interaction-Agent Architecture (CAIAA)

Adaptive HMI containing
model for cultural
differences

This architecture contains an adaptive HMI, endowed with a model (yielding parameters) for cultural (cognitive) differences (individualization), which embraces aspects of internationalization and localization as well as of personalization of software.

Dynamic adaptation of
interaction

The CAIAA allows dynamic adaptation of the (visual, haptic and audible) interaction (Graphical User Interface, Haptic User Interface, Speech User Interface) and exhibits the following features:

- History tracking (monitoring component)
- Analysis and allocation of direct hidden variables to cultural dimensions (interaction analysis component)
- Derivation of control parameters from the model for intercultural HMI design (MICHMID) about the user for HMI adaptation (adaptation decision component)
- Guiding the adaptation of the HMI (HMI adaptation component)
- Storage and retrieval of data (data management component)

Thereby, the CAIAA achieves automatic cultural adaption of the HMI for the respective user, which covers the revised principle of culturally adaptive HMI (cf. section 8.4), i.e. the automatic cultural adaptation of the HMI to the respective user by analyzing his HMI style. The HMI monitoring component serves to record the interaction data generated by the user with the system, which is stored in a database communicating with the data-managing component.

Automatic cultural adaptation of the HMI

Recording interaction data into database

The relationship between user interaction patterns and the values of the cultural dimensions can be extracted by comparing relationship tables in the database that had been determined empirically at the design phase (cf. chapters 5-7). Hence, from this, implications can be drawn for the cultural adaptation parameters that can be stored in a lookup-table (cf. Baumgartner 2003) which at runtime can be retrieved for adapting the HMI. Thereby, existing possibilities for tracing and logging user interaction events, or in general, determining and showing the user behavior with the system, serve to identify the cultural variables and their values according to the localization process.

Implications for cultural adaptation parameters comparing relationship tables from database

However, the general preparation of the system for many localized configurations has to be considered by fulfilling the requirements of software internationalization. The interaction-analysis component extracts the patterns of user interaction with the system from the monitoring component. In combination with the optional learning component, the interaction patterns can be analyzed and recognized over time by the system with respect to the identified user. This serves to generate an adequate model of the user, which also contains the cultural characteristics of the user determined at runtime. The adaptation decision component retrieves the recognized cultural characteristics from the data management component and provides the adaptation information for HMI adaptation using cultural adaptation rules. The HMI adaptation component can, therefore, adapt the HMI according to the related HMI aspects needed by the user.

To develop a general adaptability framework that is usable for all use cases, applications and systems, all discussed aspects in this work should be taken into account. For example, the concepts of localization and internationalization must be integrated (cf. section 2.3.5). Thereby, directly visible and hidden intercultural variables must be specified and implemented within the system's architecture (cf. section 2.3.4). Furthermore, adequate metrics to measure the user behavior and HMI must be used (cf. section 4.5). From this, architecture should be developed, which serves to extend and optimize the structure of the actual system.[357] The verified models now enable us to determine which

General adaptability framework

---

[357] Cf. section 8.5 in the work report.

variables of the user interaction must be recorded exactly in order to recognize the (intercultural) usability of the system (as well as system and programming errors).

Functionality of the generic adaptability framework

This framework is connected to the system via an Application Programming Interface (API) for exchanging control commands in order to provide data to the user situation model to derive adaptation objectives, adaptation means, and adaptation information and adaptation process (cf. section 2.4). The adaptation manager transforms these pieces of information into messages and sends them to the system. The system receives the messages and evaluates them based on a predefined "command language" to finally adapt HMI.[358]

CAIAA contrasted to related work

CUMO not truly adaptive

Reinecke et al. 2007 developed the cultural user model ontology at a qualitative level, which is quantitatively supported by Hofstede's indices and involved many concepts and even variables of the CAHMI approach discussed and published by the author since 2005. The main emphasis of Reinecke et al. 2007 is on user modeling and putting it into an architecture for cultural adaptivity. For that, a manual monitoring of the user is necessary using clarification dialogs at runtime. However, this is not considered truly adaptive. For example, it does not follow the revised or the general principle of adaptive HMI, because it concentrates on adaptivity triggered by cultural aspects, which can and do change over time and even worse, cannot be determined at runtime when using Hofstede's indexes (cf. section 8.1). In contrast, the optimized CAIA architecture overcomes these restrictions and problems caused by the usage of explicit cultural user models, namely the limitation from the elusive nature of cultural background as well as the constraint of the necessity to use and apply cultural dimensions.[359] The main difference of the optimized CAIAA (according to the revised principle of CAHMI) to the originally designed CAIAA[360] is that basically no explicit cultural rules are used in the adaptation rules anymore, but only implicit ones (marked grey in Figure 37).[361]

---

[358] For more information, please refer to section 8.5 in the work report as well as to Heimgärtner 2009a.

[359] The first idea for CAIAA was born in 2003 and published in Heimgärtner 2005. The successively obtained new insights regarding CAHMI during this dissertation project over the years as well as literature study about using Hofstede's cultural dimensions for HMI design discussed in section 8.1 inspired the author to revise the principle for CAHMI and enhance the CAIAA. However, still further research has to be done to improve those concepts. Some first efforts are done in section 8.5 in the work report.

[360] Cf. section 8.5 in the work report as well as Heimgärtner 2005.

[361] Some examples of the new adaptation rules are presented in section 8.4 in the work report and are implemented in the CAHMI demonstrator, which can be found in the verified connections between the PCIIs and culture in section 7.3 and in the confirmed models (MICHMID and

8.5.1   Applying CAHMI in Driver Navigation Systems

The examples of cultural differences in the map display according to information density and color-coding presented in this work (cf. section 7.1) are first
realizations on the Path-To-CAHMI (cf. section 3.3.4). However, the strong
interactive and invasive changes require systems that are more complex.
Infotainment solutions for cars and thereby communication and interaction
strategies in automotive adaptive interfaces will change dramatically in the
near future (cf. Amditis et al. 2006). Constantly, increasing functions (e.g.,
Advanced Driver Assistant Systems (ADAS) or autonomous driving, cf.
Brookhuis et al. 2001) combined with a large number of nomadic devices (e.g.,
MP3 player, personal navigation systems, mobile phones) require flexible, safe
and adaptable HMI solutions for the world market (cf. chapter 1). Therefore,
the design of future driver information and assistance systems must better
cover the culturally influenced personal preferences and needs of the drivers
using methods of cultural adaptability to broaden universal access.

Need for more complex systems in future

Furthermore, there are also some target user groups that have their own
characteristics of system use (e.g. using a driver navigation system in vehicles)
depending on their preferences (e.g., beginning drivers vs. experienced drivers,
old vs. young people, female vs. male users) that are influenced by culture. In
this sense, the meaning of the usual conception of culture as ethnically or
nationally determined is extended to the group culture and the individualistic
habits of the user (e.g., an individualistic but culturally influenced style of
using a device, interacting, driving, etc.). This means, there are many different
groups, whose members exhibit the same culture as defined in section 2.2.1,
which can be referenced by culturally adaptive systems. For example, driving
behavior includes aspects such as fast, stressed, hectic, sporty, or curvy driving
and depends e.g., on the experience of the driver (e.g., beginner, intermediate,
professional, expert etc.) or on his cultural background (using bumpers for
parking, buzzer frequency, interaction times, interaction frequencies, etc., cf.
e.g., Xie & Parker 2002 and Xie et al. 2004).[362]

Target user groups

⇨ *Individualistic habits*

Culturally influenced style of using a device

UMTM) in section 8.2. Better rules can be developed taking also into account not yet analyzed data from the second online study as well as data from new data collections in the future.

[362] Cf. also Rothengatter & Huguenin 2004 as well as Heimgärtner et al. 2007. For example, to
exemplify the different driving behavior of a bus driver in China in contrast to Germany

Integration of much more data

In addition, data from traffic, car, history logging, emotion recognition and driver verification should be used and integrated in driving preference and situation models by considering also the properties and the state of the vehicle (cf. Röse & Heimgärtner 2008). Then it is possible to compute the decisions for adapting the HMI by considering priority control, driver-load controlled information flow, information presentation preferences and calculated sensitive information. Furthermore, the relationships of secondary tasks to driver workload must also be considered and should lead finally to an optimized workload model. However, many more aspects can be considered in such systems and remain for further research. For example, the history of the driving tours contains important information about the preferences of the driver: the preferred type of routes, average speed, default tours, short or long tours or routes, along rivers or hills, etc. Also the kind and style of interaction can vary significantly (e.g., reasonable, rational, arbitrary, sequentially, fast, well considered, haptic, visual, auditory, communicative etc.). By associating these aspects with the cultural models, proposals can be made to culturally adapt the HMI and the functionality of such systems.

Modeling

⇨ Integrating cultural knowledge from the design phase

The most relevant aspects according to the requirement for the product design have to be integrated in the cognitive driver model and implemented within prototypes using databases containing the cultural differences to adjust the represented cognitive models of the user (driver) according to the desired country at runtime. For this, tables concerning the adaptation information consisting of the differences between the desired cultures (countries, ethnic groups, dialects, gender, age, preferences etc.) and the adaptation rules must already be created at the design phase (cf. Baumgartner 2003). Hence, it is very important that the actual driving situation will be taken into account (e.g., by a driving situation model) and driving safety must be granted using a driver workload model, i.e. the user may not be overloaded (or unnecessarily loaded) cognitively. Hence, cognitive modeling and system adaptability play a decisive role for a generic adaptability framework for driver navigation systems (cf. e.g. also Cacciabue 2007). Therefore, in order to direct adaptive HMI the system must analyze and integrate the driver's cognitive states through driver preferences and the driver situation model with data from several other models and sources as indicated in Figure 38.

please have a look at the video files "Chinese bus driver driving.mpg", "Chinese bus driver waiting.mpg" and "German bus driver driving.mpg" in the online appendix.

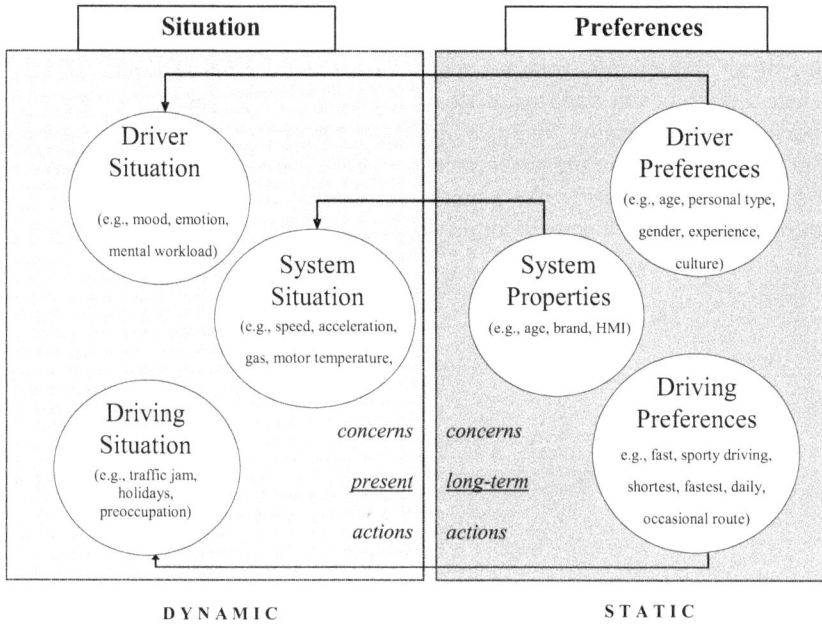

Figure 38: Criteria influencing adaptive Automotive HMI

From the plethora of models (cf. Salvucci 2006) like driving and driver situation model, driver and driving preference model, driver intention model and driver and driving interaction model as well as much data like driving history, vehicle data and environmental data (inside or outside the car, traffic, etc.), at least two models should be employed to take into account static aspects (preferences) and dynamic aspects (situation).

At least two models are reasonable

The data-oriented driving situation model describes the current driving situation which is defined by the values of the variables of the vehicle such as speed, lateral and longitudinal acceleration as well as the position of the vehicle (traffic jam, highway, parking place, etc.) or the reason for driving (business, spare time, race, etc.) and so on.

⇨ *Data-oriented driving situation model*

The driver workload model contains information about the mental or physical stress of the driver indicated by variables such as heart rate, galvanic skin response values or error clicks and task failures. A layered approach for intelligent services must be developed that comprises the architecture and the priorities of the data oriented models. For example, the driver workload model

⇨ *Driver workload model*

could be an extension of De Waard's model by "sleepy" state to include drowsiness detection (micro sleep) (De Waard 1996).[363]

Future task:
generating a model for
integrated adaptive HMI

Research should deliver further information to enable the development of these models in detail and to generate an integrated adaptive HMI model. However, this extends beyond this work and remains a task for further research. Nevertheless, the author has made some basic reflections on this topic combining the revised culturally adaptive interface agent architecture (cf. section 8.5.2 in the work report) with an universal mediator layer between basic navigation functions and HMI using the generic adaptability framework to derive a generic adaptability framework for driver navigation systems.[364]

---

[363] I thank Franziska Groenland and Hans-Wilhelm Rühl very much for discussing some important aspects regarding adaptive HMI in vehicles relevant for this dissertation project.

[364] However, the detailed GAF_{DNS} may not be published as it is property of SV.

9   Summary, Conclusion and Perspectives

"Napred meriti, potom krojiti."
(Czech saying) [365]

This dissertation represents fundamental research for culturally adaptive HMI and for further and more detailed studies in intercultural HMI design because both, most of the methodological hypotheses regarding culturally adaptive systems and the empirical hypotheses concerning dimensions relevant for HMI design (HMIDs) as well as cultural interaction indicators (CIIs) and their values have been confirmed in this work for the first time (cf. sections 6.5 and 7.6).

Fundamental research

The following items achieved in this dissertation project are new in the research for intercultural HMI design:

News value of this work

- Extending and optimizing structures, processes and methods in inter-cultural HMI research for the global market to enable an automatically parameterized adaptation of HMI to the culture of the desired target user groups by developing an approach to culturally adapt HMI (cf. chapter 3).

CAHMI

- Development of a *potential model for intercultural HMI design* (PMICH-MID) represented by a set of relevant cultural variables by analyzing the interaction behavior of users with different cultural imprint (cf. chapter 4).

(P)MICHMID

---

[365] "Measure first, and then cut." (cf. footnote 1 and file "Sprichwörter mit messen.txt" in the online appendix). The differences in the proverbs of this form possibly express the differences in precisely measuring things or the frequency of reflecting an intended action before doing it. For example, Turks measure 1000 times (according to their proverb "Measure a thousand times and cut once." (Reinsberg III, 23)) before being sure about a fact. Greeks measure 10 times ("Measure ten times and cut once."), Englishman three times ("Measure three times what you buy, and cut only once."), Swiss ("Besser zweimol gmässe as eimol vergässe." (Sutermeister, 129)) and Germans two times (in the Low German: "Bäter twêmoal möäten oss ênmoal vergöäten." (Schlingmann, 1026) and in East Frisia: "T of is prayer twêmal mäten, ace ênmal vergäten." (Schütze, IV, 292; Kern, 1290)), and Czeches one time: "Measure first, and then cut!".

IIA tool

- Implementation of a method of culture oriented design in a tool to determine cultural variables and their values for intercultural HMI design (cf. IIA tool, chapter 5). This tool is effective, efficient and meaningful within the process of intercultural HCI design because it can be used locally online worldwide and provides quantitatively comparable results.

CIIs and HMIDs

- (Quantitative) Recognition of the specific values of direct, hidden intercultural variables of interaction as a precondition for a culturally adaptive systems as well as providing default parameters called cultural interaction indicators (CIIs) categorized in HMI dimensions (HMIDs) (cf. chapter 6).

CAHMI demonstrator

- Implementation of the CAHMI principle in the "CAHMI demonstrator" running on a real mobile driver navigation system and proof that the CAHMI approach in culturally adaptive systems works in reality using this demonstrator (cf. chapter 7).

MICHMID

- Verification of parts of the PMICHMID and derivation of recommendations for intercultural (adaptive) HMI and UI design as well as using the culturally adaptive interface agent architecture (CAIAA). Extending and optimizing the principle of CAHMI to escape the problem of building complex cultural models at runtime and at the same time adapting to the culturally imprinted individual user needs (cf. chapter 8).

CAIAA

CAHMI
tool chain

Thereby, a new methodological access and several concepts, models, architectures as well as tools (e.g., IIA tool, supporting tools, cf. chapter 5) have been created that can be considered as an approach towards a tool chain for intercultural HMI design, especially for culturally adaptive systems.[366] This approach integrates internationalization (I18N) and localization (L10N) of human machine systems with cultural adaptation to reduce interventions in the source code.

---

[366] Cf. list of used and developed tools by the author in file "Used Tools.docx" in the online appendix.

The main objectives of this dissertation project have been to identify cultural differences in HCI primarily regarding hidden intercultural variables (cf. chapter 6) as well as to develop an approach to quantitatively recognize these differences in order to pave the road to culturally adaptive systems (cf. chapter 3). It was investigated whether or not users from different cultures interact differently with a computer system. The results of working on these two objectives built the basis to prove the functionality of culturally adaptive systems (cf. chapter 7). Using the methods from research literature and analytical reasoning, potential culturally sensitive parameters have been postulated (cf. chapter 4), implemented in a newly developed intercultural interaction analysis (IIA) tool and applied by measuring the interaction behavior of the test persons with a computer in relation to their culture (cf. chapter 5). It has been shown theoretically (cf. chapters 2-4) and empirically (cf. chapters 5-7) which aspects in HMI depend on culture (cf. chapter 8) and how these aspects can be adapted automatically at runtime to users of different cultures within a real mobile driver navigation system (cf. chapter 7). To verify the relationships between cultural aspects and HMI as found in the literature expressed by potential cultural interaction indicators (PCIIs) (contained in the potential model for intercultural HMI design, PICHMID, cf. section 4.5), qualitative offline pre-studies as well as two quantitatively comparable remote online studies have been conducted mainly in China and in Germany (cf. chapter 6). The IIA tool served to record and analyze the user's interaction with the system in order to identify culturally influenced variables (PCIIs) such as color, positioning, information density and interaction speed as well as their values, which enabled the verification of parts of PMICHMID to yield a model for intercultural HMI design (MICHMID) as well as preliminary design rules for intercultural HMI design (cf. chapter 8).

Main objectives of this dissertation project:

⇨ Quantitatively identifying cultural differences in HCI

⇨ Creating a path to culturally adaptive systems

Building a potential model for intercultural HMI design

Empirical verification of relationship between cultural aspects and HMI by two online studies

The analysis of the collected data from two temporally separated online studies with Chinese, German, and English speaking employees of Siemens VDO all over the world showed that there are correlations between the interaction of the users with the system and their cultural background (cf. chapter 6). There are cultural differences in HCI between the tested Chinese and German employees of SV concerning layout (complex vs. simple), information density (high vs. low), personalization (high vs. low), language (symbols vs. characters), interaction speed (higher vs. lower) and interaction frequency (higher vs. lower). Some of these aspects have been applied in use cases and implemented within the CAHMI demonstrator (cf. chapter 7).

Résumé from two online studies (n ≈ 1000)

Furthermore, the HMI dimensions (HMIDs) have been recognized by explorative factor analysis from over one hundred measurement variables (potential cultural interaction indicators (PCIIs)) as categories of HMI characteristics like information density and speed as well as interaction frequency and speed (cf. section 6.6.1).

HMI dimensions recognized by explorative factor analysis from over one hundred measurement variables

HMIDs derived from
"information" and
"interaction"

HMI dimensions (HMIDs) relevant for HMI design (cf. section 4.2) were derived from the basic dimensions "information" and "interaction" as most important for HMI design (cf. section 2.1). The definition and the evaluation of these HMI dimensions and their specific values in relation to culture results in a potential model for intercultural HMI design (PMICHMID) (cf. section 4.4). This model serves as a basis for future studies to generate principles for intercultural HMI design.[367]

PMICHMID as a basis for
creating a future theory
for intercultural HMI
design

HMI dimensions and
cultural interaction
indicators

The hypotheses behind cultural adaptivity associate the values of the HMI dimensions (HMIDs) to the values of cultural dimensions describing the culturally influenced behavior, i.e. HMI exposed to culture. The cultural interaction indicators (CIIs), which display the specific values of the HMIDs, concern information density and frequency as well as interaction speed, frequency and exactness (cf. chapter 6), i.e. mainly regarding the HMI localization levels "surface" and "interaction" (cf. section 2.3.7).

Metric for measuring
cross-cultural HCI

The results in chapter 6 partly confirmed the relationships postulated in chapter 4 based on the PMICHMID by revealing that there is a metric, which is adequate to measure cross-cultural HCI (cf. section 8.2). The values of the HMI dimensions (HMIDs) revealed tendencies in user interaction behavior (i.e., "HMI style" or "HMI characteristics",[368] cf. Figure 39) that imply recommendations for intercultural HMI design (cf. section 8.3).

---

[367] Cf. section 8.6.7 in the work report for some initial thoughts about this.

[368] Parallel to the concept of "user interface characteristics" by Marcus 2001 (cf. section 2.3.2).

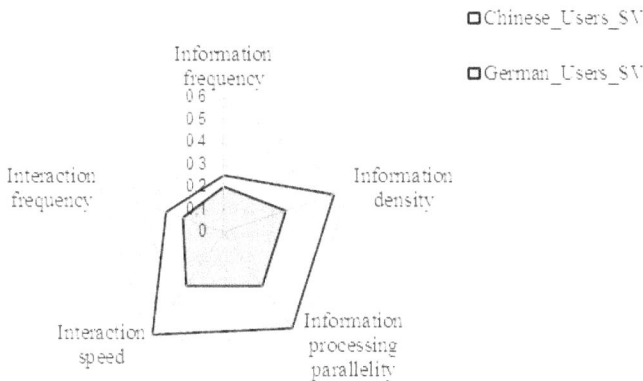

Figure 39: Specifics of HMI dimensions regarding HMI style representing culture dependent differences in user interaction with the system

Cultural interaction indicators (CIIs) also serve to see computer experience, age, gender, etc. with respect to cultural imprint, which is mostly relevant for building user models necessary for adaptive systems. Real cultural classification works because the variables (CIIs) can be selected according to the expected definition of culture (e.g., nationality). This means that with the right combination of CIIs it is possible to capture interaction differences that are culturally imprinted in the desired sense (e.g., according to nationality) (cf. section 6.3).[369] The developed metrics in this work consisting of the most discriminating CIIs (cf. section 8.2) is adequate to measure cross-cultural HCI in culturally adaptive systems (cf. sections 6.2, 6.3, 6.6.2 and 8.2).[370]

Cultural Interaction Indicators

---

[369] Or to other cultural aspects, e.g., mother tongue, country of birth, etc. or to cultural dimensions.

[370] Cf. also section 8.2.2 in the work report.

Cultural differences in HCI quantitatively measurable	In addition, the cultural differences found in HCI are quantitatively measurable by a computer system using a special combination of CIIs represented by cultural interaction patterns (CIPs) depending on the culturally imprinted interaction behavior of the user. The recognition and classification of cultural interaction patterns in HCI, i.e. cultural differences in HCI can be achieved purely *quantitatively* (cf. section 7.6). A handful CIIs are sufficient for this purpose (cf. sections 6.6.2 and 7.5). Moreover, the cultural interaction patterns representing the cultural differences in HCI and the derived CIIs are statistically sufficiently discriminating (cf. section 6.6.2) to enable computer systems to detect them *automatically* and to assign the users to a certain cultural imprint (cf. section 6.4).[371] These are preconditions for automatically adapting the system to the user by the system itself (through monitoring and evaluating the user interactions to identify the correct adaptation) (cf. section 3.2.1). Initial research has been conducted to specify the preparation time necessary for a culturally adaptive system to automatically adapt the HMI to the culturally different user needs (cf. chapter 7). The time for bootstrapping identified until now ranges between 5-20 minutes (cf. Figure 35 in section 7.4). This time can be optimized in the future by using more cultural interaction indicators and in other combinations to increase their discriminatory power. Hence, this work contributes to establish cultural adaptive systems by determining culturally different interaction patterns in HCI purely quantitatively and makes culturally adaptive systems *possible* in the first place.

Preconditions for automatically adapting the system to the user fulfilled

Initial research for system to automatically adapt HMI to user needs

Optimizing bootstrapping time

Culturally adaptive systems are possible

Culturally adaptive systems are reasonable and necessary in special situations

Moreover, culturally adaptive systems are reasonable and necessary. Hence, in situations where the user cannot change the system manually (e.g. during driving in automotive context, cf. chapter 1). Especially industry can profit from this fact.[372]

Cultural differences in HCI can be determined quantitatively by a computer system in real-time

Probably, this is one of the most important and fruitful implications of this work for further projects regarding culturally adaptive systems: Cultural differences in HCI can be determined quantitatively and automatically by a computer system at runtime. This enables the system to become more autonomous and yet make decisions without the necessity of human interpretation

---

[371] Furthermore, when reversed, cultural interaction patterns (CIPs) are also useful to identify a user (cf. section 7.5), which is necessary for the system to adapt to the right user.

[372] For example, the kind of connection of internationalization, culture, interaction, personalization, user preferences and adaptability with driver information systems is unique and represents a unique selling proposition (USP) for those OEMs in automotive industry that will integrate these concepts and provide culturally adaptive HMI. Similarly, those OEMs that apply intercultural usability engineering will have the USP of doing intercultural HMI design properly providing products to the user that he can use with ease and joy (which is a USP as well) and, therefore, remain loyal to the OEM.

at runtime. This is also an innovation of this dissertation project by integrating intercultural aspects within system architecture that is able to adapt HMI to users of different cultures.

The confirmation of the reliability of the results of the two quantitative online studies done with the IIA tool proves the validity of the methods used in this work. The following reciprocally confirming aspects attest to the high reliability and criteria validity of the statistical results obtained in this dissertation project: *Reliability of the results*

- High discrimination rate by the cultural interaction indicators of over 80% for classifying into two groups (especially for Chinese and German users, cf. section 6.6.2),
- High accordance of the HMI dimensions (HMIDs) and the cultural interaction indicators (CIIs) found by applying different statistical methods (cf. section 6.6.1),
- Highly correlated quantitatively comparable results of two temporally separated studies conducted online (cf. section 6.2).

Moreover, several results presented in this paper are in accordance with other studies, which support the correctness of their common methodology and outcome (e.g., Lewandowitz et al. 2006, Kralisch 2006 and Kamentz 2006) (cf. section 6.6.3). Furthermore, it seems that it is justified and reasonable to transfer the results of employees of SiemensVDO to all users in China (cf. section 8.1) and hence, it encourages the use of these results and recommendations for Chinese and German users (but not for other cultures) for further intercultural HMI research (e.g., to create new hypotheses). In addition, the HMI dimensions can be used in intercultural HMI design in general, i.e. for all cultures.

From the cultural interaction indicators and patterns obtained by the empirical studies (cf. Table 24 in section 6.2), their discussion (cf. section 6.6) and their verification for the MICHMID (cf. Table 48 in section 8.2), the following preliminary rules of thumb for intercultural HMI design in general can be derived (cf. section 8.3): *Design recommendations*

- Avoid too many pieces of information for German users (information density is low).
- Provide very fast system feedback for Chinese users (information frequency and interaction speed are high).
- Provide parallel working for Chinese users (information and interaction parallelism is high).
- Provide anthropomorphic agents, relationship-oriented dialogs and message content, and even chat for Chinese users (information and interaction frequency is high).

Challenges:	It was attempted to determine the effects of the culturally influencing factors known from research literature about HMI by empirical research. However, not all the obtained results were as expected (cf. section 8.1). It turned out that interaction of the user with the system in HMI is also influenced by parameters like experience or age along cultural parameters (cf. section 6.3). Hence, it is important to consider such variables very carefully along with the cultural background of the user.
⇨ HMI not only culturally influenced	

⇨ Cultural complexity

In addition, it is problematic to bring cultural models into accordance with HMI design because of cultural complexity.

⇨ Dynamic aspects of interaction only quantitatively measurable

⇨ Tools necessary

Furthermore, the experience with the methods used in this work indicates that only quantitative studies are sufficient for determining cultural differences in HMI at the interaction level because of the dynamic aspect of interaction that cannot reasonably be recognized by human beings:[373] interactional aspects are too complex and too fast to capture them without special tools (e.g., with the IIA tool, cf. section 5.2.2).

Optimizing CAHMI approach:

⇨ User interaction is inherently culturally imprinted

⇨ It is sufficient to adapt the system to the culturally influenced individual interaction behavior of the user

⇨ Cultural models reasonable but not necessary

Complexity of culture was one reason for optimizing the CAHMI approach in this work by revising the CAHMI principle (cf. section 8.4). In addition, individual adaptation embraces cultural adaptation because the individual (and its interaction behavior in HMI) is inherently culturally imprinted (cf. sections 6.4 and 8.1). For example, there are significant differences between German and Chinese users in HMI (cf. section 6.5) expressed by CIPs that are inherently culturally imprinted by user culture (cf. sections 6.2 and 6.6.2), which implies that the main requirement to achieve culturally adaptive HMI is simply to adapt HMI to CIPs (cf. section 8.4). This further reason for optimizing the CAHMI approach resulted in the extension of the revised CAHMI principle to the general principle of adaptive HMI by shifting from cultural to individual adaptation.[374] Thereby, explicit complex cultural models can or even should be dropped to adapt most exactly to the cultural needs of the user regarding HMI at the interactional level because the interaction behavior of the user is inherently culturally influenced (cf. section 8.4).

---

[373] Only about seven pieces of information can be processed by human beings at the same time (cf. Miller 1956). In addition, the information processing frequency of human beings is limited, too. It is not possible for human beings to recognize and analyze *all* available aspects while observing the user interaction with a system (e.g., including system events) because of "inherent filters" in the brain (like the principle of "selective attention", cf. Springer 2005). Therefore, tools must be used that surmount the human shortcomings.

[374] Cf. also section 8.4 as well as section 8.4 in the work report.

The following assumptions remain to be verified by future research in intercultural HMI design:[375]

Open assumptions

- Considering intercultural variables during the process of product design improves the usability of the product.[376]
- Automatic adaptation of HMI to the idiosyncrasies of cultural variables required by the user known from design phase and from analyzing the cultural characteristics at runtime is judged positively by the user because the usability of the system improves.

Other open items remaining from this work concern the optimization of the IIA tool, checking the acceptance of adaptivity using e.g. the CAHMI demonstrator or a new one, as well as optimizing (the discriminatory power of) cultural interaction indicators, HMIDs, MICHMID, UMTM and adaptation rules.[377] Furthermore, closing these open items is reasonable before further developing the model for intercultural HMI design (MICHMID) towards a theory of cultural HMI.

Open items

To put all in a nutshell, this work confirms that HMI depends on culture. This work provides fundamental research regarding the empirical proof of the existence of culturally influenced HMI dimensions. Furthermore, the results of this work proved that there are cultural differences in HCI regarding interaction speed and frequency as well as information density, frequency and parallel processing. Moreover there is a metric that can be used to measure these culturally imprinted interaction differences in HMI (even for a single user). Therefore, the empirical results produced by this work can be considered to represent the first and main step towards real culturally adaptive HMI by purely quantitatively determining cultural differences in HCI (first of all at inter-action level). However, until all open questions regarding culturally adaptive HMI systems are answered, the following Estonian proverb is valid: "Kõiki ei saa ühe mõeduga mõeta."[378]

Conclusions:

⇨ HMI is culturally imprinted

⇨ Quantitative determination of cultural differences in HMI possible

⇨ Thereby first and main step towards real culturally adaptive HMI done

⇨ Motivation for further research

---

[375] 4 of 6 assumptions, 8 of 8 presumptions, 5 of 9 empirical and 5 of 5 methodological hypotheses have been confirmed in this dissertation project.

[376] For instance, using icons and metaphors with similar intercultural meaning support comprehension of applications.

[377] Cf. also section 8.6 in the work report.

[378] "One cannot measure everyone with the same measure." (cf. file "Sprichwörter mit messen.txt" in the online appendix). However, in my view, the answers to the open questions will reveal that "one *can* measure everyone with the same measure using enough variables", which would challenge the proverb.

Appendix

Components of the Dissertation Project and Their Relationships

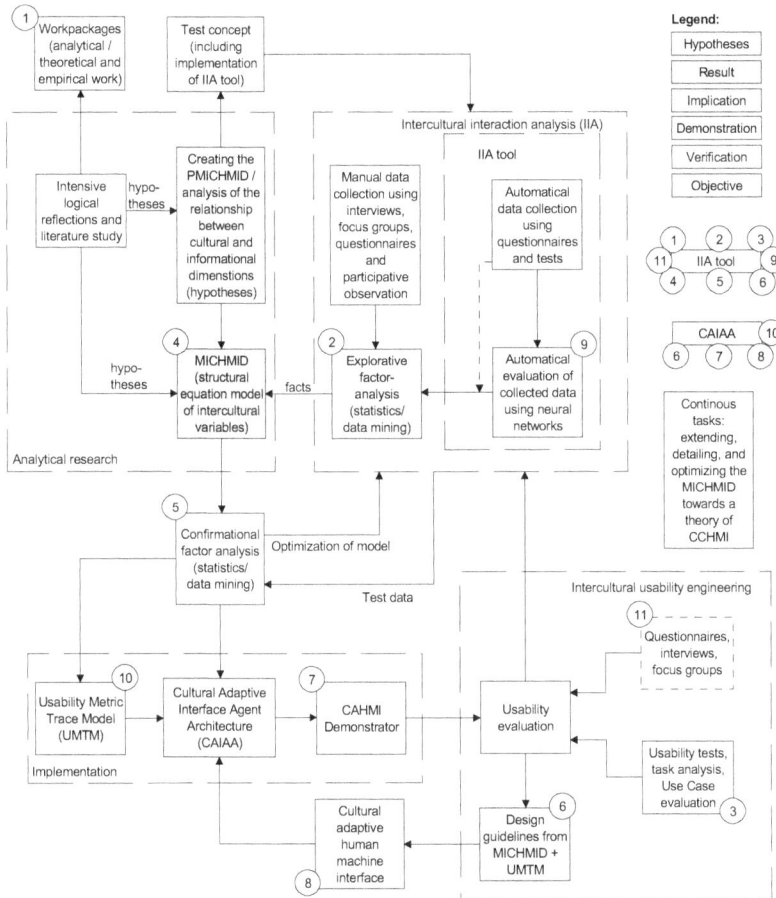

Figure 40: Components of the dissertation project and their relationships

Absolute Values from Data Collection of the Second Online Study

Table 49: Comparison of absolute values of Potential Cultural Interaction Indicators (PCIIs) between (C), (G) and (E) (Source: file "070127 Alle Daten der Haupterhebungen.sav" in the online appendix)

Parameter (measurement variable)	Short name	Group	N	Mean	Min	Max
Information speed	IS, TPI	(C)	97	88,11340206	67	97
		(G)	359	93,03064067	71	100
		(E)	420	92,86666667	67	99
		(total)	876	92,40753425	67	100
Exactness of interaction	INE	(C)	97	14,73195876	0	25
		(G)	359	17,18941504	1	30
		(E)	420	16.01190476	0	25
		(total)	876	16.35273973	0	30
Interaction speed	INS	(C)	97	83.40206186	68	94
		(G)	359	85.33983287	74	98
		(E)	420	84.20238095	73	95
		(total)	876	84.57990868	68	98
Uncertainty Avoidance Value	UV	(C)	97	11.07216495	10	45
		(G)	359	14.16713092	10	100
		(E)	420	11.7	10	68
		(total)	876	12.64155251	10	100
Power Distance Value	PDI	(C)	97	2.096456842	0.15125	8.333333
		(G)	359	1.912720669	0.226875	8.333333
		(E)	420	1.763987721	0.15125	8.333333
		(total)	876	1.861755567	0.15125	8.333333
Number of Help Initiations	HI	(C)	97	0.608247423	0	44
		(G)	359	0.094707521	0	4
		(E)	420	0.15	0	4
		(total)	876	0.178082192	0	44
Total Mouse Clicks		(C)	97	1250.309278	470	3158
		(G)	359	1398.802228	482	4079
		(E)	420	1295.452381	452	3818
		(total)	876	1332.808219	452	4079
Total Dialog Displaying Time		(C)	97	2055287.412	749937	7152408
		(G)	359	2325024.156	551562	9349684
		(E)	420	2408363.138	762531	50514861
		(total)	876	2335113.092	551562	50514861
System Mouse Speed		(C)	97	10.74226804	0	20
		(G)	359	10.98607242	6	20
		(E)	420	10.84285714	2	20
		(total)	876	10.89041096	0	20
System Mouse Keys Max Speed		(C)	97	78.7628866	0	80
		(G)	359	79.66573816	40	80
		(E)	420	80	40	120
		(total)	876	79.7260274	0	120
CPU Norm Freq		(C)	97	2184.804124	1066	3020

		(G)	359	2426.256267	600	3620
		(E)	420	2113.104762	500	3790
		(total)	876	2249.378995	500	3790
CPU Processor Count		(C)	97	1.18556701	1	4
		(G)	359	1.208913649	1	2
		(E)	420	1.138095238	1	4
		(total)	876	1.172374429	1	4
CPU Raw Freq		(C)	97	2184.556701	1064	3000
		(G)	359	2426.518106	598	3610
		(E)	420	2113.061905	498	3794
		(total)	876	2249.438356	498	3794
Screen Height		(C)	97	812.9896907	0	1050
		(G)	359	946.0557103	720	1280
		(E)	420	881.1	768	1280
		(total)	876	900.1780822	0	1280
Screen Width		(C)	97	1086.185567	0	1400
		(G)	359	1216.846797	1024	2560
		(E)	420	1163.314286	1024	1920
		(total)	876	1176.712329	0	2560
Screen Hz		(C)	97	68.45360825	0	100
		(G)	359	67.98607242	60	120
		(E)	420	67.72857143	50	100
		(total)	876	67.91438356	0	120
Memory Total Physical Memory		(C)	97	598459930.4	259457024	2145468416
		(G)	359	927486956	258457600	2147483647
		(E)	420	769105568.9	132104192	2147483647
		(total)	876	815117316.7	132104192	2147483647
Maximal Open Tasks	PT	(C)	97	4.639175258	1	13
		(G)	359	2.874651811	1	34
		(E)	420	2.780952381	1	34
		(total)	876	3.025114155	1	34
Open Tasks Before Test		(C)	97	5.154639175	1	14
		(G)	359	5.22005571	0	32
		(E)	420	5.028571429	0	32
		(total)	876	5.121004566	0	32
Exceptions		(C)	97	3.886597938	0	96
		(G)	359	1.17270195	0	59
		(E)	420	2.319047619	0	181
		(total)	876	2.02283105	0	181
Age		(C)	97	28.15463918	0	47
		(G)	359	37.74373259	17	64
		(E)	420	36.35	0	67
		(total)	876	36.01369863	0	67
Gender		(C)	97	0.24742268	0	1
		(G)	359	0.17270195	0	1
		(E)	420	0.19047619	0	1

		(total)	876	0.189497717	0	1
PC Experience		(C)	97	1.989690722	1	3
		(G)	359	2.194986072	0	3
		(E)	420	2.016666667	0	3
		(total)	876	2.086757991	0	3
Mouse Clicks	MC	(C)	97	15.16494845	7	58
		(G)	359	14.52367688	7	40
		(E)	420	14.40952381	7	46
		(total)	876	14.53995434	7	58
Textures379	(POI)	(C)	96	50.78125	0	100
		(G)	358	46.81843575	0	100
		(E)	418	42.76555024	0	100
		(total)	872	45.31192661	0	100
POI	POI	(C)	96	35.26041667	0	100
		(G)	358	19.90502793	0	100
		(E)	418	20.97607656	0	100
		(total)	872	22.10894495	0	100
Roads		(C)	96	63.33333333	0	100
		(G)	358	78.32960894	0	100
		(E)	418	76.75358852	0	100
		(total)	872	75.92316514	0	100
Road Names		(C)	96	63.70833333	0	100
		(G)	358	58.93854749	0	100
		(E)	418	65.66746411	0	100
		(total)	872	62.68922018	0	100
Restaurants	(POI)	(C)	96	49.34375	0	100
		(G)	358	35.30446927	0	100
		(E)	418	44.53349282	0	100
		(total)	872	41.27408257	0	100
Maneuvers		(C)	96	71.30208333	0	100
		(G)	358	75.31005587	0	100
		(E)	418	51.66028708	0	100
		(total)	872	63.53211009	0	100
Number of Input Characters	(KS)	(C)	96	81.08333333	0	449
		(G)	358	197.6201117	3	1634
		(E)	418	199.9832536	0	1373
		(total)	872	185.9231651	0	1634

---

[379] The measurement variables (e.g. "textures") whose short name is in parentheses (e.g., (POI) belong to the same HMI dimension ("information density", ID) as measurement variables whose short name has no tilde (e.g. "points of interest"), i.e. "textures" is representing similar properties as "points of interest", but does not have the original name "POI". For example, information density is represented by number of points of interest "POI" as well as by number of restaurants "(POI)" or textures "(POI)".

Message Distance	NIT	(C)	96	112.6875	0	200
		(G)	358	141.0502793	1	200
		(E)	418	139.3301435	1	200
		(total)	872	137.103211	0	200
Speed	TPI	(C)	96	43.66666667	0	100
		(G)	358	27.40502793	1	100
		(E)	418	33.19138756	1	100
		(total)	872	31.9690367	0	100
Display Duration	DIP	(C)	96	2351.739583	0	5000
		(G)	358	2285.455307	1	5000
		(E)	418	2199.971292	1	5000
		(total)	872	2251.775229	0	5000
Color		(C)	96	29.59375	0	100
		(G)	358	37.23184358	0	100
		(E)	418	32.18421053	0	100
		(total)	872	33.97133028	0	100
Exactness		(C)	96	17.75434028	0	29.3333333
		(G)	358	16.25814711	2.83333333	30.8333333
		(E)	418	17.15590112	0	33.75
		(total)	872	16.85321101	0	33.75
Error Clicks	EC	(C)	96	0.958333333	0	21
		(G)	358	0.335195531	0	10
		(E)	418	0.483253589	0	14
		(total)	872	0.474770642	0	21

Nationality		(C)	97	48.51546392	46	221
		(G)	359	54.91643454	3	238
		(E)	420	136.0595238	5	221
		(total)	876	93.11187215	3	238
Duration of Test	T	(C)	81	2891.12216	1167.144	9176.883
		(G)	333	3298.06382	1513.438	11372.602
		(E)	367	3420.207629	1392.375	51746.904
		(total)	781	3313.255246	1167.144	51746.904
Mouse Moves	MM	(C)	81	26316152.99	12550543	47213739
		(G)	333	22817675.32	2860105	47319927
		(E)	367	23127259.07	37093	47461605
		(total)	781	23325990.2	37093	47461605
NC Mouse Moves	(MM)	(C)	81	877607.9506	414701	1586330
		(G)	333	774016.1171	85943	1589171
		(E)	367	773284.5259	952	1592498
		(total)	781	784416.1741	952	1592498
Key Downs	KS	(C)	81	1189035.222	562109	2100155
		(G)	333	1030236.595	139018	2104594
		(E)	367	1035693.463	4230	2108949
		(total)	781	1049270.346	4230	2108949
Key Ups	KS	(C)	81	316659.358	155820	538224

		(G)	333	268083.9189	33966	539468
		(E)	367	274502.4087	651	540681
		(total)	781	276137.9475	651	540681
Lexs	KS	(C)	81	1191142.617	562594	2103718
		(G)	333	1031926.595	139157	2108157
		(E)	367	1037256.504	4230	2112512
		(total)	781	1050943.976	4230	2112512
Sems	(FI)	(C)	81	2580759.494	1237719	4573786
		(G)	333	2227836.144	269480	4581273
		(E)	367	2250449.466	4421	4594320
		(total)	781	2275065.184	4421	4594320
L Button Ups	(MC)	(C)	81	230001.5432	108333	400276
		(G)	333	198155.7327	24749	401039
		(E)	367	199888.5068	308	402054
		(total)	781	202272.8118	308	402054
L ButtonDowns	(MC)	(C)	81	301807.8272	142457	525672
		(G)	333	259875.3333	32297	526710
		(E)	367	262870.9292	388	527980
		(total)	781	265631.9475	388	527980
Mouse moves_norm	MM	(C)	81	10566.10175	2678.74576	26441.7475
		(G)	333	7529.522172	631.185570	21836.6421
		(E)	367	7992.476242	13.1361895	27343.9662
		(total)	781	8062.00244	13.1361895	27343.9662
NC Mouse moves norm	(MM)	(C)	81	352.3745459	88.3597330	886.430466
		(G)	333	255.3339416	19.2445604	741.406615
		(E)	367	267.2571543	0.33714319	929.873225
		(total)	781	271.0011733	0.33714319	929.873225
Key Downs_norm	KS	(C)	81	477.5444754	120.199243	1197.27985
		(G)	333	340.142622	31.2796895	1003.29448
		(E)	367	357.8437057	1.4980207	1210.96496
		(total)	781	362.7109291	1.4980207	1210.96496
Key Ups_norm	KS	(C)	81	127.2416387	33.2278989	315.696263
		(G)	333	88.51760639	7.78285723	258.851700
		(E)	367	94.86525242	0.23054644	309.918637
		(total)	781	95.51662395	0.23054644	315.696263
Lexs_norm	KS	(C)	81	478.3827389	120.302457	1199.56406
		(G)	333	340.6969741	31.3104567	1005.28465
		(E)	367	358.3858819	1.4980207	1213.12788
		(total)	781	363.289005	1.4980207	1213.12788
Sems_norm	FI	(C)	81	1036.522113	264.547806	2597.30333
		(G)	333	735.1380436	59.7876486	2153.45788
		(E)	367	777.7277162	1.56566182	2651.54250
		(total)	781	786.4088752	1.56566182	2651.54250

L Button Ups_norm	(MC)	(C)	81	92.40478072	23.1644233	232.768193
		(G)	333	65.38290901	5.49534847	192.981807
		(E)	367	69.08943452	0.10907573	234.279443
		(total)	781	69.92716826	0.10907573	234.279443
L Button Downs_norm	(MC)	(C)	81	121.234947	30.4455888	304.637645
		(G)	333	85.74988226	7.14046332	252.271318
		(E)	367	90.86459583	0.1374071	307.900600
		(total)	781	91.83360841	0.1374071	307.900600
Mouse Moves_L Button Downs_Ration	MM, (MC)	(C)	81	87.24194537	86.6890027	89.9013209
		(G)	333	87.84393266	86.1513165	89.9060239
		(E)	367	88.41502642	85.4310939	108.13182
		(total)	781	88.04986152	85.4310939	108.13182
M_NC_Mouse moves_Ratio	(MM)	(C)	81	30.02874082	29.6846874	30.5050085
		(G)	333	29.82483313	28.9676571	33.3797738
		(E)	367	30.48666643	29.3242350	38.9632352
		(total)	781	30.15698338	28.9676571	38.9632352

Hofstede's Scores

Table 50: Hofstede's Scores (Source: ITIM international web page of Hofstede, URL = http://www.geert-hofstede.com/hofstede_dimensions.php, last access 1/08/2011)

	PDI score	IDV score	MAS score	UAI score	LTO score
Arab World**	80	38	52	68	
Argentina	49	46	56	86	
Australia	36	90	61	51	31
Austria	11	55	79	70	
Bangladesh*	80	20	55	60	40
Belgium	65	75	54	94	
Brazil	69	38	49	76	65
Canada	39	80	52	48	23
Chile	63	23	28	86	
China*	80	20	66	30	118
Columbia	67	13	64	80	
Czech Republic*	57	58	57	74	13
Costa Rica	35	15	21	86	
Denmark	18	74	16	23	
East Africa**	64	27	41	52	25
El Salvador	66	19	40	94	
Equador	78	8	63	67	
Estonia*	40	60	30	60	

Finland	33	63	26	59	
France	68	71	43	86	
Germany FR	35	67	66	65	31
Greece	60	35	57	112	
Guatemala	95	6	37	101	
Hong Kong	68	25	57	29	96
Hungary*	46	80	88	82	50
India	77	48	56	40	61
Indonesia	78	14	46	48	
Iran	58	41	43	59	
Ireland (Rep of)	28	70	68	35	
Israel	13	54	47	81	
Italy	50	76	70	75	
Jamaica	45	39	68	13	
Japan	54	46	95	92	80
Luxembourg*	40	60	50	70	
Malaysia	104	26	50	36	
Malta*	56	59	47	96	
Mexico	81	30	69	82	
Morocco*	70	46	53	68	
Netherlands	38	80	14	53	44
New Zealand	22	79	58	49	30
Nigeria					16
Norway	31	69	8	50	
Pakistan	55	14	50	70	0
Panama	95	11	44	86	
Peru	64	16	42	87	
Philippines	94	32	64	44	19
Poland	68	60	64	93	32
Portugal	63	27	31	104	
Romania*	90	30	42	90	
Russia*	93	39	36	95	
Salvador	66	19	40	94	
Singapore	74	20	48	8	48
Slovakia	104	52	110	51	38
South Africa	49	65	63	49	
South Korea	60	18	39	85	75
Spain	57	51	42	86	
Surinam*	85	47	37	92	
Sweden	31	71	5	29	33
Switzerland	34	68	70	58	
Taiwan	58	17	45	69	87
Thailand	64	20	34	64	56
Trinidad*	47	16	58	55	
Turkey	66	37	45	85	
United Kingdom	35	89	66	35	25
United States of America	40	91	62	46	29

Uruguay	61	36	38	100	
Venezuela	81	12	73	76	
Vietnam*	70	20	40	30	80
West Africa	77	20	46	54	16
Yugoslavia	76	27	21	88	
Zimbabwe					25

* *Estimated values*
** *Regional estimated values:*

'Arab World' = Egypt, Iraq, Kuwait, Lebanon, Libya, Saudi Arabia, United Arab Emirates

'East Africa' = Ethiopia, Kenya, Tanzania, Zambia
'West Africa' = Ghana, Nigeria, Sierra Leone

Literature

Adler, N. J. (1997). International dimensions of organizational behavior. Cincinnati, Ohio, South-Western College Publ.

Adler, N. J. & A. Gundersen (2008). International dimensions of organizational behavior. Mason, Ohio u.a, Thomson South-Western.

Altarriba, J. (1993). Cognition and culture: A cross-cultural approach to cognitive psychology. Amsterdam, North-Holland.

Amberg, M., S. Fischer, et al. (2003). "Biometrische Verfahren." Studie zum State of the Art, Friedrich-Alexander-Universität Erlangen-Nürnberg, Erlangen/Nuremberg.

Amditis, A., A. Polychronopoulos, et al. (2006). "Communication and interaction strategies in automotive adaptive interfaces." Cognition, Technology & Work 8(3): 193-199.

Anderson, J. R. (1996). The architecture of cognition. Mahwah, NJ, Lawrence Erlbaum Assos. Publ.

Aranda, M. P. & B. G. Knight (1997). "The influence of ethnicity and culture on the caregiver stress and coping process: A sociocultural review and analysis." The Gerontologist 37(3): 342-354.

Arbuckle, J. L. (2005). AMOS 6.0 user's guide. Chicago, Ill., SPSS.

Austin, J. L. & E. v. Savigny (1962). Zur Theorie der Sprechakte. Stuttgart, Reclam.

Backhaus, K., B. Erichson, et al. (2006). Multivariate Analysemethoden: Eine anwendungsorientierte Einführung. Berlin, Springer.

Badre, A. & W. Barber (1998). Culturabilty: The Merging of Culture and Usabilty. Proceedings of the 4th Conference on Human Factors and the Web. NJ, USA, Basking Ridge.

Bales, R. F. (1950). Interaction process analysis: A method for the study of small groups. 1950, Cambridge, MA: Addison-Wesley.

Balzert, H. (2005). Lehrbuch Grundlagen der Informatik: Konzepte und Notationen in UML 2, Java 5, C++ und C, Algorithmik und Software-Technik, Anwendungen ; mit CD-ROM und e-learning-Online-Kurs. München, Elsevier Spektrum Akad. Verl.

Bartmann, D. (1997). PSYLOCK - Identifikation eines Tastaturbenutzers durch Analyse des Tippverhaltens. GI Jahrestagung: 327-334.

Bartmann, D., I. Bakdi, et al. (2007). "On the Design of an Authentication System Based on Keystroke Dynamics Using a Predefined Input Text." International Journal of Information Security and Privacy 1(2): 1-12.

Bartmann, D., D. j. Bartmann, et al. (2003). Authentifizierung anhand des Tippverhaltens. Bankinformatik 2004: Strategien, Konzepte und Technologien für das Retailbanking. D. Bartmann: 301-308.

Bartmann, D. & M. Wimmer (2007). "Kein Problem mehr mit vergessenen Passwörtern." Datenschutz und Datensicherheit - DuD 31(3): 199-202.

Bauer, H. (2002). Wahrscheinlichkeitstheorie, Walter de Gruyter.

Baumgartner, V.-J. (2003). A Practical Set of Cultural Dimensions for Global User-Interface Analysis and Design. Graz.

Bengler, K., M. Herrler, et al. (2002). "Usability Engineering bei der Entwicklung von iDrive (Usability Engineering accompanying the Development of iDrive)." it-Information Technology (vormals it+ ti) 44(3/2002): 145.

Bernsen, N. O., H. Dybkjær, et al. (1998). Designing interactive speech systems. London, Springer.

Berry, J. W. (2007). Cross-cultural psychology: Research and applications. Cambridge, Cambridge Univ. Press.

Beynon, M., C. L. Nehaniv, et al. (2001). Cognitive technology: Instruments of Mind–Proceedings of the International Cognitive Technology Conference, Warwick, UK: Springer-Verlag.

Bittner, K. & I. Spence (2003). Use Case Modeling, Addison-Wesley. Boston, MA.

Blank, K. (1996). Benutzermodellierung für adaptive interaktive Systeme: Architektur, Methoden, Werkzeuge und Anwendungen (Dissertationen zur Künstlichen Intelligenz; Bd. 131), Sankt Augustin: Infix.

Boling, D. M. C. (2008). Programming Windows Embedded CE 6.0 Developer Reference, Microsoft Press.

Bortz, J. & N. Döring. (2006). "Forschungsmethoden und Evaluation: Für Human- und Sozialwissenschaftler." 4., überarbeitete Auflage., from http://dx.doi.org/10.1007/978-3-540-33306-7.

Bortz, J., N. Döring, et al. (2006). Forschungsmethoden und Evaluation: Für Human- und Sozialwissenschaftler. Berlin, Springer.

Bortz, J. & R. Weber (2005). Statistik für Human- und Sozialwissenschaftler. Heidelberg, Springer Medizin.

Bossel, H. (1992). Simulation dynamischer Systeme: Grundwissen, Methoden, Programme. Braunschweig, Wiesbaden, Vieweg.

Bra, P., L. Aroyo, et al. (2004). "The Next Big Thing: Adaptive Web-Based Systems." Journal of Digital Information 5(1).

Braun, B.-M. & K. R. a. P. Rößger (2007). Localizing for the Korean Market: "Actually Being There with a Multi-method Approach. Designing for Global Markets 8, IWIPS 2007, Actually being There, 28-30 June 2007, Merida, Mexico, Proceedings of the Eighth International Workshop on Internationalisation of Products and Systems. V. Evers and C. S. a. M. A. M. R. a. E. C. M. i. a. T. Mandl, Product & Systems Internationalisation, Inc.: 55-62.

Brennan, M. & J. Hoek (1992). "The Behavior of Respondents, Nonrespondents, and Refusers Across Mail Surveys." Public Opinion Quarterly 56(4): 530-535.

Brislin, R. W. & T. Yoshida (1994). Intercultural communication training: An introduction. Thousand Oaks, SAGE Publications.

Brookhuis, K. A., D. De Waard, et al. (2001). "Behavioural impacts of Advanced Driver Assistance Systems–an overview." EJTIR 1(3): 245-253.

Brüggemann, D. (2002). Starke Gesetze der großen Zahlen bei blockweisen Unabhängigkeitsbedingungen, Universitätsbibliothek.

Brunner, G. (2005). Untersuchung der kulturellen Einflüsse auf die Mensch-Maschine-Interaktion am Beispiel von Fahrernavigationssystemen. Regensburg.

Brusilovsky, P. (1996). Adaptive Hypermedia: An Attempt to Analyze and Generalize. Multimedia, Hypermedia, and Virtual Reality. Lecture Notes in Computer Science, Springer-Verlag: 288□304.

Brusilovsky, P. & M. T. Maybury (2002). "From adaptive hypermedia to the adaptive web." Communications of the ACM 45(5): 30-33.

Bühner, M. (2004). Einführung in die Test- und Fragebogenkonstruktion. München, Pearson Studium.

Burzan, N. (2005). Quantitative Methoden der Kulturwissenschaften: Eine Einführung. Konstanz, UVK Verl.-Ges.

Byrne, B. M. (2001). Structural equation modeling with AMOS: Basic concepts, applications, and programming. Mahwah, NJ, Lawrence Erlbaum.

Cacciabue, P. C. (2007). Modelling Driver Behaviour in Automotive Environments: Critical Issues in Driver Interactions with Intelligent Transport Systems, Springer-Verlag New York Inc.

Cagiltay, K. (1999). Culture and its Effects on Human-Computer-Interaction. Proceedings of World Conference on Educational Multimedia, Hypermedia and Telecommunications 1999. B. Collis and R. Oliver. Chesapeake, VA, AACE: 1626□1626.

Callahan, E. (2005). "Cultural similarities and differences in the design of university Web sites." Journal of Computer-Mediated Communication 11(1): 239-273.

Cantù, M. (2003). Mastering Delphi 7. San Francisco, Calif., Sybex.

Capurro, R. (2006). "Towards an ontological foundation of information ethics." Ethics and Information Technology 8(4): 175-186.

Capurro, R. & B. Hjorland (2003). "The concept of information." Annual review of information science and technology 37(1): 343-411.

Card, S. K., T. P. Moran, et al. (1983). The psychology of human-computer interaction. Hillsdale, N.J., Erlbaum.

Charwat, H. J. (1992). Lexikon der Mensch-Maschine-Kommunikation. Munchen; Wien, Oldenbourg, ISBN.

Chen, M. J. (1993). "A comparison of Chinese and English language processing." Advances in psychology 103: 97-117.

Cohen, M. (1999). 101 philosophy problems, Routledge.

Cole, M. & S. Scribner (1974). Culture & thought: A psychological introduction. New York, Wiley.

Condon, J. C. (1984). With respect to the Japanese: A guide for Americans. Yarmouth, Me., Intercultural Press.

Constantine, L. L. & L. A. D. Lockwood (1999). Software for use: A practical guide to the models and methods of usage-centered design. Reading, Mass., Addison Wesley [u.a.].

Courtney, A. J. (1986). "Chinese population stereotypes: color associations." Human factors 28(1): 97-99.

Cox, T. (1993). Cultural diversity in organizations: Theory, research, and practice, Berrett-Koehler Publishers.

Cramer, P. D. T. (2008). Interkulturelle Zusammenarbeit in multinationalen Teams, GRIN Verlag OHG.

Cronbach, L. J. (1951). "Coefficient alpha and the internal structure of tests." Psychometrika 16: 297-334.

Currie, N. J. & B. Peacock (2002). International Space Station Robotic Systems Operations A Human Factors Perspective, Human Factors and Ergonomics Society.

Cyr, D. & H. Trevor-Smith (2004). "Localization of Web Design: An Empirical Comparison of German, Japanese, and United States Web Site Characteristics." Journal of the American Society for Information Science and Technology 55(13): 1199-1208.

D'Andrade, R. G. (2001). The development of cognitive anthropology. Cambridge, Cambridge Univ. Press.

Day, D. L. (1991). "The Cross-Cultural Study of Human-Computer Interaction: A Review of Research Methodology, Technology Transfer, and the Diffusion of Innovation."

De Marco, T. (1983). Controlling Software Projects: Management, Measurement, and Estimates. Prentice Hall.

De Saussure, F., C. Bally, et al. (1986). Course in general linguistics. LaSalle Ill., Open Court.

De Waard, D. (1996). The Measurement of Drivers' Mental Workload, Groningen University, Traffic Research Center.

Del Galdo, E. M. & J. Nielsen (1996). International user interfaces. New York, Wiley.

Dennett, D. C. (1998). The intentional stance. Cambridge, Mass., MIT Press.

Dieterich, H., U. Malinowski, et al. (1993). "State of the Art in Adaptive User Interfaces." HUMAN FACTORS IN INFORMATION TECHNOLOGY 10: 13-13.

DIN (1996). DIN EN ISO 9241-10 (1996): Ergonomische Anforderungen für Bürotätigkeiten mit Bildschirmgeräten – Teil 10: Grundsätze der Dialoggestaltung. Berlin, Wien, Zürich, Beuth-Verlag.

Dix, A., J. Finaly, et al. (2001). Human-computer interaction. London, Prentice Hall Europe.

Dix, A. F.; Janet E.; Abowd, Gregory D. and Beale, Russell (2007).   Human Computer Interaction [Import] [Hardcover], Prentice Hall.

Doberenz, W. & T. Gewinnus (2007). Borland Delphi 7. München, Hanser.

Dong, J. & G. Salvendy (1999). "Designing menus for the Chinese population: horizontal or vertical?" Behaviour and Information Technology 18(6): 467-471.

Dong, Y. & K.-p. Lee (2008). A Cross-Cultural Comparative Study of Users' Perceptions of a Webpage: With a Focus on the Cognitive Styles of Chinese, Koreans and Americans.

Donsbach, W. (2008). The International encyclopedia of communication. Oxford, Blackwell.

Dormann, C. (2006). Cultural Representations in Web Design: Differences in Emotions and Values. People and Computers XIX - The Bigger Picture. T. McEwan, D. Benyon and J. Gulliksen. London: 285-299.

Dormann, C. & C. Chisalita (2002). Cultural values in web site design.

Dotson, C. L. (2006). Fundamentals of Dimensional Metrology. Delmar Publishers Inc.

Dumas, J. S. & J. Redish (1999). A practical guide to usability testing. Exeter, England, Portland, Or, Intellect Books.

Dutke, S. (1994). Mentale Modelle: Konstrukte des Wissens und Verstehens. Göttingen, Verl. für Angewandte Psychologie.

Dybkjær, H. & L. Dybkjær (2004). Design and First Tests of a Chatter. Affective Dialogue Systems, Tutorial and Research Workshop, ADS 2004, Kloster Irsee, Germany, June 14-16, 2004, Proceedings. A. Elisabeth and H. Laila Dybkjær and Wolfgang Minker and Paul: 166-177.

Eckensberger, L. H. (2003). Auf der Suche nach den (verlorenen?) Universalien hinter den Kulturstandards. Psychologie interkulturellen Handelns. A. Thomas. Göttingen, Hogrefe: 165-197.

Eco, U. (2002). Einführung in die Semiotik. München, Fink.

Eibl, M., C. Wolff, et al. (2005). Designing information systems: Festschrift für Jürgen Krause.

Einstein, A. (1919). Die Relativitätstheorie, BG Teubner.

Endrass, B., M. Rehm, et al. (2008). Talk is silver, silence is golden: A cross cultural study on the usage of pauses in speech.

Ercan, E. (2005). Lokalisierung eines Fahrernavigationssystems für den asiatischen Markt bei der Siemens VDO Automotive AG. Unpublished master thesis, University of Regensburg.

Esselink, B. (1998). A practical guide to software localization: For translators, engineers and project managers. Amsterdam, Benjamins.

Esselink, B. (2000). A practical guide to localization. Amsterdam, Benjamins.

Evers, V. (1998). "Cross-cultural understanding of metaphors in interface design." Ess, C. & Sudweeks, F., Attitudes toward Technology and Communication (proceedings): 1-3.

Evers, V. (2003). Cross-cultural Aspects of User Understanding and Behaviour: Evaluation of a Virtual Campus Website by User from North America, England, the Netherlands and Japan. Proceedings of the Fifth International Workshop on Internationalisation of Products and Systems. V. Evers, K. Röse, P. Honold, J. Coronado and

D. Day. IWIPS 2003, Germany, Berlin, 17.-19. July 2003. Kaiserslautern, University of Kaiserslautern: 189-210.

Evers, V. & D. Day (1997). The Role of Culture in Interface Acceptance. Proceedings of the IFIP TC13 Interantional Conference on Human-Computer Interaction, Chapman & Hall, Ltd.: 260-267.

Evers, V., A. Kukulska-Hulme, et al. (1999). Cross-Cultural Understanding of Interface Design: A Cross-Cultural Analysis of Icon Recognition.

Eysenck, H. J. & M. W. Eysenck (1985). Personality and individual differences: A natural science approach, Plenum Press, New York.

Eysenck, M. W. & M. T. Keane (2004). Cognitive psychology: A student's handbook. Hove, Psychology Press.

Fanchen, M. & J. Yao (2007). Ganzheitliches Denken - harmonisches Handeln. Wertorientierungen der Unternehmenspraxis. T. Aigner-Hof. Münster.

Fang, X. U. (2007). "Analysis on the Metaphorical Structure of Education Discourses." Sino-US English Teaching 38/4(2): 52-56.

Fayyad, U., G. Piatetsky-shapiro, et al. (1996). "From data mining to knowledge discovery in databases." AI Magazine 17: 37☐54.

Ferber, J. (2001). Multiagentensysteme: Eine Einführung in die verteilte künstliche Intelligenz, Addison-Wesley.

Fink, G. (2001). Interkulturelles Management: Österreichische Perspektiven. Wien, Springer.

Fischer, K. (2006). What Computer Talk Is and Is not: Human-Computer Conversation as Intercultural Communication. Saarbrücken, AQ-Verlag.

Fitzgerald, W. (2004). "Models for Cross-Cultural Communications for Cross-Cultural Website Design." Institute for Information Technology, National Research Council Canada.

Floridi, L. (2004). The Blackwell guide to the philosophy of computing and information. Malden, Mass., Blackwell.

Francis, D. J. (1988). "An introduction to structural equation models." Journal of Clinical and Experimental Neuropsychology 10(5): 623 - 639.

Frey, S. & G. Bente (1989). "Mikroanalyse Medienvermittelter Informationsprozesse zur Anwendung zeitreihen-basierter Notationsprinzipien auf die Untersuchung von Fernsehnachrichten." Kölner Zeitschrift fur Soziologie und Sozialpsychologie, Sonderheft 30(1989): 515-33.

Friedersen, G.-H. & N. Lindemann (2000). Informationsfreiheitsgesetz für das Land Schleswig-Holstein (IFG-SH). Wiesbaden, Kommunal- und Schul-Verl.

Fromm, S. (2007). Datenanalyse mit SPSS für Fortgeschrittene: Multivariate Verfahren für Querschnittsdaten. Wiesbaden, VS Verlag für Sozialwissenschaften.

Fuchs, C. & W. Hofkirchner (2002). "Ein einheitlicher Informationsbegriff für eine einheitliche Informationswissenschaft." Floyd, Christiane/Fuchs, Christian/Hofkirchner, Wolfgang (Hg.): Stufen zur Informationsgesellschaft. Festschrift zum 65. Geburtstag von Klaus Fuchs-Kittowski. 65: 241-281.

Galtung, J. (1981). "Structure, culture, and intellectual style: An essay comparing saxonic, teutonic, gallic and nipponic approaches." Social Science Information 20(6): 817.

Galtung, J. (1985). "Struktur, Kultur und intellektueller Stil. Ein vergleichender Essay über sachsonische, teutonische, gallische und nipponische Wissenschaft." In: Wierlacher, Alois [Hrsg.](1985): Das Fremde und das Eigene." Prolegomena zu einer interkulturellen Germanistik: 151-193.

Gärdenfors, P. & H. Rott (1995). Belief revision, Handbook of logic in artificial intelligence and logic programming (Vol. 4): epistemic and temporal reasoning, Oxford University Press, Oxford.

Gellner, M. & P. Forbrig (2003). "ObSys–a Tool for Visualizing Usability Evaluation Patterns with Mousemaps." Human Computer Interaction: Theory and Practice.

Georgeff, M., B. Pell, et al. (1999). "The belief-desire-intention model of agency." Lecture Notes in Computer Science 1555: 1-10.

Gerken, J., P. Bak, et al. (2008). How to use interaction logs effectively for usability evaluation. BELIV'08: Beyond time and errors - novel evaLuation methods for Information Visualization (a CHI 2008 Workshop).

Görz, G. (2003). Handbuch der Künstlichen Intelligenz. München, Oldenbourg.

Gottfried, C., G. Hager, et al. (2002). Kriterienkatalog zur qualitativen Bewertung von Lernsoftware.

Graham, T. C. N., L. A. Watts, et al. (2000). A dimension space for the design of interactive systems within their physical environments, ACM New York, NY, USA.

Grice, P. (1993). Studies in the way of words. Cambridge, Mass., Harvard Univ. Press.

Grotjahn, R. (2001). Themenschwerpunkt: Leistungsmessung und Leistungsevaluation. Tübingen, Narr.

Gstalter, H. & W. Fastenmeier (1995). "Auswirkungen von Navigationsinformationen im Kraftfahrzeug: Mögliche Sicherheitseffekte, wichtiger Fahrervariablen und

Folgerungen für empirische Untersuchungen." W. Fastenmeier (Hg.): Autofahrer und Verkehrssituation. Köln: TÜV-Rheinland: 79-96.

Hackos, J. T. & J. C. Redish (1998). User and task analysis for interface design. New York, Wiley.

Haken, H. (1983). Synergetik: Eine Einführung ; Nichtgleichgewichts- Phasenübergänge und Selbstorganisation in Physik, Chemie und Biologie. Berlin West, Springer.

Hall, E. T. (1959). The Silent Language. New York, Doubleday.

Hall, E. T. (1976). Beyond Culture. New York, Anchor Books.

Hall, E. T. (1983). The Dance of Life. The Other Dimension of Time, New York: Anchorbooks, Doubleday.

Hall, E. T. (1989). The dance of life: The other dimension of time. New York, N.Y., Doubleday.

Hall, E. T. (1990). The hidden dimension. New York, NY, Anchor Books.

Hall, E. T. & M. R. Hall (1990). Understanding cultural differences. Yarmouth, Me., Intercultural Press.

Hall, E. T. & M. R. Hall (2004). Understanding cultural differences: [Germans, French and Americans]. Yarmouth, Me., Intercultural Press.

Hall, E. T. H., Mildred (1983). Verborgene Signale. Hamburg, Gruner & Jahr.

Halpin, A. W. & B. J. Winer (1957). A factorial study of the leader behavior descriptions. Leader behavior: Its description and measurement. R. M. Stogdill and A. E. Coons. Columbus, OH, Bureau of Business Research, Ohio State University.

Hamacher, N. A. (2006). Automatische kriterienorientierte Bewertung der Gebrauchstauglichkeit interaktiver Systeme. München, Dr. Hut.

Hammwöhner, R. (1997). Komplexe Hypertextmodelle im World Wide Web durch dynamische Dokumente. HIM: 109-120.

Hammwöhner, R. & R. Kuhlen (2004). Wissen in Aktion: Der Primat der Pragmatik als Motto der Konstanzer Informationswissenschaft ; Festschrift für Rainer Kuhlen. Konstanz, UVK Verl.-Ges.

Hampe-Neteler, W. (1994). Software-ergonomische Bewertung zwischen Arbeitsgestaltung und Softwareentwicklung. Frankfurt am Main, Lang.

Hansen, K. P. (2003). Kultur und Kulturwissenschaft: Eine Einführung. Tübingen, Francke.

Hasebrook, J. & A. C. Graesser (1995). Multimedia-Psychologie: Eine neue Perspektive menschlicher Kommunikation. Berlin, Spektrum Akad. Verl.

Hassenzahl, M. (2001). "The Effect of Perceived Hedonic Quality on Product Appealingness." International Journal of Human-Computer Interaction 13(4): 481-499.

Haykin, S. (2008). Neural networks: a comprehensive foundation, Prentice Hall.

Heimgärtner, R. (2001). Michael Tye: ,Phenomenal Consciousness: The Explanation Gap as a Cognitive Illusion' (1999). Kritische Diskussion der zentralen Position. Philosophische Fakultät IV. Regensburg, Universität Regensburg. BA.

Heimgärtner, R. (2002). Antirepräsentationalismus – Kognition ohne Repräsentation? Philosophische Fakultät I, Universität Regensburg. MA.

Heimgärtner, R. (2005). Research in Progress: Towards Cross-Cultural Adaptive Human-Machine-Interaction in Automotive Navigation Systems. Proceedings of the Seventh International Workshop on Internationalisation of Products and Systems (IWIPS 2005). D. Day and E. M. del Galdo. The Netherlands, Amsterdam, Grafisch Centrum Amsterdam: 97-111.

Heimgärtner, R. (2006). Measuring Cultural Differences in Human Computer Interaction as Preparatory Work for Cross-Cultural Adaptability in Navigation Systems. Useware 2006. Düsseldorf, VDI-Verl. 1946: 301-314.

Heimgärtner, R. (2007a). A Tool for Cross-Cultural Human Computer Interaction Analysis. Usability and Internationalization. HCI and Culture, Second International Conference on Usability and Internationalization, UI-HCII 2007, Held as Part of HCI International 2007, Beijing, China, July 22-27, 2007, Proceedings, Part I. N. M. Aykin, Springer. 4559: 89-98.

Heimgärtner, R. (2007b). Cultural Differences in Human Computer Interaction: Results from Two Online Surveys. Open innovation. A. Oßwald. Konstanz, UVK. 46: 145-158.

Heimgärtner, R. (2008a). A Tool for Getting Cultural Differences in HCI. Human Computer Interaction: New Developments. K. Asai: 343-368.

Heimgärtner, R. (2008b). Towards A Generic Adaptability Framework for Automotive HMI. Lübeck.

Heimgärtner, R. (2009a). "Auf dem Weg zu einem generischen Adaptivitätsframework für die Mensch-Maschine-Interaktion im Kraftfahrzeug." i-com.

Heimgärtner, R. (2009b). Identification of the User by Analysis of Human Computer Interaction. Human-Computer Interaction. Ambient, Ubiquitous and Intelligent Interaction. 13th International Conference, HCI International 2009, July 19-24, 2009, Proceedings, Part III. J. A. Jacko. San Diego, CA, USA, Springer. 5612: 275-283.

Heimgärtner, R., A. Holzinger, et al. (2008). From Cultural to Individual Adaptive End-User Interfaces: Helping People with Special Needs. Computers Helping People with Special Needs, 11th International Conference, ICCHP 2008, Linz, Austria, July 9-11,

2008. Proceedings. K. Miesenberger and J. K. a. W. L. Z. a. A. I. Karshmer, Springer. 5105: 82-89.

Heimgärtner, R., L.-W. Tiede, et al. (2007). Towards Cultural Adaptability to Broaden Universal Access in Future Interfaces of Driver Information Systems. Universal Access in Human-Computer Interaction. Ambient Interaction, 4th International Conference on Universal Access in Human-Computer Interaction, UAHCI 2007 Held as Part of HCI International 2007 Beijing, China, July 22-27, 2007 Proceedings, Part II. C. Stephanidis, Springer. 4555: 383-392.

Heimgärtner, R. & L. W. Tiede (2008). Technik und Kultur: Interkulturelle Erfahrungen bei der Produktentwicklung für China. Interkulturelle Kommunikation. O. Rösch. Berlin, Verlag News & Media. Band 6 „Technik und Kultur": 149-162.

Heinecke, A. M. (2011). Mensch-Computer-Interaktion, Springer Verlag.

Herczeg, M. (2003). "Interaktions-und Kommunikationsversagen in Mensch-Maschine-Systemen als Analyse-und Modellierungskonzept zur Verbesserung sicherheitskritischer Technologien." DGLR BERICHT 3: 73.

Herczeg, M. (2005). Software-Ergonomie: Grundlagen der Mensch-Computer-Kommunikation. München, Oldenbourg.

Herczeg, M. (2009). Software-Ergonomie - Theorien, Modelle und Kriterien für gebrauchstaugliche interaktive Computersysteme, 2009, Oldenbourg Wissenschaftsverlag GmbH.

Hermeking, M. (2001). Kulturen und Technik. München, Waxmann.

Herrmann, J., M. Kloth, et al. (1998). "The role of explanations in an intelligent assistant system." Artificial Intelligence in Engineering 12(1-2): 107-126.

Hill, T. & P. Lewicki (2006). Statistics. Tulsa, Okla., StatSoft.

Ho, R. (2006). Handbook of univariate and multivariate data analysis and interpretation with SPSS. Boca Raton, Fla., Chapman & Hall/CRC.

Hobfoll, S. E. (2004). Stress, culture, and community: The psychology and philosophy of stress, Springer.

Hodemacher, D., F. Jarman, et al. (2005). Kultur und Web-Design: Ein empirischer Vergleich zwischen Großbritannien und Deutschland. Mensch & Computer 2005: Kunst und Wissenschaft – Grenzüberschreitungen der interaktiven ART., Wien, Oldenbourg Verlag, München.

Hodicová, R. (2007). Psychische Distanz und Internationalisierung von KMU: Empirische Untersuchung am Beispiel des Sächsisch-tschechischen Grenzraumes, Duv.

Hof, A. (2007). Entwicklung eines adaptiven Hilfesystems für multimodale Anzeige-Bedienkonzepte im Fahrzeug. Regensburg, Universität Regensburg. PhD.

Hofstadter, D. R. & D. C. Dennett (1981). The mind's I. Toronto, Bantam Books.

Hofstede, G. (1984). Culture's consequences: International differences in work-related values. Beverly Hills, Calif., Sage.

Hofstede, G. (1994). VSM94: Values Survey Module 1994 Manual. Tilberg, Netherlands, IRIC.

Hofstede, G. (1997). Lokales Denken, globales Handeln: Kulturen, Zusammenarbeit und Management. München, Dt. Taschenbuch-Verl.

Hofstede, G. & G. J. Hofstede (2005). Cultures and Organizations: Software of the mind ; [intercultural cooperation and its importance for survival]. New York, McGraw-Hill.

Hofstede, G. & J. G. Hofstede (2005). Cultures and Organizations: Software of the Mind. 2nd Edition. New York, USA, McGraw-Hill.

Hofstede, G. H. (1991). Cultures and organizations: Software of the mind. London, McGraw-Hill.

Hoft, N. L. (1995). International technical communication: How to export information about high technology. New York, Wiley.

Hoft, N. L. (1996). Developing a cultural model. International users interface. E. M. Del Galdo and J. Nielsen, John Wiley & Sons, Inc.: 41-73.

Hohmann, S. (2003). Mensch - Maschine - Interface: Studien zu einer Theorie der Mensch-Interaktion. Fachbereich Geisteswissenschaften » Germanistik » Literaturwissenschaften, Duisburg-Essen. PhD.

Hollnagel, E. (1995). "The art of efficient man-machine interaction: Improving the coupling between man and machine." Expertise and Technology: Cognition & Human-Computer Cooperation: 229–241.

Holoch, F. (1999). Die Struktur von Arbeitswerten. Eine faktorenanalytische Untersuchung, Johannes Gutenberg-Universität Mainz.

Holzinger, A. (2001). Lernen: Kognitive Grundlagen multimedialer Informationssysteme. Würzburg, Vogel.

Holzinger, A. (2005). "Usability Engineering for Software Developers." Communications of the ACM 48(1): 71-74.

Holzinger, A. (2005). "Usability engineering methods for software developers." Commun. ACM 48(1): 71-74.

Holzinger, A. & K.-H. Weidmann, Eds. (2005). Empowering Software Quality: How can Usability Engineering reach these goals? 1st Usability Symposium, HCI&UE Workgroup, Vienna, Austria, 8 November 2005, Austrian Computer Society.

Homann, B. (2002). "Standards der Informationskompetenz." Bibliotheksdienst 36(5): 625-638.

Honold, P. (1999). "Cross-cultural" or "intercultural" - some findings on international usability testing. Designing for Global Markets 1, First International Workshop on Internationalisation of Products and Systems. G. V. D. G. E. M. Prabhu. IWIPS 1999, Rochester, New York, USA, Backhouse Press: 107-122.

Honold, P. (2000). Interkulturelles usability engineering: Eine Untersuchung zu kulturellen Einflüssen auf die Gestaltung und Nutzung technischer Produkte. Düsseldorf, VDI Verl.

Houghton, G. (2005). Connectionist models in cognitive psychology. Hove, Psychology Press.

House, R., M. Javidan, et al. (2002). "Understanding cultures and implicit leadership theories across the globe: an introduction to project GLOBE." Journal of world business 37(1): 3-10.

Hox, J. J. & T. M. Bechger (1998). "An Introduction to Structural Equation Modeling." Family Science Review 11: 354-373.

Hubner, W. (1990). "Ein objektorientiertes Interaktionsmodell zur Spezifikation graphischer Dialoge." Zentrum fur graphische Datenverarbeitung, Darmstadt.

Husserl, E. & D. Lohmar (2003). Phänomenologische Psychologie. Hamburg, Meiner.

Inglehart, R. (1990). Culture shift in advanced industrial society. Princeton, NJ, Princeton Univ. Press.

Inglehart, R., A. Moreno, et al. (1998). Human Values and Beliefs: A Cross-Cultural Sourcebook, University of Michigan Press.

International, D. (2003). Developing international software. Redmond, Wash., Microsoft Press.

Jacko, J. A., Ed. (2007). Human-Computer Interaction. Interaction Design and Usability, 12th International Conference, HCI International 2007, Beijing, China, July 22-27, 2007, Proceedings, Part I, Springer.

Jacko, J. A. & A. Sears (2003). The human-computer interaction handbook: Fundamentals, evolving technologies and emerging applications. Mahwah, NJ, Erlbaum.

Jäger, L., Ed. (2004). Handbuch der Kulturwissenschaften. Grundlagen und Schlüsselbegriffe. Stuttgart, Metzler.

Jagne, J. & A. Smith-Atakan (2006). "Cross-cultural interface design strategy." Universal Access in the Information Society 5(3): 299-305.

Jameson, A. (2007). Adaptive Interfaces and Agents. Human-Computer Interaction. Interaction Design and Usability, 12th International Conference, HCI International 2007, Beijing, China, July 22-27, 2007, Proceedings, Part I. J. A. Jacko, Springer. 4550: 305-330.

Jarz, E. M. (1997). Entwicklung multimedialer Systeme. Wiesbaden, Dt. Univ.-Verl. [u.a.].

Jetter, H.-C. (2004). Interkulturelles UI Design und UI Evaluation, Universität Konstanz.

John, O. P. & S. Srivastava (1999). "The Big Five trait taxonomy: History, measurement, and theoretical perspectives." Handbook of personality: Theory and research 2: 102-138.

Johnson-Laird, P. N. (1983). Mental models: Towards a cognitive science of language, inference and consciousness. Cambridge, Mass., Harvard Univ. Press.

Johnson-Laird, P. N. (1988). The computer and the mind: An introduction to cognitive science. Cambridge, Mass., Harvard Univ. Press.

Jordan, B. & A. Henderson (1995). "Interaction analysis: Foundations and practice." Journal of the Learning Sciences 4(1): 39-103.

Jürgensohn, T., K.-P. Timpe, et al. (2001). Kraftfahrzeugführung: [Gedenkband für Prof. Dr. Hans-Peter Willumeit]. Berlin, Springer.

Kamentz, E. (2006). Adaptivität von hypermedialen Lernsystemen: Ein Vorgehensmodell für die Konzeption einer Benutzermodellierungskomponente unter Berücksichtigung kulturbedingter Benutzereigenschaften. Hildesheim, Univ. PhD: 293.

Kamentz, E. & T. Mandl (2003). Culture and E-Learning: Automatic Detection of a Users' Culture from Survey Data. Proceedings of the Fifth International Workshop on Internationalisation of Products and Systems. V. R. K. H. P. C. J. D. D. Evers. IWIPS 2003, Germany, Berlin, 17-19 July 2003. Kaiserslautern, University of Kaiserslautern: 189-210.

Kamp, H. & U. Reyle (1993). From discourse to logic: Introduction to modeltheoretic semantics of natural language, formal logic and discourse representation theory. Dordrecht, Kluwer.

Kant, I. (2006). Kritik der reinen Vernunft. Stuttgart, Reclam.

Keirsey, D. M. (1998). Please understand me II: Temperament, character, intelligence. Del Mar, CA, Prometheus Nemesis.

Kenny, D. A. (1979). Correlation and Causality. John Wiley & Sons Inc. New York.

Khaslavsky, J. (1998). Integrating Culture into Interface Design. Student Posters: Design: Applications and Approaches (Summary). Proceedings of ACM CHI 98:

Conference on Human Factors in Computing Systems, Los Angeles, California, United States, ACM.

Kluckhohn, F. & F. L. Strodtbeck (1961). Variations in value orientations. Westport Conn., Greenwood Press.

Knapp, B. (2007). "Mental Models of Chinese and German Users and Their Implications for MMI: Experiences from the Case Study Navigation System." Lecture Notes in Computer Science 4550: 882.

Kobsa, A. (1990). "User modeling in dialog systems: Potentials and hazards." AI & Society 4(3): 214-231.

Kobsa, A. (1993). "Tagungsband KI-93-Workshop "Adaptivität und Benutzermodellierung interaktiven Softwaresystemen"."

Kobsa, A. & W. Pohl (1995). "The user modeling shell system BGP-MS." User Modeling and User-Adapted Interaction 4(2): 59-106.

Kobsa, A., W. Wahlster, et al. (1989). User models in dialog systems: [based on UM86, the first International Workshop on User Modeling, held in Maria Laach, Germany]. Berlin, Springer.

Kockläuner, G. (2000). Multivariate Datenanalyse. Braunschweig, Vieweg.

Koda, T., M. Rehm, et al. (2008). "Cross-Cultural Evaluations of Avatar Facial Expressions Designed by Western Designers." Lecture Notes in Computer Science 5208: 245-252.

Kohonen, T. (2001). Self-organizing maps: With 22 tables. Berlin, Springer.

Kolrep, H. & K. R. a. F. G. a. T. Jürgensohn (2003). Mobile Anwendungen im Kraftfahrzeug - Mensch-Maschine-Interaktion und Akzeptanz. Informatik 2003 - Innovative Informatikanwendungen, Band 2, Beiträge der 33. Jahrestagung der Gesellschaft für Informatik e.V. (GI), 29. September - 2. Oktober 2003 in Frankfurt am Main. K. R. Dittrich and W. K. a. A. O. a. K. R. a. W. Wahlster, GI. 35: 386-391.

Komischke, T., A. McGee, et al. (2003). Mobile Phone Usability and Cultural Dimensions: China, Germany & USA. Human Factors in Telecommunication. Proceedings of the 19th International Symposium on Human Factors in Telecommunication (HFT 03). L. Mühlbach. Berlin, Germany

Komlodi, A. (2005). Cross-Cultural Study of Information Seeking. Proceedings of the International Conference on Human-Computer Interaction (HCII 2005). First International Conference on Usability and Internationalization, Las Vegas, Nevada, USA, Springer, Berlin; New York.

Koning, H., C. Dormann, et al. (2002). Practical guidelines for the readability of IT-architecture diagrams, ACM New York, NY, USA.

Köppen, N. & H. Wandke (2002). Entwicklung eines Toolsets zur Unterstützung von Logfilestudien. Useware 2002. Düsseldorf: 27-32.

Kralisch, A. (2006). The Impact of Culture and Language on the Use of the Internet Empirical Analyses of Behaviour and Attitudes, Berlin.

Krause, J. & L. Hitzenberger (1992). Computer Talk. Hildesheim, Olms.

Krauth, J. (1995). Testkonstruktion und Testtheorie. Weinheim, Beltz Psychologie Verl.-Union.

Kritzenberger, H. (1998). Dialoge mit Computern in natürlicher Sprache, Universität Regensburg PhD.

Krömker, H. (2000). "Introduction." International Journal of Human-Computer Interaction 12(3&4): 281-284.

Kühme, T., H. Dieterich, et al. (1992). Approaches to Adaptivity in User Interface Technology: Survey and Taxonomy, North-Holland Publishing Co. Amsterdam, The Netherlands, The Netherlands.

Kuhlen, R. (1991). "Information and pragmatic value-adding: Language games and information science." Language Resources and Evaluation 25(2): 93-101.

Kulak, D. & E. Guiney (2000). Use cases: Requirements in context. Boston, Addison-Wesley.

La Cruz, T., T. Mandl, et al. (2005). Cultural Dependency of Quality Perception and Web Page Evaluation Guidelines: Results from a Survey. Designing for Global Markets 7: Proceedings of the Seventh International Workshop on Internationalization of Products and Systems (IWIPS 2005). D. Day, E. del Galdo and V. Evers. Amsterdam, The Netherlands: 15-27.

Lakoff, G. & M. Johnson (1980). "The metaphorical structure of the human conceptual system." Cognitive Science 4(2): 195-208.

Lange, K. W., K.-H. Bäuml, et al. (2005). Experimentelle Psychologie: Beiträge zur 47. Tagung Experimentell Arbeitender Psychologen 04. April-06. April 2005. Lengerich, Pabst Science Publ.

Langer, D. W. (2002). Einführung in die konfirmatorische Faktoren-und Pfadanalyse mit LISREL. Methoden V: Konfirmatorische Faktorenanalyse, Universität Halle.

Latane, B. (1996). "Dynamic social impact: The creation of culture by communication." The Journal of Communication 46(4): 13-25.

Lee, Y. (2002, 19.11.2002). "Introduction." from http://www.csulb.edu/web/journals/jecr/issues/20024/paper3.pdf.

Lee, Y. T., C. R. McCauley, et al. (1999). Personality and person perception across cultures. Mahwah, NJ, Erlbaum.

Leuchter, S. & L. Urbas (2004). "Useware Engineering mit kognitiven Architekturen." Automatisierungstechnische Praxis 46(9): 68-72.

Levine, R. (2007). Eine Landkarte der Zeit: Wie Kulturen mit Zeit umgehen. München, Piper.

Levine, R. V. & A. Norenzayan (1999). "The pace of life in 31 countries." Journal of Cross-Cultural Psychology 30(2): 178.

Lewandowitz, L., P. Rößger, et al. (2006). Asiatische vs. europäische HMI Lösungen von Fahrerinformationssystemen. Useware 2006. Düsseldorf, VDI. 1946: 279–287.

Lewin, K. (1993). Feldtheorie in den Sozialwissenschaften. Ausgewählte theoretische Schriften [Gebundene Ausgabe]. Bern, Huber Hans.

Liang, S. F. M. (2003). Cross-Cultural Issues in Interactive systems. Proceedings of the International Ergonomics. Ergonomics in the Digital. Age.

Lienert, G. A., U. Raatz, et al. (1998). Testaufbau und Testanalyse. Weinheim, Beltz Psychologie-Verl.-Union.

Luhmann, N. (2010). Soziale Systeme: Grundriß einer allgemeinen Theorie. Frankfurt am Main, Suhrkamp.

Lunde, K. (1999). CJKV information processing: [Chinese, Japanese, Korean & Vietnamese computing]. Beijing, O'Reilly.

Maier, E., T. Mandl, et al. (2005). Internationalisierung von Informationssystemen: Kulturelle Aspekte der Mensch-Maschine-Interaktion. Workshops-Proceedings der 5. fachübergreifenden Konferenz Mensch und Computer 2005. A. Auinger. Wien: 57-58.

Maletzke, G. (1996). Interkulturelle Kommunikation: Zur Interaktion zwischen Menschen verschiedener Kulturen. Opladen, Westdt. Verl.

Malinowski, U., T. Kuhme, et al. (1992). A Taxonomy of Adaptive User Interfaces. Proceedings of the conference on People and computers VII York, UK, Cambridge University Press: 391-414

Malinowski, U. & A. Obermaier (1993). Adaptivität und Benutzermodellierung - Was ist ein adäquates Modell? Tagungsband KI-93-Workshop "Adaptivität und Benutzer-modellierung interaktiven Softwaresystemen". A. e. a. Kobsa. Konstanz, Univ.-Verl. Konstanz: 61-68.

Mandl, T. (2005). "IWIPS Workshop discusses Internationalisation of Products and Systems7-9 July 2005, Amsterdam, The Netherlands." Inf. Serv. Use 25(3,4): 197-198.

Mandl, T., M. Schudnagis, et al. (2003). A Framework for Dynamic Adaptation in Information Systems. Human Computer Interaction: Theory and Practice. Proceedings of 10 th International Conference on Human-Computer Interaction, 22-27 June 2003. C. Stephandis. Crete: 425-429.

Mangold, P. (2005). Proceeding studies on behavior - not only a challenge for professional tools. Empowering Software Quality: How can Usability Engineering reach these goals? 1st Usability Symposium, HCI&UE Workgroup, Vienna, Austria, 8 November 2005. H. Andreas and W. Karl-Heinz: 127-140.

Marcus, A. (2001). Cross-Cultural User-Interface Design. Proceedings, Vol. 2, Human-Computer Interface Internat. (HCII). M. J. S. G. Smith. Conf., USA, LA, New Orleans, Lawrence Erlbaum Associates, Mahwah, NJ, USA: 502-505.

Marcus, A. (2003). "User-interface design and China: a great leap forward." Interactions 10(1): 21-25.

Marcus, A. (2006). Cross-Cultural User-Experience Design. Diagrammatic Representation and Inference: 16-24.

Marcus, A. & V.-J. Baumgartner (2004). A Practical Set of Culture Dimensions for Global User-Interface Development. Computer Human Interaction, 6th Asia Pacific Conference, APCHI 2004, Rotorua, New Zealand, June 29 - July 2, 2004, Proceedings. M. Masood and R. Steve Jones and Bill: 252-261.

Marcus, A. & E. W. Gould (2000). "Crosscurrents: cultural dimensions and global Web user-interface design." Interactions 7(4): 32-46.

Masao, I. & N. Kumiyo (1996). Impact of culture on user interface design. International users interface, John Wiley & Sons, Inc.: 105-126.

Matiaske, W. (1997). Struktur und Bedeutung von Wertorientierungen bei Managern aus der Volksrepublik China und der Bundesrepublik Deutschland.

Maturana, H. R. & F. J. Varela (1980). Autopoiesis and cognition, Reidel Dordrecht.

Maybury, M. T. & W. Wahlster (1998). Readings in intelligent user interfaces. San Francisco, Calif., Morgan Kaufmann.

Mayhew, D. J. (2008). The usability engineering lifecycle: A practitioner's handbook for user interface design. San Francisco, Calif., Morgan Kaufmann.

McTear, M. F. (2002). "Spoken dialogue technology: enabling the conversational user interface." ACM Comput. Surv. 34(1): 90-169.

Mehler, A. & C. Wolff (2005). LDV Forum Themenschwerpunkt Text mining. Frankfurt am Main, GLDV.

Michon, J. A. (1993). Generic intelligent driver support, CRC Press.

Miller, G. A. (1956). "The magical number seven, plus or minus two." Psychological review 63: 81-97.

Moeschler, J. (1989). Modélisation du dialogue: Représentation de l'Inférence Argumentative. Paris, Hermès.

Monfared, R. R. & A. West (2002). "A User-Oriented Interface Methodology for Automotive Manufacturing Machines Developed Under the Foresight Vehicle Programme."

Moosmüller, A. (2007). Interkulturelle Kommunikation: Konturen einer wissenschaftlichen Disziplin. MünsterWaxmann,.

Morris, C. W. (1988). Grundlagen der Zeichentheorie, Ästhetik der Zeichentheorie, Fischer Wissenschaft.

Mutschler, B. & M. Reichert (2004). "Usability-Metriken als Nachweis der Wirtschaftlichkeit von Verbesserungen der Mensch-Maschine-Schnittstelle."

Nagy, C. (2003). "„The hidden dimension". Kulturdimensionen als Orientierung in der interkulturellen Zusammenarbeit." Interculture-Online 5/2003: 1-4.

Nardi, B. A. (1996). Context and consciousness: Activity theory and human-computer interaction. Cambridge, Mass., MIT Press.

Nardi, B. A. (2001). Context and consciousness: Activity theory and human-computer interaction. Cambridge, Mass., MIT Press.

Nardi, B. A. & C. L. Zarmer (1991). Beyond models and metaphors: visual formalisms in user interfacedesign. Proceedings of the Twenty-Fourth Annual Hawaii International Conference on System Sciences 8-11 Jan 1991. 2: 478-493.

Naumann, J., T. Richter, et al. (2000). Content-specific measurement of attitudes: From theories of attitude representation to questionnaire design.

Neuliep, J. (2008). Intercultural communication: A contextual approach, Sage Pubns.

Neuss, R. (2001). Usability Engineering als Ansatz zum Multimodalen Mensch-Maschine-Dialog. München, Technische Universität München. PhD.

Nielsen, J. (1990). Designing user interfaces for international use. Amsterdam, Elsevier.

Nielsen, J. (2001). "Usability metrics." Alertbox Jan.

Nisbett, R. E. (2003). The geography of thought: How Asians and Westerners think differently ... and why. New York, Free Press.

Nissen, S. (2003). "Implementation of a fast artificial neural network library (fann)." Report, Department of Computer Science University of Copenhagen (DIKU) 31.

Norman, D. A. (2004). Emotional design: Why we love (or hate) everyday things. New York, Basic Books.

Norman, D. A., Draper, Stephen, Ed. (1986). User Centered System Design: New Perspectives on Human-Computer Interaction, Lawrence Erlbaum Associates.

Ou, L. C., M. R. Luo, et al. (2004). "A study of colour emotion and colour preference. Part I: Colour emotions for single colours." Color Research & Application 29(3).

Parsons (1964). The social system. New York, USA / London, Free Press of Glencoe.

Paunonen, S. V., M. C. Ashton, et al. (2001). "Nonverbal assessment of the Big Five personality factors." European Journal of Personality 15(1): 3-18.

Paunonen, S. V., M. Zeidner, et al. (2000). "The Nonverbal Assessment of Personality in Five Cultures." Journal of Cross-Cultural Psychology 31(2): 220.

Peabody, D. (1999). Nationality characteristics: Dimensions for comparison. Personality and person perception across cultures. Y. T. Lee, C. R. McCauley and J. G. Draguns. Mahwah, NJ, Erlbaum: 65-100.

Peterson, Mark F. and Kenneth L. Pike. 2002. "Emics and etics for organizational studies: a lesson in contrast from linguistics." International Journal of Cross Cultural Management 2(1): 5-19.

Piechulla, W., C. Mayser, et al. (2003). "Reducing drivers' mental workload by means of an adaptive man-machine interface." Transportation Research Part F: Traffic Psychology and Behaviour 6(4): 233-248.

Podsiadlowski, A. (2002). Multikulturelle Arbeitsgruppen in Unternehmen. Münster, Waxmann.

Preece, J. (1993). A guide to usability: Human factors in computing. Wokingham, England, Addison-Wesley.

Prendinger, H. & M. Ishizuka (2004). Life-like characters: Tools, affective functions and applications. Berlin, Springer.

Prosise, J. (1999). Programming Windows with MFC Second Edition [M/CD], Microsoft Press.

Prümper, J. (1994). Fehlerbeurteilungen in der Mensch-Computer Interaktion. Münster, Waxmann.

Rätzmann, M. (2004). Software-Testing & Internationalisierung. Bonn, Galileo Press.

Reeves, B. & C. Nass (1998). The media equation. Stanford, Calif., CSLI Publ.

Rehm, M., N. Bee, et al. (2007). Too close for comfort?: adapting to the user's cultural background, ACM Press New York, NY, USA.

Reimer, A. (2005). Die Bedeutung der Kulturtheorie von Geert Hofstede für das internationale Management, Hochsch., Fachbereich Wirtschaft.

Reinecke, K. & A. Bernstein (2007). "Culturally Adaptive Software: Moving Beyond Internationalization." Lecture Notes in Computer Science 4560: 201.

Reinecke, K. & A. Bernstein (2008). Predicting user interface preferences of culturally ambiguous users. CHI Extended Abstracts. M. Czerwinski, A. M. Lund and D. S. Tan, ACM: 3261-3266.

Reischer, J. (2002). Die Sprache: Ein Phänomen und seine Erforschung. Berlin, de Gruyter.

Reischer, J. (2006). Zeichen, Information, Kommunikation. Analyse und Synthese des Zeichen- und Informationsbegriffs. Regensburg, Universitätsbibliothek.

Revel, A. & P. Andry (2009). "2009 Special Issue: Emergence of structured interactions: From a theoretical model to pragmatic robotics." Neural Netw. 22(2): 116-125.

Rogelberg, S. G., G. G. Fisher, et al. (2001). "Attitudes toward surveys: Development of a measure and its relationship to respondent behavior." Organizational Research Methods 4(1): 3-25.

Rösch, O. (2005) "Gemeinsame Ziele – unterschiedliche Wege? Über die Gleichzeitigkeit des Ungleichzeitigen in der deutsch-russischen Zusammenarbeit " TRANS - internet journal for cultural sciences 14/2005, DOI:

Röse, K. (2001). Kultur als Variable des UI Design. Mensch & Computer 2001, Stuttgart, Teubner.

Röse, K. (2002). "Kulturmodelle und ihre Anwendbarkeit beim User Interface Design." Bedienen und Verstehen 4: 305-317.

Röse, K. (2002). Methodik zur Gestaltung interkultureller Mensch-Maschine-Systeme in der Produktionstechnik. Kaiserslautern, Univ.

Röse, K. & R. Heimgärtner (2008). "Kulturell adaptive Informationsvermittlung im Kraftfahrzeug: 12 Uhr in München – Stadtverkehr, 18 Uhr in Shanghai – Stadtverkehr." i-com 7(3 Usability und Ästhetik): 9-13.

Röse, K., D. Zühlke, et al. (2001). Similarities and Dissimilarities of German and Chinese Users. Preprints of 8th IFAC/IFIP/IFORS/IEA Symposium on Analysis, Design, and Evaluation of Human-Machine Systems. G. Johannsen. Germany, Kassel: 24-29.

Röse, K. L. L. Z. D. (2001). Design Issues in Mainland China: Demands for a Localized Human-Machine-Interaction Design. 8th IFAC/IFIPS/IFORS/IEA Symposium on Analysis, Design, and Evaluation of Human-Machine Systems. G. Johannsen. Kassel, Preprints: 17-22.

Rößger, P. (2003). An International Comparison of the Usability of Driver-Information-Systems. Proceedings of the Fifth International Workshop on Internationalisation of Products and Systems. V. R. K. H. P. C. J. D. D. Evers. IWIPS 2003, Germany, Berlin, 17–19 July 2003. Kaiserslautern, University of Kaiserslautern: 129-134.

Rößger, P. & I. Rosendahl (2002). Intercultural Differences in the Interaction between Drivers and Driver-Information-Systems. SAE World Congress.

Rothengatter, T. & R. D. Huguenin, Eds. (2004). Traffic and transport psychology: theory and application : proceedings of the ICTTP 2000, Elsevier.

Rumelhart, D. E. (1986). Parallel distributed processing: Explorations in the micro-structure of cognition. Cambridge, Mass., MIT Pr.

Salmen, A. (2002). Multimodale Menüausgabe im Fahrzeug. München, Utz Wiss.

Salvucci, D. D. (2006). "Modeling driver behavior in a cognitive architecture." Human Factors 48(2): 362.

Salvucci, D. D., E. R. Boer, et al. (2001). "Toward an integrated model of driver behavior in cognitive architecture." Transportation Research Record: Journal of the Transportation Research Board 1779(-1): 9-16.

Schlegel, T., A. Burst, et al. (2003). "Interaktionsmodelle in der Spezifikation: Von der Datenzentrierung zur Ablauforientierung (Interaction models in the requirements specification: From data centric to flow centric models)." i-com/Zeitschrift für interaktive und kooperative Medien 2(1/2003): 17-27.

Schlögl, C. (2005). "Information and knowledge management: dimensions and approaches." Information Research 10(4): 10-4.

Schlungbaum, E. (1996). Model based User Interface Software Tools: Current State of Declarative Models, Graphics, Visualization & Usability Center, Georgia Institute of Technology.

Schlungbaum, E. (1997). Individual user interfaces and model-based user interface software tools. Proceedings of the 2nd international conference on Intelligent user interfaces. Orlando, Florida, United States, ACM.

Schmack, N. & H. Wandke (1989). (In-)Konsistenz im Nutzerinterface: Effekte im Nutzerverhalten? Software-Ergonomie '89. Aufgabenorientierte Systemgestaltung und Funktionalität. Gemeinsame Fachtagung des German Chapter of the ACM und der Gesellschaft für Informatik (GI). B. d. G. C. o. t. ACM, ACM. 32: 153-162.

Schmitz, K.-D. & K. Wahle (2000). Softwarelokalisierung. Tübingen, Stauffenburg-Verl.

Schneider, W. (2008). Ergonomische Gestaltung von Benutzungsschnittstellen - Kommentar zur Grundsatznorm DIN EN ISO 9241-110. Berlin Wien Zürich, Beuth Verlag.

Schomaker, L., J. Nijtmans, et al. (1995). "A Taxonomy of Multimodal Interaction in the Human Information Processing System." Esprit Basic Research Action 8579.

Schriesheim, C. A., C. C. Cogliser, et al. (1995). "Is it "trustworthy"? A multiple-levels-of-analysis reexamination of an Ohio State leadership study, with implications for future research." The Leadership Quarterly 6(2): 111-145.

Schwartz, S. H. (1992). "Universals in the content and structure of values: theoretical advances and empirical tests in 20 countries." Advances in experimental social psychology 25: 1-65.

Schwartz, S. H. & A. Bardi (2001). "Value Hierarchies Across Cultures: Taking a Similarities Perspective." Journal of Cross-Cultural Psychology 32(3): 268.

Scollon, R. & S. Wong Scollon (2008). Intercultural communication: A discourse approach. Oxford, Blackwell.

Searle, J. R. (1992). The rediscovery of the mind. Cambridge, Mass, MIT Press.

Searle, J. R. & H. P. Gavagai (1987). Intentionalität: Eine Abhandlung zur Philosophie des Geistes. Frankfurt a.M., Suhrkamp.

Searle, J. R. & F. Kiefer (1980). Speech act theory and pragmatics. Dordrecht, Holland, Reidel.

Seitz, T., J. Balzulat, et al. (2000). "Anthropometry and measurement of posture and motion." International Journal of Industrial Ergonomics 25(4): 447-453.

Shannon, C. E. (1948). "A mathematical theory of communication." Bell System Tech. J. 27: 379-423, 623-656.

Shneiderman, B. (2002). User Interface Design, MIT Press.

Shneiderman, B. P., Catherine;Cohen, Maxine; Jacobs, Steve (2009). Designing the User Interface: Strategies for Effective Human-Computer Interaction, Addison Wesley.

Siemens-Nixdorf (1992). "IHB Internationalisierungshandbuch. Richtlinien zur Erstellung von internationalen Produkten."

Smith, A. & Y. Chang (2003). Quantifying Hofstede and Developing Cultural Finger-prints for Website Acceptability. Proceedings of the Fifth International Workshop on Internationalisation of Products and Systems. V. R. K. H. P. C. J. D. D. Evers. IWIPS 2003, Germany, Berlin, 17–19 July 2003. Kaiserslautern, University of Kaiserslautern: 89-102.

Smith, A. & F. Yetim (2004). Global human-computer systems: cultural determinants of usability. Special Issue Editorial Interacting with Computers 16 (1), 1–5, Elsevier.

Smith, R. W. & V. Bugni (2006). "Symbolic interaction theory and architecture." Symbolic Interaction 29(2): 123-155.

Sontag, C., S. Schroll-Machl, et al. (2007). Beruflich in Ungarn: Trainingsprogramm für Manager, Fach-und Führungskräfte, Vandenhoeck+ Ruprecht Gm.

Spannagel, C. (2003). Qualitative und quanitative Analyse von Interaktionsaufzeichnungen. Darmstadt, Technische Universität Darmstadt. Dipl.

Springer, A. (2005). "Wie das Selbst das Denken steuert." Der Einfluss independenten und interdependenten Selbstwissens auf die Anwendung exekutiver Funktionen zur Steuerung und Kontrolle der Informationsverarbeitung.

Stary, C. (1994). Interaktive Systeme. Wiesbaden, Vieweg.

Stengers, H., O. Troyer, et al. (2004). Localization of Web Sites: Is there still a need for it? International Workshop on Web Engineering (HyperText 2004 Conference), Santa Cruz, USA.

Stephanidis, C. (2001). User interfaces for all: Concepts, methods, and tools. Mahwah, NJ, Lawrence Erlbaum Assoc.

Stephanidis, C., Ed. (2007). Universal Access in Human-Computer Interaction. Ambient Interaction, 4th International Conference on Universal Access in Human-Computer Interaction, UAHCI 2007 Held as Part of HCI International 2007 Beijing, China, July 22-27, 2007 Proceedings, Part II, Springer.

Stephanidis, C. & A. Savidis (2001). "Universal Accessin the Information Society: Methods, Tools, and InteractionTechnologies." Universal Access in the Information Society 1(1): 40-55.

Stock, W. G. (2000). Informationswirtschaft: Management externen Wissens. München, Oldenbourg.

Straub, J. (2007). Handbuch interkulturelle Kommunikation und Kompetenz: Grundbegriffe - Theorien - Anwendungsfelder. Stuttgart, Metzler.

Strohschneider, S. (2002). Cultural factors in complex decision making. Online Readings in Psychology and Culture. W. J. Lonner, D. L. Dinnel, S. A. Hayes and D. N. Sattler. Bellingham, Washington USA, Center for Cross-Cultural Research, Western Washington University. 4/1.

Sturm, C. & C. H. Mueller (2003). Putting Theory into Practice: How to apply cross-cultural differences to user interface design? Human-computer interaction: INTERACT '03 ; IFIP TC13 International Conference on Human-Computer Interaction, 1st-5th September 2003. M. Rauterberg, M. Menozzi and J. Wesson, International Federation for Information Processing: 1051-1052.

Sun, H. (2001). Building a culturally-competent corporate web site: an exploratory study of cultural markers in multilingual web design. Proceedings of the 19th annual international conference on Computer documentation. Sante Fe, New Mexico, USA, ACM: 95-102.

Sundermeier, T. (1996). Den Fremden verstehen: Eine praktische Hermeneutik. Göttingen, Vandenhoeck & Ruprecht.

Thissen, F. (2008). Interkulturelles Informationsdesign. Kompendium Informationsdesign. W. Weber. Berlin, Heidelberg: 387-424.

Thomas, A. (1996). Psychologische Bedingungen und Wirkungen internationalen Managements analysiert am Beispiel deutsch-chinesischer Zusammenarbeit. Psychologie interkulturellen Handelns. A. Thomas. Göttingen, Bern, Toronto, Seattle, Hogrefe.

Thomas, A. & L. H. Eckensberger (1993). Kulturvergleichende Psychologie: Eine Einführung. Göttingen, Hogrefe.

Timpe, K.-P. (2000). Bewertung von Mensch-Maschine-Systemen. Düsseldorf, VDI.

Timpe, K.-P. & R. Baggen (2000). Mensch-Maschine-Systemtechnik. Symposion Publ.

Tomasello, M. (2006). Die kulturelle Entwicklung des menschlichen Denkens: Zur Evolution der Kognition. Frankfurt am Main, Suhrkamp.

Tonnis, M., J. G. Fischer, et al. (2008). "From Sensors to Assisted Driving–Bridging the Gap." Journal of Software 3(3): 71.

Trillo, N. G. (1999). The cultural component of designing and evaluating international user interfaces. Proceedings of the 32nd Annual International Conference on System Sciences, 1999. HICSS-32. Hawaii. 3: 1-6.

Trompenaars, F. (1993). Handbuch globales Managen: Wie man kulturelle Unterschiede im Geschäftsleben versteht. Düsseldorf, ECON-Verl.

Trompenaars, F. & C. Hampden-Turner (2007). Riding the waves of culture: Understanding cultural diversity in business. London, Brealey.

Van der Veer, G. C. & M. Del Carmen Puerta Melguizo (2007). Mental Models. Human-Computer Interaction. Interaction Design and Usability, 12th International Conference, HCI International 2007, July 22-27, 2007, Proceedings, Part I. J. A. Jacko. Beijing, China, Springer. 4550: 52-80.

Van Gelder, T. (1998). "The dynamical hypothesis in cognitive science." Behavioral and brain sciences 21(05): 615-628.

Van Kleek, M. & H. E. Shrobe (2007). A practical activity capture framework for personal, lifetime user modeling. In The 11th International Conference on User Modeling, Corfu. 4511: 298-302.

Vanka, S. (1999). Color Tool: The Cross Cultural Meanings of Color.

Vatrapu, R. & M. A. Pérez-Quiñones (2006). "Culture and usability evaluation: The effects of culture in structured interviews." Journal of usability studies 1(4): 156-170.

Vatrapu, R. & D. Suthers (2007). "Culture and Computers: A review of the concept of culture and implications for intercultural collaborative online learning." Lecture Notes in Computer Science 4568: 260.

VDMA (2009). Software-Internationalisierung Leitfaden. Frankfurt a.M., VDMA Fachverband Software.

Victor, D. (1997). International Business Communication. New York, Prentice Hall.

Victor, D. A. (1998). International business communication. New York, NY, Harper Collins.

Vöhringer-Kuhnt, T. (2002). The Influence of Culture on Usability, Freie Universität Berlin. M.A.

Vollhardt, J. K., K. Migacheva, et al. (2008). Social Cohesion and Tolerance for Group Differences. Handbook on Building Cultures of Peace. New York, Springer: 139-152.

Wandmacher, J. (1993). Software-Ergonomie. Berlin, de Gruyter.

Watzlawick, P. H. B., Janet; Jackson, Don D. (2011). Menschliche Kommunikation: Formen Störungen Paradoxien. Bern, Huber.

Weggel, O. (1997). Die Asiaten. München, Deutscher Taschenbuchverlag.

Wentura, D. (2005). Multivariate Datenanalyse. Vorlesungsskript zur Veranstaltung Forschungsmethoden, Universität des Saarlandes.

Wierlacher, A. & A. Bogner (2003). Handbuch interkulturelle Germanistik. Stuttgart, Metzler.

Wierzbicka, A. (1991). Cross cultural pragmatics: The semantics of human interaction. Berlin, Mouton de Gruyter.

Witkin, H. A., C. A. Moore, et al. (1977). "Field-dependent and field-independent cognitive styles and their educational implications." Review of educational research 47(1): 1.

Wittgenstein, L. & J. Schulte (2000). Tractatus logico-philosophicus. Tagebücher 1914-1916. Philosophische Untersuchungen. Frankfurt am Main, Suhrkamp.

Wittig, T. (1979). Der Dialog zwischen Mensch und Maschine. Dialoge: Beiträge zur Interaktions-und Diskursanalyse. W. Heindrichs and G. C. Rump. Hildesheim, Gerstenberg: 86-98.

Würtenberger, M., M. Heimrath, et al. (2003). "Systemarchitektur der Fahrerinformations- und Anzeigesysteme der neuen 5 er Baureihe: Moderne Bordnetztopologie und ergonomisches HMI zur Beherrschung von Komplexität und Informationsflut." VDI-Berichte 1789: 525-544.

Xie, C. & D. Parker (2002). "A social psychological approach to driving violations in two Chinese cities." Transportation Research Part F: Psychology and Behaviour 5(4): 293-308.

Xie, C., D. Parker, et al. (2004). Driver Behaviour and its Consequence: The Case of Chinese Drivers. Traffic and transport psychology: theory and application : proceedings of the ICTTP 2000. T. Rothengatter and R. D. Huguenin, Elsevier Science. 33: 193-200.

Zaphiris, P. & S. Kurniawan (2007). Human Computer Interaction Research in Web Design and Evaluation. Hershey, PA, USA, IGI Global.

Zeidler, A. & R. Zellner (1992). Software-Ergonomie. München, Oldenbourg.

Zimbardo, P. G. G., R. J. (2008). Psychologie München, Pearson Studium.

Zimmer, A. (1985). What Uncertainty Judgments Can Tell About the Underlying Subjective Probabilities. UAI '85: Proceedings of the First Annual Conference on Uncertainty in Artificial Intelligence, Rome, New York, USA. L. N. Kanal and J. F. Lemmer, Elsevier: 249-258.

Zimmer, A. (2001). Experimentelle Psychologie: Abstracts der 43. Tagung Experimentell Arbeitender Psychologen, Universität Regensburg, 9. - 11. April 2001. Lengerich, Pabst.

Zins, C. (2007). "Knowledge map of information science." Journal of the American Society for Information Science and Technology 58(4): 526-535.

Zühlke, D. (2004). Useware-Systeme für internationale Märkte. Useware-Engineering für technische Systeme. Berlin, Heidelberg, Springer: 142-164.

Zühlke, D. & K. Röse (2000). Design of Global User-Interfaces: Living With the Challenge. Proceedings of the IEA 2000/ HFES 2000 Congress, July 29th trough August 4th 2000. San Diego, California, USA. 6: 154-157.

Figures

Tables

Abbreviations

¬IN = IB	interaction break
a	Acceleration, speed per time unit (v/t)
A	Application
AHMI	Adaptive Human-Machine Interaction
AMOS	Analysis of MOment Structures
API	Application Programming Interface
BCD	Basic cultural dimension
BCD4HMI	Basic cultural dimension for HMI
BDI	Beliefs, Desires, Intentions (Model)
BVP	Blood Vein Pressure
BVR	Heart Variability Rate
C	Group of Chinese users, i.e. users that are imprinted by Chinese culture
(C)	Group of SV employees that selected Chinese as test language
CAHMI	Cultural Adaptive Human-Machine Interaction
CAIA	Cultural Adaptive Interface Agent
CAIAA	Cultural Adaptive Interface Agent Architecture
CHMID	Cultural Human Machine-Interaction Design
CHN	Chinese students & SV employees
CII	Cultural Interaction Indicator
CIP	Cultural Interaction Pattern
CMH	Culture Concerning Methodological Hypothesis
CS	Cultural standard
CV	Cultural variable
CVMH	Cultural variable Concerning Methodological Hypothesis
DA	Discriminance Analysis
Delphi IDE	IDE for Delphi
DIP	Duration of information presentation
(E)	Group of SV employees that selected English as test language
EC	Number of error clicks
EFA	Explorative Factor Analysis
EH	Empirical Hypothesis
f	Number (of events) per time unit
FAH	Fundamental Abstract Hypothesis
FH	Future Hypothesis
FI	Number of function initiations
FTE	Fortuna Tracability Evaluation
G	Group of German users, i.e. users that are imprinted by German culture
(G)	Group of SV employees that selected German as test language

G11N	Globalization
GAF	Generic Adaptability Framework
GDNS	German driver navigation systems
GER	German students & SV employees
GLOBE	Global Leadership and Organizational Behavior Effectiveness
GSR	Galvanic skin Resistance
GUI	Graphical User Interface
H	Hypothesis
HCC	Human-Computer Communication
HCI	Human-Machine Interaction
HCID	Human-Computer Interaction Design
HMID	Human-Machine Interaction Dimension
HF	Software Ergonomics, Human Factors
HHC	Human-Human Communication
HHI	Human-Human Interaction
HI	Number of help initiations
HMI	Human-Machine Interaction
HMID	Human-Machine Interaction Design
HR	Heart Rate
I	Information
I18N	Internationalization
IB = ¬IN	Interaction break
IC	Intercultural
ID	Information density
ID	Informational Dimension
IDE	Integrated development environment
IDV	Individualism Index
IDV_HS	Individualism Index according to Hofstede
IDV_SV	Individualism Index according to the studies in this work
IF	Information frequency
IH	Informational Hypothesis
IIA	Intercultural Interaction Analysis
IIA Tool	Intercultural Interaction Analysis Tool
IN	Interaction / Number of interaction cycles
INAMM	Change in the mouse movement distance per time unit
INB	Interaction break
INBIC	Time interval between two interaction cycles
INBS	Number of interaction breaks per session
INC	Sum of all interaction parameters (dimensionless)
IND	Interactional Dimension
INF	Interaction frequency
INFIE	Number of interaction events per time unit
INFMC	Number of mouse clicks per time unit
INFS	Number of interaction cycles per session
INFsystem	Number of interaction cycles initiated by the system per time unit
INFuser	Number of interaction cycles initiated by the user per time unit
INH	Interactional Hypothesis

INP	Number of simultaneous interaction events (dimensionless)
INS	Interaction speed
INSMM	Mouse movement distance per time unit
IO	Information order
IP	Information parallelism
IS	Information sequence/sequentiality
IUE	Intercultural Usability Engineering
IUID	Intercultural User Interface Design
IV	Intercultural variable
JDNS	Japanese driver navigation systems
KS	Number of key strokes
L10N	Localization
LMT	Length of mouse track
LTM	Long Term Memory
LTO	Long Term Orientation Index
LTO_HS	Long Term Orientation Index according to Hofstede
LTO_SV	Long Term Orientation Index according to the studies in this work
MAS	Masculinity Index
MAS_HS	Masculinity Index according to Hofstede
MAS_SV	Masculinity Index according to the studies in this work
MC	Number of mouse clicks per time unit
MCD	Method of Cultural Design
MCV	Model of (Inter-)Cultural Variables
MDS	Multidimensional Scaling
MFC	Microsoft Foundation Class
MH	Main Hypothesis
MH	Methodological Hypothesis
MHCV	Methodological Hypothesis Concerning Cultural Variables
MMH	Main Methodological Hypothesis
MMS	Mouse movement speed
NIT	Number of pieces of information presented per time unit
NLP	Neurolinguistic Programming
NN	Neural Networks
NVIN	Number of non-verbal interactions with the system per time unit
NVIV	Non-Visible (or Hidden) Intercultural Variable
OEM	Original Equipment Manufacturer
OSLS	Ohio State Leadership Study
PASW	Predictive Analytics Software
PCII	Potential Cultural Interaction Indicator
PDI	Power Distance Index
PDI_HS	Power Distance Index according to Hofstede
PDI_SV	Power Distance Index according to the studies in this work
POI	Points Of Interest
POI	Number of POI at the map display
PUMTM	Potential Usability Metric Trace Model
PT	Number of parallel tasks in task bar
RCAIAA	Revised Cultural Adaptive Interface Agent Architecture

RM	Number of refused system messages
ROI	Return Of Investment
S	System
SAT	Siemens Adaptive Transmission Control
SC	Skin Conductance
SE	Software Engineering
SEM	Structure Equation Model
SEM	Structural Equation Modeling
SH	Statistical Hypothesis
SPSS	Statistical Package for the Social Sciences
STM	Short Term Memory
SUI	Speech User Interface
SV	Siemens VDO
t	Time
T	Time interval from one to another time point
TDA	Time to disable virtual agents
TH	Test Hypothesis
TPI	Time between two presented pieces of information
TIB	Time interval from begin to end of one interaction cycle
TIBS	Duration of interaction breaks per session
TIC	Time interval from begin to end of one interaction cycle
TICS	Duration of interaction cycles per session
TS	Time from begin to end of one session
U	User
UAI	Uncertainty Avoidance Index
UAI_HS	Uncertainty Avoidance Index according to Hofstede
UAI_SV	Uncertainty Avoidance Index according to the studies in this work
UE	Usability Engineering
UI	User Interface
UID	User Interface Design
UM	Usability Metrics
UMTM	Usability Metrics Trace Model
USP	Unique Selling Proposition
v	Speed, spatial distance per time unit (s/t)
VIV	Visible Intercultural Variable
VSM	Value Survey Module

Index

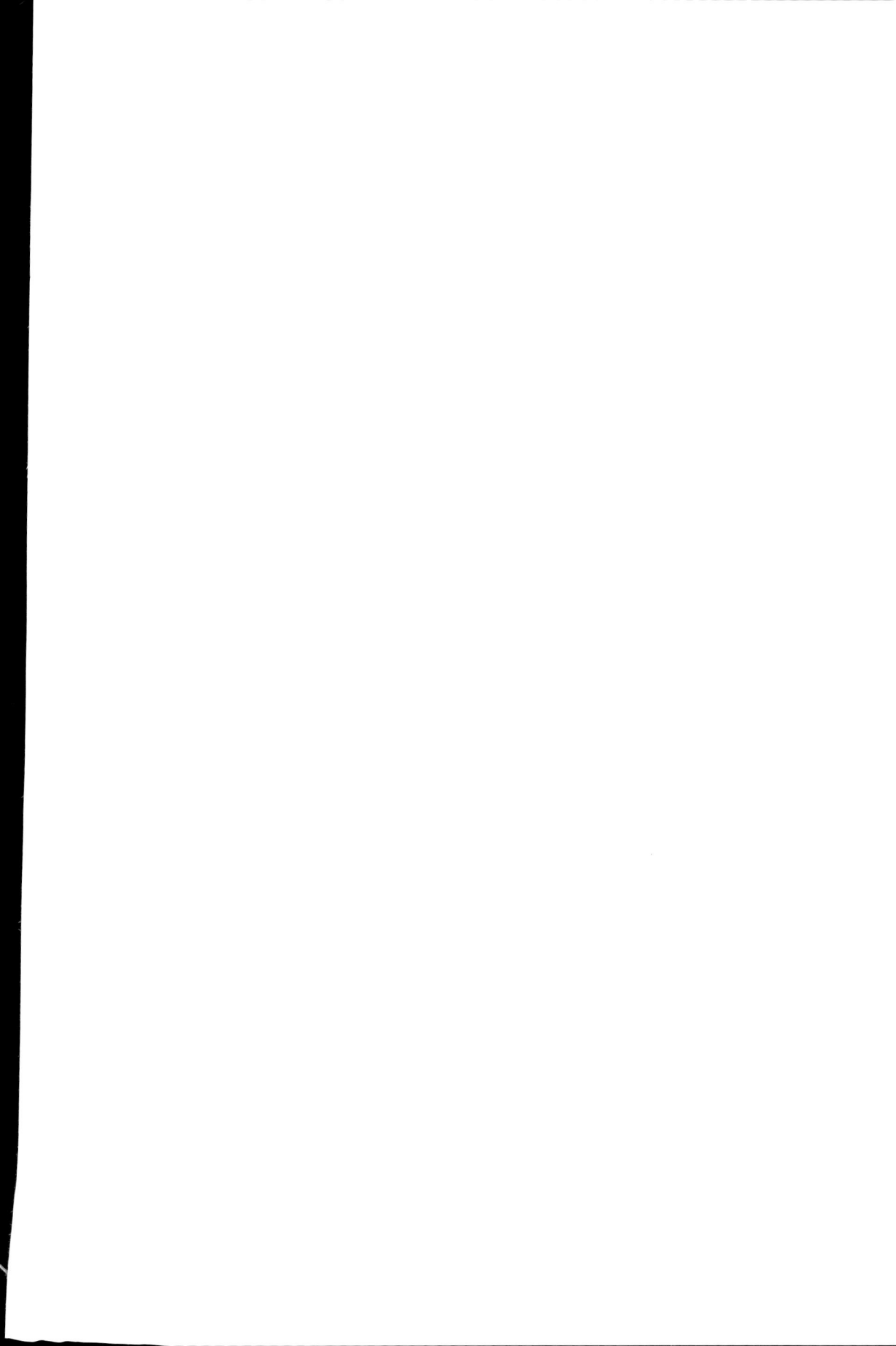

www.ingramcontent.com/pod-product-compliance
Lightning Source LLC
Chambersburg PA
CBHW081049220326
41598CB00038B/7042